Contemporary Debates in Epistemology

Contemporary Debates in Philosophy

In teaching and research, philosophy makes progress through argumentation and debate. *Contemporary Debates in Philosophy* presents a forum for students and their teachers to follow and participate in the debates that animate philosophy today in the western world. Each volume presents pairs of opposing viewpoints on contested themes and topics in the central subfields of philosophy. Each volume is edited and introduced by an expert in the field, and also includes an index, bibliography, and suggestions for further reading. The opposing essays, commissioned especially for the volumes in the series, are thorough but accessible presentations of opposing points of view.

1. Contemporary Debates in Philosophy of Religion *edited by Michael L. Peterson and Raymond J. VanArragon*
2. Contemporary Debates in Philosophy of Science *edited by Christopher Hitchcock*
3. Contemporary Debates in Epistemology *edited by Matthias Steup and Ernest Sosa*
4. Contemporary Debates in Applied Ethics *edited by Andrew I. Cohen and Christopher Heath Wellman*
5. Contemporary Debates in Aesthetics and the Philosophy of Art *edited by Matthew Kieran*

Forthcoming *Contemporary Debates* are in:

Moral Theory *edited by James Dreier*
Cognitive Science *edited by Robert Stainton*
Metaphysics *edited by Ted Sider, Dean Zimmerman, and John Hawthorne*
Philosophy of Mind *edited by Brian McLaughlin and Jonathan Cohen*
Social Philosophy *edited by Laurence Thomas*
Political Philosophy *edited by Thomas Christiano*
Philosophy of Language *edited by Ernie Lepore and Kent Bach*

Contemporary Debates in Epistemology

Edited by

Matthias Steup and Ernest Sosa

Blackwell
Publishing

© 2005 by Blackwell Publishing Ltd

BLACKWELL PUBLISHING
350 Main Street, Malden, MA 02148-5020, USA
9600 Garsington Road, Oxford OX4 2DQ, UK
550 Swanston Street, Carlton, Victoria 3053, Australia

The right of Matthias Steup and Ernest Sosa to be identified as the Authors of the Editorial Material in this Work has been asserted in accordance with the UK Copyright, Designs, and Patents Act 1988.

First published 2005 by Blackwell Publishing Ltd

4   2007

Library of Congress Cataloging-in-Publication Data

Contemporary debates in epistemology / edited by Matthias Steup and Ernest Sosa.
    p. cm. – (Contemporary debates in philosophy; 3)
  Includes bibliographical references and index.
  ISBN 1-4051-0738-3 (hardcover: alk. paper) – ISBN 1-4051-0739-1 (pbk. : alk. paper)
1. Knowledge, Theory of. I. Steup, Matthias. II. Sosa, Ernest. III. Series.

  BD161.C6545 2005
  121 – dc22

                                2004016178

ISBN-13: 978-1-4051-0738-9 (hardcover: alk. paper) – ISBN-13: 978-1-4051-0739-6 (pbk. : alk. paper)

A catalogue record for this title is available from the British Library.

Set in 10 on 12.5 pt Rotis Serif
by SNP Best-set Typesetter Ltd, Hong Kong
Printed and bound in Singapore
by COS Printers Pte Ltd

The publisher's policy is to use permanent paper from mills that operate a sustainable forestry policy, and which has been manufactured from pulp processed using acid-free and elementary chlorine-free practices. Furthermore, the publisher ensures that the text paper and cover board used have met acceptable environmental accreditation standards.

For further information on
Blackwell Publishing, visit our website:
www.blackwellpublishing.com

Contents

Notes on Contributors

Laurence BonJour is Professor of Philosophy at the University of Washington. His interests are in Epistemology, Kant, and British Empiricism. He is the author (together with Ernest Sosa) of *Epistemic Justification: Internalism versus Externalism, Foundations versus Virtues* (Blackwell, 2003).

Bill Brewer is Lecturer in Philosophy at Oxford University and Fellow of St Catherine's College. He works on philosophy of mind, metaphysics and epistemology. He is author of *Perception and Reason* (Oxford University Press, 1999), and is currently working on a book on the relation between empirical realism and various forms of externalism.

Alex Byrne is an Associate Professor of Philosophy at the Massachusetts Institute of Technology. He has published papers in the philosophy of mind, metaphysics, philosophy of language, and epistemology.

Stewart Cohen is Professor of Philosophy at Arizona State University. He is the author of many articles in epistemology, including "How to Be a Fallibilist" (*Philosophical Perspectives*, 2, 1988) and "Contextualism, Skepticism, and the Structure of Reasons" (*Philosophical Perspectives*, 13, 1999).

Earl Conee is a Professor of Philosophy at the University of Rochester. He is author, with Richard Feldman, of *Evidentialism: Essays in Epistemology* (Oxford University Press, 2004).

Marian David (PhD, University of Arizona) is Professor of Philosophy at the University of Notre Dame. He is the author of *Correspondence and Disquotation: An Essay on the Nature of Truth* (Oxford, 1994). His recent publications include an entry on

"The Correspondence Theory of Truth" in the Stanford Encyclopedia of Philosophy (http://plato.stanford.edu). His present research interests include: the role of the first-person in epistemology; the nature of propositions, facts, and truth; and the idea of truth being a goal or good to be aimed for or pursued.

Michael Devitt is a Distinguished Professor of Philosophy at the Graduate Center of the City University of New York. His main research interests are in the philosophy of language and mind, and in issues of realism. Recent publications include "The Metaphysics of Truth" (*The Nature of Truth*, ed. Michael Lynch, MIT Press, 2001) and "A Shocking Idea about Meaning" (*Revue Internationale de Philosophie*, 2001). He is currently working on *Ignorance of Language*.

Fred Dretske is Professor Emeritus, Stanford University and the University of Wisconsin. He is presently Research Scholar (occasionally doing some teaching) at Duke University. His interest in the past ten years has centered on the intersection of epistemology and philosophy of mind – in particular, self-knowledge. A collection of his essays on these topics, *Perception, Knowledge, and Belief*, was published in 2000 by Cambridge University Press.

Catherine Z. Elgin is Professor of the Philosophy of Education at Harvard Graduate School of Education. Her research focuses on understanding and its relation to issues in the epistemology, the philosophy of science and the philosophy of art. She is the author of *Considered Judgment* (1996) and *Between the Absolute and the Arbitrary* (1997).

Richard Feldman is Professor of Philosophy at the University of Rochester. His interests are in Epistemology and Metaphysics. His most recent publications include *Epistemology* (Prentice Hall, 2003), *Evidentialism* (with Earl Conee, Oxford University Press, 2004), "Chisholm's Internalism and Its Consequences" (*Metaphilosophy*, 34, 2003) and "Freedom and Contextualism," in *Topics in Contemporary Philosophy Volume II: Freedom and Determinism* (Seven Bridges Press, 2004).

Richard Foley is Professor of Philosophy, and Dean of the Faculty of Arts and Sciences, at New York University. He is the author of numerous articles in epistemology, and *The Theory of Epistemic Rationality* (1987) and *Working without a Net* (1993).

Richard Fumerton is Professor of Philosophy at the University of Iowa. He has published numerous articles in epistemology, and is the author of *Truth and Correspondence* (Rowman and Littlefield, forthcoming) and *Metaepistemology and Skepticism* (Rowman and Littlefield, 1996).

Carl Ginet is Professor of Philosophy Emeritus at Cornell University. He has published a book and some articles on epistemology and a book and some articles on free will and action theory. He is currently giving his thought primarily to topics in epistemology, particularly the kinds of non-inferential justification of belief.

Notes on Contributors

John Greco is Professor of Philosophy at Fordham University. He is the author of *Putting Skeptics in Their Place: The Nature of Skeptical Arguments and Their Role In Philosophical Inquiry* (Cambridge University Press, 2000), and co-editor (with Ernest Sosa) of *The Blackwell Guide to Epistemology* (1999). He has published a number of chapters and articles in epistemology, including "Agent Reliabilism," *Philosophical Perspectives*, 13, 1999, "Virtues in Epistemology," *The Oxford Handbook of Epistemology* (2002), and "Reid's Reply to the Skeptic," *The Cambridge Companion to Reid* (2004).

John Hawthorne is Professor of Philosophy at Rutgers University. He is the author of *The Grammar of Meaning* (with Mark Lance, Cambridge University Press, 1997), *Substance and Individuation in Leibniz* (with Jan Cover, Cambridge University Press, 1999), and *Knowledge and Lotteries* (Oxford University Press, forthcoming).

Peter Klein received his PhD from Yale and has taught at Rutgers since 1970. His work focuses on three issues in epistemology: the defeasibility theory of knowledge, skepticism, and, more recently, infinitism. Recent publications from each of the areas include: "Knowledge is True, Non-defeated Justified Belief" (*Essential Knowledge*, Longman, 2004), "Skepticism" (*The Oxford Handbook of Epistemology*, 2002), "When Infinite Regresses Are not Vicious" (*Philosophy and Phenomenological Research*, 66, 2003) and "What Is Wrong with Foundationalism Is that It Cannot Solve the Epistemic Regress Problem" (*Philosophy and Phenomenological Research*, 68, 2004).

Jonathan Kvanvig is Professor and Chair of the Philosophy Department at the University of Missouri. His research interests are in metaphysics and epistemology, as well as philosophy of religion. He has recently been working on issues surrounding the problem of the value of knowledge, having published *The Value of Knowledge and the Pursuit of Understanding* (Cambridge University Press, 2003). In addition, he has been working on the under-appreciated knowability paradox, the result of which is a book forthcoming in 2005 entitled *The Knowability Paradox.*

James Pryor received his PhD from Princeton, taught at Harvard for several years, and now teaches at Princeton. He works in epistemology and the philosophy of mind; and on related issues in metaphysics and the philosophy of language. His research focuses on perceptual justification and the nature of perceptual experience, de re thought, and our knowledge of our own mental states. He is working on a book about epistemological issues raised by Twin-Earth thought-experiments.

James van Cleve is Professor of Philosophy, Brown University, and Visiting Professor of Philosophy, University of Southern California, and is interested in epistemology, metaphysics, and the history of modern philosophy.

Jonathan Vogel is Professor of Philosophy at Amherst College. He is the author of many articles in epistemology, including "Cartesian Skepticism and Inference to the Best Explanation" (*Journal of Philosophy*, 65, 1990) and "Reliabilism Leveled" (*Journal of Philosophy*, 97, 2000).

Michael Williams holds the Krieger–Eisenhower Professorship at Johns Hopkins University. He received his BA from Oxford and his PhD from Princeton. His main areas of interest are epistemology (with special reference to skepticism), philosophy of language, and the history of modern philosophy. In addition to numerous articles, he is the author of *Groundless Belief* (Blackwell, 1977; 2nd edn, 1999), *Unnatural Doubts* (Princeton University Press, 1992; 2nd edn, 1996), and *Problems of Knowledge* (Oxford University Press, 2001).

Nicholas Wolterstorff is Noah Porter Professor Emeritus of Philosophical Theology at Yale University. Two of his recent books are *John Locke and the Ethics of Belief* (Cambridge University Press, 1996), and *Thomas Reid and the Story of Epistemology* (Cambridge University Press, 2001).

Notes on Contributors

Preface

This volume, part of Blackwell's Contemporary Debates series, is a collection of 22 essays on 11 central questions in epistemology. Each question is addressed by a pair of authors, acknowledged experts in their respective fields, who argue for clearly opposite points of view.

When reading the epistemological literature of the previous two or three decades, noting the bewildering plethora of views on "S knows that p" and seemingly endless supply of counterexamples, modifications and refinements, it is easy to lose sight of the underlying, fundamental issues. The debate format, upon which this volume is based, is ideally suited to bring these issues into clear focus, and to cast the spotlight on what the arguments are that motivate opposing points of view. Thus, we believe that this collection will enliven epistemology and make exciting reading for scholars working in the field, graduate students, and advanced undergraduates alike. If it achieves this aim, it will be due to the hard work of the contributors. We wish to thank them for their efforts, and Jeff Dean and Nirit Simon at Blackwell Publishing for guiding this project towards completion.

Matthias Steup
Ernest Sosa

PART I

KNOWLEDGE AND SKEPTICISM

Introduction

Matthias Steup

Chapter 1: Is Knowledge Closed under Known Entailment?

Sometimes our beliefs are true by chance. In such cases, they do not amount to knowledge, for if we know what we believe, it must not be by accident that what we believe is true. How can we capture what it takes to rule out such accidentality? According to Fred Dretske (1971), what rules out accidentality is the possession of conclusive reasons. Thus Dretske holds that knowing that p requires having a conclusive reason for p. He defines the concept of a conclusive reason counterfactually as follows:

> **Conclusive Reason**
> R is a conclusive reason for p = $_{df}$ If p were false R would be false (or: If p were not the case R would not be the case).

Counterfactuals are claims about what would (or would not) be the case if things were different than they in fact are. The standard method of assessing the truth value of a counterfactual is to see whether its consequent is true in the closest possible worlds in which its antecedent is true.

Suppose, prompted by a goat-in-the-field-like visual experience, E, Jim forms the belief

> G: There is a goat in the field.

On Dretske's view, Jim knows G only if his reason for G, E, is conclusive. To assess whether E is a conclusive reason for G, we must determine the truth value of the following counterfactual:

C1: If there were no goat in the field, Jim would not have E.

We could imagine fancy circumstances in which the consequent of C1 is false. For example, a Cartesian demon might manipulate Jim's brain so as to let him have E even though there is no goat in the field. But we must consider the closest possible world in which G is false. That would be a world in which everything remains unaltered except for one thing: there is no goat in the field, but instead perhaps a cow, or no such animal at all. In such a world, Jim would not have E. Instead, he would have a visual experience of an empty field, or a field with a cow in it. When assessing C1 against a world like that, it turns out true. So E is a conclusive reason for G, which is to say Dretske's theory yields the result we ought to get: G is a proposition that Jim knows.

Thinking of knowledge as requiring conclusive reasons, as Dretske does, has an important consequence: the principle that knowledge is closed under known implication – *Closure*, for short – turns out to be false. Exactly how the Closure Principle is to be articulated is a matter of some complication. A rough and ready version of it goes as follows:

Closure
If S knows that p and knows that p implies q, then S is in a position to know that q.

There is broad agreement that deducing logical consequences of our knowledge can always expand our knowledge, i.e. can always result in knowledge of these consequences. There are, however, detractors. Dretske is one of them. For if knowledge requires conclusive reasons, it turns out that sometimes we are not in a position to know the logical consequences of what we know. Here is a well known example from Dretske (1970). Visiting the zoo, you see several zebras in an enclosure. Your zebra-like visual experience, E_z, is a conclusive reason for, and thus gives you knowledge of

Z: There are zebras in the enclosure.

What makes E_z conclusive is this: the closest possible world in which Z is false is one in which there are, say, tigers in the enclosure. In such a world, you would not have E_z. Now consider the following alternative, incompatible with Z:

M: The animals in the enclosure are cleverly disguised mules.

The question is: do you know that M is false, i.e. do you have a conclusive reason for ¬M? As long as your evidence for Z consists in E_z only, you do not. The relevant counterfactual is

C2: If M were true, I would not have E_z.

Since cleverly disguised mules look exactly like zebras, you *would* have zebra-like visual experiences if M were true. So C2 is false. Hence you do not know ¬M even though you know that Z implies ¬M. Closure fails.

In his contribution to this volume, Dretske makes a case for embracing this result. Closure is bound to fail, he argues, because the ordinary things we know have heavy weight implications that are unknowable. For example, you can know that the following event took place at some time in the past: John ate all the cookies. This event implies the following *heavyweight propositions*:

There are physical objects.
There are other minds.
The past is real.

According to Dretske, there are no accredited ways of knowing such propositions. Perception can give you knowledge about external objects, but it cannot give you conclusive reasons for thinking that idealism is false. For if idealism were true, your perceptual reasons would remain the same. Your memory can give you knowledge of the past, but it can't give you conclusive reasons for thinking that the past is real. For if the world, complete with fossils and memories of the past, had come into existence five minutes ago, your memorial reasons would remain unaltered. In general terms, instruments can be reliable indicators of certain features of reality. But they cannot be indicators of their own reliability, no matter how reliable they may in fact be. It is difficult to see, then, how we could know the heavyweight implications of our ordinary knowledge. Hence we face a trilemma. It consists of the following three propositions:

A: We have lots of knowledge of ordinary things.
B: There is no way of knowing the heavyweight implications of our knowledge of ordinary things.
C: Closure.

We know that the ordinary things we take ourselves to know imply heavyweight propositions of the kind mentioned above. Thus, if B and C are true, A must be false. But unless we are attracted to skepticism, certainly we do not want to give up A. If A and C are true, B must be false. According to Dretske, rejecting B amounts to verbal *hocus pocus*. To know that the heavyweight implications of our ordinary knowledge are true, we must know that the following *skeptical alternatives* are false:

• We are deceived by a Cartesian evil demon.
• Solipsism: I am the only conscious thing in existence.
• The world sprang into existence five minutes ago, complete with fossils and memories of the past.

Each of these alternatives is designed so as to ensure that our evidence remains unaltered. As a result, we cannot have conclusive reasons for their negations. Hence, on Dretske's view, we cannot know them to be false.

So Dretske considers the denial of neither A nor B an attractive option for resolving the trilemma, and hence views Closure as the sole remaining choice for rejection. Compared with A or B, denying C, Dretske suggests, carries the smallest costs. After all, abandoning Closure does not mean that we can *never* use implications to expand our stock of knowledge. Frequently, when we know that p implies q, we *will* have conclusive reasons for both p and q. In cases like that, we are in a position to deduce q from p.

In his essay in defense of Closure, John Hawthorne begins by discussing how a plausible version of Closure is to be articulated, and then advances three main criticisms of Dretske's view. First, rejecting Closure turns out to be more costly than it may initially seem. For if Closure fails, so does the following, rather plausible principle (Distribution): if you know the conjunction of p and q and know that a conjunction implies each of its conjuncts, then you are in a position to know p (or, for that matter, q). The other two criticisms concern Dretske's distinction between ordinary propositions for which we can have conclusive reasons, and heavyweight propositions for which we can't have such reasons. According to Hawthorne's second objection, there are some heavyweight propositions for which it is possible to have conclusive reasons. For example, although you *cannot* have a conclusive reason for the proposition that your are not a brain in a vat (a BIV), you *can* have a conclusive reason for the conjunction *I have a headache and am not a BIV*. So, on Dretske's view, you cannot know that you are not a BIV, but you can know that you have a headache and are not a BIV. Third, Hawthorne argues that there are cases in which a subject fails to have a conclusive reason for a proposition that we would classify as easily knowable. His example involves various quantities of consumed salmon. It is easy to have a conclusive reason for believing that you consumed less than one pound of salmon. But if consuming a very large quantity of salmon (say 14 pounds) causes you to hallucinate that you ate very little salmon, you do not have a conclusive reason for believing that you ate less than 14 pounds of salmon. So if you suffer from this affliction, you can know that you ate less than one pound of salmon, but not that you ate less than 14 pounds. In sum, then, Hawthorne argues that conceiving of knowledge in terms of conclusive reasons bears significant costs.

Dretske's reply is simple. A convincing defense of Closure must show that there is an alternative account of knowledge that (a) succeeds in fending off skepticism and (b) does so at smaller costs than Dretske's conclusive reasons account. Hawthorne, Dretske says, has not done that. Without endorsing it, Hawthorne reviews contextualism as an alternative way of defending our ordinary knowledge against skepticism. Dretske suggests that, when comparing costs, contextualist grass is in worse shape than the grass in his yard.

Chapter 2: Is Knowledge Contextual?

Unlike Dretske, contextualists hold that Closure should be preserved. Yet they agree with Dretske that the falsehood of a skeptical alternative such as "I'm a BIV" cannot be known – at least according to the standards of knowledge in place when we worry about skeptical alternatives. But if Closure is true *and* it is true that one cannot know that one is not a BIV, then we are confronted with what appears to be an inconsistent triad of very plausible propositions:

1 I know that I have hands.
2 I do not know that I am not a BIV.
3 I know that I have hands → I know that I am not a BIV.

It is hard to see how I could fail to know that I have hands. It is also hard to see how I could know that I am not a BIV, since if I were a BIV, my evidence would not be relevantly different from what it is now. Contextualists hold, therefore, that 1 and 2 enjoy a high degree of plausibility. Now, we could secure 1 and 2 by rejecting 3. But contextualists wish to preserve Closure. Since I know that my having hands implies my not being a BIV, Closure tells us that 3 is true. But if 3 is true, either 1 or 2 must be false. It would appear, then, that if we accept Closure, we must choose between 1 and 2. Contextualists stress that simply denying either 1 or 2 is not going to be a satisfying solution to the puzzle. What we need is a solution that preserves the intuitions in light of which 1 and 2 seem both true. According to contextualism, there is such a solution. It consists of an explanation of how propositions 1–3 can all be true (Cohen, 1988, 1999; DeRose, 1995).

Sometimes two assertions seem to be inconsistent when in fact they are not. Here is an elementary example to illustrate this phenomenon, involving the indexical "I":

4 "I have a headache" ... uttered by Jack.
5 "I do not have a headache" ... uttered by Jill.

The conjunction of 4 and 5 seems to be of the form "p and ¬p," and thus inconsistent. However, a sentence such as "I have a headache" has different truth conditions when it is uttered by different speakers. If Jack has a headache but Jill does not, "I have a headache" is true when uttered by Jack and false when uttered by Jill. Consequently, if Jack has a headache and Jill does not, 4 and 5 are both true.

The word "knowledge," contextualists say, functions just like an indexical. The truth conditions of a sentence such as "I am F" depends on who asserts it. According to contextualists, the truth conditions of sentences such as "S knows that p" and "S does not know that p" depend on the context of the subjects who assert them. Let us refer to sentences that attribute knowledge (or ignorance) to a subject as *K-assertions*. Contextualists hold that whether a K-assertion is true depends on which standard of knowledge is in place in the context in which the assertion is made. In some contexts, the standards of knowledge are low; in others, they are high. In ordinary situations of daily life, the standards of knowledge are less demanding than they are in philosophical contexts. When philosophers get together and worry about skeptical alternatives, the standards rise to the maximum: the assertion that S knows that p will be true only if S can eliminate *any* alternative that is incompatible with p. In the various non-philosophical contexts of ordinary life, the standards are lower. In low-standard contexts, what is required for the assertion that S knows p to be true is merely that S can eliminate alternatives to p that are *relevant* in those contexts.

Let us see how contextualism works when we apply it to an example:

6 Alan Greenspan knows he has hands.
7 Alan Greenspan does not know he has hands.

On the face of it, 6 and 7 seem inconsistent. Contextualists hold that they need not be. Assume Jack and his friend Joe are in a bar debating, while having a beer together, what Alan Greenspan knows and what he doesn't know. Jack claims that Greenspan knows that he has hands, but doesn't know when the Dow will reach 12,000. Since neither Jack nor Joe worries about being a BIV, or any other skeptical alternative, the standards of knowledge remain low. In that context, Jack's assertion of 6 is true.

Assume further that Jill is attending a philosophy seminar on skepticism. In this context, the skeptical alternative of being a BIV becomes salient. As a result, the standards of knowledge are high. Just like Jack and Joe, Jill happens to be thinking about what Alan Greenspan knows. Noting that Greenspan cannot eliminate the possibility that he is a BIV, Jill claims that Greenspan does not know that he has hands. In that context, her assertion of 7 is true. Since Jack's assertion of 6 and Jill's assertion of 7 occur in different contexts, each of them involving a different standard of knowledge, both assertions turn out to be true.

So, according to contextualism, whether an attribution of knowledge is true depends on the standards in place in the attributor's context. To determine the truth value of a K-assertion, we must determine whether: (a) the standards in place in the attributor's context are high or low; and (b) the subject to whom knowledge is attributed meets these standards.

Let us return to the puzzle that arises from accepting Closure. If Closure is true, it would seem that either

1 I know that I have hands.

or

2 I do not know that I am not a BIV.

is false. According to contextualism, we do not have to choose between 1 and 2. In low standard contexts, we can truly assert 1 and the negation of 2; in high standard contexts, we can truly assert 2 and the negation of 1.[1] So according to the contextualist solution to the puzzle, we can preserve both our skeptical and non-skeptical intuitions. This, according to Cohen, is one of the virtues of contextualism.

What theory does contextualism compete with? In his critique of contextualism, Earl Conee argues that its plausibility must be gauged against that of *high standards invariantism*. According to this view, the truth conditions of K-assertions do not vary from context to context. Instead, there is one, and only one, standard: one that is high, but not excessively high. Call this the *unique standard*. In ordinary life, we frequently attribute knowledge to subjects who do not have knowledge according to the unique standard. When this happens, we are simply indulging ourselves in loose talk. On the other hand, when, for some p we would normally claim to know, we are confronted with the question of whether we *really* and *truly* know p, we tend to apply the unique standard and, if convinced we don't meet that standard, retract the knowledge claim. We will not, however, retract K-assertions when it comes to the best cases of perception, memory and triple checked calculations. Such cases satisfy the unique standard, and thus are genuine instances of knowledge. Skepticism denies that they are instances of knowledge, and must therefore be rejected.

Earl Conee defends high standards invariantism on the following grounds. First, it preserves conflict where genuine conflict exists. Skeptics deny our ordinary claims to knowledge. Thus we judge that propositions 1–3 form an inconsistent set. If contextualism is correct, this judgment, the truth of which should be preserved, turns out to be mistaken. Second, contextualism concedes too much to skepticism. Like other philosophical arguments, those for skepticism can be critically assessed and might be judged as wanting. They do not deserve the deference that contextualism affords them. Third, if contextualism were true, we would be faced with another paradox. If the truth conditions of K-assertions really were context-sensitive, this should be a semantic fact transparent to competent speakers. Why, then, do competent speakers fail to recognize the context sensitivity of "know," and why does contextualism elude broad acceptance within the philosophical community?

Stewart Cohen defends contextualism on the ground that it offers us a better resolution of the paradox than high standard invariantism does. In response to Conee, he makes the following points. First, when responding to the paradox, we will have to acknowledge error somewhere. It is correct that, if contextualism is true, we are mistaken in thinking that propositions 1–3 are inconsistent. But if invariantism is correct, we must judge one of these propositions to be false, although each of them is highly plausible. Second, Cohen denies that contextualism concedes too much to skepticism. Skeptical arguments are cogent arguments. They do not suffer from obvious defects. It is a virtue of contextualism that it captures what is plausible about skepticism and does so in a way that preserves our ordinary claims to knowledge. Third, Cohen argues that "know" is not the only word the context-sensitivity of which escapes competent speakers. According to flatness skepticism, nothing is really flat because no surface is entirely free of bumps. When confronted with flatness skepticism, competent speakers respond not by noticing the context-sensitivity of "flat," but by becoming convinced that, indeed, nothing is flat. Finally, Cohen suggests that the explanation of why the philosophical community did not rush to endorse contextualism is that it is a good news–bad news theory. The good news is that, in ordinary contexts, we can truly attribute to ourselves the kind of knowledge we ordinarily think we have. The bad news is that, in philosophical contexts, we cannot truly assert that we know we have hands. Most philosophers don't like to acknowledge this, so they reject contextualism.

Chapter 3: Can Skepticism Be Refuted?

I know that my having hands implies my not being a BIV. Suppose further that we accept Closure. It then follows that I either know that I'm not a BIV, or do not know that I have hands. So if we accept Closure, we face the following skeptical argument:

The BIV Argument
1 If I know that I have hands, then I know (or am at least in a position to know) that I am not a BIV.

2 I do not know that I'm not a BIV.
Therefore:
3 I do not know that I have hands.

The first premise is the result of accepting Closure. So if you accept Closure, and you think you know you have hands, you must find a good objection to 2. Dretske, as you will recall, thinks that any such objection will amount to verbal *hocus pocus*. According to Jonathan Vogel, however, there are good grounds for rejecting 2.

Suppose you don't know how to tell a goldfinch from a canary. Vogel would say that, if so, your choice between

G: This bird is a goldfinch

and

C: This bird is a canary

is evidentially underdetermined. Your evidence is not sufficient for making a justified choice between C and G. The same, the skeptic would argue, applies to the two propositions:

H: I have hands.
B: I'm a BIV.

The BIV hypothesis is designed so as to make your evidence compatible with your being a BIV. No part of your evidence, the skeptics would argue, gives you a clue as to whether or not you are a BIV. Hence your evidence underdetermines your choice between H and B. That is why you cannot know that you are not a BIV. Vogel suggests that the choice between H and B is in fact not underdetermined. You do have reasons that you could bring to bear against B.

To reject the underdetermination claim, Vogel appeals to the principle of *inference to the best explanation*: if hypothesis A explains the relevant data better than hypothesis B, then we have a reason to prefer A to B. When discussing skepticism, the relevant data are our ordinary perceptual experiences. Vogel suggests that undeveloped skeptical hypotheses – hypotheses that do not explain in detail how our experiences come about – are poor explanations, clearly inferior to the physiological explanation we can employ when we assume that the world is pretty much what we take it to be (the *real world hypothesis*, in Vogel's terminology). However, skeptical hypotheses need not suffer from a paucity of detail and a lack of sophistication. What Vogel calls the *isomorphic skeptical hypothesis* is designed to match the cause and effect relationships of the real world hypothesis. Its explanatory power seems therefore to be no less than that of the real world hypothesis. On which grounds, then, could it be rejected?

According to Vogel, the isomorphic skeptical hypothesis suffers from the following defect: though it offers us a more complex explanation of the relevant data than the real world hypothesis, it does not deepen our understanding of these data. Its increased complexity is not offset by a commensurate increase in explanatory scope and depth. But why is the isomorphic hypothesis more complex? It is more complex, according to Vogel, because it must replace genuine shapes with pseudo shapes, and genuine locations with pseudo locations. That is why we may prefer the real world hypothesis after all, and thus reject the second premise of the BIV Argument.

Unlike Vogel, Richard Fumerton does not attempt a refutation of skepticism. Instead, he examines the nature of the challenge before us when we attempt to avoid skepticism within the traditional framework of foundationalist, internalist philosophy. If we accept this framework, then, according to Fumerton, we are committed to a view that he calls *inferential internalism*. It can be stated as follows:

(i) We are acquainted with the contents of our thoughts, and thus have direct knowledge of them.
(ii) We are not acquainted with physical objects. Therefore, if we have knowledge of physical objects, it must be inferential: inferred from what we know directly on the basis of acquaintance.
(iii) Call a body of evidence obtained through acquaintance "E." Call a typical proposition about an ordinary object "O." If we can acquire knowledge of O by inferring it from E, E must make O probable, and we must *know* that E makes O probable.

Many philosophers would reject (iii). To such philosophers, Fumerton would reply as follows. Suppose a subject, S, makes a claim, C, on the basis of a body of evidence, E. Suppose further that you are given the information that S has no clue as to whether or not E makes C probable. Wouldn't you then judge that S is *not* justified in claiming C to be true, even if you are yourself convinced that E does in fact make C probable? If you would thus judge, this shows that you actually accept condition (iii).

One problem with condition (iii) is that philosophers who accept it face a regress problem. How could we ever know a proposition to the effect that E makes O probable? Suppose we acquire knowledge of

P1: E makes O probable

by inferring it from a proposition P2. In that case, (iii) requires us to know

P3: P2 makes P1 probable.

If our knowledge of P3 were inferential as well, we would have to infer P3 from a proposition, P4, and we would have to know that P4 makes P3 probable, and so forth. So if knowledge of probability were inferential, we would end up in an infinite regress. This would make it rather doubtful that such knowledge can be had. Thus the inferential internalist must, as Fumerton stresses, employ a Keynesian conception of probability, according to which we can know directly that E makes O probable. According to to Keynes, knowledge of probability can be understood in analogy to knowledge of entailment. For example, we can know directly that "p" entails "p or q." Likewise, according to Keynes, if E does indeed make O probable, we can know directly that this is so.

According to the inferential internalist, I cannot know *directly* that I am not a BIV. Thus it is not easy for the inferential internalist to avoid skepticism. If inferential internalism is correct, and if I am to know that I am not a BIV, there must be a body of evidence that makes my not being a BIV probable for me, and it must be possible for me to know directly that it makes this probable for me. That, according to Fumerton, is the challenge we face when we wish to refute skepticism.

Vogel's suggestion is that the needed body of evidence consists in the fact taht the BIV hypothesis is not as good an explanation of the relevant data as the real world hypothesis. But does it? Suppose that, all other things being equal, the simpler of two explanations is more likely to be true than the more complex one. Obviously, antiskepticism wins only if the real world hypothesis is indeed simpler than any competing skeptical hypothesis. Fumerton points out, however, that Berkeley claimed his own view of immaterialism – according to which God causes our experiences – was simpler than the competing view that our experiences are caused by physical objects. Moreover, why should we believe that the simpler of two explanations is really more likely to be true? Fumerton argues that the skeptic has every right to question the probability principles to which the non-skeptic appeals. What reasons, then, can be adduced for thinking that inference to the best explanation is a guide to truth? Vogel responds that this does indeed raise a difficult problem for the kind of antiskepticism he advocates, but registers the opinion that inference to the best explanation is in fact no more problematic than any other principle of probability.

Chapter 4: Is There *a Priori* Knowledge?

There is a large set of propositions that, according to philosophical tradition, are knowable *a priori*: knowable independently of experience. What is meant by saying that such propositions are knowable in this way is that the justification we have for believing them does not arise from experience. Thus the issue over *a priori* knowledge really concerns a distinction between two kinds of *justification*: empirical and *a priori*, the former resulting from the use of our perceptual and introspective faculties, the latter from exercising what we might call the faculty of rational insight. Typical examples of the kind of propositions claimed to be knowable through rational insight are the following:

The sum of two and two is four.
Two is an even number.
Whatever is square is rectangular.
Whatever is red is colored.
Necessarily, if "p or q" is true and "q" is false, then "p" is true.

Call such propositions PAPS: putatively *a priori* propositions. It is generally agreed that PAPS are knowable. There is skepticism about knowledge of the external world, other minds, and the past. Skepticism about PAPS, however, is rarely pursued. Indeed, considering that knowledge of PAPS includes knowledge of the laws of logic, and more specifically, knowledge of an argument's validity, it is hard to see how a skeptical argument for anything could get off the ground without the prior assumption that knowledge of PAPS is indeed possible. So the knowability of PAPS is not at issue. However, there are philosophers – advocates of radical naturalism – who question that PAPS are really known *a priori*. They can be viewed as skeptics about *a priori* knowledge, not on account of denying that we know any PAPS, but because they hold that there is no such faculty as rational insight, and consequently no such thing as *a priori* knowledge. According to such philosophers, all knowledge, including that of PAPS, is empirical.

In the two essays on the issue of *a priori* knowledge, Laurence BonJour represents the traditional point of view, and Michael Devitt makes the case for radical naturalism. For defenders of *a priori* knowledge, the chief task is to explain how *a priori* justification comes about. According to BonJour, justification for an *a priori* proposition, p, results from grasping that p is necessarily true. We recognize p as a necessary truth, and thus are supplied with a reason for accepting p. For opponents of *a priori* knowledge, the task is twofold. First, they must give an account of how empirical knowledge of PAPS is possible. Second, they must explain why PAPS cannot be known through rational insight. Devitt attempts to dispose of the first task by appeal to the thesis of holism, proposed by Duhem and Quine: beliefs face the tribunal of experience not individually but only as a system. PAPS are part of our belief system. Since any belief within such a system may be revised in light of experience, it follows that there is empirical justification for PAPS.

However, from the thesis of holism, it does not follow that, in addition to holistic empirical justification, there is not also *a priori* justification for PAPS in the form of rational insight. Thus Devitt offers a second, main argument. *A priori* justification in the form of rational insight is, he claims, utterly obscure. Although we lack a well developed theory of empirical justification, it is nevertheless well understood what such justification at bottom amounts to. But as far as rational insight is concerned, we face an unexplained mystery. Not only do we not have a well developed account of it, we do not even understand how we *could* acquire knowledge of external, worldly facts without the help of experience. In short, there is a significant discrepancy between empirical justification and *a priori* justification. The latter is deeply mysterious, the former not at all.

BonJour denies such discrepancy. Empirical justification, at least when it comes to indirect empirical knowledge, is no less problematic than *a priori* justification. In response to Devitt's appeal to holism, BonJour claims that Devitt begs the question. If the premise of holism is to yield the conclusion that PAPS are justifiable empirically, we must assume the additional premise that a conflict between a PAP and a set of experiences must always be decided in favor of the latter. But this is just what is at issue, and what a traditional philosopher would deny. Moreover, BonJour argues that even if we grant the premise of holism, we still need *a priori* knowledge. According to a Quinean epistemology, there are certain features of belief systems that count in favor of their truth; for example, simplicity, fecundity, explanatory strength. How can we justify the claim that such features are really indicators of truth? If we cannot do this *a priori*, we must infer it within our holistic belief system. But any such procedure would be viciously circular. It follows that the holistic naturalist cannot explain why holistic justification supplies us with a reason for thinking that the holistic belief system is true. Skepticism is the inevitable outcome.

BonJour, then, denies that holism can account for our knowledge of PAPS. In response, Devitt argues for three claims:

(i)   For holistic evidence to justify our beliefs, it is not necessary for us to know that the items that constitute holistic evidence are indicators of truth.

(ii) The holistic naturalist is committed not to premise circularity, but to rule circularity only, which, unlike the former, is benign.

(iii) BonJour's rationalist defense of apriority requires rule-circularity no less than holistic naturalism, and thus is committed to viewing such circularity as benign.

BonJour rejects each of these claims. First, he insists that an evidential item, E, can justify our acceptance of p only if we know that E is reason for thinking that p is true. Second, he denies that rule circularity is benign. Finally, he argues that *a priori* justification through rational insight does not raise circularity problems because it is immediate, non-propositional, and thus atomistic.

Note

1   It is, however, not entirely clear whether it is possible truly to deny 2 in a low standard context. Let "B" stand for the proposition that I am a BIV. Can I attribute to myself knowledge of ¬B while remaining in a low standard context? Perhaps merely thinking about the envatment possibility makes the skeptical alternative of being a BIV salient, thus creating a high standard context. If this is so, it remains doubtful that one can ever *truly* attribute to oneself (or to anyone else, for that matter) knowledge of ¬B.

References

Cohen, S. (1988) How to be a fallibilist. *Philosophical Perspectives*, 2, 581–605.
Cohen, S. (1999) Contextualism, skepticism, and the structure of reasons. *Philosophical Perspectives*, 13, 57–89.
Dretske, F. (1970) Epistemic operators. *Journal of Philosophy*, 67, 1007–23.
Dretske, F. (1971) Conclusive reasons. *Australasian Journal of Philosophy*, 49, 1–22.
De Rose, K. (1995) Solving the skeptical problem. *Philosophical Review*, 104, 1–52.

Is Knowledge Closed under Known Entailment?

The Case against Closure

Fred Dretske

Closure is the epistemological principle that if S knows that P is true and knows that P implies Q, then, evidentially speaking, this is enough for S to know that Q is true. Nothing more is needed. If S believes Q on this secure basis – on the basis of two things he knows to be true – then S knows that Q is true. One knows everything that one knows to be implied by what one knows.

It is important to distinguish closure from *modus ponens*, a principle of logic that it superficially resembles. Closure is stronger. *Modus ponens* says that if P is true, and if P implies Q, then Q must be true. Closure tells us that when S knows that P is true and also knows that P implies Q, then not only must Q *be* true (*modus ponens* gets you this much), S must *know* it is true.[1]

Why must S know Q to be true? Why does one have to know everything one knows to be implied by what one knows? One doesn't, after all, have to regret everything one knows to be implied by what one regrets. Tom regrets drinking three martinis last night, but he doesn't regret what he knows to be implied by this – drinking *something* last night. Nor does he regret the reality of the past even though he knows that drinking three martinis last night implies that the past is real. If

   (R) S regrets P
         S knows that P implies Q
         Therefore, S regrets Q

is not a valid argument, why should

   (K) S knows P
         S knows P implies Q
         Therefore, S knows Q

be accepted as valid?

This question defines the issue between John Hawthorne and me. I will be taking the negative side of the debate: knowledge is *not* closed under known logical implication. (K) is *not* a valid argument. There are things we know to be implied by what we know that we do not know to be true. Just as a great many conditions I do not regret have to exist (and I know they have to exist) in order for the condition I regret to exist, a great many conditions I do not know to exist have to exist (and I know they have to exist) in order for the conditions I know to exist.

1 Transmissibility

Let me begin this examination by talking about a problem that is closely related to closure: transmission of evidential warrant. I shall come back to closure later (in sections 2 and 3).

Our ways of discovering P are not necessarily ways of discovering what we know to be implied by P. From the fact that you know that P implies Q, it does not follow that you can see (smell, feel, etc.) that Q just because you can see (smell, feel, etc.) that P. Despite knowing that cookies are objective (mind-independent) objects, I can see (roughly: tell by looking) that there are cookies in the jar without being able to see, without being able to tell by looking, that there are mind-independent objects. A claim to have found out, by looking, that there are cookies in the jar is not a claim to have found out, by looking, that there is a material world. Maybe one has to know there are physical objects in order to see that there are cookies in the jar (we will come back to that), but one surely isn't claiming to see that there are physical objects in claiming to see there are cookies in the jar. After all, hallucinatory cookies "in" hallucinatory jars can look exactly like real cookies in real cookie jars. So one cannot, not by vision alone, distinguish real cookies from mental figments. One cannot *see* that the world really is the way it visually appears to be. A way of knowing there are cookies in a jar – visual perception – is *not* a way of knowing what one knows to be implied by this – that visual appearances are not misleading.

The claim to have found out, by visual means, that there is still wine left in the bottle ("Just look; you can see that there is") is not a claim to have found out, at least not by visual means, what you know to be implied by this – that it, the liquid in the bottle, is not merely colored water. You know it is wine because, let us suppose, you tasted it a few minutes ago. That you learned it is wine, and not merely colored water, by tasting does not prevent you from now (minutes later) seeing that there is still some wine left in the bottle. Seeing that P does not mean you can see that Q just because you know P implies Q.

In *Seeing and Knowing* (1969) I tried to describe this phenomenon by introducing a technical term: *protoknowledge*. Protoknowledge was a word I made up to describe things that had to be true for what you perceived to be true but which (even if you knew they had to be true) you couldn't perceive to be true. That there are material objects has to be true for there to be cookies in the jar (and, hence, for you to see that there are cookies in the jar), but it isn't something you see to be so. It is a piece of (what I was calling) protoknowledge. When you see, just by looking, that there is wine in the bottle, the fact that it is not colored water is also protoknowledge. It has to be true for there to be wine in the bottle (what you perceive to be so), but it is not a fact that (normally) you can see to be so. In describing how one knows there is still wine left in the bottle one is not (not normally) describing how one knows it is not merely colored water.

Now, thirty years later, as a result of work by Davies (1998, 2000) and Wright (2003), there is, I think, a more revealing way of making this point. The idea is that some reasons for believing P do not *transmit* to things, Q, known to be implied by P. In normal circumstances – a wine tasting party, say – one's reasons for thinking there is wine left in the bottle do not transmit to, they are not reasons for believing, what you know to be implied by this – that the liquid in the bottle is not merely colored water. Having already tasted it, you may know that it is wine and not just colored water, but the point is that your reasons for believing the one (visual) are not reasons for believing the other (gustatory). Colored water in the bottle would look exactly the same as the wine. The reasons you have for believing what you say you perceive (there is wine left in the bottle) are not *transmitted* to this known consequence (that it is not merely colored water) of what you perceive.

The non-transmissibility (to many of the known consequences) of most of our reasons for believing P is an absolutely pervasive phenomenon. I will, in this section, spend a little more time harping about it since I think it critical for evaluating the plausibility of closure. Non-transmissibility does not itself imply the failure of closure since, as our wine example illustrates, even when S's reasons for believing P do not transmit to a known consequence, Q, it may be that S must still know Q (perhaps on the basis of other reasons) in order to know P. Even though S cannot see that it is wine, not just colored water, it may turn out (this is what closure tells us) that S must know (perhaps by earlier tasting) that it is not colored water if he is now to see (hence, know) that there is wine left in the bottle. Nonetheless, once one appreciates the wholesale failure of evidential transmission, the failure of closure is, if not mandatory, easier to swallow. Or so I will argue.

As we have already seen, perception, our chief (some would say our only) route to knowledge of the world around us, does not transmit its evidential backing to *all* the known consequences of what is perceived. We can see (hear, smell, feel) that P, but some of the Qs that (we know) P implies are just too remote, too distant, to inherit the positive warrant the sensory evidence confers upon P. When Jimmy peeks into the cookie jar and, to his delight, sees that there are cookies there, his visual experience of the cookies, the evidential basis for his knowledge that there are cookies there, is not evidence, not a reason to believe, that there is a physical reality independent of Jimmy's mind. Jimmy's experience of the cookies may be good reason to believe there are cookies in the jar, but it is not a good reason to believe that idealism is false. And it is not a good reason to believe that idealism is false even if Jimmy understands that cookies are mind-independent objects and that, therefore, what he sees to be the case (that there are cookies in the jar) implies that idealism is false. Looking in the cookie jar may be a way of finding out whether there are any cookies there, but it isn't – no more than kicking rocks – a way of refuting Bishop Berkeley.

So perceptual reasons – the sense experiences on which we base everyday perceptual judgments – do not transmit their evidential force to all the known consequences of the judgments they warrant.

(T) R is a reason for S to believe P
      S knows that P implies Q
      R is a reason for S to believe Q

is not a valid argument. When we perceive that P, there are, so to speak, *heavyweight* implications of P that cannot be perceived to be so. There is transmission to *lightweight* implications, of course. If I can see that there are cookies in the jar, I can certainly see that the jar isn't empty, that there is something in the jar. For perception, though, there are *always* heavyweight implications, known implications to what one perceives (P) that one's perceptual reasons for P are powerless to reach. If there is any doubt about this, simply imagine Q to be a condition S knows to be incompatible with P but which, because of (perhaps extraordinary) circumstances, has the same sensory effects on S as P. Though incompatible with P, Q (as so specified) will look (feel, sound) exactly the same to S as P. Q is, as it were, a perceptual twin of P. With such a Q, S will not be able to perceive ~Q though he perceives P and knows that P implies ~Q.

Skeptics have used this formula to manufacture heavyweight implications for all our ordinary perceptual claims. No matter what you purport to know by perception, perception will not be the way you know that you are not being deceived by a Cartesian demon. It will not be the way you know you are not a disembodied brain in a vat being caused (by suitably placed electrodes) to experience the things an ordinary veridical perceiver experiences. One cannot see (hear, smell, feel, etc.) that one is not in this unfortunate position even though one knows one cannot be in this position and still be seeing (hearing, etc.) the things one believes oneself to be seeing (hearing, etc.). You can't *see* that you are not dreaming.

2 Closure

What does this have to do with closure? When you know that P implies Q, closure tells us you have to know Q to know P. It doesn't tell us that the reasons that promote your belief that P into knowledge that P must themselves promote your belief (assuming you have it) that Q into knowledge that Q. Maybe the reasons (see section 1) for P don't transmit to Q. Very well. Then closure tells us that if you know P you have to have *other* reasons (or, if reasons are not always required, whatever else it takes) to promote your belief that Q into knowledge that Q. But – or so closure says – you have to have *something* to make your belief that Q into knowledge in order to know P. If you don't, then – too bad – you don't know that P. Nothing I have said so far challenges this claim.

Is this true? Is it true that someone (who knows that cookies are material objects) cannot see that there are cookies in the jar unless he or she knows that there is a physical, mind-independent, world? That they are not being misled by some clever deception? In Dretske (1970) I asked the same question about my ability to see that an animal is a zebra without knowing it was not a cleverly painted mule. It seemed to me then, as it still seems to me today, that if this is true, if knowledge is closed under known implication, if, in order to see (hence, know) that there are cookies in the jar, wine in the bottle, and a zebra in the pen, I have to know that I am not being fooled by a clever deception, that the "appearances" (the facts on which my judgments are based) are not misleading, then skepticism is true. I never see (to be so), and hence do not know (to be so), what I think and say I see (to be so).[2] This is not to deny that we know – and, perhaps, necessarily know – *most* of the implications of what we know. But not *all* of them. There are some things – *heavyweight* implications – we needn't know even though we know our knowledge depends on their truth.

Though I haven't performed a scientific study, my impression is that most philosophers (who bother thinking about it) believe that this is preposterous. Feldman (1999) thinks that abandoning closure is "one of the least plausible ideas to gain currency in epistemology in recent years." DeRose (1995) finds it "intuitively bizzare" or "abominable." Fumerton (1987) thinks the failure of closure is a "devastating objection" and BonJour (1987) a *reductio ad absurdum* to any theory that implies or embraces it. Most philosophers, of course, are eager to reject skepticism. Rejecting closure as a way around skepticism, though, is quite another matter. As these reactions indicate, many philosophers are unwilling to do it. Skepticism is bad, yes, but for many philosophers, not *that* bad. Not bad *enough* to justify rejecting closure. That would be like rejecting logic because it gave us conclusions we didn't like.

Some of these reactions are, I think, a bit overdone. To deny closure is not to say that you can *never* know (find out, discover, learn) that Q is true by inferring it from a P that you know to be true. It is merely to deny that this can be done for *any* Q. Nor is denial of closure a way of embracing (without further explanation) DeRose's (1995) abominable conjunctions. Statements like "I know I have hands, but I do not know that I am not a handless brain in a vat" (a statement that denial of closure accepts as being possibly true) are clearly ridiculous. We can all agree about that. The question, however, is not whether anyone would ever say it (or, if they did, whether they would be greeted by stares of incomprehension) but whether it might be true if they said it. "The refrigerator is empty, but has lots of things in it" is also an abominable conjunction. It might, nonetheless, be true. There may be no food or other items normally stored in refrigerators inside (thus making the refrigerator empty in the normal way of understanding what isn't in empty refrigerators), but it may, nonetheless, be filled with lots of gas molecules (perfectly respectable things). The abomination in saying a refrigerator is empty but has lots of things in it comes not from any logical defect (there are lots of empty things that have gas molecules in them – pockets, classrooms, warehouses, etc.), but from a violation of normal expectations. In describing an object as a refrigerator (and not, say, a metal container) one is led to expect that the things that are in (or, in the case of its being empty, not in) it are the sorts of perishable items normally stored or preserved in refrigerators. To then include (second conjunct) gas molecules as things in refrigerators is to flout this entirely reasonable expectation about what sorts of things are to be counted as things for purposes of describing the contents of refrigerators. Why isn't it ridiculous, for exactly the same reason, to say one knows one has hands but doesn't know one isn't a handless brain in a vat? The second conjunct introduces possibilities normally assumed to be irrelevant (not counted as possibilities) by someone who asserts the first conjunct.

This is only to say (Grice 1967) that there are logical abominations (self-contradictory) and conversational abominations (perfectly consistent, and therefore possibly true statements, that violate conventional expectations). To say that S knows that there are cookies in the jar but doesn't know he isn't hallucinating them is certainly to say something absurd, but why suppose its absurdity is such (i.e. logical) as to render the statement incapable of being true? To demonstrate logical incoherence would require a theory about what it takes (and doesn't take) to know something, and we are back to where we started: assessing the status of closure.

So I don't think we (e.g. John Hawthorne and I) can just match brute intuitions on closure. Yes, closure sounds like an eminently plausible principle. Everything else being equal, then, we ought to keep it. But everything else *isn't* equal. It is also plausible (some would say it was entirely obvious) that we know things about our material surroundings – that (when we see them for ourselves) there are cookies in a jar, zebras in the zoo, people in the room, and cars on the street. And it isn't at all clear that we can have such knowledge while, at the same time, retaining closure. Something has to give. This reasoning won't impress a skeptic, of course, but, if a case could be made for the claim that a rejection of closure was not just *a* way to avoid skepticism (most philosophers would agree with this) but the *only* way to avoid skepticism, it should carry weight with philosophers who find skepticism as "bizarre" or "abominable" as the denial of closure. This will be my strategy in the remainder of this paper. The only way to preserve knowledge of homely truths, the truths everyone takes themselves to know, is, I will argue, to abandon closure.

Philosophers, though, will insist that there are other, less costly, ways of dealing with skepticism, ways that do not require the rejection of closure. One of the popular maneuvers is to make knowledge attributions sensitive to justificational context. In ordinary contexts in which knowledge claims are advanced, one knows (such things as) that there are cookies in the jar and (at the zoo) zebras in the pen. In such ordinary contexts one normally has all the evidence needed to know. One sees the cookies and the zebras and, given the absence of any special reason to doubt, this (for reasonably experienced adults) is good enough to know. So skepticism is false. Do these reasonably experienced adults also know, then, that they are not being deceived by some kind of fake? That the sensory evidence on which they base their judgments is not misleading? That there really is a material world? That they are not a brain in a vat? Well, yes (so closure is preserved), but – and here is the kicker – only as long as they don't seriously consider these heavyweight implications or say that they know them to be true. For once they think about them or say they know them to be true, the context in which knowledge claims are evaluated changes and knowledge evaporates. In this altered context (no longer an ordinary context) one doesn't know that one is not being deceived because new alternatives (that one *is* being deceived), possibilities one cannot evidentially eliminate, have been introduced. Therefore (closure forces one to say) one no longer knows that there are cookies in the jar and zebras in the pen. One gets to know about cookies and zebras only as long as one doesn't think about or claim to know what, according to closure, one has to know in order to know such mundane things. According to this way of dealing with skepticism, philosophers who spend time worrying about heavyweight implications (How do I know I'm not dreaming? How do we know there is a material world?) are the most ignorant people in the world. Not only don't they know these heavyweight implications (maybe no one does), they don't (like everyone else) know the things (that there are cookies in the jar, zebras in the pen) that imply them. This, of course, includes almost everything they thought they knew.

This result, it seems to me, is pretty bizarre – *more* bizarre, in fact, than abandoning closure. It is a way of preserving closure for the heavyweight implications while abandoning its usefulness in acquiring knowledge of them. One knows (or is evidentially positioned to know) heavyweight implications only so long as one doesn't think about them or say that one knows them to be true. I think we can do better than this. By suitable restriction of closure (to lightweight and middleweight implications) we can have most of our cake (the only part worth eating) and eat it too.

Before launching this argument, though, let me mention a theoretical consideration that deserves attention in this regard. It is not, in the end, decisive on the issue of closure, but it is certainly relevant and with some readers it may carry weight. It does with me.

There is what I (and a great many others) regard as a plausible approach to the analysis of knowledge that leads quite naturally (not inevitably,[3] but naturally) to a failure of closure. If knowledge that P requires one (or one's evidence) to exclude not all, but only all relevant, alternatives to P, then, it seems, one is committed to a failure of closure. The evidence that (by excluding all relevant alternatives) enables me to know there are cookies in the jar does not enable me to know that they (what I see in the jar) are not papier mâché fakes since papier mâché fakes are not (usually) a relevant alternative. So the evidence that gives me knowledge of P (there are cookies in the jar) can exist without evidence for knowing Q (they are not fake) despite my knowing that P implies Q. So closure fails.

Although this is, as I say, a natural line of reasoning, it isn't very effective against the skeptic if the only reason for embracing a relevant alternative analysis of knowledge is that it captures common-sense (basically antiskeptical) intuitions about when and what we know. If, that is, one's reasons for accepting a relevant alternatives analysis of knowledge is that it accords with our ordinary practice of claiming to know something (that there are cookies in the jar) without having specific evidence against possible mistakes (that, for example, they are not papier mâché fakes), then the argument against closure becomes too tightly circular to be effective against a skeptic. One uses premises – basically what is ordinarily regarded as the kind of evidence good enough to know – that no self-respecting skeptic would concede.

A dialectically more effective strategy is to provide an independent (of skepticism) analysis of knowledge that yields the result that only certain alternatives (to what is known) are evidentially relevant. This is the strategy adopted in Dretske (1969, 1970, 1971) and Nozick (1981). If knowledge is belief based on the kind of conclusive reasons I describe in Dretske (1971), for instance, then closure fails. Things turn out this way because one can have conclusive reasons, R, for P (R is a conclusive reason for P = $_{df}$R would not be true unless P were true) without having conclusive reasons for known consequences of P. For example,

(C) It would not look to me as though there were cookies in the jar if there weren't cookies in the jar.

can be true – thus making the look of the jar (roughly: my experience of the jar) a conclusive reason for believing there are cookies in it – while

> (C*) It would not look to me as though there were cookies in the jar if there were cleverly made papier mâché cookies in the jar.

is false – thus preventing the experience from being a conclusive reason for believing what I know to be implied by there being cookies in the jar – that they are not merely papier mâché fakes in the jar.

Unfortunately, though, the world has not rushed to embrace this theory of knowledge (or its information-theoretic successor in Dretske, 1981). Nonetheless, I think many of the arguments for something like a counterfactual condition on knowledge are good arguments, and I have yet to see effective counterarguments.[4] I won't, however, recapitulate the history here. One doesn't make reasons better by repeating them. Suffice it to say that if one is sympathetic to something like (C) as a condition on seeing (hence, knowing) that there are cookies in the jar, one has taken a critical step towards denying closure. One has accepted a condition on knowledge that need not be, and often isn't, satisfied by known consequences of what is known.

3 Heavyweight Implications

I argued in section 1 that some ways – the perceptual ways – of coming to know P do not transmit evidential grounding for P to all the known implications of P. Ordinary things we come to know by perception always have heavyweight implications that are out of range: we cannot see (hear, smell, or feel) that they are true. If closure is not to result in complete skepticism about the external world, then, it seems that there must always be other ways of knowing that these heavyweight implications are true. I can see that there are cookies in the jar, but I cannot see that there is an external world. So if we have to know there is an external world in order to see there are cookies in a jar, as closure tells us we must, then there must be other (than visual) ways we know that there is an external world. There must be a way other than perception in which I know that I'm not a brain in a vat, that I'm not being massively deceived, that solipsism is false, that it is not all just a dream. What might these other ways of knowing be?

It is hard to see what other ways there could be since every way of knowing either fails to reach these heavyweight implications or generates its own heavyweight implications. *No* evidence[5] transmits to *all* the implications of what it is evidence for.

Testimony, for instance, is considered to be an important source of knowledge that is distinct from perception. I didn't see the tire for myself, but I know it is flat because she told me it was flat. That is how I know. Yet, although I know that tires are material objects, I can learn, by being told, that I have a flat tire without thereby learning that solipsism is false – that there is something else in the universe besides me and my own ideas. No one, as I recall, ever told me there was something else besides me in the universe, but, if someone (a philosophy professor?) did, it is hard to believe that *that* is the way I learned there are other minds and a material world. Yet being

Chapter One

told is the way I come to know things – a great many things – that I know imply there is a material world. That there is a material world is something we know to be implied by what we are told (flat tires *are* material objects independent of me and my own thoughts and experiences) but it is not something we learn by being told. So, if closure holds, testimony – and, remember, this includes not only books, newspapers, and television but virtually our entire educational system – cannot be a source of knowledge unless we have some *other* way of finding out there is a material world. Some *other* way of discovering that solipsism is false.

Or consider memory. Although memory is not generally considered a way of *coming* to know (it is more like a way of *preserving* knowledge acquired by other means) it, too, has its heavyweight implications. Whatever cognitive mechanisms enable a person to preserve, by memory, the knowledge that P do not enable the person to preserve a knowledge of P's known consequences. If you remember having granola for breakfast this morning, then you know you had granola for breakfast this morning.[6] If you remember going to the bank before stopping at the bakery, then you know you went to the bank before stopping at the bakery. But, as we all know, we couldn't have had granola for breakfast this morning, or stopped at the bank before going to the bakery, unless time, the succession of events, and, in particular, the past is real. That the past is real, however, is not something one remembers. It doesn't sound like something one *can* remember. This implication is more like a presupposition – something one simply takes for granted – in remembering the nitty gritty details of personal history – that one had granola for breakfast or went to the bank before going to the bakery. For most of the things we remember (*most* but perhaps not all: we sometimes remember what we are supposed *to do*) the reality of the past is a heavyweight implication. It is something we know to be implied by things we remember, but it is not itself something we remember. Our way of preserving knowledge is not a way of preserving what we know to be implied by what we preserve. If closure is true, though, we cannot remember what we had for breakfast this morning unless we know the past is real. Since memory isn't a way of finding out the past is real, what, then, is the method we have for finding this out? Perception? Testimony? Fossils? I don't think so. Neither did Bertrand Russell when he wondered how we could know the world wasn't created minutes ago complete with history books, fossils, and memory traces. If there is a past, fossils, memory, and history books tell us what happened in it – the historical details, as it were – but they cannot tell us what is implied by the existence of these details: that there actually was a past.

Instead of trying to catalogue all the different ways of coming to know – probably a hopeless task, anyway – let me try approaching this topic from a more general standpoint. Generally speaking, when we come to know that P is true, there is always some indicator, some source of information, that "tells us" P is true. In the case of direct perception, this is an experience of the very condition "P" describes. We come to know there are cookies in the jar by seeing (experiencing) the cookies themselves. In testimony the information arrives by more indirect means: friends, teachers, radio and television newscasters, witnesses, books, newspapers, and magazines act as intermediaries. The information arrives in verbal form: someone tells me – perhaps by scribbling a note – that so-and-so happened. We also rely on natural signs – tracks in the snow, rings in the stump, cloud formations, facial expressions, and spontaneous behavior (yawns, sneezes, etc.). Photographs and measuring instruments indicate, they carry information about, conditions we do not – sometimes cannot – directly perceive. In each case, our way of coming to know that P always seems to depend on there being something that, by its revealing properties, indicates that P is true. There is always something that brings this information to us. It is important, therefore, to understand that the relationships we describe by speaking of one thing *indicating* or *carrying information* about another condition, P, are relations that do not relate this thing to (all) the known implications of P. Though we rely on a measuring instrument to indicate the value of Q – that it is, say, 5 units – the measuring instrument does not indicate, does not carry information, that Q is not being misrepresented. The position of a pointer (pointing at "5") on a well functioning meter indicates that the value of Q is 5 units, but it does not thereby indicate that the instrument is not broken, not malfunctioning, not misrepresenting a value of 2 units (say) as 5 units. Even when instruments (and this includes the human senses) are in perfect working order, they do not – they cannot – carry information that what they are providing is genuine information and not misinformation. That isn't an instrument's job. The job of a Q-meter is to tell us about Q, not about its reliability in providing information about Q. So even though we know that if Q really is 5 (as the meter says), then Q can't be 2 being misrepresented (by the meter) as 5, the meter gives us the first piece of information (tells us that Q is 5) without giving us the second piece of information: that Q isn't really 2 being misrepresented as 5. That isn't information the Q-meter supplies. It is a heavyweight implication of the information a Q-meter supplies. Anyone who really wanted to know whether the instrument was misrepresenting Q (when it registered "5") should not look more carefully at the pointer. A pointer pointing at "5" does not carry *that* information. The information it carries (when things are working right) is that Q is 5, not that Q doesn't just appear to be 5.

This is true of all indicators, all sources of information. That is why there is nothing in the world – either mental or material – that indicates that there is a material world. Nothing in the present that indicates there is a past. Skeptics, of course, have known this for a long time. Indicators carry information about cookies in jars, wine in bottles, and zebras in pens, not information about the heavyweight implications of these facts. That is why fuel gauges indicate, and thereby tell you, that you have gas in your tank without telling you that there is a material world (something implied by there being gas and gas tanks). That is why rings in the stump can indicate the age of a tree without indicating that the past is real. That is why birth certificates can provide information about when someone was born without providing information that the world (complete with birth certificates) was not created this morning. If there is an answer to skepticism about the past or about the material world, the answer will not be found by examining birth certificates or looking at tree stumps. If there is a past, if that heavyweight implication (of a tree being 200 years old or a person being 84 years old) is true, tree rings and birth certificates will not tell us it is true. That is something we take for granted *in*, not something we find out *by*, counting tree rings and reading birth certificates.

Insofar, then, as any accredited way of knowing P depends on information delivered about P, I conclude that *none* of our accredited ways of knowing about our material world are capable of telling us that there is a material world, none of the accredited ways of finding out about what people feel and think are ways of finding out that they are not mindless zombies, and none of the accepted ways of finding out what, specifically, happened yesterday are ways of finding out that there was a yesterday. If this is true, it leaves us with a choice. Either

(1) *Skepticism*: we retain closure and accept skepticism. I cannot know P, for any P, unless I know all the (known) implications of P. But I can't know all these. There is nothing I am aware of that indicates (carries information) that the heavyweight implications are true. So (given closure) we don't know any of the things – and this includes most things – that imply these heavyweight truths.

or

(2) *Denial of closure*: we preserve ordinary knowledge by denying closure. We don't have to know the heavyweight implications of P to know P. I don't have to know I am not a deluded brain in a vat to see (hence, know) that there are cookies in the jar. I can, and often do, get information about P sufficient unto knowing that P is true without getting information about the heavyweight implications of P.

For anyone who thinks they know something about the material world, the choice is easy. Closure must be denied. There are some (known) implications of what we know – the heavyweight implications – that we do not have to know to be true in order to know to be true what implies them.

There is, though, another possibility. The choice between (1) and (2) is so painful that some philosophers prefer to try wriggling between the horns of this dilemma. Perhaps we can keep closure *and* have knowledge if we are willing to extend – by an act of courtesy, as it were – knowledge to heavyweight implications. Though I typically have no evidence that I am not being systematically deceived by the facts on which I base my belief that P,[7] it might still be argued that our knowledge of heavyweight implications is special. Even though none of our accredited ways of knowing transmits evidence to them, we nonetheless get to know them anyway. These are things we get to know without having reasons to believe them, without being able to eliminate the possibilities (e.g. that I *am* being deceived) they directly compete with. Though I can't know they are zebras (not elephants or giraffes) in the pen without being able to distinguish (at this distance, in these circumstances) zebras from other sorts of animals, I can (according to the present hypothesis) know that they are not painted mules even though I can't (at this distance, in these circumstances) distinguish zebras from painted mules.

This strikes me as, at best, a bit of verbal hocus pocus designed to avoid skepticism while retaining closure. We have our cake and eat it too by simply stipulating that we know whatever we know to be implied by what we know even though we have no identifiable way of knowing it. In rejecting this option I assume, of course, that the visual appearance of a zebra – the sort of perceptual condition that normally leads one to say one can see that it is a zebra – is not evidence, is not itself a reason to think, that the zoo authorities did not replace the zebras with mules painted to

Is Knowledge Closed under Known Entailment?

look like zebras. I assume that the appearance of cookies in a jar, the sort of condition that prompts one to say one can see there are cookies in the jar, is not itself a reason to believe that the experience of the cookies is not misleading or delusory in some way.[8] Given these assumptions, it seems to me preposterous – abominable, if you will – to insist that we nonetheless know we are not being deceived in these ways because we know that *not* being deceived in these ways is implied by what our experience normally leads us to believe – that there are zebras in the pen and cookies in the jar. Despite its philosophical credentials (Moore, 1959), that sounds like chutzpah, not philosophy, to me.

Notes

1 I hereafter drop the distracting reminder that S, if he believes Q, must base his belief in Q on the two facts he knows to be true: (1) P, and (2) If P then Q.

2 The parenthetical "to be so" is important. Skepticism is irrelevant to what *objects* I see, whether, for instance, I see cookies in the jar, wine in the bottle, and zebras at the zoo. What I don't see if skepticism is true are *the facts* – the fact that there are cookies in the jar, wine in the bottle, and a zebra in the pen. One doesn't have to see (hence, know) these facts to see the objects that figure in these facts. Perception of objects (events, states of affairs, conditions) is immune from skeptical challenge.

3 Stine (1976), Cohen (1988, 1999) and Lewis (1996), while adopting a relevant alternative account of knowledge, retain closure by embracing a fairly radical form of contextualism. DeRose (1995) gives an externalist form of contextualism and argues that it retains closure while avoiding skepticism. For a general survey and discussion of options see Brueckner (1985).

4 Except for Martin (1975), which forced me to adopt an information-theoretic formulation of "conclusive reasons." See, also, Martin (1983), where the same example is used against Nozick (1981). An oft mentioned criticism is that the theory is subject to the sorts of counterexamples (unpublished) Saul Kripke gave of Robert Nozick's (1981) theory. I do not think these examples work against my own theory even though there is a superficial similarity between Nozick's and my accounts (we both use counterfactuals to express the required relations between knower and known). Since I am not relying on this theory to defend my rejection of closure, a detailed defense of the theory is out of place here. For the cognoscenti, though, I say this much. When there are, in the relevant neighborhood, fake barns but no fake *red* barns (so that something might look like a barn without being a barn, but nothing would look like a red barn without being a red barn), it turns out that on Nozick's theory you can track (Nozick's term) red barns (you wouldn't believe it was a red barn unless it was a red barn) without tracking barns. Thus, you can know of a red barn you see that it is a red barn but not that it is a barn. This result is an embarrassment even for someone (like Nozick) who denies closure. The example, however, is not effective against a "conclusive reason" (or information-theoretic) style analysis since these theories are formulated in terms not of a *belief* tracking a condition, but of one's reasons or evidence (the condition causing you to believe) tracking the condition. S knows it is a barn if that feature of the evidence causing S to believe it is a barn would not exist if it were not a barn. In the case of perception, if its looking like a red barn is what is causing S to believe it is a barn, then S has conclusive reasons to believe it is a barn: it would not look that way (like a red barn) unless it was a barn, and its looking like a red barn is what is causing S to believe it is a

barn. Hence, he knows it is a barn. If, on the other hand, it is merely the building looking like a barn that is causing S to believe it is a barn (its color being irrelevant to the causing of the belief) then S does not know it is a barn. His experience carries the information that it is a barn (since it looks like a red barn to him and its looking like a red barn carries the information that it is a barn), but that isn't the aspect of experience that is causing him to believe. Knowledge is *information-caused belief* and in this second case the information (that it is a barn) isn't causing the belief. All this should be evident to anyone who has thought about an example Alvin Goldman (1975) introduced years ago. Even if I mistakenly take wolves to be dogs so that my belief that x is a dog does not "track" dogs in my environment I can nonetheless know of a dachshund, seen at close range in broad daylight, that it is a dog. What is crucial to knowing the dachshund is a dog is that it has a distinctive look (it is, in this respect, like a red barn), a look that only (dachshund) dogs have. If it is this distinctive look that causes me to believe it is a dog, I know it is a dog no matter how confused I am about wolves – no matter how much my beliefs about dogs fail to "track" dogs (no matter how many false dog beliefs I have).

5 Except, possibly, logically conclusive evidence. I ignore this possibility since no one, I assume, thinks we have logically conclusive reasons for beliefs about the external world, the past, and other minds – the sorts of beliefs to which skepticism is typically directed.

6 One can, of course, *think* one remembers P without knowing P. One can even do it when P is false. But this is best described as *ostensible*, not genuine, memory. If one truly remembers P, P is not only true, one knows it is true.

7 I think it is begging the question to object by saying that deception is most improbable. Yes, it is most improbable *given what we take ourselves to know about ourselves and the world we live in*, but, given the hypothesis in question, what allows us to help ourselves to this knowledge (about ourselves and the world we live in) to estimate the probabilities? Even if we helped ourselves to this (disputed) knowledge, we would still be left with the question: is the estimated improbability enough to say we know the hypothesis is false? I know the probabilities of my winning the lottery are vanishingly small, but that doesn't mean I know I'm going to lose.

8 Some philosophers, I know, would not grant me these assumptions. Klein (1981, 1995), for instance, argues that despite having nothing to show in the way of specific evidence for thinking the zoo authorities have not put a disguised mule in the zebra pen, one can nonetheless know they didn't do it because one can see that it is a zebra and one knows that if it is a zebra the zoo authorities didn't do that. Knowing that not-Q is implied by what one knows is good enough to know not-Q even if one cannot distinguish not-Q (it isn't a disguised mule) from Q (it is a disguised mule) and, therefore, has nothing to show for one's belief that not-Q. In the end, it may come down to a matter of taste (I hope not), but this view is as hard for me to swallow as others tell me the rejection of closure is for them.

References

Brueckner, A. (1985) Skepticism and epistemic closure. *Philosophical Topics*, 13, 89–117.

BonJour, L. (1987) Nozick, externalism, and skepticism. In L. Luper-Foy (ed.), *The Possibility of Knowledge*. Lanham, MD: Rowman & Littlefield.

Cohen, S. (1988) How to be a fallibilist. *Philosophical Perspectives*, 2, 91–123.

Cohen, S. (1999) Contextualism, skepticism, and the structure of reasons. In J. Tomberlin (ed.), *Philosophical Perspectives*. Atascadero, CA: Ridgeview.

Davies, M. (1998) Externalism, architecturalism, and epistemic warrant. In C. Wright, B. C. Smith and C. Macdonald (eds), *Knowing Our Own Minds*. Oxford: Oxford University Press.

Davies, M. (2000) Externalism and armchair knowledge. In P. Boghossian and C. Peacocke (eds), *New Essays on the A Priori*. Oxford: Oxford University Press.

DeRose, K. (1995) Solving the skeptical problem. *Philosophical Review*, 104(1), 1–52.

Dretske, F. (1969) *Seeing and Knowing*. Chicago: University of Chicago Press.

Dretske, F. (1970) Epistemic operators. *Journal of Philosophy*, 67, 1007–23.

Dretske, F. (1971) Conclusive reasons. *Australasian Journal of Philosophy*, 49, 1–22.

Dretske, F. (1981) *Knowledge and the Flow of Information*. Cambridge, MA: MIT Press/A Bradford Book.

Feldman, R. (1999) Contextualism and skepticism. In J. Tomberlin (ed.), *Philosophical Perspectives*. Atascadero, CA: Ridgeview.

Fumerton, R. (1987) Nozick's epistemology. In S. Luper-Foy (ed.), *The Possibility of Knowledge*. Lanham, MD: Rowman and Littlefield.

Goldman, A. (1975) Discrimination and perceptual knowledge. *Journal of Philosophy*, 73, 771–91.

Grice, P. (1967) William James lectures at Harvard.

Klein, P. (1981) *Certainty: A Refutation of Skepticism*. Minneapolis: University of Minnesota Press.

Klein, P. (1995) Skepticism and closure: why the evil demon argument fails. *Philosophical Topics*, 23(1), 213–36.

Lewis, D. (1996) Elusive knowledge. *Australian Journal of Philosophy*, 74(4), 549–67.

Martin, R. (1975) Empirically conclusive reasons and scepticism. *Philosophical Studies*, 28, 215–17.

Martin, R. (1983) Tracking Nozick's sceptic: a better method. *Analysis*, 43, 28–33.

Moore, G. E. (1959) A proof of the external world. In *Philosophical Papers*. London: George Allen & Unwin.

Nozick, R. (1981) *Philosophical Explanations*. Cambridge, MA: Harvard University Press.

Stine, G. C. (1976) Skepticism, relevant alternatives, and deductive closure. *Philosophical Studies*, 29, 249–61.

Tomberlin, J (ed.) (1999) *Philosophical Perspectives*. Atascadero, CA: Ridgeview.

Wright, C. (2003) Some reflections on the acquisition of warrant by inference. In S. Nuccetelli (ed.), *New Essays on Semantic Externalism, Skepticism, and Self Knowledge*. Cambridge, MA: MIT Press/A Bradford Book.

The Case for Closure

John Hawthorne

Introduction

Fred Dretske's discussion provides us with a case against epistemic closure that is, on its face, rather compelling. In brief, he reasons as follows. (1) There are various "heavy-weight" propositions, such as that I am not a brain in a vat, that I cannot come to know through use of my perceptual capacities. (2) Nor can I come to know them *a priori.* So (3) I can't know them at all. But (4) rampant skepticism is unacceptable. I can come to know all sorts of ordinary propositions, such as that I have a hand, that there are cookies in my cupboard, that I used to frequent the Harborne fish and chip shop, and so on. But (5) those ordinary propositions are known by me to entail various heavyweight propositions of the sort that (by (1) and (2)) can't be known by me. So (6) it is false that knowledge transmits over known entailments.

Those who deny skepticism but accept closure – of whom there are many – will have to explain how we know various "heavyweight" skeptical hypotheses to be false. As Dretske sees it, this leads us to indulge in "verbal hocus pocus," twisting and contorting the concept of knowledge to fit the twin desiderata of closure and anti-skepticism. Others reject (4), opting for skepticism. But Dretske, reasonably enough, expects most of us – even closure-lovers – to agree that acceptance of wholesale skepticism is even more "abominable" than a denial of closure. It would appear, then, that we have three choices: (a) abominable skepticism; (b) verbal hocus pocus; (c) the abandonment of the initially plausible sounding closure principle. Dretske hopes that we will come away feeling that the sober option is to abandon closure. Despite its self-confessed costs, his position is a seductive one.

In the remarks that follow, I shall not attempt definitive resolution of the very troubling issues that Dretske's admirable discussion raises. If there were some easily accessible locus of reflective equilibrium in the vicinity, we would surely have reached it by now. But each of the resolutions to the trichotomy carries undeniable costs.

My task here is not, then, to defend a particular resolution to the kind of puzzle that motivates Dretske to abandon closure. Rather it is to question the merits of his own preferred, closure-denying package. Once the force of a suitable epistemic closure principle has been properly appreciated and the untoward consequences of Dretske's own views have been properly exposed, the costs of Dretske's preferred package can be seen to be quite considerable.

In the discussion below, I shall proceed as follows. Having in section 1 said a little about the closure principle I am most interested in, I shall in section 2 underscore the intuitive cost of abandoning that principle. In section 3, I shall point to some difficulties attending to the project of devising a restricted version of closure. In section 4, I shall make some brief remarks about the kind of puzzle that motivates Dretske to abandon closure.

1 Versions of Epistemic Closure

Epistemic closure is sometimes formulated as the principle (or, more accurately, schema) that

(1) (S knows P and Necessarily (P ⊃ Q)) ⊃ S knows Q

But this simple formulation does not present a defensible principle: if the relevant conditional is unknown to the subject, we should hardly be surprised if he were to know its consequent though not its antecedent.[1]

Recognizing this, others formulate epistemic closure as the principle that

(2) (S knows P and S knows that Necessarily (P $\supset$ Q)) $\supset$ S knows Q.[2]

But that doesn't seem right either. If one knows P and the relevant conditional, one still might not know Q on account of not having performed the relevant deductive inference. Knowing the logical consequences of what one knows takes cognitive labor.

Dretske is well aware of all this, of course, and formulates a more guarded version of the closure principle:

(3) If one knows P and one knows that Necessarily (P $\supset$ Q), one has all that it takes, evidentially speaking, to know that Q.[3]

Here is the picture. Suppose one has a body of evidence such that, were one to base a belief on that evidence, one would thereby come to know P. Even if one doesn't so form a belief, it is nonetheless natural to say that one has all it takes, evidentially speaking, to know P.

But version (3) of the closure principle invites at least two sorts of objections other than those that concern Dretske in his discussion.[4]

The first flows from the thought that one cannot always know the logical consequences of the propositions that one knows on account of the fact that small risks add up to big risks. Such a thought flows naturally from the view that knowledge that P requires that the epistemic probability of P be above a certain threshold N (where N is less than 1). I myself am not especially attracted to this "threshold conception" of knowledge. But if one were to embrace such a conception, then (3) would only be acceptable under the somewhat unrealistic idealization that one knows all necessary truths with certainty. And this is unrealistic. Suppose someone who is quite reliable tells me that the atomic number of calcium is 20. Suppose I know for certain that that if calcium has atomic number 20 then it necessarily has that number. If my rational credence that he is telling the truth is less than one, then the same is intuitively so for the proposition

Necessarily (Calcium exists $\supset$ Something with atomic number 20 exists)

So if one embraces the threshold conception of knowledge, (3) is unacceptable. This problem can be sidestepped by moving to (3′):

(3′) If one knows P and knows with *a priori* certainty that Necessarily P $\supset$ Q, one has all that it takes, evidentially speaking, to know Q.

A second sort of worry, which confronts both (3) and (3′) turns on some delicate issues about the relationship between logical consequence and rationality. Consider the following case, which builds on Saul Kripke's famous Paderevski example (see Kripke, 1979). Suppose I overhear someone (who is utterly trustworthy) say "Fred Paderevski is Bob Paderevski's brother" and I accept that sentence. I overhear someone else (who is utterly trustworthy) say "Ivan Paderevski is Fred Paderevski's father" and also accept that sentence. However, I do not realize that the token "Fred Paderevski" as used by the second individual corefers with the token of "Fred Paderevski" used by the first.

Having accepted the second sentence, I apply the necessity of origins principle and go on to accept "Necessarily if Fred Paderevski is Bob Paderevski's brother, Ivan Paderevski is Bob Paderevski's father." Now many of us hold a conception of belief attribution according to which an onlooker could truly say "John knows that Bob Paderevski is Fred Paderevski's brother and John knows that necessarily, if Bob Paderevski is Fred Paderevski's brother, then Ivan Paderevski is Bob Paderevski's father."[5] But it is quite clear that I am in no position to know that Ivan Paderevski is Bob Paderevski's father. (I am agnostic, after all, as to whether the name "Fred Paderevski" as used by the first interlocutor is coreferential with the name "Fred Paderevski" as used by the second interlocutor.) And without getting fully clear on what "evidentially speaking" is supposed to amount to, it seems at least dubious whether I "have what it takes, evidentially speaking, to know that Ivan Paderevski is Bob Paderevski's father." There is plenty more to say here, but because the issues that primarily concern Dretske do not turn on these matters, I will leave things somewhat hanging. Suffice it to say there is a good case to be made that, even if one is ideally rational, one will often be in no position to recognize the logical consequences of one's knowledge on account of diverse modes of linguistic representation of the propositions known.

If the closure debate were over (3) or (3′), then I would be the wrong recruit for defending closure. Fortunately, the issues just raised about Dretske's preferred formulation are somewhat tangential to the core of the debate. Here is a version that avoids these issues:

(4) If one knows P and competently deduces Q from P, thereby coming to believe Q, while retaining one's knowledge that P, one comes to know that Q.[6]

(Why "while retaining one's knowledge that P"? Well, one might competently deduce Q but have gotten counterevidence to P by the time one comes to believe Q.)

The "Paderevski case" does not pose problems for (4), since in that case a competent deduction to the consequent of the conditional is, intuitively, not available. And (4) offers in any case a more satisfying development of the closure intuition. The core idea behind closure is that we can add to what we know by performing deductions on what we already know. The idea that knowing both P and Necessarily P ⊃ Q is evidentially sufficient for knowing Q is, it seems to me, parasitic on the idea that *a priori* deduction from P yields knowledge of the propositions so deduced. My concern, then, will be to defend (4), rather than Dretske's own stated target, (3). To do so is not to frame the issue unfairly. The concerns that Dretske raises about closure carry over perfectly well to (4), and most of what I shall say in response carries over perfectly well to Dretske's criticisms of (3).

It is worth noting in passing that there is a more ambitious version of closure than (4), one that generalizes to deductions with more than one premise, namely:

(5) If one knows some premises and competently deduces Q from those premises, thereby coming to believe Q, while retaining one's knowledge of those premises throughout, one comes to know that Q.

Is Knowledge Closed under Known Entailment? | 29

Like (4), (5) has great prima facie intuitive plausibility. Indeed, (4) and (5) seem to originate from the core idea that one can add to what one knows by deductive inference from what one already knows. But defending (5) requires additional work. In particular, one has to confront the concern already mentioned, that "small risks add up to big risks," a concern that has no force against (4).[7] One has to also confront intuitive counterevidence arising from consideration of particular cases: allowing that a businessmen knows that he will meet X on Monday, Y on Tuesday and so forth, it still seems outrageous to allow that he knows some long conjunction of those claims, since the possibility that one of the people on the list pulls out sick seems not to be one that can be disregarded. So defending (5) requires, on the one hand, a conception of epistemic risk according to which knowledge involves no risk[8] and, on the other, some satisfactory resolution of the counterintuitions generated by a consideration of cases. I will not undertake any such defense here.

2 In Favor of Closure Principle (4)

Dretske and I would *both* agree that (4) is intuitive. It is unquestionably odd to concede that someone knows some P, to recognize that the person went on to realize that some Q follows from P and to believe Q on that basis, but to deny that the person knows Q.[9]

Now as Dretske points out, there are claims that are "conversational abominations" but that are perfectly true nevertheless. The contrast between truth and conversational propriety is, indeed, a very important one. For example, it is odd to actually assert "I know I have a hand" in nearly all ordinary conversational contexts. But we should not let such facts about conversational impropriety induce us into questioning the truth of "I know I have a hand." Might a parallel diagnosis be applied here? It seems not. In the case of "I know I have a hand," one can produce a convincing account in terms of the conversational mechanisms that Grice described concerning why the relevant speech is true though infelicitous. Roughly, we can presume participants in the conversation already know that I know that I have a hand and that, in keeping with mutually accepted conversational maxims, they will reckon that I am trying to be informative in my utterances. But "I know I have a hand" would only be informative if there were some real question as to its truth. So if I utter "I know I have a hand" then I can only be reckoned a cooperative conversant by my interlocutors on the assumption that there was a real question as to whether I have a hand. If there is no real question, my utterance misleadingly suggests there is such a question – hence the infelicity in most contexts. But what sort of mechanism could explain why "He knew P and deduced Q from P but didn't know Q" is true but conversationally infelicitous? No analogous Gricean narrative seems to be available here.

Moreover, the relevant infelicity intuitions arise not merely at the level of conversation but at the level of thought. If I think someone knows P and deduced Q from P, then I will not merely reckon it inappropriate to say "He still doesn't know Q": I will actually form the belief that he does know Q. Correlatively, when I reflect on principle (4), I form the belief that it is obviously correct. If an utterance u means P, then conversational mechanisms may explain away why we don't utter u even though it is correct, but they will not explain why we believe that which is expressed by the negation of u.

Consider by analogy the transitivity of the *taller than* relation. Suppose, somehow, that the taller than relation isn't transitive. If God told me such a thing, I would not conclude that I had been guilty merely of conversational abominations in making utterances that presupposed its transitivity. On the contrary, I would conclude that I had some seriously mistaken beliefs about the nature of the *taller than* relation. The closure principle seems to me like that. If Dretske is right, then I am prone to forming false beliefs – some involving conditionals, some not – about what others know by applying a closure principle that does not have full generality.

So our commitment to something like (4) cannot be explained away by appeal to pragmatic mechanisms. But let me be honest here. While principle (4) is compelling, it is not as *manifestly* obvious as the transitivity of the *taller than* relation. We would think it ridiculous if someone were to write a paper challenging the latter. And while we might say, by way of rhetoric, that Dretske is being ridiculous in denying (4) (or its counterpart (3)), the cases seem different. Perhaps, then, we should work to provide some supplementary considerations that reinforce our commitment to (4)'s intuitive status. Here are two lines of thought to that end.

Argument (A): closure and distribution

Begin with a principle that seems extremely compelling.

> *The Equivalence Principle*: If one knows *a priori* (with certainty) that P is equivalent to Q and knows P, and competently deduces Q from P (retaining one's knowledge that P), one knows Q.

Interestingly, Dretske's reasons for denying closure have no force against the Equivalence Principle. His argument against closure relies on the following idea. Following recent usage, let us say that R is "sensitive" to P just in case were P not the case, R would not be the case. Suppose one believes P on the basis of R, and that P entails Q. R may be sensitive to P and still not to Q. But notice that where P and Q are equivalent, there can be no such basis for claiming that while R can underwrite knowledge that P, it cannot underwrite knowledge that Q. We may thus safely assume that Dretske will accept the Equivalence principle. Here is a second, equally compelling, principle:

> *Distribution*: If one knows the conjunction of P and Q, then as long as one is able to deduce P, one is in a position to know that P (and as long as one is able to deduce Q, one is in a position to know that Q).

(Often a stronger principle is defended: that if one knows P and Q, one knows P and one knows Q. I do not need that here, though I do not wish to question it here either.)

Distribution seems incredibly plausible. How could one know that P and Q but not be in a position to know that P by deduction? Dretske, however, is committed to denying distribution. Suppose one knows some glass g is full of wine on the basis of perception (coupled, perhaps, with various background beliefs). The proposition that g is full of wine is *a priori* equivalent to the proposition

g is full of wine and ~g is full of non-wine that is colored like wine.

So by equivalence one knows that conjunction. Supposing distribution, one is in a position to know that

~g is full of non-wine that is colored like wine.

But the whole point of Dretske's position is to deny that one can know the latter in the type of situation that we have in mind.

What does this show? I do not offer the argument as a decisive refutation of Dretske's position. What we learn is that in giving up closure we are forced to give up another extremely intuitive and compelling principle, namely the distribution principle. If we are to play the game of counting costs, it must surely be reckoned a significant cost of Dretske's view that he must eschew Distribution.[10]

Argument (B): knowledge and assertion

An idea with growing popularity among epistemologists is that there is a fundamental tie between knowledge and the practice of asserting (see Unger, 1975; De Rose, 1996; Williamson, 2000). Of course, we sometimes assert that which we do not know. But it seems that when we do, we at least represent ourselves as knowing, a fact that is in turn explicable by Timothy Williamson's conjecture that it is the fundamental norm of assertion that one ought not to assert that which one does not know. Combine this thesis with Dretske's view and additional oddities arise. Suppose Q is a "heavyweight" consequence of P and S knows P and also that P entails Q. I ask S whether she agrees that P. She asserts that she does: "Yes," she says. I then ask S whether she realizes that Q follows from P. "Yes," she says. I then ask her whether she agrees that Q. "I'm not agreeing to that," she says. I ask her whether she now wishes to retract her earlier claims. "Oh no," she says. "I'm sticking by my claim that P and my claim that P entails Q. I'm just not willing to claim that Q." Our interlocutor now resembles perfectly Lewis Carroll's Tortoise, that familiar object of ridicule who was perfectly willing to accept the premises of a *modus ponens* argument but was unwilling to accept the conclusion (see Carroll, 1895). If we embrace the thesis that knowledge is the norm of assertion, then a Dretske style position on closure will turn us into a facsimile of Carroll's Tortoise.

3 Heavyweight Propositions and Conclusive Reasons

Dretske does not deny that deductive inference often succeeds in adding to our stock of knowledge. But he restricts its knowledge-extending scope: deductive inference adds to our knowledge in just those cases where the deductively reached conclusion is not a "heavyweight" proposition. Prima facie, the picture is quite attractive. Most deductive extensions of our belief set involve no heavyweight propositions. And in those cases, Dretske allows, the conclusions can be known as long as the premises are too. Though closure fails in full generality, it holds as a *ceteris paribus* generalization. Admittedly, in those special cases where we do arrive at heavyweight propositions, deductive inference does not extend knowledge. But it is not as if we are ordinarily misled here. On the contrary, inner alarm bells go off. If, having formed the belief that she is sitting, an ordinary person is invited to infer that she is not a brain in a vat (with an accompanying explanation of what that hypothesis involves), she may well not embrace that conclusion, even though it is a deductive consequence of what she just claimed. On the contrary, she will likely say, "Gee, I can't know that." It begins to look as if our actual practice conforms fairly well to what Dretske's principles would predict.

But matters become more complicated when we explore the concept of a "heavyweight" proposition. Let us begin with a somewhat vague, but nevertheless workable, gloss on the crucial notion. Let P be a "heavyweight proposition" just in case we all have some strong inclination to think that P is not the sort of thing that one can know by the exercise of reason alone and also that P is not the sort of thing that one can know by use of one's perceptual faculties (even aided by reason). Rough and ready as the characterization is, it captures a familiar category. And Dretske is just right when he points out that we all have some strong inclination to think that we cannot know by perception that we are not looking at a white thing illuminated by a red light (when in fact something looks red), that we are not brains in vats, that we are not looking at a cleverly disguised mule (instead of a zebra), and so on. And he is right when he points out that we all have a strong inclination to say that we cannot know such propositions by rational reflection either. In conceding this, I am not claiming that we do not know such things. But I am conceding that I have an immediate and strong inclination to say that I do not know such things in a way that I do not, for example, have any such immediate inclination to say that I do not know that I am working on a computer right now. Of course, I might derivatively generate some inclination to say that I do not know the latter via reflection on the former. But in the case of the former, doubts are natural and immediate, whereas in the case of the latter, doubts tend to be derivative. We should all at least agree that the relevant contrast is a salient fact about human psychology and that it is one of the bases of epistemic puzzlement. Let us call those propositions that generate immediate epistemic doubt "manifestly heavyweight propositions."

In response to the phenomenon of manifestly heavyweight propositions, one familiar reaction is to combat the inclinations towards doubt. Another is to allow doubt to spread to more humdrum propositions so that skepticism prevails. A third less familiar response is Dretske's – to reject closure and to offer a theoretical characterization of those propositions for which closure fails.

But the problem with this sort of approach is that the set of knowledge-eluding propositions identified by the theoretical characterization turns out to be markedly different from the set of manifestly heavyweight propositions that motivated the approach in the first place. Consider, by way of example, Robert Nozick's approach, in its simplest version. Nozick is initially taken with the idea that a necessary condition for knowing P is the following:

If P were not the case, S wouldn't believe P.

But such a principle will rule out knowledge of many non-heavyweight propositions as well. Suppose a real dog and a fake cat are in a room, the former keeping the latter from view. I look at the dog and form the belief that there is a dog in the room. From this, I infer there is an animal in the room. Suppose further that if there hadn't been a dog in the room, I would have seen the fake cat and formed the belief that it was a (real) animal. Then my belief that there is a dog in the room passes the Nozick test but my belief that there is an animal in the room does not. But my belief that there is an animal in the room in no way involves a heavyweight proposition. Examples such as this one put considerable pressure on closure-challengers like Nozick to "fix" their accounts of the necessary conditions on knowledge.[11] The aim of the game is to provide an account that precludes inference from what is known to manifestly heavyweight propositions but that allows inference from what is known to those that are not. If I point out that by the theorist's lights I can know that I have hands but not that I am not a brain in a vat, the theorist will welcome the result. But if I point out that by the theorist's lights there are situations where I can know that there is a cat in front of me but not that there is an animal in front of me, the theorist will hardly celebrate this result. On the contrary, he will scurry back to the epistemological laboratory to contrive an account that delivers the welcome result while avoiding the embarrassing one. Time and again, closure-deniers fail to pull this off. I believe that Dretske's own preferred account of knowledge offers an instance of this pattern of failure.

To begin, let us get clear about the form of his account. Dretske begins with the idea that to know that P one has to "rule out" or "exclude" all relevant alternatives to P. He claims in passing that this approach to the analysis of knowledge leads "quite naturally (not inevitably, but naturally)" to a denial of closure. I find this claim hard to evaluate without a clear sense of what "ruling out" or "excluding" amounts to. One very natural gloss on "ruling out P" is "knowing not-P." On this gloss, the suggestion is that for each P that one knows at t, there are some propositions incompatible with P the falsehood of which one has to know at t as well. Whether or not this is true – though I doubt that it is – I doubt that this is the intended meaning. Perhaps "rule out" means "to be able to know not-P" or "have what it takes, evidentially speaking, to know not-P." Assuming suitable deductive prowess, the suggestion that knowing P entails one can rule out relevant alternatives to P hardly encodes a challenge to closure. Indeed, assuming closure, one would, on this construal, be encouraged to think that if one knows P one can know the falsehood of any old alternative to P, relevant or not.

Fortunately, Dretske offers us a positive constraint on knowledge that bypasses this issue and that does indeed yield the result that closure fails.[12] The constraint is based on the idea of "conclusive reasons." Suppose I believe P on the basis of reasons R. Dretske tells us that if I know P, then I would not have reasons R unless P.

Let us say that reasons R are conclusive for P just in case this condition is satisfied. Suppose it is a necessary condition for knowledge that one's reasons are conclusive. Then, assuming we are not skeptics, and assuming a very natural gloss on one's reasons and the relevant counterfactuals, closure does indeed fail. Suppose A believes there is a zebra in the cage (and that this is the only animal in the cage) and A's reasons *e* are a set of zebra-ish experiences (coupled, perhaps, with some background beliefs). It is natural to suppose that if there weren't a zebra there, A wouldn't have had *e* (and if there were other animals there as well, A wouldn't have had *e* (either). So A's reasons are conclusive. Let us assume further that A knows on some occasion that the only animal in the cage is a zebra, her reasons being roughly as just described.[13] (This is, of course, an additional assumption. The conclusive reasons principle, as we have formulated it, is only a necessary condition on knowledge.[14]) A then deduces and comes to believe that there is no non-zebra in the cage cleverly disguised as a zebra. Let us suppose, as is natural, A's reasons are one or both of *e* and her belief that the only animal in the cage is a zebra. But if there were a cleverly disguised mule in the cage, she might well still have believed there was a zebra in the cage and that it was the only animal. So A does not have conclusive reasons for her belief that there is no cleverly disguised mule in the cage.[15] The necessary condition is not satisfied and so she does not know.[16]

Note further an obvious advantage of the Dretske approach over the simple version of the Nozick approach, one that Dretske is fully aware of.[17] Return to our "fake cat" case (see Dretske, note 4). One would not wish to concede in that case that one knows that there is a dog in the room but does not know that there is an animal in the room. But Dretske is not forced to such a concession. Suppose one's reasons for believing that there is an animal in the room are one or both of: (a) doggish experiences; (b) the belief that there is a dog in the room. If there were no animal in the room one would not have had *those* reasons for believing there to be an animal in the room (though one might have had others). So one turns out to have conclusive reasons for believing that there is an animal in the room. No embarrassing concession is mandated.

Nevertheless, embarrassment is close at hand. It seems evident that Dretske's account is designed to deliver the conclusion that one knows ordinary propositions and their non-manifestly heavyweight consequences, while remaining ignorant of their manifestly heavyweight consequences. But it does not come close to delivering that result. It turns out that we all too often have conclusive reasons for manifestly heavyweight propositions (in which case Dretske has not in fact provided an effective barrier to knowing such propositions), and all too often lack conclusive reasons for *a priori* consequences of known propositions, even though those consequences are not manifestly heavyweight. In these cases, not surprisingly, it is embarrassing to stick to one's theoretic guns and deny that the consequences are known.

Category 1: manifestly heavyweight with conclusive reasons

Case 1. As the discussion above in effect revealed, there are many conjunctions that are manifestly heavyweight but for which I have conclusive reasons. Thus, while I might lack conclusive reasons for the proposition ~I am a brain in a vat, I will (supposing I have a headache) have conclusive reasons for I have a headache and ~I am a brain in a vat. My reasons for that conjunction include my headache. Were the conjunction false, I would not, then, have had my reasons. (The closest worlds where that conjunction is false are ones where I do not have a headache. Stated without recourse to possible worlds language: were that conjunction false, it would be because I didn't have a headache.)

My putative knowledge of that conjunction cannot, then, be challenged on the grounds that I lack conclusive reasons. But the proposition that I am credited with knowing is every bit as apt to raise inner alarm bells as the proposition that ~I am a brain in a vat and will thus come out as manifestly heavyweight.

Case 2. I go to the zoo and see a bird flying around in a cage. I form the belief that I am not looking at an inanimate object cleverly disguised to look like an animate object. That is intuitively a manifestly heavyweight proposition. But suppose (as seems reasonable) that while it is just about possible to make an inanimate object appear like a flying bird, there are much easier ways to make an inanimate object look like an animate object. For example, it is much easier to pull off the task of creating an inanimate object that looks like a turtle than to pull off the task of creating an inanimate object that looks like a flying bird. Suppose then that "at the closest worlds" where there is an inanimate object in the cage, there is nothing that looks like a bird in the cage: instead there is something that looks like a far more sedate animal. Suppose, as seems plausible, my reason for thinking that there I am not looking at a cleverly disguised inanimate object in the cage is that I have experiences as of a bird flying around. Then I have conclusive reasons, in Dretske's sense, for the proposition that there is no cleverly disguised inanimate object.

Case 3. I see a cookie. I form the belief that there is a mind-independent object that is roughly five feet in front of me. My sense is that Dretske wishes to classify such high-filutin' theoretically loaded beliefs as "heavyweight." But that one does not come out as heavyweight by the conclusive reasons test. For presumably the closest worlds where there is no mind-independent physical object five feet in front of me are not ones where some bizarre metaphysics holds but, rather, worlds with laws like this one where there is no physical object at all in front of me. Alternatively put: if there weren't a mind-independent object about five feet in front of me, that would be because that region of space was unoccupied. But if that had happened, then (in the normal case) I wouldn't have had the experiences as of a cookie five feet away from me.

Category 2: not manifestly heavyweight but lacking conclusive reasons

Case 1. I eat some salmon for dinner. I am no glutton. I eat a modest quantity and form the belief that I have eaten less than one pound of salmon. I infer that I have eaten less than 14 pounds of salmon. In fact my perceptual system is very reliable indeed. In those nearby possible worlds where I feast on salmon and eat, say, a pound and a half, I do not believe that I have eaten less than a pound. Dretske, no skeptic, will happily concede that I know that I have eaten less than a pound of salmon. Suppose (and for all I know this is correct) that while it is utterly unlikely that any human being would eat over 14 pounds of salmon, doing this would induce (among other things) severe hallucinations. Indeed, it might even induce the hallucination that one had eaten a rather small quantity of salmon.[18] Thus it might be true that if, God forbid, I had eaten over 14 pounds of salmon, I may have had the eaten-less-than-one-pound-ish visual experiences that I have at the actual world. Thus while it may be true that I would not have had my reasons R for believing that I have eaten less than a pound of salmon unless I had, it is not true that I would not have had my reasons R for believing that I have eaten less than 14 pounds of salmon unless I had. The apparatus (in conjunction with the verdict that I know, in the given case, that I have eaten less than a pound of salmon) delivers the embarrassing result that I know that I have eaten less than a pound of salmon but not that I have eaten less than 14 pounds (even though I believe the latter and have deduced it from the former).

Case 2. I think on Monday that I am going to meet you on Wednesday on the basis of familiar sorts of reasons. (Fill them out in a natural way.) I meet you on Wednesday. It is natural to say, in many such cases, that my belief on Monday was a piece of knowledge. Consider now the counterfactual: if you hadn't met me on Wednesday, I would not have had those reasons on Monday for thinking that you would meet me on Wednesday. I do not find that counterfactual very compelling. (I have a strong inclination not to "backtrack" when evaluating the counterfactual – in effect accepting David Lewis's (1973) advice to hold the past relative to time t fixed when evaluating counterfactuals concerning t.) So my reasons turn out not to be conclusive, since they fail Dretske's counterfactual test.[19]

(There is an additional worry in the vicinity: counterfactuals are slippery and our modes of evaluating them very shifty. Dangerous, then, to build an account of knowledge on them unless one is happy for the truth of knowledge claims to slip and slide with the varying similarity metrics that may guide verdicts about counterfactuals. Let me illustrate with a case. Suppose, unknown to me, the beach is closed when the authorities believe the neighboring waters to be shark-infested. I go to the beach and ask "Is the water shark-infested?" The lifeguard says "no." Now if the lifeguard had believed the waters to be shark-infested, he wouldn't even have been on duty that day – the beach would have been closed. In that case I wouldn't have even gotten to ask him that question. Now consider the counterfactual "If the waters had been shark-infested, the lifeguard wouldn't have said that they weren't." Our evaluation fluctuates according to what we hold fixed. If we hold fixed that I am talking to a lifeguard, then, intuitively, the counterfactual comes out false. Meanwhile, if we are allowed to backtrack, imagining that I wouldn't have even reached the beach if the waters had been shark-infested, the counterfactual comes out true. Yet the parameter on which the truth of the counterfactual depends seems not to be one upon which the truth of the knowledge claim "I now know that the water is not shark-infested" similarly depends.)

The cumulative lesson is clear enough. Dretske's machinery is intended to align itself with our instinctive verdicts about what we can and cannot know by perception and reason. But, quite simply, it draws the can/cannot line in a very different place than intuition does. Of course, one might retreat to an account that gets more intuitively satisfying results by brute force, along the lines of:

> If one knows P and deduces Q from P then one knows Q, unless Q is a manifestly heavyweight proposition.

But we should all agree that this would be rather unsatisfying. But it remains an open question whether any reasonably satisfying non *ad hoc* restriction on closure is available. Epistemologists far too often assume that a discrepancy in our epistemic intuitions about pairs of cases can be accounted for in terms of interesting structural differences between the cases – differences in the pattern of counterfactuals and so on – without paying due attention to the myriad ways in which our perceptions of epistemic risk are at the mercy of incidental features of the way that the case is framed, of distortions induced by particularly vivid descriptions of this or that source of error, and so on (see Kahneman et al., 1982, 2000). I myself hold out very little hope for a plausible restriction on closure that allows with the skeptic that we are in no position to know we are not brains in vats but that allows deduction to extend knowledge in the normal case.

I close this section with one final intuition pump. Child A visits the zoo and is told by his trustworthy parent that he will get a prize if the first animal he sees is a zebra. The parent adds that the child may get a prize anyway. But whatever else, the child will definitely get a prize if the cage at the zoo entrance contains a zebra. Child B visits the zoo and is told the same thing by his parent. The parents of A and B consult. Parent A is both a philosopher and very generous. He has in fact decided that he will give child A a prize just as long as the cage at the zoo entrance does not contain a mule cleverly disguised as a zebra. (He resolves to check with the honest zookeeper before dispensing the prize.) The parent of B is less generous and less imaginative. He resolves to give child B a prize iff the first animal is either a zebra or a lion. The parents consult. Since they are walking together, they realize that if the second child wins a prize the first will also – that, indeed, it is easier for A to win a prize than for B to win a prize. They tell this to the children (though they do not explain in detail why that discrepancy obtains). The parents are very trustworthy, transmitting knowledge by testimony. Thus child A knows (a) if the cage at the zoo entrance contains a zebra, he will get a prize, (b) if the cage at the zoo entrance contains a zebra, B will get a prize, and (b) if child B gets a prize, child A will get a prize. Child B knows (a) that if the cage at the zoo entrance contains a zebra, he will get a prize, (b) that if the animal is a zebra, A will also get a prize, and also (c) that if he, B, gets a prize, child A will get a prize.

They see a zebra. Child A knows there is a zebra there. Child B knows there is a zebra there. Child A infers (a) that he will get a prize and (b) that B will get a prize. Child B infers (a) that he will get a prize and (b) that A will get a prize. Apply the Dretske machinery and we get some curious results. A does not know he will get a prize, it would seem. For if A weren't to get a prize it would be because he saw a cleverly disguised mule, in which case A would still think he was going to get a prize. But A knows B will get a prize! Furthermore, A knows that it is easier for A to win a prize than for B to – and in particular, that if B gets a prize, A will get a prize. B, meanwhile, does know that he will get a prize and knows that if he will get a prize, then so will A – since he also knows that the rules of the game are that A is guaranteed a prize if B wins. But, by parity of reasoning, B does not know that A will get a prize. At best, these conclusions are a bit dizzying.

4 Residual Puzzles

Suppose we do not embrace Dretske's rejection of closure. We are still left with the puzzle that led him to the rejection in the first place. Let us focus on an example. Suppose I learn from a reputable newspaper that Manchester United beat Coventry City. That piece of information, in combination with the fact that the newpaper says that Manchester United beat Coventry City, entails that

> ~Due to a misprint, the newspaper said that Manchester United beat Coventry City when in fact Manchester United lost to Coventry City.

Call this proposition "Misprint." On the one hand, it seems odd to suppose that one can know Misprint in advance of reading the newspaper; on the other, it seems odd to suppose that one can come to know Misprint by looking at the newspaper.[20]

One prima facie attractive way out is that of the contextualist. Roughly, the contextualist says that the standards for knowledge ascription vary according to what the ascriber is worried about. If one worries about misprints, one's standards for knowledge ascriptions in testimony cases go up, and that is why we balk at *saying*, in the case described, that one knows Misprint upon looking at the newspaper. But the contextualist saves closure: in contexts where such worries are salient, the ascription "He knows the Manchester United result" is also false. So we are not left ascribing knowledge to the premises of a deductive argument while denying knowledge of the conclusion.

I am by no means convinced that contextualism holds the key to Dretske's puzzle. But Dretske's own way with contextualism is too quick, betraying a flawed understanding of that approach. He attributes to the contextualist the thesis that reasonably experienced adults know such things as that there are cookies only as long as they do not seriously consider the heavyweight implications of such beliefs. This is wrong. Contextualism says that the standards of "know" are *ascriber* sensitive. Suppose that A isn't considering heavyweight possibilities but that B is. In particular suppose that B believes P and also goes on to believe some heavyweight consequence of P by deduction. Suppose A says (1) "B knows P" and, moreover, (2) "B knows anything he has deductively inferred from P and thereby come to believe." If B is in a context where "A knows P," in her mouth, expresses a truth, then she will be in a context where (2), in her mouth, expresses a truth as well. That the *subject* of a knowledge ascription attends to heavyweight propositions does not undermine knowledge ascriptions by an ascriber who does not worry about this or that skeptical scenario. Indeed, in the case just described, the standard contextualist will allow that the extension of "knows" in the mouth of A may include the pair ⟨B, Q⟩, where Q is a heavyweight proposition. Relatedly, it is simply not correct that contextualism delivers the result that "philosophers are the most ignorant people in the world."

Contextualism remains one prima facie promising avenue for resolving Dretske's puzzle. Are there others? Without pretending to be able to resolve perennial problems in a few short paragraphs, let me at least gesture at one other move that is perfectly consistent with closure.

Begin with the humble phenomenon of epistemic anxiety, cases where human beings really begin to have genuine doubts about what they believe. Suppose, for example, I worry that my partner is going to leave me or that the plane I am on is going to crash. In such situations, I may still have the betting inclinations symptomatic of a believer. For example, despite my worries, I may be willing to bet heavily on the plane's safe arrival. But it is an obvious feature of the way the concept of knowledge works that in such a situation one is not inclined to self-ascribe knowledge of the proposition that is the target of one's anxiety. This might be accounted for variously. Perhaps knowledge requires a kind of conviction that is incompatible with such anxiety. Or perhaps instead, while knowledge is in fact compatible with such anxiety, the latter is constituted in part by a belief that one doesn't know.[21]

Notice that such anxiety, once generated and unalleviated – either by informal therapy or by a simple shift of attention – tends to spread. If one has it about Q and P entails Q, one acquires it with respect to P (when the question arises). Someone might know that his partner will never leave him and this may entail that she will never leave him for Mr X. But if he runs though the relevant inference, that may induce anxiety about both the inferred proposition and the original (we all know how to fill in the details!)

On such a picture, there are two sorts of situations. On the one hand, there are standard cases where deductive inference adds to our stock of knowledge. On the other, there are situations where deductive inference brings to light sources of anxiety that may, in some way or other, undercut the epistemic status – or at least the believed epistemic status – of one's premises. An account of the human epistemic condition should give due place to both mechanisms. But it remains unclear to me whether a denial of epistemic closure would have any useful role to play in any such an account.[22] On the contrary, the reality of closure explains the epistemic goodness of deductive inference as well as why epistemic anxiety tends to spread.

But still, what of the puzzle itself? Do I know Misprint in advance? And then, by parity of reasoning, can I have contingent *a priori* knowledge that one is not a brain in a vat? Or is it that, as long as anxiety can be kept at bay, we can know the latter only by perception in combination with deductive inference (intuitions and Bayesian style arguments to the contrary notwithstanding[23])? Better that we appreciate (with Dretske) the force of this problem than rush too quickly to try to solve it.[24]

Notes

1 There are those who adopt a conception of thought according to which the thought that P is identical to the thought that Q just in case P and Q are true in the same possible worlds. From that perspective, (1) may be more motivated. After all, if P entails Q, then the thought that P is necessarily equivalent to the thought that P and Q. So if one knows P and P entails Q, one automatically knows that P and Q since the thought that P and Q just is, from this perspective, the thought that P. Assuming that knowledge distributes over conjunction – that is, that if one knows P and Q, one knows P and knows Q – then (1) is secured. But, despite its distinguished list of adherents, such a conception of belief is a deviant one, and I shall not pursue it here.

2   See, for example, Dretske (1971), Stine (1976), Nozick (1981), Cohen (1988), and Richard Feldman (1999).

3   Note that this principle allows for the possibility of some pair P, Q such that P entailed Q but that it was impossible to know P without already knowing Q. Thus the principle at least allows that there be a knowable P and an entailed Q such that deductive inference from P to Q was not a possible route to knowing Q.

4   There are other, less decisive, worries as well. Suppose I know P and know that necessarily P ⊃ I will never perform a deductive inference again. Is it intuitive to say still that I have all it takes, evidentially speaking, to know the consequent?

5   For helpful discussion of the relevant issues, see Kripke (1979) and Soames (2000).

6   This is a (slightly improved) version of Williamson (2000, p. 117), restricted to single premise inferences. Williamson has an insightful take on the root of epistemic closure intuitions, namely the idea that "deduction is a way of extending one's knowledge," one that I take on board in what follows. The notion of "competent deduction" could obviously do with some elaboration, though I won't attempt that here. Another general issue worth considering (raised in correspondence by Jonathan Kvanig) is whether, in a case where Q is competently deduced from P, a (misleading) defeater for Q – that destroys knowledge of Q – is automatically a defeater for knowledge of P.

7   This may be a little quick: one might worry that an exercise of one's deductive capacities that in fact is competent carries a risk of being incompetent. I shall not address that worry here.

8   Such a conception is, for example, defended by Williamson (2000), who explicitly adduces it in defense of generalized closure.

9   I leave out the "retaining all along" clause for ease of exposition.

10 A similar line of thought shows that Dretske is committed to denying a seemingly humble, restricted version of closure, namely addition closure – that if one knows P then by deduction one can know P or Q. See my *Knowledge and Lotteries* (forthcoming). Nozick (1981) is willing to abandon distribution along with closure. I await Dretske's opinion on the matter.

11 In Nozick's own case (1981), the "fix" to these anticipated worries famously took the form of an appeal to methods: one knows P, only if, were P false, one wouldn't have believed P by the same method. It is not my purpose to immerse myself in the details of Nozick's account here, though many of the remarks that follow are pertinent.

12 The main ideas are laid out in Dretske (1971).

13 Of course, we epistemologists are often a little lax in our closure-illustrating examples. We may say that the proposition that I have a meeting tomorrow strictly entails that I will not die beforehand, ignoring the possibility that I reincarnate, or go through with the meeting as a ghost. We may say that the proposition that I am seeing a zebra in the cage entails that I am not seeing a cleverly disguised mule, ignoring the possibility that the cage is itself a cleverly disguised mule or else that the mule is cleverly disguised by being inserted within a zebra that is somehow kept alive. So most illustrations of deductive closure aren't really illustrations of deductive closure. Let us trust that such sloppiness is neither here nor there.

14 Best to avoid the pitfalls of devising a necessary and sufficient condition here.

15 I am assuming that claims of the form "P wouldn't be the case unless Q were the case" entail "If Q weren't the case P wouldn't be the case." Dretske certainly relies on such an entailment in generating anti-closure results from his formulation of a conclusive reasons requirement. For the record, I am open to being convinced that "unless" counterfactuals have special features that make trouble for that purported entailment, though I doubt that this would bolster Dretske's cause.

Is Knowledge Closed under Known Entailment?

16 Obviously, there are those who will insist on an externalist notion of reasons according to which, say, the fact that there is a zebra may count as a reason (when I see that there is a zebra). If one opted for this notion of reasons, then I may after all have conclusive reasons for thinking that I am not seeing a cleverly disguised mule. (And, *pace* Dretske, note 5, one's reasons would be logically conclusive.) I shall not pursue the matter further here.

17 Note that this simulates some of the work of Nozick's own appeal to methods.

18 I could run the case with pints of beer, which may be more easily grasped (as long as it is agreed that the world where I drink enough beer to hallucinate that I have drunk a normal amount is a distant one!).

19 Note that Dretske is happy enough to use his conclusive reasons framework to explain why I do not know that I will win the lottery (see Dretske, 1971, and "The case against closure," note 7). But it may well be that for any belief about the future, there are outcomes with a real – though low – probability that, if actualized, will render the belief false. The small chance of winning the lottery means, for Dretske, that we do not know we will lose. But what of the small chance postulated by quantum mechanics of the cup flying sideways if I drop it? And what of the small chance that I will have a fatal heart attack? We are in need of an explanation as to how the cases are supposed to be different, unless skepticism about the future is to be embraced. I discuss these issues at length in *Knowledge and Lotteries* and "Chance and counterfactuals" (forthcoming).

20 A natural application of Bayesian confirmation theory supports this latter contention. Supposing one's conditional probability of Misprint on the newspaper saying that Manchester United beat Coventry City is N (where N is presumably less than 1), then since one's conditional probability of Misprint on the newspaper denying Manchester United beat Coventry City is 1, one's new rational credence on the evidence that the newspaper said Manchester United beat Coventry City will drop from somewhere between N and 1 to N. (One's new rational credence will be obtained by conditionalization. One's old rational credence will be one's rational expectation that the newspaper will deny that Manchester United won plus N multiplied by one's rational credence that the newspaper will say that Manchester United won, assuming (somewhat unrealistically) that it is certain that the newspaper will deliver a verdict on the matter. If not, adjust "deny" to "not say.")

21 Perhaps instead, while one knows and believes one knows, this kind of situation is one where certain beliefs, albeit temporarily, no longer control one's behavior. There are no doubt fertile connections here between epistemology and the relevant issues in philosophical psychology.

22 Of course, if one thought knowledge required a kind of conviction over and above "belief" in the ordinary sense, then one would slightly reformulate (4) so that it only covers cases where deductive inference produces the suitable kind of conviction.

23 One way to resist is to insist that one's body of evidence is misdescribed by such arguments. That, I take it, is the strategy suggested by Williamson (2000). Perhaps, when I see that there is a table, my evidence is not merely that I seem to see a table, but that there is a table. I shall not explore the matter further here.

24 Thanks to Fred Dretske, Peter Klein, Jonathan Kvanig, David Manley, Ernest Sosa, Timothy Williamson, and especially Tamar Gendler for helpful comments and conversation. The ideas in this essay overlap in places with material in my *Knowledge and Lotteries* (forthcoming).

References

Carroll, L. (1895) What the Tortoise said to Achilles. *Mind*, 4, 278–80.

Cohen, S. (1988) How to be a fallibilist. *Philosophical Perspectives*, 2: 91–123.

DeRose, K. (1996). Knowledge, assertion and lotteries. *Australasian Journal of Philosophy*, 84, 568–80.

Dretske, F. (1970) Epistemic operators. *Journal of Philosophy*, 67, 1007–23.

Dretske, F. (1971) Conclusive reasons. *Australasian Journal of Philosophy*, 49, 1–22.

Feldman, R. (1999) Contextualism and skepticism. *Philosophical Perspectives*, 13, 91–114.

Hawthorne, J. (forthcoming) Chance and Counterfactuals. *Philosophy and Phenomenological Research*.

Hawthorne, J. (forthcoming) *Knowledge and Lotteries*. Oxford: Oxford University Press.

Kahneman, D., Slovic, P. and Tversky, A. (1982) *Judgment under Uncertainty: Heuristics and Biases*. Cambridge: Cambridge University Press.

Kahneman, D. and Tversky, A. (2000) *Choices, Values and Frames*. Cambridge: Cambridge University Press.

Kripke, S. (1979) A puzzle about belief. In A. Margalit (ed.), *Meaning and Use*. Dordrecht: Reidel.

Lewis, D. (1973) *Counterfactuals*. Cambridge, MA: Harvard University Press.

Nozick, R. (1981) *Philosophical Explanations*. Oxford: Oxford University Press.

Soames, S. (2002) *Beyond Rigidity*. Oxford: Oxford University Press.

Stine, G. C. (1976) Skepticism, relevant alternatives, and deductive closure. *Philosophical Studies*, 29, 249–61.

Unger, P. (1975) *Ignorance: A Case for Skepticism*. Oxford: Oxford University Press.

Williamson, T. (2000) *Knowledge and Its Limits*. Oxford: Oxford University Press.

Reply to Hawthorne

Fred Dretske

John Hawthorne does an admirable job of describing the "costs" connected with my rejection of closure. These costs are, I admit, significant. I would not be willing to pay this price if I thought there were alternatives that were less expensive. Philosophy is a business where one learns to live with spindly brown grass in one's own yard because neighboring yards are in even worse shape. From where I sit, the grass on the other side of the fence looks worse than mine.

One option, of course, is skepticism. Though some may be willing to embrace it, John and I agree that this is a last resort. If the *only* choices are skepticism or the rejection of closure, then – too bad – we had better learn to live without closure (distribution, etc.).

As a historical footnote, I wasn't led to deny closure because it represented a way around skepticism. I was led to it because it was a result of what I took to be a plausible condition on the evidence (justification, reasons) required for knowledge. If your reasons for believing P are such that you *might* have them when P is false, then they aren't good enough to *know* that P is true. You need something more. That is why you can't know you are going to lose a lottery just because your chances of losing are 99.99 percent. Even with those odds, you still might win (someone with those odds against him *will* win). That is why you can't learn – can't come to know – that P is true if all you have to go on is the word of a person who might lie about whether or not P is so. This is just another way of saying that knowledge requires reasons or evidence (in this case, testimony) you wouldn't have if what you end up believing were false. You can learn things from people, yes, but only from people who wouldn't say it unless it were true.

John (in section 3) does a beautiful job in showing the problems with this obvious (to me) condition on knowledge. I had grappled with some of these problems myself, but others, I confess (even after 30 years of defending the view) were completely new to me. Contrary to what he suggests (case 2 in category 2, section 3), though, I think the counterfactual condition accords with common and widespread intuitions about knowledge of the future. In my more careful moments, I prefer to say (on Monday) not that I know that I will be in my office on Wednesday, but that I know that is where I intend or plan to be on Wednesday. I retreat to this more cautious claim because I realize that my reasons for thinking I will be in my office on Wednesday are reasons I would have on Monday even if a Tuesday accident were to prevent me from being there on Wednesday. As long as I might not make it to the office, I do not know I will be there. How could I? One doesn't, generally speaking, have conclusive reasons for believing that something will happen. Death may be an exception, but I doubt whether taxes are. I'm a bit of a skeptic about the future.

But John is certainly right when he says that these counterfactuals are a slippery and shifty business. So a theory of knowledge that appeals to them is exposed to examples of the embarrassing sort that he describes. This, I confess, is a problem. It is not *always* a problem. Sometimes this shiftiness in the way we understand the counterfactual reflects quite neatly – or so I think – the shiftiness and subtlety in our judgments about exactly what and exactly when someone knows something. Does S, standing at the stove watching water boil, know that the water is boiling? Can he see that it is boiling? Well, would it look that way if it weren't boiling? If it wouldn't, he can see that the water is boiling. He can know this despite not being able to see – perhaps not even knowing (but just correctly assuming) – that it is water (not gin) he sees in the pot. The relevant counterfactual is: would the water (not just anything) look that way if it weren't boiling. If *this* counterfactual is true, one can know the water is boiling without knowing (at least not by seeing) that it is water that is boiling since, given the look of things, it could be gin (vodka, pear juice, etc.). I think this example is related in interesting ways to John's lifeguard example, but I won't take the time to spell out the details.

So sometimes the counterfactual condition captures important distinctions. But not always. As John points out, we sometimes seem to have conclusive reasons for believing "manifestly" heavyweight propositions and lack them for clearly lightweight propositions. So things don't sort out as neatly as I would like.

But let's look at the neighbors' yards. How green is their grass? John does not undertake to propose or to defend any particular solution to the problems for which the denial of closure represents an answer. Without endorsing it, however, he suggests that despite my low opinion (and "flawed understanding") of contextualism, this approach to understanding knowledge offers some promise in this regard. We can keep closure and avoid skepticism if we think of knowledge as relative to attributional context. To say that it is relative to attributional context is to say that whether S knows something – that she has two hands, for instance – depends on the context of the person who is saying S knows it. If I, a philosopher, worried about brains in vats and Cartesian demons, say it, then S doesn't know she has two hands. At least what I say when I say she doesn't know it is true. Why? Because, assuming S is in no position to know she isn't being deceived by a Cartesian demon, then, given closure, neither can she know that she has two hands. If she knew she had two hands, she would be able to infer, and thereby come to know, by closure, that she isn't being deceived by such a demon into falsely believing she has two hands. So when I say she doesn't know she has two hands, what I say is true. Neither do I know I have two hands. Nobody knows it. Skepticism is true. At least it is true when I assert it. But if S, an ordinary person on the street, someone without the least tincture of philosophy, says she knows that she has two hands, what she says is true. She attributes knowledge to herself in an ordinary, practical, context in which demons and handless-brains-in-vats are not relevant possibilities. They aren't alternatives she means to be excluding, evidentially, when she attributes knowledge to herself. So what she says is true, and it is true, mind you, even when she attributes this knowledge to me, the philosopher pondering skepticism in the seminar room. Whether I know that I have two hands depends not on what alternatives I (the attributee) take to be relevant, but on what possibilities S, the attributor, takes to be relevant. So, if we imagine S (with no tincture of philosophy) asserting that skepticism is false or (given that she probably doesn't understand what skepticism is) that she and most other people know a great many things about the world, she speaks truly. Skepticism is false when *S* is the speaker.

So who, according to contextualism, is right? Am I, a philosopher, right when I (given my context) say that nobody knows they have hands. Or is S right? We are, I'm afraid, both right. And that is where my low opinion of contextualism comes from. The only people who can truly assert that skepticism is false are those, like S, who don't understand what skepticism is or those who understand it but who steadfastly ignore as irrelevant (for purposes of attributing knowledge to themselves and others) exactly those possibilities the skeptic insists are relevant.

I don't really consider this to be an answer to skepticism or, if it is, it is merely a backhanded way of denying closure. It looks to me as though contextualism succeeds in keeping closure (I use John's improved statement of closure, i.e. (4)) only by denying it a role in reaching conclusions about the heavyweight propositions the skeptic is concerned with. If you actually try to use closure to conclude from the fact that you have two hands that you are not being massively deceived, then you automatically change the context in which you attribute knowledge to yourself (the context is now one in which the possibility of being deceived in this undetectable way is being explicitly raised) and, given closure (and the fact that you can't know you aren't being deceived in this undetectable way), you cease to know the premise (that you have two hands) you used to reach that heavyweight conclusion. So, despite reaching this heavyweight conclusion in a perfectly respectable way from a premise you (when you started) knew to be true, you do not wind up knowing that the conclusion is true – that you aren't being deceived. Instead, you lose the knowledge of the premise (that you have two hands) you used to reach that conclusion. This grass doesn't look very green to me.

Is Knowledge Contextual?

Contextualism Contested

Earl Conee

It should be helpful to situate epistemic contextualism ("EC") in a broader context. Epistemology will creep gradually into the discussion.

Most broadly, semantic contextualism is the thesis that something semantic about a symbol varies with some differences in contexts that involve tokens of the symbol. The kind of semantic contextualism of most direct interest to epistemologists asserts that different sentence tokens of the same type have different truth conditions. That is, some differences in the context where a sentence is used affect which conditions must obtain in the world for the use of the sentence to state a truth.

For instance, the sentence "Smith's thimble is large enough" uncontroversially displays this variation. Let's consider a context in which Smith's friends are discussing whether the thimble fits her. A friend says, "Smith's thimble is large enough." Assuming that Smith's thimble is an ordinary one that Smith has used comfortably for years, the friend states something true by uttering this sentence token. Suppose that the same sentence is uttered simultaneously by a household mover. He has been talking about items that are sizable enough to require two movers to carry, and he mistakenly thinks that Smith has a gigantic thimble. The claim made by that token of the sentence does not state a truth.

In this example the context of the subject of the sentence, the thimble, does not vary. What does vary is the context in which the sentence is used. This is called variation in the "attributer" context, or "attributer relativity." Variations that affect truth conditions in the context of the subject of the sentence are called "subject" contextual variations, or "subject relativity." We shall be focusing on claims of attributer relativity.

Indexical expressions provide other illustrations of uncontroversial attributer relativity. Words like "I," "you," and "it" in a sentence contribute to the sentence's having different truth conditions in different contexts. For instance, the first-person pronoun, "I," is the subject of a sentence that is used to state a truth only if the predicate of the sentence is true of the one who is asserting something with the sentence.

The clear attributer relativity of truth conditions for sentences with a pronoun might seem at first glance to show that attributer relativity is of negligible philosophical interest. No doubt "You are happy" makes a true claim just in case the individual addressed by the attributer is happy. The philosophical questions about persons seem entirely unaffected by the innocuous contextualist claim about how the pronoun "you" refers to them. Is a person a material object, an immortal soul, or something else? Does a person exist as a fetus in early pregnancy? Are the mental properties of a person identical to physical properties? The contextualism is neutral about all of this.

On second thought, though, the general conclusion is too hasty. The contextualism seems to take a side in some philosophical controversies. It claims that sentences of the form "I am F" are true just when the one using the sentence is F. If this is correct, then apparently there has to exist some such entity as the one who is using the sentence for any of these sentences to be true. Yet this runs contrary to no-self theories. They say that there are no such beings as ones who use sentences. According to one no-self view, experiences exist. When these experiences bear certain relations to one another, such as later conscious episodes bearing a "recollective" relation to earlier experiencings, we say that the experiences have "the same subject." That is not strictly true. There is no one entity that undergoes the experiences. There are just particular events of experiencing and relations among them.

Thus, our supposedly bland semantic claim – that sentences with first-person pronoun subjects say something true just when the predicate is true of one using the sentence – appears to conflict with this no-self view. So the semantics now seems to take a philosophical side. Perhaps the claim that epistemic terms exhibit attributer relativity will likewise turn out to exclude some existing philosophical options.

But on third thought, the assertion of first-person pronoun attributer relativity is no particular threat to the no-self view. The contextualist semantic claim employing the phrase "the one using the sentence" is among the claims that the no-self theory addresses. Our sample version of the theory declares that all such statements are false. To be plausible, the theory must also give some explanation of how such statements are often reasonable to make, in spite of their falsity. Whatever the explanation is, we should expect it to carry over to the assertion of first-person pronoun attributer relativity. The fact that this is a semantic assertion does not make it less likely that the theory can explain its plausibility.

The final merits of no-self views lie in the details of their defensibility. Generally, we see that semantic assertions are neither automatically irrelevant nor immediately decisive.

This illustration should be borne in mind as we consider EC. Many epistemological issues may be unaffected by the existence of attributer relativity in the truth conditions of sentences that include epistemic terms. By itself this is neither a strength nor a weakness in either EC or the unaffected theories. An EC thesis may have some substantial epistemic implication. The implication in conjunction with some epistemological theories may appear to induce surprising truth-values. This result need not lead sensible proponents of the affected theories to give them up. They may be able to interpret the sentences to explain away any difficulties.

Another non-epistemic example of purported attributer relativity illustrates how contextualism characteristically copes with certain sorts of conflict. Suppose that Robinson is Chair of the Boring Committee ("BC"). At the time for a meeting of the BC, Robinson sees that all of the members of the BC are in the room. He declares, "Everyone is present." The members present would be led by this to think that the membership of the BC is present. Yet "everyone," the subject term of Robinson's sentence, seems to be about every person in the world. Of course none of the members of the BC is led to believe that every person in the world is present.

One reasonable semantic hypothesis is that quantifiers like "everyone" have a contextually narrowed range. A use of a sentence with the subject "everyone" states a truth just when the predicate of the sentence is true of all of the people who are made relevant by the context of use. In Robinson's context, his "everyone" would be restricted to all who are members of the BC.

Though this attributer relativity is a reasonable hypothesis, such examples can also be accommodated while allowing that "everyone" always ranges over, well, everyone. One alternative view is that sentences with "everyone" typically are overly general and therefore false. But people who hear such claims immediately ignore those who are irrelevant to the purposes at hand. This practice of ignoring is widely taken for granted. That makes such false claims efficient ways to communicate something that is about only those who are in the group of contextually determined interest.

An asset of this contextually unvarying ("invariantist") semantic view of such sentences emerges in the following continuation of the example. Suppose that someone on the BC, say Stickler, opposes Robinson's claim. Stickler says, "No, what you said is not true, because not everyone is here. The Pope is not here." Probably Stickler's comment would come off as unamusing, at best. But it is not easy to see that Stickler is saying something false.

Quantifier contextualists can find truth in Stickler's comment. They can say that Stickler has shifted the conversational context, perhaps by mentioning the Pope, someone who is not in the group previously assumed to be relevant. So in Stickler's mouth "everyone" ranges over a wider group, perhaps all people worldwide. Thus, in that context it is correct for Stickler to assert "not everyone is here." The contextualist can note that this is compatible with the truth of the claim made by Robinson with "everyone," on the grounds that Robinson's claim had a crucially narrower contextually determined range.

This contextualist response does not wholly avoid the difficulty, though. The response finds a truth in the claim made by Robinson and it finds a truth in a claim made by Stickler. The remaining difficulty is this. It seems that Stickler was entirely accurate (though unamusing, unhelpful, and maybe obtuse). Yet the contextualist view does not find only truth in what Sticker says. Stickler said that Robinson's original claim was untrue. The contextualist view that we are considering must disagree with this. The contextualist must say that Stickler himself is wrong on that point, because the truth conditions of Robinson's original claim were met. The contextualist view implies that the original claim was true if and only if the members of the group in question were all there, and they all were. So our impression that Robinson was entirely accurate must be erroneous.

It is not obvious how best to interpret quantifiers in cases like this. The contextualist position may be overall best. In any event, contextualism applied to quantifiers displays a characteristic feature. Contextualism finds truth at the expense of contradiction. That has a nice constructive ring to it. But it runs a risk of interpretive failure. Concerning some cases in which one sentence seems to be used to deny something that another sentence says, contextualists characteristically allege that they are not really flat denials. This happens whenever there is a difference in what the contextualism counts as a semantically relevant context. Any such contextual difference implies that the two claims do not just contradict one another, even if one sentence used seems to negate the other.[1] Most commonly, contextualist proposals yield compatible truth conditions for the sentences. For instance, they say that Robinson and Stickler can both be right about those whom they respectively call "everyone."

Moral relativists are the contextualists of ethical theory. They hold roughly that something about the context of a moral evaluation, perhaps something in the culture or the personal values of the evaluator, contributes to the truth conditions of the resulting evaluation. Moral relativists have always been a relatively small and besieged group, though not lacking in able philosophers. The reason seems to be this. The prevalence of fundamental disagreements about moral evaluations is a virtually ineluctable element of the ethical situation. Among non-philosophers there are vigorous disputes about capital punishment, the treatment of animals, gun control, and so forth. Or, at least, their exchanges give every appearance of being disputes, and the participants clearly regard them as such. Among philosophers there are vigorous disputes among consequentialists, Kantians, virtue theorists, and divine command theorists. Or, at least, they certainly seem to disagree. In both cases the disputants often speak from more or less different cultural and personal backgrounds. When these differences are ones that a moral relativist claims to be crucial, the relativist cannot find contradictory claims, and may find only compatible claims. Yet it is deeply dubious that any such conciliatory interpretation is correct. Moral relativism has some resources to try to explain away the appearance of disagreement. But often it seems clear both that the disputants are fully competent with the language they are using and that those on each side fully intend to use it to deny what the other side affirms. These facts are hard for a relativist to explain away. These cases are trouble for moral relativism.

To the extent that apparent disagreement over epistemic claims is similarly witting and heartfelt, it is similarly difficult to find credible a reconciling EC interpretation. Some arguments about skepticism appear to have that character. Like moral relativists, EC theorists can work to explain away the appearance of contradiction or disagreement. But also as in the moral case, often it seems clear that competent speakers use words with the intent to be discussing the same thing and to be respectively affirming and denying something about it. These cases are trouble for EC.

Finally by way of preliminaries, we should be alert to a misleading temptation. It is tempting to think that semantic contextualism is obviously correct for all evaluative expressions. It is a plain fact that people routinely apply differing standards of evaluation in different contexts. For instance, suppose that Jones works on a Sabbath.

Smith counts Jones as "evil" because Jones is thereby disobeying a strict edict of Smith's religious faith. Robinson denies that Jones is "evil" because Jones's work is intended to promote a social cause that Robinson admires. Numerous similar examples exist for evaluations of beauty, humor, morality, and many other things. In particular, the application of differing standards of judgment plainly occurs as well in epistemic evaluations, such as attributions of knowledge, justification, and good reasoning. Are these contextually varying truth conditions in action?

Not necessarily. The fact that different standards are routinely applied in making an evaluative judgment does not imply the correctness of semantic contextualism about the contents of the judgment. To see this, note that differing standards are routinely applied in making judgments that are uncontroversially context-invariant. For instance, usually the genuineness of a purported piece of US currency is judged by a quick look, sometimes it is judged by a more careful inspection, and occasionally it is rigorously judged using a high-tech device. In spite of these differing standards, the content of the uses of "genuine US currency" is clearly the same. Other examples abound.

Thus, we cannot validly infer that contextual differences yield differing truth conditions simply because differing standards are often applied. For semantic contextualism to be correct, there must be something else about an expression, something beyond its susceptibility to differing standards of judgment, that makes the truth conditions of tokens of the expression differ with context.

Epistemic Contexualism

The most widely discussed form of EC holds that the truth conditions for tokens of sentences that include "knows" (and cognate expressions) vary with the attributer's context. Broadly speaking, what varies with some differences in the context in which a "knows" sentence is used is the strength of the epistemic position that the subject of the sentence must be in, in order for the sentence to assert a truth.

Many versions of EC share this core. Typically, the strength of epistemic position required is said to vary in a range that allows, at its low end, many true attributions in everyday contexts concerning ordinary judgments based on perception, memory, testimony, and perhaps also inductive generalization and high probability. At the high end of the range of variation, the typical EC truth conditions are demanding enough to make true many skeptical denials of "knowledge" of the external world.

This range corresponds to a genuine phenomenon of "knowledge" attributions. Fluent English speakers regularly make confident "knowledge" attributions about numerous routine matters of daily life: the color of a shirt when it is seen in good light, the occurrence of a death when it is read about in a newspaper, the identity of the first US President when it is recalled from some source or other, the sum of two large numbers when they are totaled on a calculator, and so on. Fluent speakers typically become increasingly hesitant about "knowledge" attributions as the practical significance of the right answer increases. Fluent speakers typically doubt or deny "knowledge" attributions when coming to grips with impressive skeptical arguments.

The heart of the contextualist explanation of this phenomenon is that people are responding in an approximately accurate way to shifting standards for correct "knowledge" attributions. In the context of everyday life, "knowledge" attributions have truth conditions that are weak enough to be met by seeing a color in good light, reading a report in a reliable publication, recalling a famous historical fact, adding on a calculator, and so forth. As the truth-value of a proposition matters more, the context shifts so that the truth conditions for "knowledge" of the proposition require somehow excluding ever more potential sources of error. In a context where skeptical considerations are prominent, the skepticism somehow gives rise to truth conditions for "knowledge" attributions that are so demanding that external world beliefs do not meet them.

There are two noteworthy ways in which the contextualist explanation of this phenomenon involving "knowledge" attribution could be misleading.

Loose Talk

The first way that EC could be misleading is by being fundamentally mistaken. It may be that all "knowledge" attributions have the same truth conditions, but people apply contextually varying standards for making the attributions. The most plausible unvarying standard for truth is very high, but not unreachably high. In ordinary contexts, when nothing much turns on it, people will claim knowledge, and attribute knowledge to themselves and others, in belief and in speech, on a basis that is significantly weaker than what is actually required. This is an efficient way to communicate assurance about the proposition and to facilitate taking it for granted.

According to the view now under consideration, fluent speakers actually realize, at least tacitly, that this knowledge ascription is just loose talk. The realization is shown by the fact that, if asked whether some proposition to which knowledge is ascribed on some such basis is *really* known, or *truly* known, or *really and truly* known, fluent speakers have a strong inclination to doubt or deny that it is.[2] Only the most conspicuous facts of current perception, the clearest memories, triple-checked calculations, and the like will often pass some such "really and truly" test. The present view has it that the answer to this "really and truly" question reveals what a speaker judges to be knowledge when she is trying her best to apply her best thought as to what is the actual standard for the truth of a "knowledge" attribution.

A contextualist has a ready explanation for the results of this "really and truly" test. The explanation is that raising a question about "knowledge" using these words serves to impose more stringent truth conditions. So it is no wonder that propositions that pass previous, more lenient standards are no longer said to be "known."

There is an important liability of this contextualist response. There are many big topics that receive similar results on the "really and truly" test. For instance, when fluent speakers consider whether they are "really and truly" happy, or they consider who are "really and truly" their friends, or they consider what is "really and truly" worth striving for, they tend to have doubts about their previous casual attributions of happiness, friendship, and worthwhile goals. It is possible that the English terms for these categories of happiness, friendship, and so forth all have contextually varying truth conditions, and that the standards are raised by these "really and truly" questions. But that is not what seems to be happening as we ponder these questions. It seems that our aim is to set aside loose talk about an important topic and tell the truth about it, the very same topic that was previously more casually discussed. The contextualist who holds that the "really and truly" test changes the truth conditions is bound to count this view of what we are doing as a mistake.[3] That is a liability.

Strict Truth

The second way in which contextualism about "knows" may be misleading would be by being correct. The reason why this might mislead is that it might suggest that the correctness of EC has a significant implication concerning some philosophical issue about knowledge. The fact is that the truth of EC in general would have no such implication.

For instance, suppose that "really and truly" does constitute a context in which "know" has truth conditions with different and higher standards than those of ordinary uses of "know." It may be that all philosophical discussion of knowledge is carried on in that one context. That is, it may be that every issue about knowledge, from the Gettier problem to the extent of scientific knowledge, from the nature of justification to the merits of external world skepticism, has been discussed solely in this single "really and truly" context. Granting epistemic contextualism, this claim of a single philosophical context has some plausibility. Philosophy generally gets going only when we get serious about a topic. So it may be that "really and truly" is one colloquial way to direct attention to the truth conditions that arise when we take this philosophical sort of attitude toward our investigation.

If all of this is so, then "knows" is context sensitive. But appreciating that fact would tell us nothing new about our philosophical issues. All sides to the philosophical disputes would have been discussing the same thing all along. At most, we would have reason to avoid importing into philosophical discussions of knowledge examples in which "knows" is less scrupulously applied. Given the correctness of EC, these may well not be cases of the philosophical topic of knowledge. Not relying on such cases is sensible. But we have reason not to rely on them in any event. Whether or not EC is correct, relatively casual uses of a term are more likely to be mistakes.

More detailed contextual views have more philosophically consequential implications. For instance, some EC views say enough about what differentiates contexts, and what the differing truth conditions are, to imply that skeptics and non-skeptics typically operate in contexts that make each position correct about what it typically calls "knowledge." The present point is only that contextualism in general says nothing about when there are context shifts. So even if they exist, they may not affect philosophical questions about knowledge.

Again, suppose that EC is correct in broad outline, but now suppose that philosophy does not set a single context. In skeptical contexts, the requirements for "knowledge" are severe; in various non-skeptical contexts, including some in which philosophical issues are under discussion, the requirements are variously less severe. There are still no immediate epistemological consequences, even for the merits of external world skepticism. The severe requirements of skeptical contexts might be satisfiable by felicitous external world judgments, the standards actually imposed by skeptics to the contrary notwithstanding. The outline of one such possibility is this. It might be that in skeptical contexts, only 100 percent of the right sort of probability is enough. But it is enough (along with true belief). There need not also be something that skeptics often require: internally possessed evidence that excludes all possibility of false belief. Skeptics see various ways in which our judgments often both lack this probability and are possibly false. Skeptics draw the extreme conclusion that the external world judgments must have the support of entailing evidence. But perhaps external world judgments are in the right way 100 percent probable when they are correctly causally connected to the fact known.[4] This might occur only in optimal cases of perception and memory. The skeptical context would set the 100 percent probability requirement, while the skeptic would mistakenly impose a more stringent standard. EC does not imply that skeptics have infallible theoretical insight into the truth conditions for "knows" that hold when they are being skeptical.

Again, EC leaves the main epistemological issues unresolved. Only versions that are specific about the contextual truth conditions do more. Those versions must be defended on their own particular merits. The general thesis of EC is neutral about the epistemically consequential details.

A Delicate Balance

EC has never been obviously true. In this way it differs from the contextual variation in truth conditions exhibited by indexicals and comparatives like "large" and "near." EC is defended not by direct semantic reflection among fluent speakers, but by its explanatory strengths. The classic explanatory role is to explain how both ordinary "knowledge" attributions and skeptical arguments denying "knowledge" can seem so plausible. The classic contextualist view is that each is correct. The reason is that ordinary "knowledge" ascriptions often meet the truth conditions of "knows" in everyday contexts, while skeptical denials of "knowledge" are right according to the truth conditions for "knows" operative in their contexts.

This reason does not quite yield the data to be explained. The data are the *plausibility*, or the *reasonableness*, of both ordinary "knowledge" attributions and skeptical "knowledge" denials. The classic contextualist proposal offers us a way to have those claims come out *true*. In order to use this truth to account for the plausibility in question, the explanation must add something about how the truth engenders the plausibility.

The most straightforward way to do this is to add something along the following lines. When we are thinking about ordinary speakers, and skeptics, are we in some way cognizant of the truth conditions of their respective "knowledge" ascriptions? We are in some way cognizant that the respective truth conditions are met. And so we find the respective claims plausible.

This explanation attributes to us some sort of grip on the contextual variation in standards for "knowledge" ascriptions. We are not said to think explicitly that there is a contextual variation. But we are supposed to be guided by our understanding of "knows" to count some differences in context as decisive to truth when we make our plausibility judgments.

The problem is to understand how the correctness of EC can be so difficult to recognize that it has been missed entirely until lately, and many philosophers who consider it still sincerely deny it. How can it be that fluent English speakers are well enough attuned to this variation for it to guide some of their plausibility judgments, while none noticed that "knows" is context-sensitive until recently, and some are unable to recognize this by semantic reflection, even under the tutelage of a contextualist?

There is no contradiction in this. It is not a hopeless situation for EC. There may be some adequate psychological explanation of how one can have a concept that one commonly applies in a context-sensitive way, while being unable to spot this feature of the concept when one tries. It is difficult to understand this sort of grasp, though. For a start, it would be nice to be shown other examples of concept possession with *almost* these same features, say, examples where the context sensitivity is sufficiently hidden to have been universally overlooked but is eventually recognizable by virtually all proficient speakers. The oddity of this sort of grasp of a concept poses a challenge to EC. It is another liability of the view.[5]

Notes

1 Contextualists find differences in truth conditions. This does not automatically make the claims compatible. However, if there is any contextual variation in truth conditions, then the two claims are not the direct contradictories of one another that they seem to be. Also, denials of contradiction are what a straightforward application of contextualism engenders. It is possible to add a special provision for disputes. A special provision might claim that in a dispute something overrides each speaker's separate context in determining truth conditions. It might be claimed that this yields one context for both of the pair of syntactically contradictory utterances. This sort of view will have a hard time locating one interpretation that is credible for both utterances, while otherwise interpreting in the spirit of the contextualism. Why does the basis for the unifying interpretation override the particular contexts of use only in disputes, and not everywhere? Furthermore, justifying this sort of special provision is especially difficult when uses of syntactically contradictory sentences are not public, but rather formulate successive thoughts by someone weighing the merits of opposing positions. There is no intuitive third context to appeal to in assigning unifying truth conditions, while the successive contexts seem tied for suitability as context determiners.

2 "Really" by itself, and "truly" by itself, sometimes seem to function as intensifiers, as in "a really hot day," and "a truly long drive." But "really and truly" seems rather to function as a way to get serious about the truth of the modified claim. Similarly functioning terms include "actually" and "genuinely." "Really and truly" will be the phrase of choice here.

3 The contextualist who denies that the "really and truly" test changes the truth conditions seems to have no reasonable principled way to say why the truth conditions do change in skeptical contexts.

4 This is very roughly the position of Fred Dretske about knowledge in general, in his *Knowledge and the Flow of Information.*

5 The negative perspective on contextualism that I express in this exchange has been influenced by the work of several philosophers. The following essays have been most influential: Schiffer (1996), Sosa (2000), and Feldman (2001).

References

Feldman, R. (2001) Skeptical problems, contextualist solutions. *Philosophical Studies*, 103, 61–85.
Schiffer, S. (1996) Contextualist solutions to scepticism. *Proceedings of the Aristotelian Society*, 96, 317–33.
Sosa, E. (2000) Skepticism and contextualism. *Philosophical Issues*, 10, 1–18.

Contextualism Defended

Stewart Cohen

1 Contextualism and Skeptical Paradoxes

Contextualism has been proposed as a way to resolve stubborn epistemological paradoxes. Where P is some common-sense proposition about the external world (e.g. I see a zebra) and H is some skeptical hypothesis (e.g. I do not see a cleverly disguised mule), the paradox takes the following form:

(1) I know P.
(2) I do not know not-H.
(3) I know P only if I know not-H.

These propositions constitute a paradox because each is independently very plausible, yet jointly they are inconsistent. Because our intuitions about knowledge lead to paradox, skepticism threatens.

Most philosophers who consider this paradox are unwilling to accept skepticism. Instead, they attempt to provide an antiskeptical resolution of the paradox. But one cannot satisfactorily respond to the paradox by simply denying one member of the inconsistent set. The paradox arises because each proposition seems true. To resolve the paradox, one must explain the intuitive appeal of the denied proposition. Otherwise, we have no explanation for how the paradox arises. So an antiskeptical resolution must resolve the paradox in a way that preserves the truth of (1) while explaining the appeal of the propositions that threaten a skeptical result, i.e. (2) and (3).

One robust feature of our intuitions regarding (1) to (3) is that they tend to vacillate. We begin by confidently holding (1), that we know many things about the world.

Chapter Two

Under pressure from skeptical arguments, we see the appeal of (2). Given that (3) is compelling, and that (3) and (2) entail the falsity of (1), we begin to waver in our assent to (1). But we find this unsatisfactory given our common-sense rejection of skepticism. But again (1) together with (3) entails that (2) is false. But when we consider the skeptical arguments for (2), we tend to fall back into a skeptical frame of mind.

The contextualist resolution of the paradox proposes that we take these intuitions at face value. Rather than rejecting one of these intuitions as mistaken, contextualism attempts to explain away the apparent inconsistency of our intuitions by arguing that they reflect the contextually varying truth-conditions for knowledge ascriptions. Contextualism holds that ascriptions of knowledge are context-sensitive – that the truth-value of sentences of the form "S knows P" depend on contextually varying standards for how strong one's epistemic position with respect to P must be in order for one to know P.

There are various ways of cashing out this notion of the strength of one's epistemic position. But contextualist resolutions of the paradox are alike in holding that the context of ascription determines which proposition of the skeptical paradox gets denied. According to contextualism, in everyday contexts (2) is false, in stricter "skeptical contexts (1) is false, but in no context is (3) false. This resolution of the paradox explains the appeal of skeptical arguments by allowing that the claims of the skeptic are true, relative to the very strict context in which they are made. But the resolution is antiskeptical in that it preserves the truth of our everyday knowledge ascriptions relative to the everyday contexts in which they are made. In essence, contextualism concedes that there is some truth to skepticism, but contains the damage by holding that the skeptical claims are true only relative to atypically strict contexts.

2 Alternative Accounts

We can think of contextualism as involving two theses:

(a) Ascriptions of knowledge are context-sensitive.
(b) The context-sensitivity of knowledge ascriptions provides the basis for resolving the skeptical paradox.

Criticisms of contextualism can challenge (a), or grant (a) while denying (b). Earl Conee raises criticisms of both kinds.

Conee challenges (a) by arguing that there are alternative ways of accounting for our intuitions that saddle us with the paradox. He suggests the possibility that the truth conditions for knowledge ascriptions are invariant – most plausibly "very high, but not unreachably high" – but that the standards for making appropriate, though not strictly speaking true, attributions vary with context. In everyday contexts, "when nothing much turns on it" people will ascribe knowledge to themselves and others on a basis that is "significantly weaker than what is actually required." But competent speakers realize that this is loose talk, as evidenced in their willingness to withdraw their claims when challenged as to whether the proposition is "really and truly" known. Conee notes that "only the most conspicuous facts of current perception, the clearest memories, triple-checked calculations and the like" will pass the "really and truly" test.

Conee's point here is that there is nothing in the intuitive data to support contextualism over this alternative account. But although the account Conee suggests is consistent with the intuitive data, I don't see that this account does explain the intuitive data as well as contextualism. The problem for Conee's alternative is that competent speakers, under skeptical pressure, tend to deny that we know even the most conspicuous facts of perception, the clearest memories, etc. For the contextualist, this is because the strictness of the standards in skepticism make our skeptical denials true, in those contexts. But Conee's alternative incorrectly predicts that we should hang on to such knowledge ascriptions, even in the face of skeptical "really and truly" challenges.

As Conee notes, the contextualist should say that when one applies the "really and truly" test, one is in fact raising the standards, and in this new context, the truth conditions for sentences of the form "S knows P" are so strict as to falsify the ascriptions. This would seem to commit the contextualist to taking a similar line for a whole host of predicates that behave similarly when subjected to the "really and truly" test, e.g. happy. But according to Conee, that is not what seems to be happening when we consider questions like "Am I really and truly happy?" It seems to us that we are setting aside loose talk and trying to get to the truth of the matter. According to Conee, this is a liability for contextualism.

There is no doubt that when one is in what the contextualist wants to view as a high standards context, one has a feeling of enlightenment regarding the correct application of the predicate in question. We feel as if we are seeing the truth of the matter that has, up until that point, eluded us. So we have the "witting and heartfelt" sense that, contrary to what contextualism holds, our skeptical judgments conflict with our previous everyday judgments. So the contextualist has to argue that we are in all of these cases mistaken in our metajudgment that our skeptical judgments conflict with our earlier judgments. Conee holds that this is a liability for contextualism. But the extent to which this is a liability will depend on the plausibility of attributing to us this kind of mistake. I will return to this issue below.

Conee goes on to raise objections to (b). He suggests two ways in which contextualism might be misleading, even if it turns out that ascriptions of knowledge are context-sensitive. First, it might be the case that the skeptic (or the skeptic in us) is mistaken in thinking that the stricter skeptical standards are unsatisfiable. Second, it may be that all philosophical discussions are carried out in one strict, "really and truly" context. If either of these possibilities obtains then the fact that ascriptions of knowledge are context-sensitive will not, by itself, settle the main *philosophical* questions about knowledge.

Conee is right that even granting the context-sensitivity of knowledge ascriptions, nothing strictly follows about what the standards are in particular contexts. That is, (b) is logically stronger than (a). For the contextualist solution to work, it must be that the standards in everyday contexts are low and attainable, and the standards in skeptical contexts are high and unattainable. The contextualist proposes that if we take our shifty intuitive judgments, both skeptical and commonsensical, at face value, then we get just those results.

Of course, the contextualist has no *proof* that our intuitive judgments are correct. What contextualism offers is a non-skeptical way to resolve the skeptical paradox. It proposes an explanation of our inconsistent inclinations that accounts for the appeal of skeptical arguments, while still preserving the truth of our everyday knowledge ascriptions. Now for all that, contextualism may be false. But the fact that it can do this much shows that there is much to recommend it. In the end, whether contextualism should be adopted depends on how it compares with other proposals for resolving the paradox.

This brings us back to Conee's proposals. The first is that the standards are context-sensitive, but we are mistaken in thinking that the strict skeptical standards are not met. Perhaps this is so. But absent some defense of a particular proposal as to how we are mistaken, as to how we can satisfy what appear, in some contexts, to be the very strict standards for knowledge, the proposal does not count for much. (Conee mentions Dretske's information-theoretic account, but I don't think he is seriously endorsing it.) At best, it shows how the falsity of the contextualist solution to the epistemological paradox is consistent with the thesis that ascriptions of knowledge are context-sensitive. And this is something the contextualist can concede.

Moreover, even if we had a plausible account of how we could meet the stricter standards, such an account would have to explain why we were inclined to make the mistake of thinking that we cannot meet those standards, when in fact we can. Recall that these are intuitive judgments. It is not clear that our intuitive skeptical judgments are made on the basis of some false theory we hold about what is required for knowledge. If the correct theory entails that our skeptical intuitions are mistaken, the question still remains as to why we have those intuitions. Only with such an explanation would we have a resolution of the paradox.

Conee's second proposal is that although the standards for knowledge vary across contexts, there is a single standard that is always in effect in philosophical discussions of knowledge, "from the Gettier problem, to the extent of scientific knowledge, from the nature of justification to the merits of skepticism all have been discussed solely in the 'really and truly' context." This is another possibility wherein "knowledge" is context-sensitive, but that fact has no implications for important philosophical issues.

Again, Conee is correct that nothing philosophically significant strictly follows from the thesis that ascriptions of knowledge are context-sensitive. The point of contextualism is to provide an explanation for the intuitive data in a way that can explain the appeal of skepticism while still preserving the truth of our everyday knowledge ascriptions. The fact that contextualism can provide such an explanation does not entail that it is the only possible account, even on the supposition that ascriptions of knowledge are context-sensitive. So we need to compare the relative merits of competing accounts.

An important fact about our epistemological intuitions is that even when we are discussing philosophy, we vacillate between thinking that we know and thinking that we do not. When we discuss the Gettier problem, we readily allow that we know all sorts of things. We use these intuitions about when we know as data in constructing our theory of knowledge. But when we discuss skepticism, we have intuitions that we don't know the very things we thought we knew when discussing the Gettier problem.

How do we explain this shiftiness in a way that avoids skepticism while still explaining its appeal? Contextualism proposes a way to do this in terms of contextually shifting truth-conditions. The view that Conee mentions provides no such explanation. Since our intuitions vacillate even in philosophical contexts, if, as Conee suggests, there is a single standard for all such contexts, then some of those intuitions are mistaken. But which ones are mistaken, and why, if they are mistaken, do we have them? Conee's suggestion is merely the bare statement of a possibility that leaves entirely open whether skepticism is true, and if not, why we find it appealing. Thus the contextualist explanation of our intuitions, while not entailed by the thesis that ascriptions of knowledge are context-sensitive, has much more to recommend it than the possibility that Conee raises.

3 Is the Contextualist Model Coherent?

Of course, a theory's explanatory power does not count for much if the theory is independently implausible. And Conee argues that contextualism taken as a whole entails an implausible story about competent speakers. He notes that contextualism explains the appeal of the premises of the skeptical paradox by arguing that each is in fact true, relative to a particular context. Thus contextualism must hold that the appeal of the premises of the paradox reflects our grasp of their truth conditions. So it must be that judgments of competent speakers, to the extent that their judgments are so guided, are sensitive to the contextual shifts in the truth conditions.

But at the same time, contextualism involves a kind of error theory with respect to certain metajudgments about knowledge. According to the view, when we are in skeptical contexts where (1) is false, we mistakenly think our denial of (1) conflicts with our everyday assent to sentences of that form. That is, we fail to recognize the context-sensitivity of our own judgments even though we grasp, in some sense, their shifting truth conditions. Conee claims that this account of competent speakers is "difficult to understand" and challenges the contextualist to provide other examples of our use of context-sensitive predicates that fits the model the contextualist proposes in the case of "knows."

As I have argued, there are precedents for the contextualist model (see Cohen, 1999, 2001). Consider ascriptions of flatness. You can lead competent speakers to question their everyday ascriptions of flatness by making salient "bumps" that ordinarily we do not pay attention to. As Peter Unger demonstrated, taking this strategy to the extreme, e.g. by calling attention to microscopic surface irregularities, one can lead competent speakers to worry whether anything is really flat (Unger, 1975). But Unger's case for flatness skepticism is interesting precisely because many who feel the pull of flatness skepticism look back on their previous flatness ascriptions and think they may have been wrong.

Should we worry that all along we have been speaking falsely when we have called things "flat"? Surely not. Philosophical reflection will convince most that ascriptions of flatness are relative to context-sensitive standards. Roads that count as flat in a conversation among Coloradans do not generally count as flat in a conversation among Kansans. And while one can truly ascribe flatness to a table in everyday conversations, one might not be able to truly ascribe flatness to that same table when setting up a sensitive scientific experiment. If we implicitly raise the standards high enough (by making salient microscopic bumps), then perhaps, relative to that context, no physical surface really is flat. But of course, that does not impugn our ascriptions of flatness in everyday contexts where the standards are more lenient.

So the controversy over whether anything is flat can be resolved by noting that ascriptions of flatness are context-sensitive. And to the extent that competent speakers' ascriptions of flatness are guided by these contextually shifting truth conditions, they in some sense grasp those truth-conditions. But then why can we get competent speakers to question their everyday flatness ascriptions by implicitly raising the standards? It must be that although competent speakers are guided in their flatness ascriptions by contextually shifting truth-conditions, such speakers can fail to realize that their flatness ascriptions are context-sensitive. And because they can fail to realize this, they can mistakenly think that their reluctance to ascribe flatness, in a context where the standards are at the extreme, conflicts with their ascriptions of flatness in everyday contexts. That is to say, they conflate the proposition expressed by "X is flat" at a strict context, with the proposition expressed by that sentence at a more lenient context. And this is precisely what the contextualist argues occurs in the case of knowledge ascriptions.[1]

Having said that, I should note that there is an important difference between the two cases. Contextualist theories of flatness ascriptions, once proposed, gain easy and widespread acceptance among most people. But, as Conee points out, contextualist theories of justification/knowledge do not. This is something a contextualist – one like me anyway who relies on the analogy – needs to explain.

One thing the contextualist can say here is that there are varying degrees to which competent speakers are blind to context-sensitivity in the language. Thus, while everyone can readily see the context-sensitivity of indexicals like "I" and "now," it can take some amount of reflection to convince most that "flat" is context-sensitive. And for a term like "knows," it may be very difficult even after some amount of reflection for competent speakers to accept context-sensitivity. It may take subtle philosophical considerations concerning the best way to resolve a paradox in order to "see" the context-sensitivity of "knows."

Here is a somewhat speculative attempt to explain why it is difficult to accept that "knows" (and "justified") is context-sensitive. Justification and knowledge are normative concepts. To say that a belief is justified or constitutes knowledge is to say something good about the belief. We value justification and knowledge. But contextualist theories are deflationary. Contextualism about knowledge says that most of our everyday utterances of the form "S knows P" are true, even though the strength of S's epistemic position in those instances does not meet our highest standards. In the same way, contextualism about flatness says that most of our everyday utterances of sentences of the form "X is flat" are true, even though X's surface may fall short of perfect flatness.

In other words, contextualism is a "good news, bad news" theory. The good new is that we have lots of knowledge and many surfaces are flat; the bad news is that knowledge and flatness are not all they were cracked up to be. We find this much easier to accept in the case of flatness than knowledge, because ascriptions of flatness do not have the normative force that ascriptions of knowledge/justification do.

Note

1 A perhaps less clear case involves ascriptions of solidity. With the rise of our understanding of atomic physics, it became clear that many of the objects we think of as solid actually contain quite a bit of empty space. This led some people to conclude that no physical objects are solid. Others found this conclusion to contradict common sense. No doubt some vacillated between agreeing with the conclusion and rejecting it. Again, I assume that philosophical reflection will convince most that the correct thing to say here is that ascriptions of solidity are context-sensitive. Here it seems most plausible to view ascriptions of solidity as involving a kind of implicit quantification and the context as governing a shifting domain. So for x to be solid, it must contain no spaces between its parts. But what counts as a part depends on the context. If this is correct, then we have another case where competent speakers' judgments are guided by contextually shifting truth conditions, but the speakers are unaware of this fact.

References

Cohen, S. (1999) Contextualism, skepticism, and the structure of reasons. *Philosophical Perspectives*, 13, 57–89.

Cohen, S. (2001) Contextualism defended: comments on Richard Feldman's "Skeptical problems, contextualist solutions." *Philosophical Studies*, 103, 87–9.

Unger, P. (1975) *Ignorance: A Case for Skepticism*. Oxford: Oxford University Press.

Contextualism Contested Some More

Earl Conee

Stewart Cohen offers EC as a way to solve an epistemological problem that he counts as a paradox. Here is the standard illustration of the problem. While I see an animal in a zoo enclosure:

(1) I know that I see a zebra.
(2) I do not know that I do not see a cleverly disguised mule.
(3) I know that I see a zebra only if I know that I do not see a cleverly disguised mule.

Stew reports that our intuitions about the truth of (1) to (3) robustly tend to vacillate. We are drawn to (1) by common sense. Skeptical arguments lead us to (2). (3) is compelling all along, and inferences from (3) and each of (1) and (2) lead us to the denial of the other.

Stew's EC theorist has it that each of (1) and (2) is true at a context from which it is found intuitive. The intuitive appeal of (1) is to be explained by the proposal that there are relatively lenient truth conditions for (1) in everyday contexts. The plausibility of a skeptical conclusion is to be explained by the proposal that skeptical claims that imply (2) are true at contexts with relatively strict truth conditions for sentences using "know."

As I write, a painting is in the news. Thoughts about the reports provide a model of an intellectual conflict similar to (1) to (3) that does not allow a contextualist resolution.

> A woman bought a painting for $5. It is a large canvas covered with bright squiggles and blotches of paint. Eventually the woman happened to contact an art professor about it. She was led to believe that the artist might well be the renowned twentieth century American painter, Jackson Pollock. An expert found a Pollock fingerprint in the paint. He declared it a genuine Pollock. An art institute examined the painting. After careful study, the institute announced that the painting is not by Pollack. There the matter stands.[1]

Considering the case, I vacillate between two conclusions.

> C1: The painting is by Jackson Pollock.
> C2: The painting is not by Jackson Pollock.

On different bases, each seems true. I am tempted to accept C1 when I think:

> How could Pollock's fingerprint get in a painting that looks like a Pollock to an expert, if Pollock didn't paint it? There is no other plausible way.

I am tempted to accept C2 when I think:

> The art institute has its reputation at stake. They are aware of the fingerprint evidence. Yet they say that the work is not by Pollock.

I incline toward C1 again when I note that the art institute is relying heavily on the lack of an established history for the work, while I doubt that it is peculiar to lose track of one painting. I incline toward C2 again when I note that I may know little of the reputable art institute's full grounds for their negative conclusion. I alternate between C1 and C2 on the basis of these reasons. I become perplexed and reluctant to judge.

This is no paradox. There is a straightforward empirical fact of the matter (leaving vagueness aside). I happen to have pretty strong evidence for each conclusion with no overriding consideration. I alternate between C1 and C2 by employing different standards of judgment, each of which is normally sufficient for reasonable belief. Some of my standards make a mistake here. This is not mysterious. We have no good grounds to think that such standards are universally correct.

Is Knowledge Contextual?

Finally about this case, a reconciling contextualist interpretation of my perplexity is out of the question.[2] The thoughts that I formulate with C1 and C2 are incompatible. Now let's return to Stew's (1) to (3), and its EC resolution.

Intuitive responses do incline us toward accepting (1) and (2), though we can become perplexed and reluctant to judge. It may be misleading to classify the responses as intuitions. Neither (1) nor (2) is just credible on its own. Each seems true, when it does, on the basis of something else. The bases differ. (1) seems true when we naively consider the facts of an ordinary zoo visit. (2) seems true partly as a consequence of plausible skeptical reasoning. For instance, a typical key premise alleges that a visitor to the zoo has no evidence that distinguishes the animal seen from a cleverly disguised mule.

The appeal of (1) and (2) derives in one way or another from other considerations. I shall call any such basis a "standard for judgment." It is of some importance that the plausibility of (1) and (2) derives from standards for judgment, that this joint plausibility is perplexing, and that we have no reason beyond the limited credibility of our standards to regard them is unerring. This all makes (1) to (3) significantly like my C1 and C2. There the truth conditions do not vary. I am drawn to C1 and C2 by credible but fallible standards, while I have no overriding evidence about which standards support a falsehood. The counterpart invariantist view of (1) to (3) beckons.

Does EC have an explanatory advantage? The EC resolution is crucially incomplete. Where (1) to (3) seem true, an EC theorist locates satisfied truth conditions. But satisfied truth conditions do not explain plausibility. What directly explains the plausibility to a person of a sentence is whatever leads the person to regard the sentence as true. An explanation of plausibility must cite something that influences the person's thinking.

Presumably EC theorists will supplement their explanation with claims about our use of common-sense standards for judging (1) and skeptically encouraged standards for judging (2). To involve varying truth conditions in the account, EC theorists will also claim that our standards are sufficient for the truth of (1) and (2) in their respective contexts. They might say that we regard each context's truth condition itself as our standard there.

Imputing a standard for judgment yields the same immediate explanation of plausibility, whether or not we add that it establishes truth. So the distinctive EC claim that our standards establish the truth of (1) and (2) is idle for this explanatory purpose.

Some of the standards have a notable vulnerability that EC overlooks. Our inclination toward (2) results from some more or less philosophical reasoning. It is alluring enough to draw us toward (2). But like most alluring philosophical arguments, it is subject to reasonable objection. At best, its success remains in doubt. EC sweeps the doubts aside and declares that the reasoning in support of (2) yields genuine truth conditions for knowledge. No philosophical reasoning deserves such deference.

Is the EC claim that the relevant standards establish truth an asset on other grounds? A complete account of our responses to (1) to (3) also says why we reasonably and confidently employ the pertinent standards. EC theorists can hold that our standards for judging (1) and (2) are somehow tacitly acquired in learning the meaning of "know." They might say that our learning partly consists in acquiring a rule for accessing a context's truth condition, and the rule yields the standards that make (1) and (2) plausible to us. EC theorists can then hold that the analytic link of these standards to the meaning of "know" explains why the standards seem so trustworthy to us.

Invariantists can offer a better explanation of our reasonable confidence in the standards. Invariantists can observe that although the standards that we apply to (1) and (2) may include ones we are taught in learning "know," they are not therefore semantically guaranteed to be necessary or sufficient conditions for the application of the term. They can be stereotypes offered to guide usage, well supported rules of thumb, or apparent implications of convincing theories. Nothing readily available shows us which appealing standards fail here. An account along these lines explains the attractiveness of (1) and (2) in a way that better accommodates other features of the situation. Allowing our standards to be fallible lets us be right about the conflict that we see among the propositions that attract our acceptance as we consider (1) to (3).

Brief Replies

R1. Stew's EC is the conjunction of

(a) Ascriptions of knowledge are context-sensitive,

and

(b) The context-sensitivity of knowledge ascriptions provides the basis for resolving the skeptical paradox.

Stew writes that I opposed (a) by offering a particular invariantist view of knowledge to account for "our intuitions that saddle us with the paradox."

I did not offer the invariantist view to explain what Stew regards as our intuitions about knowledge. As may now be clear, I believe that those intuitive responses have no simple connection to the actual conditions on knowledge. I offered the view as a possibility about the nature of knowledge that accords with our having a specific intelligent basis for a variety of the knowledge attributions that the view counts as false. The basis is that those attributions are efficient loose talk. The "really and truly" test is supposed to show that this status is how we ourselves think of the attributions in our best moments.

R2. Stew suggests that there is a telling vacillation in intuitive knowledge judgments within philosophy. During Gettier problem discussions we readily allow that we know many things, while discussions of skepticism give rise to intuitions that we do not know those things. EC can offer shifting truth conditions within philosophy to explain the vacillation. I discussed the possibility of a context-sensitive view of "knows" that finds within philosophy no variation of truth conditions. This view leaves the vacillation unexplained.

I was thinking of EC as Stew's (a) only. I presented the particular context-sensitive view of "knows" as an example of how (a) could be true while leaving philosophy unaffected. In support of this sort of context-sensitivity, I offered just the observation that philosophy seems to occupy a "serious" context.

What does account for the vacillation within philosophy? When we consider the Gettier problem, most of us (some philosophers are spoilsports about this) apply common-sense standards for knowledge. Any of them will do. When we think hard about skepticism, we tend to apply more severe standards. (Here too there have been spoilsports, notably G. E. Moore.) These are reasonable proclivities, if only because the standards are initially plausible. Philosophers' use of such standards explains the vacillation. Any claimed connection between this variation in our standards and the actual truth conditions requires argument.

R3. Stew offers a speculative account of why some find it difficult to accept EC (where EC is understood as the conjunction of (a) and (b)). We regard knowledge as a good thing. If EC is true, our external world "knowledge" is not so hot. We only meet disappointing truth conditions. Some hold out against EC to avoid this disappointment.

Probably this accounts for some resistance to EC. It does not hit home with me. My resistance derives primarily from two sources. First, it seems to me that skeptical views deny the very knowledge that is otherwise widely affirmed. EC implies otherwise. On further reflection, the thoughts continue to seem incompatible.

Explanatory success could conceivably outweigh this reflective liability. That brings us back to points about explaining our knowledge attribution inclinations. Invariantists can credibly explain our reasonable confident use of the varying standards for judgment that EC theorists invoke.[3] The distinctive EC thesis is that some of our relatively high standards, and some of our less high standards, are contextual truth conditions, or derive from them. This gives an EC explanation no advantage. It incurs the costs of caving in to dubious skeptical reasoning and requiring some durable impressions of incompatibility to be errors.

Notes

1   Some of these claims about the case may turn out to be inaccurate. By the time you read this, the question may well be settled. In any event, the example as described serves to make the point.
2   The sentence types display some contextual variation. "The painting" has different referents in different contexts and probably the name "Jackson Pollock" does too. But to formulate my thoughts with C1 and C2, we must hold fixed the referents of those two expressions. The resulting thoughts are irreconcilable.
3   Toward providing an invariantist explanation of our attitudes to the standards, I have just mentioned stereotypes, rules of thumb, and inference from theories. An adequate explanation would elaborate. The point is only that some invariantist explanatory possibilities are at least as initially credible as the envisaged EC account.

Contextualism Defended Some More

Stewart Cohen

1 When Should We Appeal to Contextualist Resolutions of Philosophical Paradoxes?

Earl Conee raises important issues about when we should appeal to a contextualist resolution of a philosophical problem. He argues, in effect, that contextualists are too quick to appeal to a contextualist resolution of our conflicting intuitions regarding knowledge. His strategy is to present another case that he argues is structurally identical to the knowledge case where a contextualist resolution looks to be uncalled for. This, he argues, should make us question the validity of appealing to a contextualist resolution of the knowledge case.

Conee's case involves a conflict over whether a particular painting is by Jackson Pollock. On the one hand, an expert testifies that the painting contains Pollock's fingerprint. On the other hand, an art institute has testified that the painting is not by Pollock. This leads us to vacillate over whether or not the painting is by Pollock.

About this case, Conee makes the following points:

(a) Different considerations pull us in different directions regarding a particular matter of fact.
(b) The considerations in both directions are fallible but we have no overriding basis that tells in favor of one set of considerations over the other.
(c) We find this situation perplexing.

All the same, according to Conee, "This [case] is no paradox. There is a straightforward empirical fact of the matter (leaving vagueness aside)."

Conee then notes that the skeptical paradox is like his Pollock case in respect of (a) to (c). But, Conee argues, there is no temptation in the Pollock case to appeal to a contextualist semantics for the predicate " . . . is by Pollock." Clearly here, the truth conditions are invariant. And this, he argues, should lead us to question whether a contextualist resolution of the skeptical case is correct.

Conee is surely correct that we should not necessarily be attracted to a contextualist solution anytime we have a case that satisfies (a) to (c). And I agree that a contextualist resolution of the Pollock case would be very implausible. But I will argue that there are important disanalogies between the two cases that make a contextualist resolution of the skeptical case plausible.

Perhaps the most important difference is that, as Conee himself points out, there is nothing paradoxical about the question of whether the painting is by Pollock. It is a straightforward empirical matter. Our only problem is that we lack empirical information – information that presumably would settle the matter.

But the knowledge case is not a straightforwardly empirical matter. The question about whether we know is arguably not an empirical question. In fact, there need not be any disagreement between skepticism and common sense about any empirical fact. In the skeptical case, the issue is conceptual. Different considerations pull us in different directions concerning whether or not a particular set of empirical facts is properly classifiable as an instance of knowledge.

Conee questions whether it is correct to call our conflicting responses about the knowledge case "intuitions." For our each response is not "credible on its own," but rather based on "something else." I agree that our responses are based on various considerations. Our response that we know we see a zebra is based on the facts of the case as described. Our response that we don't know we don't see a cleverly disguised mule is based on the appeal of various skeptical principles. But I don't see that they are not intuitions. Our response that we know we see a zebra is an intuitive judgment about whether the concept of knowledge applies in a particular case. And our response that we don't know we don't we are not seeing a cleverly disguised mule is an intuitive judgment about the cogency of a particular argument. The fact that nothing empirical is at stake makes it appropriate to think of these responses as intuitive judgments.[1] And the fact that the Pollock case is clearly empirical makes it clear that our conflicting judgments in that case are not intuitive. We cannot decide by intuition whether or not a particular painting is a Pollock.

So there is an important difference between the Pollock case and the skepticism case. The former involves empirical judgments about an empirical matter of fact, whereas the latter involves intuitive judgments about whether a conceptual matter, or to ascend semantically, about whether a particular predicate applies. Of course, even if we are dealing with intuitive judgments concerning the application of a predicate, it does not follow that a contextualist treatment is called for. There must be a semantical model of the predicate that makes a contextualist treatment plausible. Different contextualists have proposed different models.

Lewis argues that ascriptions of knowledge involve an implicit quantification (Lewis, 1996). S knows P just in case S's evidence eliminates every alternative. But what counts as an alternative that S's evidence must eliminate depends on context. So for Lewis, the context-sensitivity of "knows" is a function of contextual restrictions on the domain of quantification.

On my own view, the context-sensitivity of knowledge is inherited from one of its components, i.e. justification (Cohen, 1999). In general, when a predicate has both a comparative form and a simpliciter form, context will determine the degree to which the predicate has to be satisfied in order to be satisfied *simpliciter*. So, for example, context determines how flat a surface must be in order to be flat *simpliciter*. Analogously, context will determine how justified a belief must be in order to be justified *simpliciter*. So if justification is a constituent of knowledge, and "justified" is context-sensitive, that provides some reason to think "knows" will be context-sensitive.

So this makes for another important difference between the skeptical paradox and Conee's Pollock case. Contextualists about knowledge have provided semantic models for "knows" that explain its context-sensitivity in a way that allows the dispute about knowledge to be resolved. But I can see no way to model the predicate " . . . is by Pollock" that would explain the sort of context-sensitivity required to resolve the dispute over whether the painting is a Pollock.

2 Explaining the Skeptical Paradox: Contextualism versus Invariantism

Conee also argues that the contextualist does not really explain the appeal of the sentences that constitute the skeptical paradox. On the contextualist view, those sentences come out as true, in those cases where they strike us as true. But Conee notes that "satisfied truth conditions do not explain plausibility." According to Conee, the contextualist needs an explanation of the plausibility of those sentences involving " . . . something that influences the person's thinking."

But he then goes on to explain quite well how a contextualist can explain the appeal of the sentences that constitute the paradox:

> EC theorists can hold that our standards for judging (1) and (2) are somehow tacitly acquired in learning the meaning of "know." They might say that our learning partly consists in acquiring a rule for accessing a context's truth condition, and the rule yields the standards that make (1) and (2) plausible to us. EC theorists can then hold that the analytic link of these standards to the meaning of "know" explains why the standards seem so trustworthy to us.

I could not have said it better myself. But Conee goes on to argue that invariantists can offer a better explanation of our intuitions regarding the sentences constituting the paradox.

> Invariantists can observe that although the standards that we apply to (1) and (2) may include ones we are taught in learning "know," they are not therefore semantically guaranteed to be necessary or sufficient conditions for the application of the term. They can be stereotypes offered to guide usage, well supported rules of thumb, or apparent implications of convincing theories. Nothing readily available shows us which appealing standards fail here. An account along these lines explains the attractiveness of (1) and (2) in a way that better accommodates other features of the situation. Allowing our standards to be fallible lets us be right about the conflict that we see among the propositions that attract our acceptance as we consider (1) to (3).

So on Conee's view, it is better to explain our intuitions about the sentences (1) to (3) in a way that allows us to be wrong about them. By so doing we can vindicate our judgment that our skeptical endorsement of (2) conflicts with our common-sense endorsement of (1). Recall that on the contextualist view, that judgment is a mistake that results from conflating contexts.

So here we have a clear contrast between the contextualist response to the paradox, and Conee's invariantist account. On the contextualist view, our first order judgments (1) to (3) are correct. More specifically, our judgment that (1) is true is correct when evaluated at everyday contexts, our judgment that (2) is true is correct when evaluated at stricter skeptical contexts, and our judgment that (3) is true is correct at every context. But our metajudgment that (1) to (3) are inconsistent is a mistake. On the invariantist view, we are correct in our metajudgment that (1) to (3) are inconsistent, but we are mistaken in at least one of our first-order intuitive judgments concerning (1) to (3).

Each view provides an explanation for the sort of mistake it attributes to us. On the invariantist view, our mistaken endorsement of both (1) and (2) results from the fallibility of stereotypes, rules of thumb, and our ability to see logical implications.

On the contextualist view, our mistaken judgment that (1) conflicts with (2) results from our conflating contexts. And the contextualist can appeal to the very same kind of mistake in the case of the puzzle concerning flatness to avoid the charge of special pleading.[2]

So which explanation is better, the invariantist or the contextualist? It is important to see that the contextualist explanation of our intuitions in the paradox, if correct, constitutes a resolution of the paradox. It resolves the apparent inconsistency of (1) to (3) in a way that accounts for the cogency of skeptical arguments without compromising our strong sense that we know much about the world.

But the invariantist explanations suggested by Conee do not, in themselves, resolve the paradox. According to those explanations, there is a genuine conflict between our common-sense judgment that (1) is true and our skeptical judgment that (2) is true. Owing to the use of stereotypes, or rules of thumb, etc., we are mistaken in at least one of those judgments. The problem is that we are unable to determine which is the mistaken judgment. As Conee notes, "Nothing readily available shows us which appealing standards fail here." In the end, contextualism will have to be weighed against worked-out versions of invariantism which explain which standards fail and why.[3]

3 Objections to Contextualism

Conee mentions two reasons in particular to worry about the feasibility of a contextualist resolution of the paradox: "It incurs the costs of caving in to dubious skeptical reasoning and requires some durable impressions of incompatibility to be errors." Let's take these in reverse order.

As Conee says, contextualism holds that our impression that (1) to (3) are inconsistent is an error. But (1) to (3) constitute a paradox, precisely because we have the "durable impression" that each is true and that as a set they are inconsistent. But any response to the paradox will require that at least one of these impressions is erroneous. While the contextualist holds that our impression that (1) to (3) are jointly inconsistent is in error, the invariantist holds that our impression that they are all true is in error. Moreover, as I argued earlier, the contextualist can bolster the plausibility of attributing such a mistake to us by appealing to an analogous mistake in our sometimes paradoxical thinking about flatness.[4] So I don't see that contextualism here is at a comparative disadvantage.

In what way is the skeptical reasoning dubious? Surely there is no obvious error in the reasoning. Otherwise we would not be stuck with a stubborn paradox. We might say the reasoning is dubious in that we are confident that the conclusion is false. Surely this is true. Again, the reason we are stuck with the paradox is that we find the conclusion of the skeptical argument to be intuitively unacceptable.

Does contextualism cave in to skeptical reasoning? Yes and no – the former because contextualists allow that the sentences expressing skeptical conclusions are true, evaluated at skeptical contexts, the latter because the contextualists hold that those very same sentences are false when evaluated at everyday contexts.

Does this concede too much to the skeptic? Of course, this is something about which reasonable people can disagree. But by my lights, what is truly surprising and intuitively repugnant about skepticism is the thought that all along in our everyday lives, when we have been uttering sentences of the form "S knows P," we have been speaking falsely. Contextualism denies that this is so.

Contextualism does explain the stubborn appeal of skeptical arguments by allowing that there is some truth in skepticism. But the strategy of the contextualist is to limit the damage. So although contextualism does concede there is some truth in skepticism, it limits the damage by showing how this concession still allows for the truth of our everyday knowledge ascriptions. To me this is no worse than conceding that in certain limited and unusual contexts, we can truly say "Nothing is flat," while at the same time holding that many of our everyday utterances of the form "X is flat" are true.

Notes

1 Of course there is a general problem about what an intuition is, but to discuss it would go beyond the scope of this essay, not to mention my understanding.
2 I discuss the "flat" case in my first contribution to this exchange. The contextualist need not hold that our first-order knowledge ascriptions are infallible. The contextualist need only hold that the explanation of what is occurring in the skeptical paradox is that our judgments reflect our grasp of the correct standards for the context.
3 I am indebted to Earl Conee here for helping me to see this issue more clearly.
4 Again, see the first response to Conee in this exchange.

References

Cohen, S. (1999) Contextualism, skepticism, and the structure of reasons. *Philosophical Perspectives*, 13, 57–89.
Lewis, D. (1996) Elusive knowledge. *Australasian Journal of Philosophy*, 74, 549–67.

CHAPTER THREE

Can Skepticism Be Refuted?

The Refutation of Skepticism

Jonathan Vogel

I

We take ourselves to know a lot about the world, and it would be profoundly disturbing if we didn't. To deny that we enjoy such knowledge is to endorse *skepticism* about the external world.[1] Skepticism is philosophically important because a gripping line of thought seems to show that it is correct.

The argument that supports skepticism is one of the most famous in the history of philosophy.[2] It turns on the possibility that we might be victims of some kind of massive sensory deception. Consider two situations. In one, everything is normal and you see a bridge. In the other, you are the subject of an awful experiment. Your brain is isolated in a laboratory vat and fed completely delusory sensory inputs. These inputs make it appear to you as though there were a bridge before you, even though there isn't. It may well seem that you have no way of knowing which of these two situations you're in. So, in particular, you don't know that there is really a bridge before you. This line of thinking generalizes. If you don't know that you're not the victim of massive sensory deception, then you're unable to know virtually anything at all about the world. Skepticism prevails.

That is the gist of the "deceiver argument" (as I shall call it), but there are various details that need to be taken into account. I think we can understand better what is at stake by comparing the deceiver argument with an ordinary case in which someone fails to know. Imagine that you're in the kitchen, and the toaster suddenly stops working. It could be that the toaster itself has burned out. However, it could also be that the toaster is all right, but a fuse has blown instead. You are, then, faced with two competing hypotheses as to what caused the toaster to shut off.[3] If you have no further relevant information, you have no basis for accepting one hypothesis over the other. Any choice on your part would be arbitrary. I will say that, in such a situation, your choice of hypothesis is *underdetermined*. If, despite such underdetermination, you guess that the toaster shut off because the fuse blew, you wouldn't *know* that – even if, luckily, your guess turned out to be correct. This sort of example supports the view that knowledge is governed by the following general principle:

> *Underdetermination principle* (UP): If q is a competitor to p, then one can know p only if one can non-arbitrarily reject q.

Rejection of q would be arbitrary in the relevant sense just in case q is, from an epistemic standpoint, no less worthy of belief than p. So, we have:

> *Underdetermination principle* (UP, alternate version): If q is a competitor to p, then a subject S can know p only if p has more epistemic merit (for S) than q.

What factors add to or subtract from epistemic merit is a crucial, but controversial, matter. I address it below.

With these points in hand, we can set out the deceiver argument more rigorously, as follows.

(1) Consider any proposition *m* about the world I ordinarily believe (hereafter, "mundane propositions"). In order to know that *m*, my belief that *m* must not be underdetermined.
(2) My belief that *m* is underdetermined.
(3) Therefore, I don't know that *m*.

Premise (1) may be seen as a straightforward application of the underdetermination principle. According to that principle, underdetermination is inimical to knowledge. Premise (1) makes the point that we fail to know any mundane proposition for which there is a competitor of equal epistemic merit. Premise (2) is the claim that all mundane propositions face a competitor of just that sort. The competitor is that one is the victim of massive sensory deception, as described above (I will call this the "skeptical hypothesis"). The conclusion (3) is that we lack knowledge of mundane propositions in general, which is to say that skepticism about the external world holds. Now, the deceiver argument is logically valid. To refute it, we would have to successfully challenge one of its premises. Premise (1), and the underdetermination principle that underwrites it, seem unassailable.[4] So, a satisfactory response to the deceiver argument will have to show that premise (2) is false, or at least not adequately supported.

But satisfactory to whom? The deceiver argument explicitly or tacitly depends on various epistemic principles. One is the underdetermination principle. In determining whether underdetermination exists, other principles will be brought to bear. Now, I take it that we are committed to a body of epistemic principles that govern what we count as knowledge, justified belief, and the like. The deceiver argument may be construed as (putatively) proceeding from just those principles. Thus understood, the argument is an attempt to show that, by our own lights, we lack the knowledge of the world we think we have. I will call this position *domestic skepticism*. Domestic skepticism is concessive, but dangerous. It is concessive, in that it doesn't contest the legitimacy of the epistemic principles we embrace and employ. But it is also danger-ous, in the sense that it would be deeply unsettling, or worse, if we have no knowl-edge of the world, according to our own accepted view of what knowledge is and what it requires. On the other hand, if it emerges that our epistemic principles don't have that consequence after all, domestic skepticism has been refuted.[5]

My primary concern here will be with domestic skepticism. However, there are other forms skeptical thinking might take. Someone might contest not only our ordinary judgment that we have knowledge of the world, but also the legitimacy of the prin-ciples on which we rely in making that judgment. I will call this more extreme posi-tion "exotic" skepticism. It won't matter to an exotic skeptic that our knowledge claims accord with our epistemic principles, since the latter themselves are supposed to be questionable in some way. Thus, a reply that answers the domestic skeptic will seem to the exotic skeptic like our pointlessly patting ourselves on the back. I will return to the difference between domestic and exotic skepticism in section III.

II

The case for skepticism depends on the status of premise (2) of the deceiver argument, and the status of that premise depends on whether mundane propositions have more epistemic merit than the skeptical competitors they face. Philosophical opinion varies widely and sharply on this point. One can distinguish the following positions, among others. (a) We have no basis whatsoever for rejecting skeptical hypotheses, if such hypotheses really do compete for our acceptance. Skepticism is at least "condition-ally correct," and it can't be refuted.[6] (b) While no particular evidence counts against skeptical hypotheses, epistemic rationality permits us or requires us to reject such hypotheses out of hand. "A reasonable man does not have certain doubts," as Wittgenstein said (Wittgenstein, 1972, Remark no. 220). (c) What licenses us in main-taining belief in mundane propositions, and rejecting skeptical hypotheses, isn't a special antiskeptical epistemic principle, but a broader principle of methodological conservatism. Methodological conservatism is, roughly, the doctrine that we are enti-tled to maintain beliefs we already have, all other things being equal. Since we have already accepted mundane propositions, rather than any skeptical competitor, the former have a kind of epistemic merit the latter don't. (d) Experience itself provides immediate justification for the acceptance of mundane propositions. On one way of framing this approach, it is a fundamental epistemic principle that if it appears to S that F, S is justified in believing that F. Insofar as experience justifies believing F, F is epistemically more meritorious than the hypothesis of massive sensory deception, and there is no underdetermination (see Pryor, 2000). (e) It has been argued that skep-tical hypotheses are "dialectically" or "pragmatically" self-refuting, or even logically inconsistent. If this is so, and our mundane beliefs aren't similarly defective, then our mundane beliefs are certainly superior to their competitors.[7]

I regard these views as worthy of serious consideration, but, in my judgment, all of them are ultimately untenable.[8] The alternative I favor may be outlined as follows: when one is choosing between competing candidates for belief A and B, one has good reason to accept A rather than B, if A provides a better explanation of a relevant body of facts than B does. That is, I uphold the legitimacy of what is known as *inference to the best explanation* (hereafter, "IBE"). Skeptical hypotheses are less successful than our mundane beliefs in explaining a relevant body of facts, namely, facts about our mental lives.[9] Because of this disparity, we have reason to favor mundane propositions over their skeptical competitors, and the choice between them isn't underdetermined after all. Therefore, premise (2) of the deceiver argument is false, and skepticism stands refuted.[10] This approach faces some significant obstacles, however. There is unclarity about what counts towards explanatory goodness, and about how such goodness could be assessed or compared – there is even substantial disagreement as to what constitutes an explanation at all.[11] I certainly don't propose to resolve these difficulties here. Rather, in what follows, I will make some specific assessments of explanatory goodness that I take to be plausible in their own right.

A further complication is that the skeptical hypothesis that one is the victim of massive sensory deception could be developed in any number of ways. Presumably, these will vary with respect to their degree of explanatory goodness. Consider what I will call the "minimal skeptical hypothesis" (MSH). The content of the MSH is just that your experience is caused in a delusory manner, and no more: with respect to every Z, if it appears to you that Z, then something causes it to appear to you *falsely* that Z. (If you like, you can embellish the MSH a little by adding that the cause is an evil demon or the computer of a mad neuroscientist.) It seems to me that the MSH has little, if any, explanatory power. The putative explanations it offers are impoverished and *ad hoc*. According to the MSH, it appears to you that Z because something causes it to appear to you falsely that Z. That is like explaining that you fell asleep because of the action of something with a dormitive virtue – i.e. like saying that you fell asleep because something caused you to fall asleep – which is practically no explanation at all.[12]

However, I have offered no reason to suppose that all skeptical hypotheses have to fail as badly as the MSH. The possibility apparently lies open that a skeptical hypothesis could posit a nexus of causes and regularities that is as cohesive and economical as the body of our ordinary beliefs about the world. Call this body of beliefs the "real world hypothesis" (RWH). In fact, it seems that the skeptic could take over the causal-explanatory *structure* of the RWH, but substitute within it reference to objects and properties other than the ones we take to be real. For example, suppose you move your hand so as to pet a cat, which purrs in response. The motion of your hand (H) causes your (V) visual experience as of a hand moving, and it causes (C) the cat to purr. The cat itself causes you to have (P) an auditory experience of a gentle rumbling. But now imagine that the brain-in-a-vat skeptical hypothesis were true, and that the computer has a file (H*) that stands in for your hand and another file (C*) that stands in for the cat. (H*), rather than a real hand, causes (V) and also activates (C*) the cat-file in a particular way. The cat-file, in turn, causes (P) your auditory experience of a purring sound.[13] I will call a skeptical competitor of this sort the "isomorphic skeptical hypothesis" (ISH). The relationships among causes and effects according to the ISH match those of the RWH. To that extent, it seems, the explanations provided by the one are no better or worse than the explanations provided by the other. There is, then, no difference in explanatory success that favors the RWH over the ISH.

So far, we have considered two ways the skeptic might proceed. Either he deploys the MSH (or some variant of it) as a competitor to the RWH, or he puts forward a skeptical hypothesis that is structurally identical to the RWH. The MSH differs in structure from the RWH, but is explanatorily inferior to it. The ISH is supposed to have the same structure as the RWH, and, consequently, explain just as well as the RWH does. But it may seem that the inadequacies of the MSH needn't carry over to every other skeptical competitor that differs in structure from the RWH. So there could be some such competitor that equals the RWH in explanatory merit.

There are several points to make in response to this suggestion. First, a certain class of skeptical hypotheses (the MSH and its ilk) may be rejected on explanatory grounds. Formulations of the deceiver argument typically invoke skeptical hypotheses of just this kind, and those versions of the argument *are* refuted by the appeal to explanatory considerations. Second, the claim that, for some particular hypothesis H, there is a competitor that differs in structure from H, but equals H in explanatory merit, is by no means trivial and cannot be taken for granted. Adducing an equally good, structurally different competitor to a given hypothesis requires one to undertake substantive theory-construction, which is by no means guaranteed to succeed.[14] Finally, as I will suggest below, the RWH enjoys certain explanatory advantages over skeptical hypotheses. There is no reason to suppose that these advantages are offset by unspecified *disadvantages* attaching to the RWH, which a structurally different skeptical competitor will somehow manage to avoid. Hence, it is doubtful that one could cobble together a structurally different skeptical competitor to the RWH that will succeed in matching the RWH in explanatory merit.

To provide a setting for further argument, it will be helpful to say something more about the nature of our problem and its solution. As I see things, the underlying motivation for skepticism is that perception, the ultimate source of whatever empirical knowledge we have, is a causal relation. Our perceptual experiences are the effects of the world upon us. In general, causal relations are contingent, so there seems to be no bar in principle to anything causing a given effect. Various skeptical hypotheses serve to make us vividly aware of this point in the perceptual case. Our perceptual experiences could be caused by familiar sorts of things in the world, but those experiences could also be caused by radically different sorts of things (a computer, a demon). In the same way, it seems that specifying any wider structure of causal relations and regularities doesn't fix which properties and objects participate in that structure. Unfamiliar properties (e.g. a computer disk's magnetic patterns, a demon's mental states) could stand in for the familiar ones invoked by the RWH, without any additional loose ends or explanatory regularities. The result would be a skeptical hypothesis that has the same structural explanatory virtues as the RWH.

At the same time, though, there is a natural impression that a good explanation for why X behaves like something that is F is that X is, indeed, F. An explanation of why something that *isn't* F nevertheless behaves as though it were F seems bound to involve greater complications. However, someone with Humean scruples may well find such talk, as it stands, mysterious and misguided. She will think that X's being F by itself implies nothing about how X "behaves." X's being F doesn't determine what regularities X enters into, including whether X appears to us to be F or not.

The issues here are deep and hard, but I want to suggest that explanatory considerations can still do the requisite antiskeptical work.[15] Even though the ISH is supposed to share the structure of the RWH, it is meant to be a thoroughgoing competitor to it. That is, the ISH is required to explain the character of our experience as successfully as the RWH does, while positing a very different disposition of matter in space. Rather than there being ordinary arrangements of ordinary-shaped objects, there is just your brain, its vat, and the computer with which it interacts.[16] Now, the ascription of shapes and locations to things does a great deal of explanatory work for us. The ISH has to achieve the same explanatory success by ascribing properties other than shape and location to some other kind of object. Call these alternative properties "pseudo-shapes" and "pseudo-locations." My proposal is that skeptical hypotheses are bound to suffer an explanatory disadvantage insofar as they have to make do with pseudo-shapes and pseudo-locations instead of genuine shapes and locations.

The disadvantage is a lack of simplicity. It is, in principle, a defect to proliferate explanatory apparatus without any commensurate increase in the depth or scope of what is explained. So, other things being equal, a hypothesis that invokes fewer explanatory regularities is preferable to a competitor that invokes more. I take it that we are able to recognize differences of this sort and choose between hypotheses accordingly. For example, we find a version of mechanics that provides a uniform account of terrestrial and celestial motion preferable to a mechanics that invokes one set of laws governing the former and another set of laws governing the latter. Similarly, we accept that most people who seem comfortable really are so, rather than "super-spartans," i.e. people who are in great pain, yet have the desire and fortitude not to manifest it in any way.[17] I believe that the RWH is more economical than the ISH in much the same way, and so the RWH may be favored over the ISH on explanatory grounds.

In previous work, I tried to establish that result as follows (Vogel, 1990). It is, I claimed, a necessary truth that two distinct objects can't be in the same place at the same time.[18] This truth about location is deeply ingrained in our understanding of the world. If I walk two blocks north and then two blocks west, while you walk two blocks west and then two blocks north, we encounter the very same thing, whatever it may be, when we arrive. In the RWH, such facts are explained by the necessary truth that if X has the property of being located at a genuine location L, and Y is distinct from X, then Y doesn't have the property of being located at L. Now, where the RWH says that two objects don't have the same location at the same time, the ISH must say that two pseudo-objects don't have the same pseudo-location at the same time. But in so doing, the ISH must invoke an extra empirical regularity, since it is metaphysically possible for distinct objects to share any property other than location.[19] To make this point more vivid, imagine that the nefarious computer in the skeptical scenario keeps track of the "location" of "your hand" by writing coordinates in the hand-file, and likewise for the pseudo-location of other pseudo-objects. The same coordinates could be written in two different files. It is therefore an additional empirical regularity, rather than a necessary truth, that different pseudo-objects have different pseudo-locations, i.e. that they are not, so to speak, "double-booked."[20]

The details of this argument raise a number of questions.[21] But even if this particular line of thought doesn't serve as a definitive response to the skeptic, it illustrates a crucial difficulty the skeptic faces. Some relations between properties are necessary. To that extent, properties have what might be called a "modal configuration." If F and G are properties whose modal configurations are different, one can't simply substitute reference to G for reference to F within a hypothesis, and assume that the structure of the original can be preserved. My argument about the role of location-properties in the RWH was meant to exploit that fact. The idea was that the modal configuration of location-properties includes their being uniquely instantiated, i.e. that necessarily, if x is located at L, then nothing else can be located at L. No other genuine property P is such that, necessarily, if x is P, then nothing else is P. Hence, a version of the ISH which adverts to other properties in place of location-properties must add some empirical "exclusion principle" for these pseudo-locations to explain why no two items share the same pseudo-location. The upshot would be that substitution of reference to pseudo-locations rather than genuine locations in the ISH doesn't permit preservation of the explanatory structure of the RWH. More generally, the ISH will fail to match the RWH in explanatory adequacy unless the properties invoked by the ISH have exactly the right modal configurations. I see no reason to believe that this requirement can be met, and substantial reasons to doubt it.[22] Considerations of explanatory adequacy will, then, favor the RWH over the ISH.[23]

Here is where we stand. Skeptical hypotheses usually discussed, such as the MSH, are underdeveloped, explanatorily impoverished, and thus defective. The question then arises whether there is a superior skeptical hypothesis which could compete on equal terms with the RWH. My answer is no.

III

The ground gained so far is significant, but not unlimited. We have a refutation, or the outline of a refutation, of a certain kind of skepticism: domestic skepticism about the external world, motivated by the underdetermination principle. I have assumed that, since the skepticism under consideration is domestic skepticism, a reply may freely appeal to whatever epistemic principles we ordinarily accept, including principles of IBE. But the status of IBE itself is controversial, and some will doubt that an appeal to explanatory considerations has much force against the skeptic.

A principal criticism directed against IBE is that epistemic justification would be worthless unless beliefs that are so justified are thereby more likely, or have a greater tendency, to be true. Now, suppose H_1 provides appropriately simpler, hence better, explanations of a given domain than H_2 does, so that IBE underwrites the choice of H_1 over H_2. This choice seems to presume that the simplicity of an explanation is a guide to truth, i.e. that the world is likely to be simple in the ways we appreciate. But, the criticism goes, such a presumption is nugatory – it is a kind of wishful thinking that the world is nice and neat. Since simplicity and truth seem to be independent, explanatory success gives us at best pragmatic, rather than epistemic, reasons to favor one hypothesis over another. The upshot for skepticism is that, if the hypothesis that you are the victim of massive sensory deception is more complex than the real world hypothesis, the former may suffer some pragmatic disadvantage (it may be more cumbersome, inelegant, or the like). Nevertheless, you don't have genuinely epistemic justification for rejecting that hypothesis, and the deceiver argument can still go through.

The issues raised by this kind of argument are various and difficult, and I can't hope to do them justice on this occasion. But I would like at least to register the opinion that, in the end, IBE is no more suspect than other kinds of inductive confirmation. IBE licenses the acceptance of hypotheses that aren't entailed by the evidence that supports them, as any sort of inductive confirmation does. For example, consider an application of induction by enumeration. Observations that the roses in the yard have all been red in the past is evidence for the conclusion that the roses in the yard will be red next season. But the proposition that all the roses in the yard have been red in the past doesn't entail that all the roses in the yard will be red next season. IBE and enumerative induction have still more in common. The criticism of IBE just considered was that acceptance of a hypothesis because of its simplicity presupposes that simplicity is a guide to truth, and that such a presupposition amounts to a kind of wishful thinking that the world is nice and neat. But one might say with equal justice that enumerative induction presupposes that the observed is a guide to the truth about the unobserved, and that this presupposition, too, is a kind of wishful thinking that the world is nice and neat. To this extent, IBE appears to be on a par with other forms of inductive confirmation.[24]

Given the assumption that knowledge requires justification, there are now three positions in play: skepticism about the external world, skepticism about IBE, and skepticism about induction in general. In my view, the relations among them are as follows. If you aren't a skeptic about IBE, you can reject skepticism about the external world. If, however, you are skeptical about IBE for the reasons given above, you will also be a skeptic about induction of all kinds (and presumably about the external world, too). So far, I haven't offered any reply to skepticism about induction, nor will I attempt to do so. Instead, I'll make some comments that are meant to illuminate, rather than settle, some of the issues now before us.[25]

(1) One can take a sunny view of the situation, according to which there can be no rationally compelling challenge to our basic epistemic principles. A critic might reject our principles, or be committed to principles that conflict with ours. But the mere fact that someone else disagrees with us hardly shows that we must be wrong. If anything, we should stand by our own principles, and regard the critic's stance as mistaken. Assuming then that our epistemic principles include or imply the canons of IBE and induction in general, their legitimacy isn't open to serious question. To use the terminology introduced above, skepticism about IBE is exotic and, consequently, may be ignored. The same goes for skepticism about induction more broadly.[26]

(2) This response may strike some as unsatisfactory. For one thing, it may be disappointing that we are unable to establish the correctness of our epistemic principles *vis-à-vis* others, from some kind of "neutral" standpoint. In addition, the line of criticism directed against IBE and induction at the beginning of this section may seem to have some weight, and just setting it aside may appear superficial or obtuse. But exactly what is at issue here is somewhat cloudy. One sharpening of the concern about the connection between justification and truth is what I have termed the *problem of misleading evidence* (see Vogel, forthcoming a, b). Suppose your evidence E

inductively confirms hypothesis H, so that you're justified in believing H. Presumably, you're justified in believing propositions logically weaker than H, including –(E & –H).[27] If (E & –H), then H is false despite your having good evidence for H. We could say that, in such a case, your evidence is misleading with respect to H. Now, we're supposing that you're justified in believing –(E & –H), i.e. that your evidence *isn't* misleading with respect to H. That is a proposition about the world, so you're not justified in believing it unless you have evidence that supports it. It may appear, though, that the only pertinent evidence you have is E. That looks like trouble, because it is hard to see how E could be evidence that E itself isn't misleading with respect to H. But if you have no evidence at all for –(E & –H), it seems that you're not justified in believing –(E & –H). It follows that you're not justified in believing H, and the result is a thoroughgoing skepticism about induction. As far as I'm concerned, whether the problem of misleading evidence is a serious threat to inductive knowledge, and, if so, how to respond to it, remain open questions.

(3) In his contribution to this volume, Richard provides a searching and distinctive treatment of motivations for a general skepticism about (non-deductive) "inferential justification." According to Richard, someone who rejects externalist accounts of justification must accept that

> When one's justification for believing P involves *inference* from E [one's evidence for P], a constituent of that inferential justification is a justified belief that E does indeed make probable P. . . . We could, of course, *infer* that the probability connection holds from some other proposition we believe, F, but then we would still need reason to think that F makes likely that E makes likely P. Eventually, however, inferential internalists will need to find some proposition of the form E makes likely P that we can accept without inference.

Substantive propositions of that sort look to be very hard to come by.[28] In that event, skepticism about induction immediately follows. Now, I'm not confident that I grasp exactly what Richard means by "makes probable," but structurally this challenge resembles the problem of misleading evidence. The former makes having evidence for "E makes probable H" a condition for justified belief that H; the latter makes having evidence for "E isn't misleading with respect to H" a condition for justified belief that H. The two requirements are also similar in spirit, or so it seems to me.[29] Thus, I'm inclined to think that there will be a satisfactory response to Richard's challenge if and only if there is a satisfactory response to the problem of misleading evidence – assuming that a response is necessary at all.[30]

This reservation reflects uncertainty as to the status of the demand that, if S's believing E justifies S's believing H, then S must have evidence for the proposition that E makes probable H (hereafter, "Fumerton's requirement," or FR). I take Richard's view to be that, given the falsity of externalism, FR holds. This means, at a minimum, that FR is a condition on what *we take to be* inferentially justified belief. FR is an epistemic principle we accept. Richard maintains that FR leads to skepticism, in the absence of *a priori*, non-inferential justification for judgments of the form *E makes probable H*. Suppose all that is so. The result is *domestic* inductive skepticism, insofar as such skepticism follows from epistemic principles to which we are committed.

Now, there is at least some reason for denying that FR is a condition for justification, as we understand it. Consider the total body of evidence (TE) available to a subject S. When S has inductive justification for a proposition H, TE confirms but doesn't entail H.[31] According to FR, S still needs reason to think that TE makes probable H. And, since TE doesn't entail H, S presumably needs some additional *evidence* that the making-probable relation holds between TE and H. But S can have no such evidence, since, by assumption, TE is S's total evidence. FR, then, seems to be unsatisfiable in principle. So, if we have a *coherent* conception of justification, it can't include FR. That result, in turn, favors the view that skepticism stemming from FR is exotic, not domestic.[32]

But maybe justification as we conceive it *is* subject to FR, and it undoes itself in the way just described. Our situation with respect to epistemic justification would then be something like the one we face with respect to the concept of a set, in the face of Russell's Paradox, or with respect to the concept of truth, in the face of the semantic paradoxes. After the bad news is in, we can try to minimize our disappointment by seeking out a successor concept that does a good part of the work done by its untenable predecessor. The question in the present case would then be whether our concept of justification, shorn of FR, is enough like the original for us to care about it as before. If so, the encounter with the sort of skepticism Richard envisions might end in partial concession rather than full capitulation.

IV

In this essay, I have argued that some kinds of skepticism need to be refuted, and can be. Other kinds of skepticism can't be refuted, but needn't be. I hope, and want to suggest, that the division is exhaustive.[33]

Notes

1 Generically, skepticism is the denial that we have some kind of knowledge (or, maybe better, the denial that we have some kind of knowledge one might sensibly suppose we have). The rejected body of knowledge might be identified by subject matter (skepticism about the external world, skepticism about the past) or by mode of acquisition (perception, induction). When I talk about "skepticism" as such, I mean skepticism about the external world. In addition, I assume here that knowledge requires justification, so that the denial that we have justification for a body of beliefs implies the denial that those beliefs count as knowledge. For more on these matters, see Richard's helpful discussion, and section III below.

2 What follows is an updated version of Descartes's "Evil Genius" argument in the First Meditation.

3 For simplicity, I'm ignoring the possibility that the toaster shut off because it burned out *and* also because the fuse blew. I'm proceeding as though the two hypotheses are *competitors*, in the sense that the truth of one is logically incompatible with the truth of the other.

4 For discussion of these issues, see Vogel (forthcoming b).

5   Richard considers the investigation of various conditional claims of the form *If such and such principles hold, skepticism follows*. His characterization of the way I understand the situation is helpful, except for two things. First, I don't think I've misidentified the epistemic principles to which we're committed, being "stingy" about excluding "*sui generis* epistemic principles of perception" (see Vogel, 1997). Second, I'm not sure how Richard distinguishes "conceptual requirements for knowledge and justified belief" from "the legitimacy of certain basic sorts of inference." Thus, I don't see that there are two different ways of drawing a distinction between domestic and exotic skepticism.

6   For extended, critical discussion, see Williams (1992).

7   For extended, critical discussion, see Greco (2000).

8   For my evaluation of these views, see Vogel (1993, 1997).

9   Whether there is such a body of facts to be explained is disputed by Williams (1992) and Byrne (forthcoming). For a response, see Vogel (1997).

10 Other authors have advanced different replies to skepticism that, in one way or another, appeal to IBE. Two recent contributions are those due to BonJour (1998) and Peacocke (forthcoming).

11 For different views about what an explanation is, see Pitt (1988).

12 My discussion blurs some important distinctions. At least some explanations are explicitly causal, where the *explanans* is a cause of the *explanandum*. I assume that at least some explanations involve the subsumption of the *explanandum* under some law or regularity, either explicitly or because causation itself requires nomological support. In the text, I make no attempt to sort this out.

13 The terms of the causal relation are usually taken to be events, not things. The scrupulous reader may make the necessary adjustments to the text.

14 Otherwise, science would be even harder than it is. For example, proponents of steady-state cosmology would have been able to explain the presence of background radiation as well as proponents of the Big Bang. Then, too, the job of defense attorneys would be far easier than it actually is.

15 According to the view known as "structural realism," we can know that things in the world have at least some relational properties, but we are unable to know what intrinsic properties they have. A structural realist might then deny that we have reason to accept the RWH rather than the ISH. I take it Richard is sympathetic to such a position. But if shape is an intrinsic property of bodies, then a structural realist of this stripe has to say that we don't know what shapes things have, which is a more skeptical outcome than I would like to see. Matters here are complicated, however, involving among other things questions about the identity conditions for properties that I cannot discuss in any detail.

16 The difference in purely spatial features of our environment doesn't exhaust the disagreement between the ISH and the RWH. But I think that if skepticism about the spatial configuration of the external world can be refuted, dealing with whatever else remains of external world skepticism would be relatively easy.

17 The example is from Lewis (1980).

18 By "distinct" I mean at least that the objects have no parts in common at the time in question. So, if you think that a statue and the mass of clay from which it is fashioned aren't identical, the statue and mass of clay still wouldn't count as distinct, in the way that I'm employing the term. If your favored ontology allows for object-stages, the thesis is meant to imply that there can't be two distinct object-stages at the same place at the same time.

19 On the relation between simplicity and necessary truth see Glymour (1984), and below (compare Sober, 1988).

20 A bit more precisely: an account according to which X has the property of being at a location L will explain more economically why X behaves as though it has that property

than an account according to which X really doesn't have the property of being at location L, but rather has a pseudo-location which corresponds to L.

21　Mark Johnston and Philip Bricker have cautioned that there may be counterexamples to the claim that the co-location of distinct objects is impossible. Ned Hall and Tim Maudlin have suggested that the propensity of bodies to exclude one another is a matter of the dynamics governing those bodies, and thus not necessary.

22　Here is the sort of thing I have in mind. I am inclined to think that spatial properties are such that, necessarily, they conform to some kind of geometry, and their so doing enters into the modal configurations of those properties. A relatively clear – although somewhat out of the way – case in point may be the following. Consider the property of being a perfect solid. In Euclidean space, there are exactly five perfect solids, so the determinable *perfect solid* has precisely five determinates. Suppose the RWH invokes the fact that something is a perfect solid in giving an explanation (say, of why the chances that each side of an object will come up on a toss are equal). To maintain structural parity with the RWH, the ISH would have to invoke some other property (the property of being a "pseudo-perfect-solid") with exactly five determinates, while avoiding other difficulties. I see no reason to think that this condition can be met. The sort of difficulty I am raising here is analogous to that facing the possibility of spectrum inversion: color-properties bear complex relations to one another, such that a simple substitution of one for another in an account of color experience may not be feasible. See Hardin (1997).

23　There may be another way of arguing for the same result, which moves in something like the opposite direction from the foregoing. The ISH isn't merely a competitor to the RWH, but is something like a simulacrum of it. As the ISH more closely resembles the RWH in structure, the question of what makes the ISH *different* from the RWH becomes more pressing. The problem, loosely speaking, is that the ISH needs to specify how things that behave as though they are F still *aren't* F, without taking on unwanted encumbrances.

24　There are other notable objections to IBE, including those due to Van Fraassen. For a survey and discussion of these, see Ladyman et al. (1997). I should note that Van Fraassen would reject the view that IBE is no worse off than any any other kind of ampliative inference, and that Richard agrees with Van Fraassen at least that far.

25　One important difference is that the deceiver argument works by invoking the underdetermination principle. Richard examines skepticism about induction (and the external world) motivated by what he calls the principle of inferential justification. For a discussion of these issues, see Vogel (forthcoming b), and below.

26　This position is similar to the one adopted by P. F. Strawson (1952), although it doesn't include Strawson's view that claims about inductive support are analytic. Strawson undertakes to show in some detail how various motivations for inductive skepticism covertly distort or diverge from our ordinary understanding of what is required for epistemic justification. Those efforts bolster the judgment that skepticism about induction is invariably exotic in character.

27　That is, it is not the case that E is true while H is false. This is a more precise rendering of what it is for the world to be "nice and neat."

28　Richard also stresses that the justification for the underpinning propositions must be *a priori*, which if anything makes it less plausible that there are such propositions.

29　See Vogel (forthcoming b) for discussion of what I take to be the likeness of the two. But there are differences, as I note there.

30　But some caveats are called for. First, adopting some kind of holism might block the threat Richard envisions, although it is somewhat harder to see how holism could help with the problem of misleading evidence. Second, the link between justification for H and justification for –(E & –H) is secured by the eminently plausible principle that justification is

closed under known logical implication. What underwrites the connection between justification for H and justification for (E makes probable H) is somewhat harder to see, and
is perhaps more tenuous.

31   I take it Richard would not protest at this point, in light of his reply to a criticism by
Michael Huemer.

32   *One* way to read FR is that it covertly appeals to a deductivist view of confirmation, as
follows. Whenever E is inductive evidence for H, FR finds E insufficient, and demands
further evidence (for the proposition that E makes probable H). So, the import of FR is
that inductive evidence is never sufficient for justification; only deductive evidence would
really do. Richard agrees that the standard of justification for knowledge should not rise
that high, although I take it he would reject the way I have characterized FR. Points related
to this one, and the one in the text, may also provide some refuge from the problem of
misleading evidence.

33   I would like to thank Philip Bricker, Richard Feldman, Michael Glanzberg, Ned Hall, Mark
Johnston, Tom Kelly, Tim Maudlin, Richard Moran, Bernard Nickel, Ted Sider, and Steve
Yablo for their kind help. I have been very fortunate to work with Richard Fumerton,
Ernest Sosa, and Matthias Steup on this project. Finally, I'm deeply grateful to Neil
Harpster for his extraordinary efforts on the side of the angels.

References

BonJour, L. (1998) *In Defense of Pure Reason*. Cambridge: Cambridge University Press.

Byrne, A. (forthcoming) How hard are the skeptical paradoxes? *Noûs*.

Glymour, C. (1984) Explanation and realism. In J. Leplin (ed.), *Scientific Realism*. Berkeley:
University of California Press.

Greco, J. (2000) *Putting Skeptics in Their Place*. Cambridge: Cambridge University Press.

Hardin, C. L. (1997) Reinverting the spectrum. In A. Byrne and Hilbert (ed.), *Readings on Color,
Volume I*. Cambridge, MA: MIT Press.

Ladyman, J., Douven, I., Horsten, L. and van Fraassen, B. (1997) A defence of Van Fraassen's
critique of abductive inference: reply to Psillos. *Philosophical Quarterly*, 47, 305–21.

Lewis, D. (1980) Mad pain and Martian pain. In N. Block (ed.), *Readings in Philosophy of
Psychology, Volume I*. Cambridge, MA: Harvard University Press.

Peacocke, C. (in preparation) Explaining perceptual entitlement.

Pitt, J. (ed.) (1988) *Theories of Explanation*. Oxford: Oxford University Press.

Pryor, J. (2000) The skeptic and the dogmatist. *Noûs*, 34, 517–49.

Sober, E. (1988) Let's razor Occam's razor. In *Reconstructing the Past: Parsimony, Evolution,
and Inference*. Cambridge, MA: MIT Press.

Strawson, P. F. (1952) *Introduction to Logical Theory*. London: Methuen.

Vogel, J. (1990) Cartesian skepticism and inference to the best explanation. *Journal of Philosophy*, 87, 658–66.

Vogel, J. (1993) Dismissing skeptical possibilities. *Philosophical Studies*, 70, 235–50.

Vogel, J. (1997) Skepticism and foundationalism: a reply to Michael Williams. *Journal of Philosophical Research*, 11–28.

Vogel, J. (forthcoming a) Subjunctivitis. *Philosophical Studies*.

Vogel, J. (forthcoming b) Skeptical arguments. *Philosophical Issues*.

Williams, M. (1992) *Unnatural Doubts*. Oxford: Blackwell.

Wittgenstein, L. (1972) *On Certainty*. New York: Harper and Row.

find and hold ground favorable to the engage-
insists on unacceptably strong standards for
aims victory when those standards are not met.
at he calls *exotic* skepticism from what he takes
ersions. I join with Jonathan in an attempt to
sonably demand of a successful refutation of
ian and I agree on a great many issues, but may
understand epistemic probability and the need
quirement of acquiring ideal justification.[1] I will
the prospects of avoiding skepticism within the
m that Jonathan discusses.

hallenge

nge one should probably first attempt to discover
dermining *knowledge*, or has the more ambitious
ef. We can also distinguish *global* skepticism from
tic with respect to *knowledge* claims that we don't
now that we don't know anything (though we might
global skeptic with respect to *justified belief* claims
we are not even justified in believing that we have
been relatively few global skeptics with respect to
respect to justified belief. The global skeptic with
bviously deal with the charge of epistemic self-
obal justification skepticism will have premises that
cannot be jus⋯   the conclusion of the argument is true. It is not clear
that that fact entitles one to ignore the arguments, but it puts the most extreme of
skeptics in an awkward position to say the least. In any event, even rather radical
skeptics tend to at least implicitly suppose that they can know truths about their subjective experience and recognize the distinction between legitimate and illegitimate
reasoning.

Local skeptics are skeptics with respect to knowledge or justified belief about some
particular *kind* of truth: for example truths about the external world, the past, the
future, other minds, theoretical entities posited by physics, and so on. Like Jonathan,
I will often take, as our paradigm of a local skepticism, skepticism with respect to
truths about the external world. The skeptic with respect to knowledge of the external world claims that one cannot know (or sometimes with added emphasis, know
with certainty) any truths about the physical world. Before investigating this claim,
we should decide what conditions we need to meet in order to satisfy our skeptic that

we do indeed possess the knowledge in dispute. Suppose that our skeptic insists that we know only when we possess justification that precludes any possibility of error. If we agree, the skeptic might seem to face relatively smooth sailing. The justification I have for believing that I am seated in front of a computer is precisely the same sort of justification that I would have had were there no computer there and were I instead suffering a massive and vivid hallucination (or were I a brain in a vat, a victim of demonic machination, an inhabitant of the *Matrix* world, etc.). My justification for believing that the computer exists, therefore, does not entail the existence of the computer.

The above argument is not uncontroversial. Williamson (2000), Brewer (1999), and others, for example, argue that we might be unable to *recognize* crucial and dramatic differences between epistemic situations in which we find ourselves. We might not be able to tell, for example, the difference between a situation in which we are directly confronted with the computer (a situation in which the computer itself is literally a *constituent* of our visual experience) and a situation in which we are merely hallucinating the computer. Our perceiving that there is a computer in front of us might *in fact* generate a kind of justification that guarantees the computer's existence and, trivially, provide us with evidence of precisely the sort Descartes sought that guarantees the computer's existence.[2] For those of us who find the skeptic's challenge interesting, however, it is difficult to take this idea seriously. While we may be unable to tell the difference between epistemic situations that are only marginally different, it still seems utterly puzzling as to how we could be so incompetent as to fail to notice the difference between two experiential situations that Williamson (and other direct realists) claim should get *radically* different philosophical analyses.

In any event, for the purposes of this debate I will simply presuppose (and Jonathan, I understand, will not dispute) that we can easily imagine skeptical scenarios that are epistemic counterparts to veridical perception, scenarios in which we would possess precisely the same kind and strength of justification for the same kind of beliefs about our physical environment that we would possess were our perceptions veridical. We will agree here, therefore, that we cannot avoid knowledge skepticism with respect to the physical world if we understand knowledge as requiring justification so strong that it eliminates the possibility of error.

Of course, the moral most contemporary epistemologists draw is that we should reject Cartesian standards for knowledge. Our only hope of avoiding skepticism with respect to knowledge of the external world (the past, the future, other minds, and so on) is to accept more relaxed standards for knowledge. While Jonathan and I may end up disagreeing on whether or not one can defend weaker requirements for knowledge, that disagreement is probably unimportant for this debate. I think we do agree that the most interesting epistemological question is whether we can find justification that makes likely for us the truth of what we believe. As a result I'm going to frame the skeptical challenge employing the concept of justification with the understanding that if one can know without possessing justification that guarantees the truth of what one believes, the discussion could just as easily take place employing the concept of knowledge.

Underdetermination

If we switch our focus from knowledge to justified belief then what should one be expected to show in order to defeat skepticism? Here, I agree completely with Jonathan that the issue is best understood in terms of underdetermination. He suggests two principles. While he states the principles in terms of knowledge, one can easily reformulate them to concern justification instead:

UP1: If q is a competitor to p, then there is justification for one to believe p only if one can non-arbitrarily reject q.

UP2: If q is a competitor to p, then there is justification for S to believe p only if p has more epistemic merit for S than q.

For these purposes, competitors to p include all contraries of p and any other proposition whose truth would render highly unlikely the truth of p.[3]

UP1 and UP2 state only a *necessary* condition for S's possessing justification for believing P. A skeptic might want to remind us that for S to possess justification for believing P, there must be an epistemically non-arbitrary way of rejecting the *disjunction* of competitors to p. This is particularly important to remember in evaluating arguments to the best explanation. To have justification for accepting a given explanation h for some data e one must have more reason to accept h than the *disjunction* of competing explanations. When the skeptic comes up with competitors to the hypotheses of common-sense beliefs, therefore, one must be very careful not to assign these competitors *any* sort of significant possibility of being true. The disjunction of a large number of very unlikely hypotheses is still often very likely to be true.

The nice thing about framing the debate in terms of underdetermination is that we beg no question against the skeptic. We meet the skeptic on a level playing field. If we are to take seriously the epistemic challenge of skepticism, we must insist on no burdens of proof. The beliefs of common sense are not epistemically innocent until proven guilty, and skeptical scenarios are not epistemically guilty until proven innocent.

Choosing from among Competitors

How are we supposed to figure out whether a hypothesis of common sense satisfies the above requirements? Well, if we are foundationalists, we need both a metaepistemological account of non-inferential justification and a normative epistemological account of what we are non-inferentially justified in believing.[4] If beliefs about the external world end up in the class of beliefs that are non-inferentially justified, and the skeptic's competitors to those beliefs do not, then the skeptic loses. One takes the propositions of common sense and employs closure to reject the skeptic's competitors.[5]

Given my own views about non-inferential justification, propositions about the physical world (the past, the future, other minds) do *not* get included in the class of propositions for which we possess non-inferential justification. I can't argue here for my version of foundationalism. The view I defend (1995 and elsewhere) is very traditional and now very unpopular. In short, I hold that one is only non-inferentially justified in believing a proposition p when one is directly acquainted with the fact that p while one has the thought that p and one is acquainted with a correspondence between the thought and the fact. Because I think that one can possess in hallucinatory experience the *same* justification that one possesses in veridical experience for believing truths about one's physical environment, I don't think one can be directly acquainted with facts about physical objects.

Jonathan wants to remain neutral on many of the most fundamental questions concerning the *structure* of justification (the debate between foundationalists and coherentists), and even neutral on the question of what we should take to be the class of beliefs non-inferentially justified if we endorse foundationalism. But because he thinks that his approach to meeting the skeptical challenge through argument to the best explanation works from within quite different frameworks, I think he would not object to my presupposing for the purposes of this debate a foundationalism that takes as its base propositions restricted to the phenomenal (the world of appearance).

So how do we move beyond our foundational justification for believing some proposition e to justified belief in a proposition of common sense, say a proposition describing our immediate physical environment? The two most obvious suggestions are these:

1: For S to have justification for believing p on the basis of e, e must make epistemically probable p (where e's entailing p can be viewed as the upper limit of e's making p probable).

2: For S to have justification for believing p on the basis of e, S must be aware of the fact that (have justification for believing that) e makes probable p.

Elsewhere, I have called (2) *inferential internalism* (see Fumerton, 1995, chapter 3). Notice that the inferential internalist does *not* endorse the general principle that to be justified in believing P one must be justified in believing that one is justified in believing P. Nor does he endorse the principle that to be inferentially justified in believing P one must be justified in believing that one is inferentially justified in believing P. *Those* principles seem destined to generate vicious regress.[6] The inferential internalist insists only that when one's justification for believing P involves *inference* from E, a *constituent* of that inferential justification is the justified belief that E does indeed make probable P. One must *see* the connection between one's evidence and one's conclusion before one can justifiably draw the conclusion from one's evidence.

If we are foundationalists and we accept inferential internalism, then there isn't just one potentially vicious regress of justification we need to end with non-inferential justification. To be sure, in order to have inferential justification for believing P, we must be able to trace our justification for believing P back to some proposition for which we have non-inferential justification – a proposition that will serve as our premise. But we also need to cauterize a threatening regress concerning the justification we need for believing that our premise makes probable our conclusion. We could, of course, *infer* that the probability connection holds from some other proposition we believe, F, but then we would still need reason to think that F makes likely that E makes likely P. Eventually, however, inferential internalists will need to find some proposition of the form E makes likely P that we can justifiably believe without inference. And, indeed, the *key* to meeting the skeptical challenge for the inferential internalist centers on the ability to find non-inferential justification for accepting probability connections between our available evidence and the propositions of common sense.

Leaving aside for now the issue of how to understand epistemic probability, why should one embrace inferential internalism? Why shouldn't we view the inferential internalist's demands on inferential justification as exotic, as demands that simply *invite* skepticism? Well, consider the astrologer who predicts the future based on beliefs about the positions of planets relative to one another. It seems obvious that a *sufficient* condition for rejecting astrological inferences as rational is that the astrologer has no reason to believe that the positions of planets relative to one another makes *likely* any of his predictions. If a detective infers from someone's appearance that the person is guilty of a crime, one will surely demand evidence for supposing that appearances of this kind are correlated with guilt before one will concede the rationality of the conclusion. These commonplace examples and indefinitely many others like them surely indicate that we *do* embrace the inferential internalist's account of what is necessary for inferential justification.

Mike Huemer (2002) has objected plausibly to the above arguments for inferential internalism. He argues that the examples used to make initially attractive the principle are misleading in that they inappropriately characterize the evidence from which one infers the relevant conclusion. Even astrologers don't think that they can legitimately infer their predictions from propositions describing the positions of planets and the birth dates of people, *and from that information alone.* It should be a truism that much of the argument we actually give outside of a philosophical context is highly compressed, highly enthymematic. As we ordinarily use the term "evidence," we certainly do characterize litmus paper's turning red in a solution as evidence that the solution is acidic. The approach of very dark clouds is evidence of an approaching storm. A footprint on a beach is evidence that someone walked on the beach recently. But it is surely obvious upon reflection that one's evidence for believing that the solution is acidic, for example, is not the color of the litmus paper *by itself.* To legitimately draw the conclusion one would need an additional *premise*, most likely a premise describing a correlation between the color of litmus paper in a solution and the character of that solution.

Once one realizes that the reasoning discussed above is enthymematic, one is positioned to respond to that appearance of an argument for inferential internalism. It *is* necessary to have some justification for believing that there is a connection between positions of planets and the affairs of people, the approach of dark clouds and storms, footprints on a beach and the recent presence of people before drawing the respective conclusions, but *only* because propositions describing connections or correlations of the relevant sort are implicitly recognized as critical *premises*. Internalists and externalists alike share the foundationalist's insight that inferential justification is parasitic upon the justification we possess for believing the relevant premises of our arguments. If the astrologer is relying on an unstated, but critical, premise describing correlations between astronomical facts and the lives of people in reaching her conclusion, she will, of course, need justification for believing that *premise*. But that in no way suggests that when we have fully described *all* of the relevant premises from which a conclusion is drawn, we should require that the person who draws that conclusion have additional evidence for believing that the premises make probable the conclusion. The existence of the relevant connection between premises and conclusion is enough.

One can make just as strong a case for inferential internalism, however, by focusing on non-enthymematic reasoning. Consider the case of someone who infers P from E where E logically *entails* P. Is the inferential internalist right in maintaining that in order for S to believe justifiably P on the basis of E, S must be aware of the fact that (or at least have a justified belief that) E entails P (or alternatively, that the inference in question is legitimate)? The answer still seems to me obviously yes. We can easily imagine someone who is caused to believe P as a result of believing E where E does in fact entail P, but where the entailment is far too complicated for S to understand. Unless S sees that P follows from E, would we really allow that the inference in question generates a justified belief? Or to make my case a bit stronger, would we allow that the person who reaches the conclusion has philosophically relevant justification or ideal justification – the kind of justification one seeks when one searches for philosophical assurance.

Summarizing, I'm not at all sure that the inferential internalist is imposing unreasonably exotic requirements on justification, at least if the justification we seek is justification that provides assurance from the first person perspective. I would allow that one might well acknowledge *derivative*, less demanding concepts of justification. Elsewhere (Fumerton 2004), I have argued that one might allow that when one is caused by the fact that E to believe P, when the fact that E is the truth-maker for the proposition that E and the proposition that E makes probable P (either alone or with other propositions in our background evidence), one has a *kind* of justification for believing P. It is not the kind of justification I think the *philosopher* seeks, and to determine if we have it, we still need a justified belief of the sort sought by the inferential internalist.

The Analysis of Epistemic Probability

Whether or not we adopt inferential internalism, we need an analysis of the probability connection that by itself or as the object of awareness is partially constitutive of inferential justification. There are at least two quite different approaches one might take to analyzing the epistemic probability with which philosophers are concerned. One approach attempts to understand what it means to say of our evidence that it makes probable a conclusion in terms of epistemic evaluation of belief. Crudely, E makes probable P when one's justification for believing E gives one justification for believing P (were E the only evidence one possesses). A philosopher taking this approach must analyze epistemic concepts without appealing to the concept of epistemic probability.

On the other approach, one appeals to an allegedly prior and more fundamental understanding of the relation of making probable holding between propositions in order to explicate inferential justification. On this approach, one's inferential justification for believing P on the basis of E is constituted by either the existence of, or, according to the inferential internalist, our *awareness* of, a probability connection holding between propositions. Just as one proposition or conjunction of propositions can entail another, so also one proposition or conjunction of propositions can make probable another. Just as there are deductively valid arguments whose deductive validity is not analyzable by epistemic concepts, so also there are valid non-deductive argument forms whose legitimacy depends on relations between the *contents* of premises and conclusions.

In what follows, I'm going to assume without argument that this last approach is correct. It is simply hard for me to believe that the justificatory status of inferentially justified beliefs is not fundamentally derived from relationships between that which is believed. Put another way, it is surely a feature of the *arguments* whose premises and conclusions are believed that is key to understanding the justificatory status of the beliefs formed in the conclusions as a result of justified belief in the premises.

But what is the best way of understanding the relation of making probable that holds between certain propositions? This debate has a long history, one that predates, but in many ways foreshadows, the now more familiar contemporary internalist/externalist controversies in epistemology.[7] Painting with a very broad stroke, one can attempt to analyze probability claims in epistemology on the well known model of relative frequency that is offered as a way of interpreting claims about the probability of an individual or event having a certain characteristic. On a very crude interpretation of the frequency theory, to say of something that it is probably G is always elliptical for a more complex relativized claim of probability. One must refer the individual a that is G to some reference class F, and the more perspicuous statement of the probability claim is one about the probability of a's being G relative to its belonging to the class F. The truth conditions for the claim of relative probability are determined by the percentage of Fs that are G. The higher the percentage of Fs that are G the more likely it is that something is G relative to its being F.

One could borrow at least the spirit of the relative frequency interpretation of probability and apply it to relations between propositions in the following way. We could suggest that in claiming that P is probable relative to E we are simply asserting that E and P constitute a pair of propositions, which pair is a member of a certain class of proposition pairs such that, when the first member of the pair is true, usually the second is. Thus in saying that a's being G is probable relative to its being F and most observed Fs being G, I could be construed as claiming that this pair of propositions is of the sort: most observed Xs are Y and this is X/this is Y, and most often it is the case that when the first member of such a pair is true, the second is. Similarly, if I claim that my seeming to remember eating this morning (E) makes it likely that I did eat this morning (P), I could be construed as asserting that the pair of propositions E/P is of the form S seems to remember X/X, such that most often when the first member of the pair is true, the second is.

The above view obviously resembles, at least superficially, the reliabilist's attempt to understand justified belief in terms of reliably produced beliefs. And it encounters many of the same difficulties. Just as the relative frequency theory of probability must inevitably move beyond actual frequencies in defining probability, so both the above account of epistemic probability and the reliabilist will inevitably be forced to move beyond actual frequencies in order to define the relevant epistemic probability/reliability. Just as reliabilism must deal with the generality problem, so the above approach to understanding epistemic probability as a relation between propositions must deal with the problem of how to choose from among alternative ways of characterizing the class of propositions pairs to which a given pair belongs. Just as many reliabilists are troubled by the implications of their view for what to say about worlds in which demons consistently deceive epistemically faultless believers, so a frequency theory of epistemic probability must deal with similar alleged counterintuitive consequences about what is evidence for what in demon worlds. Lastly, and most importantly for this debate, both reliabilism and the frequency theory of epistemic probability will be anathema to the inferential internalist who is convinced that one needs non-inferential *access* to probability connections in order to gain philosophically satisfying inferential justification. The inferential internalist who is a foundationalist will need to end a potential regress when it comes to gaining access to probabilistic connections. If one's model for foundational knowledge is something like knowledge of truths made true by facts with which one is directly presented, there seems no hope that one will get *that* kind of access to either the reliability of a belief-forming process or a probability relation (understood in terms of frequency) holding between propositions.

One of the historically most interesting alternatives to the frequency interpretation of epistemic probability is a view developed some eighty years ago by Keynes (1921). Keynes wanted to model epistemic probability on entailment. He held that just as one can be directly aware of the entailment holding between two propositions, so one can also be directly aware of a relation of making probable holding between two propositions. There are, of course, obvious differences between entailment and making probable. From the fact that P entails Q it follows that the conjunction of P with any other proposition entails Q. From the fact that P makes probable Q, it doesn't follow that P together with anything else makes probable Q. But for all that, we could still take making probable to be an *a priori* internal relation holding between propositions (where an internal relation is one that necessarily holds given the existence and non-relational character of its relata). P and Q being what they are, it cannot fail to be the case that P makes probable Q. (It might also be true that P, R, and Q being what they are it cannot fail to be the case that (P and R) makes probable not-Q.)

Against the Keynesean, one might argue that it is patently absurd to suppose that making probable is an internal relation holding between propositions. Such a view yields the absurd consequence that claims about evidential connections are necessary truths knowable *a priori*. If anything is obvious it is that the discovery of evidential connections is a matter for *empirical* research. While the objection might seem initially forceful, one must remember the point we conceded in considering Huemer's objections to inferential internalism. There is certainly no necessary evidential connection between litmus paper's turning red in a solution and the solution's being acidic, between dark clouds and storms, between footprints on a beach and the prior presence of people. But then on reflection, we decided that it is misleading to characterize the litmus paper, dark clouds and footprints as the evidence from which we infer the respective conclusions. What we call evidence in ordinary parlance is just a *piece* of the very elaborate fabric of background information against which we draw our conclusions. So we shouldn't *expect* to find Keynesean probabilistic connections holding between, for example, the proposition that the litmus paper turned red and the proposition that the solution is acidic.

Where *should* we look for a plausible example of Keynes's relation of making probable? The obvious, though perhaps not all that helpful, answer is that we should look for it wherever we have what we take to be legitimate, *non-enthymematic* and *non-deductive* reasoning. The trouble, of course, is that philosophers don't agree with each other about what constitutes legitimate though deductively invalid reasoning. One might look at the relationship between the premises and conclusion of an enumerative inductive argument. Less plausibly, perhaps, one might think about the connection between the proposition that I seem to remember having an experience and the proposition that I had the experience. Still more problematically, we might suggest that my seeming to see something red and round necessarily makes probable that there is something red and round.

The view that there is an internal relation of making probable that holds between propositions is just what the inferential internalist *desperately* needs in order to avoid vicious regress. As we saw, if inferential internalism and foundationalism are true, then unless we are to embrace a fairly radical skepticism, we must find some proposition of the form E makes probable P that we can justifiably believe without inference. Since most foundationalists will concede that there are at least some propositions of the form E *entails* P that one can know without inference, the closer we can make our analysis of making probable resemble our analysis of entailment, the more plausible will be the claim that we can know without inference propositions of the form E makes probable P.[8] As I implied earlier, I think that *if* there is a solution to skepticism it involves the ability to know *a priori* epistemic probability claims. But that is a very big *if* indeed, and the reason I think skepticism looms so ominously on the horizon is that it is difficult to convince oneself that one is acquainted with the relevant probability connections.

Another Sort of Domestic Skepticism

Suppose one cannot convince oneself either that there are relations of epistemic probability holding between propositions or that we have access to such relations. Is there further discussion we might have with the skeptic? Jonathan and I agree that skepticism about the knowledge that Descartes sought is not worth fighting. I'm not sure whether or not we agree that skepticism that presupposes inferential internalism is interesting. In any event, *these* issues concern the potentially exotic nature of *conceptual* requirements for knowledge and justified belief. As I understand Jonathan, however, there is yet another way of distinguishing between exotic and domestic skepticism. The domestic skeptic is prepared to *give* us the legitimacy of certain basic sorts of inference and will argue that even with these argument forms at our disposal we will be unable to generate the conclusions of common sense from the available evidence. Now the inferential internalist discussed above will allow the use of an argument form only if you can know that the premises make probable the conclusion. You can have inferences from memory, for example, only if you know that your seeming to remember that you had some experience makes likely that you had the experience. You can legitimately employ inferences of enumerative induction only insofar as you can discover the probability connection between premises and conclusions of inductive inference. And the same would be true of the reasoning to the best explanation that Jonathan sees as our best hope of getting justification for beliefs about our physical environment.[9] Before we can even assess the plausibility of the claim that the premises of arguments to the best explanation make probable their conclusions, we would need, of course, a very clear understanding of the *structure* of such arguments.

Whether or not there exists a rich enough array of legitimate and accessible non-deductive reasoning to generate conclusions of common sense, we certainly *can* still ask *conditional* questions of the following form: *assuming that* this or that form of reasoning is legitimate, can we non-arbitrarily choose the hypotheses of common sense over various skeptical hypotheses? Of course, if one includes among the inference forms described in the antecedents of the conditionals Chisholm-style epistemic principles whose formulations are tailor-made to avoid skepticism, the project might seem to lose interest. If, for example, it is conceded that it is epistemically permissible to infer that there is something red and square before one when it appears to one as if there is something red and square, then it will come as no surprise that sense perception will generate many of the conclusions of common sense. If one tries to get reasons for believing in the physical world employing only inferences of memory and enumerative induction, the project will be uphill. If one adds to these sorts of available arguments, reasoning to the best explanation, perhaps one might stand a better chance.

Again, I would emphasize that a reasonable skeptic should have no objection in principle to carrying on discussion concerning the plausibility of relevant *conditionals* asserting what one would be justified in believing were certain inferences legitimate. That same skeptic has every right to insist, however, that one can and ultimately *must* ask questions concerning the legitimacy of the reasoning referred to in the antecedents of the conditionals.

We can also make a distinction between domestic and exotic skeptics based on which principles of reasoning the skeptic is willing to presuppose as unconditionally true. We will, of course, still need some *principled* way of figuring out which presuppositions define the domestic skeptic. Jonathan obviously wants reasoning to the best explanation in the mix, and would probably appreciate an epistemic principle licensing conclusions about the past based on memory. He *wouldn't* insist that the domestic skeptic grant us *sui generis* epistemic principles of perception. One philosopher's domestic species of skeptic, however, is another philosopher's exotic skeptic. Jonathan would be characterized by many (not by me) as being unreasonably parsimonious in the epistemic paths he allows us to travel in an attempt to leave our foundations. One *could* try to single out the relevant presuppositions that define reasonable domestic skeptics by appealing to psychological facts about what inferences people actually employ, but here one must surely worry about the possibility that we find ourselves immersed in an irrational society that employs without hesitation fallacious reasoning.

Reasoning to the Best Explanation

I haven't addressed the question of whether one could defeat skepticism with the array of argument types Jonathan wants the skeptic to allow us. As Hume (1888, p. 212) so eloquently argued, we don't have a hope of getting justified belief about the external world if all we can rely on is memory and enumerative induction (where the premises of our inductive arguments are restricted to descriptions of correlations between experiences). I have argued elsewhere (1980) that there may be no legitimate form of reasoning to the best explanation understood as an alternative to inductive reasoning. I have further argued (1992) that even if we suppose that reasoning to the best explanation is an independent and legitimate argument form, it is far from clear that we can use it to arrive at the truths of common sense. In particular, it is hard to see how Berkeley's hypothesis that God directly produces in us sensations that come and go in certain predictable ways is inferior to the hypothesis that it is material objects playing that causal role. Berkeley himself claimed that his view was simpler. While he posited just two kinds of things – minds and ideas/sensations – the materialist posits three – minds, ideas/sensations, and material things.[10]

So again, *if* we give ourselves access to past experience through memory, enumerative induction as a way of projecting past correlations found between experiences into the future, and the prima facie plausibility of the claim that there are causal explanations for the occurrence of contingent phenomena, and, perhaps, even that we know somehow that simpler, more comprehensive explanations are true more often than complex, less comprehensive explanations, what are the prospects of successfully arguing for the common-sense view of the world over skeptical alternatives? Leaving aside the threat of Berkeley's idealism, a great deal depends on what we take propositions about the physical world to assert. If, for example, we embrace some form of representative realism and view common sense as vindicated only if there exist objects that are in some sense accurately *represented* by sense experience, then in addition to the competitors described by exotic skeptical scenarios, one must worry about the now familiar, but at one time quite disconcerting, fact that science *itself* seems to indicate that the physical world is quite different from anything we took it to be.[11] The solid table is mostly space. Its straight edges, when seen under high magnification, are decidedly crooked. The color that we think is *on* the object disappears under that same magnification. Although we are now used to these discoveries, one might well conclude that science has already undermined the common sense of *representative* realism.

On the other extreme, we might adopt Hylas's last suggestion (in the second of the *Dialogues*) before capitulating completely to Philonous's idealism. Hylas wondered why we couldn't think of matter as that, *whatever* it is, that is causally responsible for sensations coming and going in the familiar ways they do. If encouraged to pursue this idea, he would probably have been willing to offer further *negative*, and also very general *causal*, characterizations of these material things – they are not minds, there are many discrete objects, each with its own causal powers and so on. But on the view, our concept of a physical object involves no characterization of its *intrinsic*, *non-relational* properties. The world of external things is exhausted, both conceptually and epistemically, by their causal powers. On *this* conception of physical objects, the prospects of avoiding skepticism are far brighter, but only because we require so little of the causes of experience in order for the beliefs of common sense to be vindicated.[12]

Whatever answer we give to these conditional questions, however, I want to stress one last time that we are only postponing the skeptic's final offensive. We will be asked about the truth of the antecedents of these conditionals, and we had better be prepared to indicate what we take their truth-makers to be and how we think we can get access to them.

Notes

1   The fact that I refer to this justification as ideal might already be a warning that Jonathan (and others) may characterize its requirements as exotic.
2   On Williamson's view evidence is identified with knowledge. A perception of a computer provides a *context*, he thinks, in which one can know that the computer exists. That the computer exists is now part of our evidence and it trivially entails its own truth.
3   So, for example, the hypothesis that I am dreaming right now is a competitor to the proposition that there is a computer before me insofar as the truth of that hypothesis (together with the evidence in my possession) makes very unlikely the truth of the proposition that the computer exists. Alternatively, one might restrict competitors to contraries and include the negation of the proposition under skeptical attack as a conjunct of the description of the skeptical scenario.
4   If we are *not* foundationalists, we probably won't take the problem of skepticism seriously. The skeptic knows full well that skeptical scenarios are not going to cohere well with what we believe. I know from conversation with him that Jonathan isn't so sure that the skeptical problems disappear from within the framework of a coherence theory.
5   The closure principles states that if one is justified in believing P and knows that P entails Q then one has justification for believing Q. The principle of closure has been called into question, but the bottom line is that if a philosopher advances a view that forces us to reject closure, that should be taken as a reductio of that philosopher's view.
6   Again, for a discussion of reasons to reject global access requirements, weak and strong, for justification see Fumerton (1995, chapters 3 and 4).
7   One of the most interesting debates that has clear implications for the internalism/externalism controversy can be found in Keynes (1921) and Russell (1948, part V).
8   Notice that the Keynesean approach to understanding probability does not require that for one to be inferentially justified in believing P on the basis of E one must know or be able to formulate general principles of probability. One might be able to see the connection between particular propositions without seeing how to generalize. An analogous point holds of entailment. One can see that P entails Q without being able to see that entailment as an instance of *modus ponens*, *modus tollens* or any other general *kind* of entailment.
9   Vogel's (1990) defense of reasoning to the best explanation as the way in which to respond to the skeptic is by far the most careful and well developed in the literature.

10 Of course, a great deal depends on how one counts kinds. The mind of God, while a mind, isn't a whole lot like our minds.

11 See Eddington (1929) and Russell (1972, lecture IV) for further discussion of the idea that science undermines common sense.

12 For a defense of the claim that we do understand claims about the physical world this way, see Fumerton (1985, 2002, chapter 6).

References

Brewer, B. (1999) *Perception and Reason*. Oxford: Oxford University Press.

Chisholm, R. (1977) *Theory of Knowledge*, 2nd edn. Englewood Cliffs, NJ: Prentice-Hall.

Eddington, A. S. (1929) *The Nature of the Physical World*. New York: Cambridge University Press.

Feldman, R. and Conee, E. (1998) The generality problem for reliabilism. *Philosophical Studies*, 89, 1–29.

Fumerton, R. (1980) Induction and reasoning to the best explanation. *Philosophy of Science*, 47, 589–600.

Fumerton, R. (1985) *Metaphysical and Epistemological Problems of Perception*. Lincoln: University of Nebraska Press.

Fumerton, R. (1992) Skepticism and reasoning to the best explanation. *Philosophical Issues*, 2, 149–69.

Fumerton, R. (1995) *Metaepistemology and Skepticism*. Lanham, MD: Rowman and Littlefield.

Fumerton, R. (2002) *Realism and the Correspondence Theory of Truth*. Lanham, MD: Rowman and Littlefield.

Fumerton, R. (2004) Achieving epistemic ascent. In J. Greco (ed.), *Sosa and His Critics*. Oxford: Blackwell.

Goldman, A. (1979) What is justified belief? In G. Pappas (ed.), *Justification and Knowledge*. Dordrecht: Reidel.

Goldman, A. (1986) *Epistemology and Cognition*. Cambridge, MA: Harvard University Press.

Goldman, A. (1988) Strong and weak justification. *Philosophical Perspectives*, 2, 51–69.

Huemer, M. (2002) Fumerton's principle of inferential justification. *Journal of Philosophical Research*, 27, 329–40.

Hume, D. (1888) *A Treatise of Human Nature* (ed. L. A. Selby-Bigge). Oxford: Oxford University Press (1978).

Keynes, J. (1921) *A Treatise on Probability*. London: Macmillan.

Russell, B. (1948) *Human Knowledge: Its Scope and Limits*. New York: Simon and Schuster.

Russell, B. (1972) *Our Knowledge of the External World*. London: Allen and Unwin.

Vogel, J. (1990) Cartesian skepticism and inference to the best explanation. *Journal of Philosophy*, 87, 658–66.

Williamson, T. (2000) *Knowledge and Its Limits*. Oxford: Oxford University Press.

Yourgrau, P. (1983) Knowledge and relevant alternatives. In R. Audi (ed.), *Synthese, Special Issue: Justification and Empirical Knowledge*.

CHAPTER FOUR

Is There *a Priori* Knowledge?

In Defense of the *a Priori*

Laurence BonJour

The official subject of this debate is the existence of *a priori* knowledge. But the main focus of my discussion will in fact be not *a priori knowledge*, but *a priori jus-tification* – or rather, more specifically, *a priori reasons* for believing something to be true. In approaching the issue in this way, I am assuming both (i) that justifica-tion is one of the requirements for knowledge (the only one to which the issue of *a priori* status is relevant) and (ii) that justification in the relevant sense consists in having a good reason for thinking that the belief in question is true. But having stated these two background assumptions, I will say nothing further in support of them here.

The view I will defend is that *a priori* reasons, in a sense yet to be clarified, do exist (and in consequence that a version of epistemological rationalism is true). But the idea of an *a priori* reason (and also the associated rationalist view) has been under-stood in a number of different ways, and I will not be defending all of the specific claims that have been associated with this sort of position. My aim is to defend what I take to be a relatively minimal version of the idea of an *a priori* reason (and of rationalism): more or less the most minimal version that is both philosophically interesting and reasonably faithful to the historical dialectic. All this will take some explanation.

The Nature of *a Priori* Reasons

As I will understand it here, the concept of an *a priori* reason has two basic elements, one negative and one positive, the negative one initially more obvious, but both in the end equally essential. Negatively, an *a priori* reason for thinking that a claim is true is one whose rational force or cogency does not derive from *experience*, either directly (as in sense perception) or indirectly (as by inference of any sort – deductive, inductive, or explanatory – whose premises derive their acceptability from experience). That such a reason is in this way independent of experience does *not* mean that someone who has undergone no experience of any sort could be in possession of it, since the possession of an *a priori* reason requires understanding the claim for which it is a reason, and experience, even experience of some fairly specific sort, might be required for that. Nor does the idea of an *a priori* reason, when understood in this way, imply either: (i) that experiences of some sort could not also count for or against the claim in question; or (ii) that such experiences could not override, perhaps even more or less conclusively, the *a priori* reason in question; or still less (iii) that an *a priori* reason renders the claim certain or infallible. All of these further claims *might* be true in some cases (though not, I believe, in all or even most), but they in no way follow from or are essential to the basic idea of an *a priori* reason itself.

What then counts, for these purposes, as *experience*? Obviously the paradigm cases are the various sorts of sense experience, including such things as kinesthetic experiences of bodily orientation in addition to those deriving from the five standard senses. But, in opposition to a number of recent discussions, I would argue that *introspective* awareness of one's thoughts, sensations, and other mental states should also count as a variety of experience, and the reasons for belief that such experience provides as empirical rather than *a priori*. Introspective experience may not depend on clearly identifiable sense organs, but it is still pretty clearly an awareness of temporally located contingent facts that depends on causal relations between those specific facts and the correlative state of awareness; it is thus far more analogous to sense experience than it is to the sort of experiential process, if it should even be called that, that is involved in the most paradigmatic cases of allegedly *a priori* reasons. And basically the same thing is true of even the reason for belief in one's own existence that is supplied by the Cartesian *cogito*, since this is based on introspective awareness of the occurrence of specific thoughts and sensations.

Turning to the positive aspect of the concept of an *a priori* reason, the traditional view, which I believe to be essentially correct, is that in the most basic cases such reasons result from direct or immediate insight into the truth, indeed the necessary truth, of the relevant claim. (A derivative class of *a priori* reasons, about which little will be said here, results from similar insights into the derivability of a claim from one or more premises for which such *a priori* reasons exist or from a chain of such derivations. And a *partially a priori* reason may result from an *a priori* insight into the derivability of a claim from others established on broadly empirical grounds.) Though the term "intuition" has often been used to refer to such insights, I will refer to them simply as "*a priori* insights," thus, I hope, avoiding any confusion with the other uses of the rather slippery term "intuition."

Here it is important to be clear at the outset that insights of this sort are not supposed to be merely brute convictions of truth, on a par with the hunches and fears that may simply strike someone in a psychologically compelling way. On the contrary, *a priori* insights at least purport to reveal not just *that* the claim is or must be true but also, at some level, *why* this is and indeed must be so. They are thus putative insights into the essential nature of things or situations of the relevant kind, into the way that reality in the respect in question *must* be.

Is There *a Priori* Knowledge?   99

One other point about the nature of *a priori* insights should also be briefly mentioned. For a variety of reasons, but most fundamentally because of the role that such insights are supposed to play in deductive inference, it is often and quite possibly always a mistake to construe them as *propositional* in form. The problem here is essentially the one pointed out long ago by Lewis Carroll: at least in the most fundamental sorts of cases (think here of *modus ponens*), the application of a propositional insight concerning the cogency of such an inference would require either a further inference of the very sort in question or one equally fundamental, thereby leading to a vicious regress. Instead, I suggest, the relevant logical insight must be construed as non-propositional in character, as a direct grasping of the way in which the conclusion is related to the premises and validly flows from them. And once the need for this non-propositional conception of *a priori* insight is appreciated in the context of deductive inference, it seems to me in fact plausible to extend it to many other cases as well; in particular, it seems plausible to regard the most fundamental insights pertaining to each of the examples listed in the following section as non-propositional in character.[1]

The Argument from Examples for the Existence of *a Priori* Reasons

Why then should it be thought that reasons having this *a priori* character genuinely exist? One reason is that there seem to be many, many examples of propositions for which there are clear and obvious reasons of this sort. Here the most obvious examples come from mathematics and logic, but there are others of many widely varying kinds. For present purposes, a misleadingly short list, reflecting some of the main types, will have to do:

(1) $2 + 3 = 5$.
(2) All cubes have 12 edges.
(3) For any propositions P and Q, if it is true that P or Q and it is false that P, then it is true that Q.
(4) If object A is larger in a specified dimension (length, area, volume, etc.) than object B and B is in turn larger in that same dimension than object C, then A is larger in that dimension than C.
(5) No surface can be uniformly red and uniformly blue at the same time.

My basic claim is that anyone who understands and thinks carefully about each of these propositions will be able to see or grasp immediately that it must be true, that it is true in any possible world or situation – and that the same thing is also true of indefinitely many further examples of these sorts and others. The central rationalist thesis I am defending is that this sort of seeing or grasping constitutes, other things being equal, a good, indeed overwhelmingly compelling, reason for thinking that the claim in question is true, albeit not a reason that is capable of being stated as a separate proposition. Moreover, while independent experiential reasons might also be found for some or all of these propositions, insights of this basic sort do not depend on experience in any discernible way.

Examples like these, which could be multiplied more or less without limit, provide, I claim, compelling evidence for the existence of *a priori* reasons (and, given the assumptions enunciated earlier, for *a priori* justification and knowledge). One who wishes to reject this conclusion (and who does not adopt the quixotic stance of denying that we have good reasons for thinking that any of these propositions are true) is obligated to offer some alternative account of those reasons, one that makes them dependent on experience after all, initial appearances to the contrary. My view is that there is no such specific and detailed account of examples like these that has any real plausibility.

One other point is worth adding, before turning to other arguments in favor of the existence of *a priori* reasons. What is perhaps most misleading about the list of examples given here is that, being chosen for their obviousness, they are far from being the most philosophically interesting cases of *a priori* reasons. I believe in fact that there are many more interesting albeit less obvious examples as well: claims about the unlikelihood of complex coincidences of various kinds;[2] certain moral claims; metaphysical claims about matters such as the structure of time and space; and many, many others.

Dialectical Arguments for the Existence of *a Priori* Reasons

While the foregoing argument from examples for the existence of *a priori* reasons strikes me as pretty compelling, it is, from a dialectical standpoint, still capable of being resisted. An opponent might deny that we have good reasons for at least some of the propositions in question, dismissing the intuitive impression to the contrary as an illusion of some sort, and might also appeal to some account of how and why our reasons for the rest of them are really at bottom empirical. I find such views extremely implausible, but there is no doubt that they are dialectically tenable as long as it is only such apparent examples of *a priori* reasons that are in question. But there are also other arguments of a more dialectical character for the rationalist view, which I want now to consider. These still do not make the rejection of *a priori* reasons completely impossible to maintain, but they make clear the intolerably high skeptical price of rejecting the existence of such reasons.

I will consider two closely related arguments of this dialectical sort. The first is concerned with the relation between experience and certain of the beliefs which it intuitively seems to justify. On any account of the justificatory force of experience, there will be some beliefs whose justification derives from a direct relation to experience and others whose relation to experience is less direct. The most straightforward version of this picture would be a broadly foundationalist view in which the more directly justified beliefs are justified by the content of experience alone, without the need for any reasoning or any further premises. Despite much recent criticism, I myself do not see how to avoid a view of this general kind, while retaining the view that experience does indeed in some way justify beliefs. But even if this is mistaken and there is some more complicated story to be told concerning the directly justified beliefs, the problem to be described here will still arise about the justification of beliefs for which experience provides justification but *not* in a direct or immediate way.

Where exactly the line between the beliefs that are directly justified by experience and those that are not actually falls is a difficult issue, which need not be resolved here. All that matters for present purposes is that the class of beliefs that are broadly empirical but clearly *not* justified by a direct relation to experience is extremely large and important, something that is so for any conception of the scope of direct experiential justification that has ever been seriously advocated. On any such view, this indirectly justified class of beliefs will include at least: (i) beliefs about the unobserved past; (ii) beliefs about unobserved situations in the present; (iii) beliefs about the future; (iv) beliefs in laws of nature and similar sorts of generalizations; and (v) beliefs about unobservable entities and processes, such as those described by theoretical science. Taken together, beliefs of these various kinds are obviously fundamental to our picture of the world and our place in it.

But how can experience provide justification for beliefs of these kinds, if not directly? The only possible answer to this question, I submit, is that experience can provide a good reason for thinking that a belief in this category is true only if we have a logically prior good reason for believing some conditional proposition having a conjunction of beliefs for which there are direct experiential reasons as antecedent and the further belief we are focusing on as consequent – for only this can establish the connection between experience and something that it does not justify in the more direct way. Here it will make the issue clearer to suppose that the antecedent of our conditional is in fact a conjunction of *all* the propositions for which there are direct experiential reasons, even though most of these will be irrelevant to any particular consequent.

What sort of reason could we have for thinking that a conditional proposition of the indicated sort is true? If all of the things for which there are direct experiential reasons are already contained in the antecedent and if the consequent genuinely goes beyond the content of the antecedent (as only some highly implausible reductionist view could deny for the sorts of claims in question), then experience can offer no direct reason (and no indirect reason without assuming some other conditional of the same sort) for thinking that such a conditional proposition is true. It follows at once that the justification for a conditional proposition of this sort, if there is any, can only be wholly or partially (via some other such conditional) *a priori* in character. In this way, the blanket rejection of the very existence of *a priori* reasons leads to a deep and pervasive version of skepticism, one in which we have no reason for thinking that any of the various seemingly empirical claims that are not directly justified by experience are true. And this is a result that seems far too extreme to be acceptable.

Note that I have couched the entire argument in terms of reasons for thinking that the various beliefs are true and not in terms of knowledge. Thus it would be possible for a defender of a view that does not appeal to such reasons in its account of knowledge – such as a version of externalism – to hold that we may have knowledge of such matters, while still denying the existence of *a priori* reasons. But the admission that we have no reasons of any sort for thinking that such beliefs are true, even while insisting that we still have knowledge in a sense that does not involve such reasons, still constitutes in itself a very deep and implausible version of skepticism – especially when it is added, as it should be, that we also have in the same way no reasons to think that the requisite conditions for knowledge, whatever they may be, are *themselves* satisfied (since there are no plausible views in which these conditions are ones whose satisfaction could be directly established by experience).

The second dialectical argument, which I have space here only to indicate briefly, is in effect a generalization of the first. It questions whether any view that denies the existence of *a priori* reasons can account in any satisfactory way for *reasoning* itself. Here the fundamental point is that a reasoned or argumentative transition from a claim or group of claims to some further conclusion relies again on there being a good reason for thinking that a conditional claim is true, in this case one having the conjunction of the premises as its antecedent and the conclusion in question as its consequent. That such a conditional is true (or probably true) is in general not the sort of thing that could be directly established by experience, while to say that it is itself arrived at via some further process of reasoning is only to raise the identical issue about that previous step. My suggestion is that if we *never* have *a priori* reasons for thinking that if one claim or set of claims is true, some further claim must be true as well, then there is simply nothing that genuinely cogent reasoning could consist in. In this way, I suggest, the rejection of *a priori* reasons is tantamount to intellectual suicide.

A Priori Reasons without *a Priori* Insight: Moderate Empiricism

In the space remaining, I will look briefly at two opposing positions. While virtually all serious epistemologists up to the time of Hume and Kant were rationalists in essentially the sense advocated here, the dominant position since that time and especially in the past century has been a version of empiricism, one that concedes the existence of *a priori* reasons of a sort, but claims that when properly understood, such reasons do not have the epistemological and metaphysical significance that is attributed to them by the rationalist. Instead, according to this *moderate empiricist* view, *a priori* reasons, rather than constituting insights into reality, reflect only linguistic or conceptual conventions or are merely matters of definition.

The basic idea of moderate empiricism is to explain *a priori* reasons in a way that drastically undercuts their significance. For this purpose, the most standard version of moderate empiricism appeals to the concept of *analyticity*, holding both (i) that all propositions for which there are genuine *a priori* reasons are analytic, and (ii) that an *a priori* reason for an analytic proposition does not require the sort of insight into the character of reality advocated by the rationalist. The problem for a would-be moderate empiricist is to find a univocal conception of analyticity in relation to which *both* of these two claims can be plausibly defended. In fact, moderate empiricists have put forth not one, but many different and not obviously equivalent conceptions of analyticity, and have tended to shift illegitimately among them depending on which of these two theses they are defending at any particular moment.

When the various conceptions of analyticity have been sorted out, they fall, I suggest, into two main groups. Some conceptions are *reductive* conceptions: they explain some cases of *a priori* reasons by appeal to other cases, while providing in principle no way to account for the latter cases. Here the most obvious example is the Fregean conception of an analytic proposition as one that is reducible via definitions or synonyms to a proposition of logic (where it is the propositions of logic that remain unaccounted for). Other conceptions of analyticity in effect lose sight of the main epistemological issue altogether by equating analyticity with one of the features that a proposition for which there is an immediate *a priori* reason undeniably has according to the rationalist account, without realizing that this fails to yield an independent account of the *a priori* reason. The plainest example of this mistake is the view that identifies an analytic proposition with one that is "true by virtue of meaning": once reductive accounts are set aside, this turns out to amount to nothing more than the view that one who understands such a proposition can see directly or intuitively that it is true, where this is really just a misleading restatement of the rationalist view, not an alternative to it. In this way, I suggest, the moderate empiricist view turns out under scrutiny to be epistemologically bankrupt.[3]

The Rejection of *a Priori* Reasons: Radical Empiricism

A more radical alternative is to reject the very existence of any sort of a priori reasons, a view that has been advocated by Quine. There are two main questions that need to be asked about this more radical empiricist view. One is what the arguments for it, and against the existence of *a priori* reasons, are supposed to be. A second is whether, especially in light of the dialectical reasons in favor of *a priori* reasons offered above, it is possible for radical empiricism to offer a non-skeptical epistemology.

Quine himself tends to assume that anyone who defends the idea of an *a priori* reason must be a moderate empiricist, and some of his arguments (in particular the famous "circle of terms" argument in Quine, 1961) really apply only to that view and are thus irrelevant here. When these are set aside, the only very clear argument that remains is one that appeals to the Duhemian thesis that claims about the world cannot be experimentally tested in isolation from each other but only in larger groups. Quine's extreme version of this thesis is the holistic claim that nothing less than "the whole of science" can be meaningfully confronted with experience. From this he infers that any claim in the total "web of belief," including those for which there are allegedly a priori reasons, might be "given up" in order to accommodate "recalcitrant experience," and so, apparently, that such a priori reasons do not exist after all (see Quine, 1961). But this conclusion simply does not follow, even if the holistic view is accepted. Quine is in effect assuming that the *only* reasons relevant to retaining or giving up a claim in the "web of belief" have to do with accommodating experience, but this is just to beg the question against the existence of independent, *a priori* reasons for or against such claims. And if this assumption is not made, then the rationalist can freely admit that holistic empirical reasons of this sort may count against a claim for which there is an *a priori* reason (or the reverse), with the ultimate outcome depending on their relative weight in a particular case – though he will also insist (see below) that the very connections among beliefs that result in the holistic web can only be understood as *a priori* in character.

The other main issue concerning Quine's radical empiricism is whether it can offer a genuinely non-skeptical epistemology. While the details of Quine's view are quite obscure, it is clear that a claim is supposed to be justified in virtue of being an element of a system of beliefs, some of whose members are appropriately related to experience and which as a whole satisfies certain further criteria, such as simplicity, scope, explanatory adequacy, fecundity, and conservatism. Consider then the conditional proposition that if a claim satisfies all of the conditions thus specified, then it is likely to be true, and ask what reason there is for thinking that this conditional proposition is itself true. Clearly such a proposition is not directly justified by experience, and to appeal to its inclusion in such a system of belief would be plainly circular. Thus either there is an *a priori* reason (whether immediate or resulting from a more extended *a priori* argument) for thinking that this conditional proposition is true or there is no reason at all. If the latter is the case, then Quine's view fails to yield genuine justification, while if the former is the case, then his rejection of *a priori* reasons is mistaken. In this way it can be seen that the idea of an *a priori* reason is both indispensable for any justification beyond that yielded by direct experience and at least as well understood as the idea of holistic empirical justification, which turns out in fact to depend upon it. (It is worth adding that similar points could also be made about the claim that the various Quinean criteria are themselves satisfied.)

Notes

1   This point did not emerge clearly in my fuller discussion of the *a priori* in BonJour (1998); for further discussion, see Boghossian (2001), together with my reply to Boghossian in BonJour (2001b).
2   Which are the basis, in my view, for the justification of induction (see BonJour, 1998, chapter 7).
3   See BonJour (1998, chapter 2), for a much fuller discussion of this view and its problems.

There Is No *a Priori*

Michael Devitt

1 Introduction

It is overwhelmingly plausible that *some* knowledge is empirical, "justified by experience." The attractive thesis of naturalism is that *all* knowledge is; there is only one way of knowing.[1] But this naturalism seems to be refuted by intuitions about a range of troublesome examples drawn from mathematics, logic, and philosophy. Thus, how could experience have anything to do with justifying the belief that 5 + 7 = 12? Furthermore, it does not seem *possible* that such knowledge could be revised in the same sort of way that "All swans are white" was by the sighting of black swans in Australia. It seems that the troublesome knowledge *must* be justified in some other way, justified *a priori*.

So we have a motivation for abandoning naturalism and accepting the thesis that some knowledge is *a priori*. Yet there is a consideration against this thesis: the whole idea of the *a priori* seems deeply obscure. *What is it* for a belief to be justified *a priori*? What is the nature of this non-empirical method of justification? Without satisfactory answers the *a priori* is left mysterious.

In light of this, a naturalistic critic of the *a priori* faces two tasks: to undermine the motivation by showing that the troublesome knowledge could be empirical after all; and to demonstrate the obscurity of the *a priori*. Success in the second task would show that an *a priori* explanation of the troublesome knowledge, indeed of anything, was very unpromising. Success in the first task would show that an empirical explanation was available. So we would have a nice abduction for naturalism: the *best* explanation of that knowledge is that it is empirical.

But, first, a preliminary point. Our concern is with the *justification* of beliefs, not with their *source*. Experience is clearly not the source of many mental states: they are innate. Perhaps some of these are justified beliefs (although I doubt it). If so, the naturalist insists, beliefs of that sort were somehow justified by the experiences (broadly construed) of our distant ancestors and we have inherited that justification via natural selection.

Drawing on earlier works (Devitt, 1996, 1997, 1998, 2002), I shall attempt the two tasks. I shall conclude by considering Laurence BonJour's (1998, 2001a, b) thorough and vigorous defense of the *a priori*.

2 Motivation

The naturalistic alternative. Our aim is to provide an alternative naturalistic account of the troublesome examples of allegedly *a priori* knowledge. With the help of Quine (1961, 1966, 1969, 1975), and before him Duhem (1954), I think that we can do this.[2]

The key to the naturalistic alternative is breaking free of the naive picture of justification suggested by the swan example. We must view justification in a more holistic way: beliefs, even whole theories, face the tribunal of experience not alone, but in the company of auxiliary theories, background assumptions, and the like. Much evidence for this "Duhem–Quine thesis" has been produced by the movement in philosophy of science inspired by Kuhn (1962). In light of this, we have no reason to believe that whereas scientific laws, which are uncontroversially empirical, are confirmed in the holistic empirical way, the laws of logic and mathematics are not; no reason to believe that there is a principled basis for drawing a line between what can be known this way and what cannot; no reason to believe that there is, in Quine's vivid metaphor, a seam in the web of belief.

Quine is fond of an image taken from Otto Neurath. He likens our web of belief to a boat that we continually rebuild while staying afloat on it. We can rebuild any part of the boat – by replacement or addition – but in so doing we must take a stand on the rest of the boat for the moment. So we cannot rebuild it all at once. Similarly, we can revise any part of our knowledge – by replacement or addition – but in so doing we must accept the rest for the time being. So we cannot revise it all at once. And just as we should start rebuilding the boat by standing on the firmest parts, so also should we start rebuilding our web. So we normally take the propositions of logic and mathematics for granted. Still, each of these propositions is in principle revisable in the face of experience: taking a stand on other such propositions, and much else besides, we might contemplate dropping the proposition.

Given this naturalistic alternative, we have no need to turn to an *a priori* explanation of our knowledge of mathematics, logic, and the like. The original intuitions were really that this knowledge is not justified in some *direct* empirical way. Those intuitions are preserved. Yet we can still see the knowledge as empirical: it is justified empirically in an *indirect* holistic way.

I shall develop this account by answering objections.

> Objection 1: "You are surely not suggesting that these few hand-waving remarks about the empirical nature of mathematics come close to solving the epistemological problem of mathematics."

No, I am not. But there are two reasons why this is beside the point. First, as Georges Rey (1998) is fond of pointing out, we are not close to solving the epistemological problem of *anything*. Since we do not have a serious theory that covers even the easiest examples of empirical knowledge – examples where experience plays its most direct role – the fact that we do not have one that covers the really difficult examples from mathematics hardly reflects on the claim that these are empirical too. We all agree that there *is* an empirical way of knowing. Beyond that, the present aim needs only the claim that the empirical way is holistic. *We have no reason to believe that a serious theory would show that, whereas empirical scientific laws are confirmed in the holistic empirical way, the laws of mathematics are not.*

Second, there is a special reason for not expecting the epistemological problem of mathematics to be anywhere near solved: the *metaphysical* problem of mathematics – what mathematics is *about* – remains so intractable. How could we solve the epistemological problem when we remain in such darkness about the metaphysical one? *We no longer have any reason to think that, if we solved the metaphysical problem, the epistemolical problem would not be open to an empirical solution.*

> Objection 2: "We need to explain our knowledge of *necessities*; for example, that *necessarily* $5 + 7 = 12$, that *necessarily* all bachelors are unmarried. Yet all we can know from experience is how things are – how they are in the actual world – not how they *must* be – how they are in all possible worlds."

But why should we accept that necessities can only be known *a priori*? Prima facie, *some* necessities are known empirically; for example, that water is necessarily H_2O and that Hesperus is necessarily Phosphorus. Indeed, science seems to be discovering necessities all the time. Now, one might respond that what science discovered was only that water *is* H₂O, not that it *necessarily* is; the necessity is not an empirical discovery. But, again, why should we accept this? Certainly, we do not simply *observe* the necessity of water being H₂O. But we do not simply observe most scientific facts: we discover them with the help of a lot of theory. And that, according to the naturalist, is how we discover necessities. More needs to be said of course, but to say it we would need to take a stand on the *metaphysical* problem of necessity. That problem is another difficult one. There is no reason to believe, however, that if we solved it we would not be able to explain our knowledge of necessities empirically. The situation for that knowledge is analogous to that for our knowledge of mathematics.

> **Objection** 3: This objection concerns logic. It arises out of the dominant theme of BonJour's defense of the *a priori*: that "the rejection of any sort of *a priori* justification leads inexorably to a severe skepticism" and to the undermining of "reasoning or argument in general" (BonJour, 2001a, pp. 625–6). BonJour's discussion suggests the following objection. "On your Quinean alternative, experience justifies beliefs in the interior of the web via links with beliefs at the periphery, via links with beliefs 'close to experience.' But these justifications depend on the links themselves being justified: clearly a belief is not justified by other beliefs unless those others give it *genuine support*. The objection to your alternative is then: the justification of these links has to be *a priori*; it could not come from experience." Indeed, BonJour (2001b, p. 679) claims, "if there is no *a priori* insight . . . no prediction will follow any more than any other . . . any . . . sort of connection between the parts of the system will become essentially arbitrary." "[T]he rejection of all *a priori* justification is tantamount to intellectual suicide" (BonJour, 2001a, p. 626). In brief, the objection is that logic must be seen as *a priori* because we need logic to get evidence for or against anything.

Many would agree with this objection. I have three responses. But first I will give what I hope is some fairly uncontroversial background.

The links that hold the web of belief together reflect a set of rules that are part of "an evidential system" (Field, 1996, 1998). As a result of nature and nurture each person embodies such a system which governs the way she arrives at her beliefs about the world. A system must include dispositions to respond selectively to perceptual experiences and to infer according to certain rules. A likely example of a rule is *modus ponens*. So, a person embodying an evidential system *S* containing this rule is disposed to infer according to the pattern:

> If *p* then *q*,
> *p*,
> So, *q*.

Now, the objection is surely right in claiming that for a person using *S* to have justified beliefs, its rules have to be good ones. This is not to say that she must know the epistemological theory,

> *T*: *S* is a good evidential system,

for her beliefs to be justified. So it is not to say that she must know

MP: *Modus ponens* is a valid inference

for her beliefs to be justified by *modus ponens* arguments. Indeed, as Lewis Carroll made clear a century ago, the demand for this sort of extra premise in an argument leads to a regress (see Boghossian, 2001, for a discussion). And it is just as well that our person is not required to have this epistemological knowledge for, if she is an ordinary member of the folk, she is unlikely to have given such matters much thought. Still, it is certainly appropriate *to* give them thought. So it is appropriate for the person to stand back from her arguments and ask some epistemological questions. What are the rules of S? This is a question in *descriptive* epistemology. Are the rules of S good? How do we know T and MP? These are questions in *normative* epistemology. Any answers to such questions will be further beliefs, additions to her web. I take the point of the objection to be that normative answers must be obtained by *a priori* insight.

Because *modus ponens* is a deductive rule, it is a rather misleading example of a system's rules. Given any theory and a body of evidence that it entails, we can easily construct rival theories that entail the same evidence. So we need more than deductive rules to choose between these theories and avoid skepticism: we need non-deductive "ampliative" rules. And these are rules that we don't have much insight into, whether *a priori* or not. It is largely because of this ignorance that, as already noted, we lack a serious epistemological theory. We can, of course, wave our hands and talk of enumerative induction, abduction, simplicity, and the like, but we are unable to characterize these in the sort of detail that would come close to capturing the rules that must constitute our actual evidential systems; for example, we are unable to specify when an explanation is good, let alone the best, or when we should take the belief that all observed Fs have been G to justify the belief that all Fs are G. Aside from that, some of these vague rules are controversial; for example, scientific realists love abduction, Bas van Fraassen does not. In sum, when we move beyond deduction, we have few if any specific and uncontroversial rules to be insightful about. The non-skeptics among us will share the very general insight that, *whatever the rules of our evidential system may be*, those rules are for the most part pretty good. So, if S is that largely unknown system, we believe T.

Response 1. Is the objection claiming that T is known *a priori*? If so, the claim hardly seems tempting. It seems more plausible to view our general insight that T is true as supported by the empirical success of S, whatever S may be. Similarly, someone afloat on a boat may not know the methods by which it was built but, noting its seaworthiness, infers that the methods, whatever they were, are good. In sum, when we focus on the largely unknown ampliative parts of S, our confidence in S seems as empirical as anything. To that extent, T does not even appear to be supported by *a priori* insight.

"But what about the specific deductive rules that we do have insight into, rules like *modus ponens*? Even if our overall confidence in S is empirical, our confidence in these deductive parts is *a priori*. We know MP *a priori* at least."

Response 2. But why must we see the support for the deductive rules as different in principle from that for the ampliative rules? They are all rules of S, they are all needed to avoid skepticism, and we can see them all as supported by the overall empirical success of *S*. Then the justification of the deductive parts of *S* is no different in principle from that of the ampliative parts. Similarly, all parts of *S* are empirically *revisable*. Thus, suppose that experience leads us to abandon *T* in favor of *T'*, a theory that recommends an evidential system *S'* built around a non-classical logic. Then clearly we should use *S'* instead of *S*. In this way our logical practices are themselves open to rational revision in the light of experience. These practices are far from "arbitrary": they are recommended by an experience-based epistemology.

Still, many will feel that I have not yet got to the heart of the objection. "On the one hand, you talk of *T* being supported by the empirical success of *S*. Yet that alleged support must come via *S* itself. So, the attempt to support *T* is circular. On the other hand, you talk of the possibility of experience leading us to abandon *T* in favor of *T'*. Yet experience must be brought to bear on *T* by using *S* and so could not show that *T* is false and hence that we ought not to use *S*. The attempt to refute *T* is self-defeating."

Response 3. In considering the circularity charge we need to follow Braithwaite (1953, pp. 274–8) in distinguishing "premise-circularity" from "rule-circularity." An argument is premise-circular if it aims to establish a conclusion that *is assumed as a premise in that very argument*. Premise-circularity is clearly reprehensible. But my argument for *T* is not guilty of it because it does not use *T* as a premise. An argument is rule-circular if it aims to establish a conclusion that *asserts the goodness of the rules used in that very argument*. My argument tries to establish *T* which asserts the goodness of *S*, the system used in that argument to establish *T*. So the argument is certainly rule-circular. This is worrying initially but is there a good reason to think that it is in fact reprehensible? I agree with those who have argued that there is not (Van Cleve, 1984; Papineau, 1993; Psillos, 1998). Guided by the Neurath image, we accept the non-epistemological part of our web for the moment and seek to justify the epistemological part, *T*. And that justification is governed by just the same rules that govern the justification of anything, the rules of *S*.

The self-defeat charge is also worrying initially. Yet there are reasons for thinking that we can indeed show an evidential system to be defective using that very system.

First, it seems undeniable that our evidential systems have changed. (i) A good deal of the impressive scientific progress over the past three centuries has been in improved methodologies: we have learnt a vast amount not only about the world but also about how to learn about the world. As a result, much education of the young scientist is in these methodologies: think of physics and psychology, for example. (ii) Educated folk have tried to adjust their thinking in light of evidence that we normally tend toward certain sorts of irrationality; for example, counter-induction, and ignoring base rates in thinking about probabilities. (iii) Even our deductive practices have been affected by the rise of modern logic.

Next, the process of making any of these system changes must have been governed by some evidential system, the one that was then current. So, that system was used to establish an epistemological thesis that led to the system's replacement. These examples give us good reason to think that an evidential system could be used rationally to undermine itself. Accepting the non-epistemological part of our web and governed by *S* as usual, we find *T* wanting and so replace it and the system *S* that it recommends.

Despite this response, worries about circularity and self-defeat may persist. It helps to remove them to note that if the worries were appropriate, analogous ones would be just as appropriate *if T were justified by a priori insight*. For, if *T* were thus justified, *a priori* insights would be part of our evidential system *S*. We could then generate a circularity worry. The argument for *T*, which asserts the goodness of *S*, uses part of *S* to establish *T*. And we could generate a self-defeat worry. The *apriorist* must allow that we could abandon *T* in favor of *T'* on the basis of *a priori* insight, part of *S*. So *S* is used to establish *T'*, which leads to its own replacement. If these circularity and self-defeat charges are unworrying for the *apriorist*, the analogous ones are surely so for the naturalist.

Faced with the circularity and self-defeat charges we could conclude that our evidential system *is* unjustified. But this throws the baby out with the bathwater. Although the charges are worrying in the beginning, I have argued that they should not be in the end. In any case naturalism and *apriorism* are on an equal footing in dealing with them.

Objection 4. "Suppose that it really is the case that any belief can be confirmed or disconfirmed by experience in the Duhem–Quine way. This does not show that agreement with experience is the *only* consideration relevant to the belief's rational acceptance and rejection. Hence it does not show that there is no *a priori* justification. By supposing that it does show this you beg the question."

The objection misses the main point of the naturalistic alternative. That point is not to show that there is no *a priori* knowledge but to remove the motivation for thinking that there must be. Everyone agrees that there is an empirical way of knowing. The Duhem–Quine thesis, supported by the history of science, is that this way of knowing is holistic. I have argued that our troublesome knowledge of mathematics, logic, and the like can be accommodated within this holistic empirical picture. We are far short of a detailed epistemology for this knowledge, of course, but we are far short of a detailed epistemology for any knowledge. Now, if I am right about all this, we have clearly removed the theoretical need to seek another, *a priori*, way of knowing. This is certainly *part* of the case against the *a priori*, but it cannot stand alone. The rest of the case is that the whole idea of the *a priori* is deeply obscure.

BonJour and many others will think that this empirical justification of the troublesome knowledge is inadequate. They will demand a justification that is stronger and that can only be met by appeal to the *a priori*. I think that this demand might be rational if there were any grounds for optimism about the *a priori*. But, I shall now argue, there are no such grounds, only grounds for pessimism. If this is right, the demand is not rational.

3 Obscurity

The aim in this section is to show that the whole idea of the *a priori* is too obscure for it to feature in a good explanation of our knowledge of anything. If this is right, we have a nice abduction: the *best* explanation of all knowledge is an empirical one.

We are presented with a range of examples of alleged *a priori* knowledge. But what are we to make of the allegation? What is the nature of *a priori* knowledge? We have the characterization: it is knowledge "*not* derived from experience" and so *not* justified in the empirical way. But what we need if we are to take the *a priori* way seriously is a *positive* characterization, not just a negative one. We need to describe a process for justifying a belief that is different from the empirical way and that we have some reason for thinking is actual. We need some idea of what *a priori* knowledge *is* not just what it *isn't*.

Why? After all, I have been emphasizing how little we know about *empirical* justification. So why pick on the *a priori*? The answer is that there are two crucial differences in the epistemic status of the two alleged methods of justification. First, the existence of the empirical method is not in question: everyone believes in it. In contrast, the existence of the *a priori* way is very much in question. Second, even though we do not have a serious theory of the empirical way, we do have an intuitively clear and appealing general idea of this way, of "learning from experience." It starts from the metaphysical assumption that the worldly fact that *p* would make the belief that *p* true. The empirical idea then is that experiences of the sort that would be produced by that fact are essentially involved in the justification of the belief. In contrast, we do not have the beginnings of an idea of what the *a priori* way might be; we lack not just a serious theory but *any idea at all*.

The difficulty in giving a positive characterization of *a priori* knowledge is well demonstrated by the failure of traditional attempts based on analyticity. Let the example of alleged *a priori* knowledge be our belief that all bachelors are unmarried. According to the tradition, the content of the concept ⟨bachelor⟩ "includes" that of ⟨unmarried⟩, thus making the belief analytic. This seemed promising for an account of *a priori* knowledge because it was thought that, simply in virtue of *having* a concept, a person was in possession of a "tacit theory" *about* the concept; in virtue of having ⟨bachelor⟩, a person tacitly knew that its content included that of ⟨unmarried⟩. So a person's conceptual competence gave her privileged "Cartesian" access to facts about concepts. The required non-empirical process of justification was thought to be one that exploited this access, a reflective process of inspecting the contents of concepts to yield knowledge of the relations between them, which in turn yielded such knowledge as that all bachelors are unmarried. This alleged process is that of "conceptual analysis."

Even if we grant that we have this Cartesian access to conceptual facts, the account fails. These facts would not justify the proposition that all bachelors are unmarried *unless the proposition that all unmarrieds are unmarried were justified*. But where does the justification for this proposition come from? It does no good to say, rightly, that the proposition is a *logical* truth, for what justifies logical truths? No satisfactory non-empirical account has ever been given of how they can be justified. Without such an account we have not described a non-empirical way of knowing.

In any case, we should not grant the Cartesian view that competence gives privileged access to contents, despite its great popularity. I urge a much more modest view of competence according to which it is an *ability or skill* that need not involve any tacit theory, any semantic propositional knowledge; it is knowledge-how not knowledge-that (Devitt, 1996). Why then should we believe the immodest Cartesian view, particularly since it is almost entirely unargued?

The content of a person's thought is constituted by relational properties of some sort: "internal" ones involving inferential relations among thoughts and "external" ones involving certain direct causal relations to the world. Take one of those relations. Why suppose that, simply in virtue of her thought having that relation, reflection must lead her to *believe that* it does? Even if reflection does, why suppose that, simply in virtue of that relation partly constituting the content of her thought, reflection must lead her to *believe that* it does? Most important of all, even if reflection did lead to these beliefs, why suppose that, simply in virtue of her competence, this process of belief formation *justifies* the beliefs and thus turns them into *knowledge*? The supposition seems to be gratuitous. We need a plausible explanation of this allegedly non-empirical process of justification.

4 BonJour's Rationalism

I turn finally to BonJour's wonderfully forthright approach to the *a priori*. First, he has no more faith in attempted explanations in terms of analyticity than I have and gives an excellent critique of their failings (BonJour, 1998, chapter 2). Indeed, he is rather contemptuous of these attempts to make the *a priori* palatable to the modern mind. BonJour is an unabashed old-fashioned rationalist (apart from embracing the fallibility of *a priori* claims). He rests *a priori* justification on "rational insight": "*a priori* justification occurs when the mind directly or intuitively sees or grasps or apprehends . . . a necessary fact about the nature or structure of reality" (BonJour, 1998, pp. 15–16). So, our problem of explaining the *a priori* becomes that of explaining rational insight. Where is the *justification* to be found in this quasi-perceptual process of apprehending a necessary fact?

BonJour (1998, p. 107) is only too well aware that most philosophers find this rationalism extremely mysterious. In response, he offers the beginnings of an explanation based on the unpopular thesis that a thought's content is an intrinsic property of the thought (ibid., pp. 180–6). In my view (Devitt, 1990, 1996, 2001), this thesis thoroughly deserves its unpopularity. Aside from that, the explanation based on it is very obscure, as commentators have pointed out (Boghossian, 2001; Rey, 2001). But we need not dwell on this explanation because BonJour himself does not claim much for it. Indeed, he accepts that "we do not presently have anything close" to an adequate explanation of rational insight (BonJour, 2001b, p. 674). That seems to leave rationalism in trouble. Not according to BonJour (1998, p. 31): "the supposed mystery pertaining to rationalism . . . has been . . . greatly exaggerated"; allegations that rationalism is "objectionably mysterious, perhaps even somehow occult . . . are very hard to take seriously" (ibid., pp. 107–8); "the capacity for rational insight, though fundamental and irreducible, is in no way puzzling or especially in need of further explanation" (ibid., p. 16).

What is the source of this extraordinary confidence in an unexplained and apparently mysterious capacity? It comes partly, of course, from the earlier-noted view that to deny the *a priori* is to commit "intellectual suicide." But it comes also from "the intuitive or phenomenological appearances" of rational insight (ibid., p. 107): BonJour thinks that these appearances, when examining examples of alleged *a priori* knowledge, provide a prima facie case for rationalism that is "extremely obvious and compelling" (ibid., p. 99).

So, BonJour thinks that there just *has* to be rational insight even if we can't explain it. In contrast, I think, for the reasons set out in section 2, that there does not have to be, and the apparent hopelessness of explaining rational insight shows that there isn't any. I shall end with a few more remarks about that hopelessness.

First, a word on the phenomenology. BonJour denies that there is any mystery in "our cognitive experience" (ibid., p. 108) when we have "direct insight into the necessary character of reality" (ibid., p. 107). He may be right. But the mystery lies in the claim that *this experience is an a priori insight*. Nothing in the phenomenology supports *that* or, indeed, *any* view of what justifies the insight. In particular, it does not show that the insight is not justified in a holistic empirical way. This theoretical issue is way beyond anything in the phenomenology.

Turn next to that theoretical issue. A human mind/brain forms beliefs about the external world. In virtue of what is any belief justified and hence likely to be true? We have a rough idea of where to find an empirical answer. We look at the way in which the beliefs are related to the experiences that the world causes. Justified beliefs are appropriately sensitive, via experience, to the way the world is. Many instruments – thermometers, voltmeters, etc. – are similarly sensitive to the world. Of course, the mind/brain differs from these instruments: beliefs are much more complex than the "information states" of instruments and their sensitivity to the world is mediated, in a holistic way, by many others. Still, the mind/brain is similar enough to the instruments to make empirical justification quite unmysterious, despite the sad lack of details.

The contrast with *a priori* justification is stark. What sort of link *could* there be between the mind/brain and the external world, other than via experience, that would make states of the mind/brain likely to be true about the world? What non-experiential link to reality could support insights into its necessary character? There is a high correlation between the logical facts of the world and our beliefs about those facts which can only be explained by supposing that there are connections between those beliefs and facts. If those connections are not via experience, they do indeed seem occult.

At this point, it remains a mystery what it would be for something to be known *a priori*. Any attempt to remove this mystery must find a path between the Scylla of describing something that is not *a priori* knowledge because its justification is empirical and the Charybdis of describing something that is not knowledge at all because it has no justification.[3] The evidence suggests that there is no such path. Hankering after *a priori* knowledge is hankering after the unattainable.

The nice abduction is established: our knowledge of mathematics, logic, and the like cannot be explained *a priori*; an empirical explanation of it is the best.[4]

Notes

1 BonJour (1998) calls this *epistemological* naturalism "radical empiricism." It should not be confused with *metaphysical* naturalism, a reductive doctrine like physicalism.

2 Although Quine's influence on the views I will present is large and obvious, I am not concerned to argue that these views are precisely his nor to defend everything he has to say on the *a priori* and related topics.

3 I argue (1998), in effect, that Rey's attempt (1998) to give a reliablist account of the *a priori* falls victim to Charybdis.

4 Thanks for comments from John Bigelow, Thomas Bontly, Radu Dudau, Hartry Field, Gilbert Harman, Frank Jackson, Hilary Kornblith, David Papineau, Stathis Psillos, Elliott Sober, Kim Sterelny, and Stephen Stich.

Reply to Devitt

Laurence BonJour

Professor Devitt's case against the *a priori* involves two main points: (i) that all genuine knowledge, including "troublesome examples" like the ones cited in my initial essay, can be accounted for entirely in empirical terms, at least mainly via an appeal to what he refers to as the "holistic empirical way" of knowing, so that an appeal to the *a priori* is unnecessary and unmotivated; and (ii) that the idea of *a priori* knowledge or justification or reasons is "deeply obscure," too obscure to provide a satisfactory explanation of anything, even if there were anything further that needed to be explained. I will respond to these in turn.

(i) Devitt asserts in several places that the existence of empirical knowledge is not in question. This is indeed obviously true if by "empirical knowledge" is meant knowledge whose justification depends at least *partially* on experience. But if it means knowledge whose justification derives *entirely* from experience, with no need for any *a priori* element, then it is far from clear that there is very much such knowledge and not entirely beyond question that there is any at all. In particular, the justification of scientific laws is *not* "uncontroversially empirical" in this latter sense, since inductive reasoning or something like it is also required. Thus, contrary to what Devitt sometimes seems to suggest, the central issue as regards his point (i) is not just whether the "holistic empirical" view can account for the "troublesome examples", but whether it can account for the justification of at the very least large portions of our apparent knowledge in an *entirely* empirical way.

Here the fundamental question is what holds together the various elements of the holistic system to which he appeals (including "auxiliary theories, background assumptions, and the like") so that the whole system (and not just its "edges") connects with experience in such a way as to yield a good reason for thinking that some particular belief or theory embedded in it is true (where these connections, as Devitt notes, will involve much more than logic in the narrow sense). The connections that are relevant to any particular issue of justification may be thought of piecemeal in terms of various logical and quasi-logical relations between them or they may be summed up into one overall conditional as at the end of my initial essay, but either way some reason is seemingly needed for thinking both that various specific connections hold and that when taken together they are of the right sort for the overall system to confer justification on those of its elements that are not matters of direct experience. And it is hard to see how such reasons can be anything but *a priori*, since they are surely not a matter of direct experience (and cannot without circularity be based on any appeal to the holistic picture itself).

Devitt offers two main responses to this sort of objection, neither of which seems to me to be satisfactory. (His other response, the second in his list, is a response to an intermediate rejoinder and does not bear directly on the main issue.) The first response is that we are unable to characterize in detail the specific rules, over and above formal logic in the narrow sense, that we follow in arriving at our "web of belief," and so cannot plausibly be said to have *a priori* insight into their correctness; and it is most implausible that we have any such insight into the general claim (Devitt's *T*) that our overall system of rules is a good one. I agree that we have no insight of the latter sort; indeed any claim of this sort could, as far as I can see, be justified only indirectly by appeal to more specific claims about the particular rules involved. But is it really so clear that we have no insight into the correctness of the specific rules that we use, even if we are unable to formulate those rules in precise detail? That when a scientist reasons inductively or abductively, he has no insight into the cogency of his reasoning, but is simply flying blind, doing what (for whatever reason) comes naturally, but with no reason to think that it is likely to take him in the direction of the truth? I myself find this picture most implausible. But the further thing to be said is that if it is right, then the result is simply skepticism, since this lack cannot be remedied in the way that Devitt suggests: by reasoning that the empirical success of our system of rules is best explained by the supposition that it is generally a good one. For that sort of abductive argument – like the one that Devitt uses at the end to arrive at his main conclusion – is equally one that on his view we have no reason to think is cogent.

Devitt's second main response attempts to answer the charge that it is circular to appeal to the very set of holistic rules whose correctness is at issue in establishing that correctness. (Note that, contrary to what he suggests, the abductive argument for *T* just discussed does not in fact do this in any very clear way.) Devitt follows Braithwaite in distinguishing "premise-circularity from "rule-circularity," with the point being that while premise-circularity is clearly objectionable, this is not so clearly true of rule-circularity. Though I have no space for an extended discussion, this point seems to me to be clearly and indeed obviously mistaken. If the issue is whether following that set of rules, operating in the way that the "holistic empirical" approach sanctions, gives us any reason to think that our results are true, it is obviously no help at all to be told that the claim that those results are likely to be true (or that the rules are good ones) can be arrived at by employing the very rules whose truth-conduciveness is in doubt. Such an argument may not beg the question in quite the sense that a premise-circular one does, but it is just as unsatisfactory in relation to the question at issue. (Much of this also applies to the issue of self-defeat, though I again have no space to go into that issue in any detail. I think that changes in our system of rules obviously occur, but that such change is less holistic than Devitt would have it and so does not raise issues of circularity: the rule or alleged insight being rejected does not contribute to the reason for its rejection.)

Devitt adds the further remark that the same issue about circularity would apply to the appeal to *a priori* insight, but this also seems to me mistaken. He has in mind a view according to which the overall claim *T* is justified by *a priori* insight, and I have already rejected that. Beyond that, the basic point is that *a priori* insight is atomistic rather than holistic in character, so that neither the issue of circularity nor that of self-defeat applies in any clear way. Alleged *a priori* claims can be defeated by a combination of other such insights (plus, sometimes, empirical premises), but the main positive case for such a claim rests only on the immediate insight itself.

Thus the basic point of the objection to the holistic empirical view seems to me to remain unscathed: such a view can give no satisfactory account of how the fact that a belief satisfies its requirements constitutes a reason to think that it is true – or indeed of how we can have reason to think that its requirements are indeed satisfied. In this way, such a view leads only to a deep and pervasive skepticism.

(ii) Devitt's second main point is that the idea of *a priori* justification – that is, of an *a priori* reason – is "deeply obscure," where the obscurity in question seems to be at least primarily that the source of justification has not been adequately explained. Granting that empirical justification is also not very well understood, Devitt nonetheless claims that there are "two crucial differences" between empirical and allegedly *a priori* justification that make the lack of understanding more telling in the latter case. The first is that "the existence of the empirical method is not in question." But given the argument of my initial contribution and of part (i) of this reply, the existence of *purely* empirical justification for any claim that is not a matter of direct observation is very much in question – indeed seems to be clearly ruled out. And the existence of *partially* empirical justification, I have argued, must depend on *a priori* justification and so can hardly be taken as a reason for skepticism about it. This conclusion is reinforced by Devitt's second "crucial difference": that we have "an intuitively clear and appealing general idea" of how empirical knowledge and justification are possible, namely that experiences produced by the fact that would make the belief true are what justifies it. Plainly this applies only to the (relatively rare) cases in which experiential justification is direct and does nothing to illuminate the more indirect cases. Thus Devitt's "two crucial differences" do very little to show that there is any special problem with the *a priori*.

Beyond that, what does the alleged "mystery" really amount to? Devitt seems to me to be simply rejecting the idea that merely finding something to be intuitively necessary can ever constitute in itself a reason for thinking that it is true – albeit one that is defeasible by further considerations (which would themselves ultimately depend on further such insights). My contrary suggestion would be that apart from the limited class of claims that are directly justified by experience, there is in the end simply no other form that a reason for thinking that something is true, whether atomistic or holistic in character, could possibly take. To be sure, such insights can be combined in complicated ways to yield more elaborate arguments of various sorts, but in the end the various steps in such arguments, together with any premises or principles that they invoke, can only be justified by appeal to the very same sort of *a priori* insight – if, that is, they are to be justified at all. No doubt it would be nice to have a fuller, richer account of *a priori* insight and how it works. But given both intuitively compelling examples and an argument showing such insight to be essential to any but the most minimal cognitive functioning, the absence of such an account does not yield in any clear way a reason for denying its existence.

Reply to Bonjour

Michael Devitt

"There Is no *a Priori*" is, in effect, partly a response to the main arguments in Laurence BonJour's "In Defense of *a Priori* Reasons." So this reply is largely to his "Reply to Devitt."

My essay has two criticisms of the *a priori*: (i) we don't need it because all justification could be empirical; (ii) the whole idea of the a priori is deeply obscure.

The central issue over (i) concerns rule-circularity and self-defeat. I shall focus on rule-circularity, as does BonJour. An argument is rule-circular if it aims to establish a conclusion that asserts the goodness of the rules used in that very argument. I claimed (Response 3) that although rule-circularity is initially worrying it is not in fact reprehensible. I cited some arguments for this claim but did not give any myself (although I did give one for self-defeat, for the view that rules could govern a procedure that supplies a rational basis for their own revision). BonJour rejects my claim as "clearly and indeed obviously mistaken" but also gives no argument. What hangs on this unargued matter?

First, if naturalism needs to rely on a rule-circular argument, my claim had better be right. Now, taking S to be the set of rules constituting our actual evidential system, I did accept that my naturalistic argument for the epistemological thesis

> T: S is a good evidential system

was rule-circular. But, interestingly, BonJour's discussion raises the possibility that this acceptance was too hasty. After all, the metaphor of Neurath's boat suggests that the epistemological claim that *a certain one* of S's rules, say R, is good could be justified by an argument that uses *other* rules of S but not R itself; thus perhaps one could use inductive and deductive rules to justify abduction. There would be nothing circular about that. So if we could do that for claims about *each* rule of S in turn, we could justify T without rule-circularity. And the justification would be naturalistically kosher. Still, accomplishing this does seem a very tall order, particularly when one remembers that S must contain rules governing the choice between T and a rival T' that recommends a different system S'. Given our ignorance of S we cannot be certain that the naturalist must accept rule-circularity but I think it very likely that she must.

Second, if rationalism *also* needs to rely on a rule-circular argument then *BonJour* had better hope that I am right about them! I argued that rationalism does indeed rely on rule-circularity. BonJour disagrees. His "basic point is that *a priori* insight is atomistic rather than holistic in character." So, we justify the overall claim *T* only indirectly by justifying particular claims about the rules that make up *S* with the result "that neither the issue of circularity nor that of self-defeat apply in any clear way." BonJour is wrong about this.

S is a system of rules for belief-formation. We all agree that *S* includes rules governing responses to perceptual experiences, ampliative rules, and deductive rules. According to the rationalist, *S* also includes a rule yielding *a priori* insights. Now the challenge posed by the skeptic is to say why any rule, *R*, is good. BonJour responds to this challenge by appealing largely, if not entirely, to *a priori* insight; the mind directly or intuitively grasps the necessary fact that *R* is good. Whatever its other problems, there need be no circularity about this *provided R is not the rule for a priori insight itself.* Where *R* is that rule, the rule-circularity is obvious. So BonJour's move to atomism does not avoid rule-circularity.

Criticism (i) aimed to show that all beliefs could be justified empirically, thus removing the motivation for the *a priori*. Among these beliefs are epistemological ones about the goodness of rules for belief formation. I doubt that all these epistemological beliefs could be justified empirically if rule-circularity is disallowed but there is no reason to think that they could not if rule-circularity is allowed. BonJour is in no position to disallow rule-circularity because his own rationalism depends on it. For, if he had a justification for believing that *a priori* insight was a good method of belief formation, the justification would be an *a priori* insight.

In response to (ii), BonJour continues to minimize the obscurity of the *a priori*, wondering what its "alleged 'mystery'" really amounts to. It is important to note something he *does not* do: he does not attempt an explanation that might reduce the mystery. We should not be surprised at this failure if I am right that nothing *can* reduce the mystery.

In charging that the *a priori* is deeply obscure I am, according to BonJour, "simply rejecting the idea that merely finding something to be intuitively necessary can ever constitute in itself a reason for thinking that it is true." But I am not simply rejecting this: I am *demanding an explanation of how it could be so.* How could this intuitive process *justify* something unless the process is empirical? The *a priori* is mysterious because we do not have even a hint of a satisfactory answer. It seems like magic that a process in someone's mind can justify her belief in an external worldly fact without that justification arising from some sort of experiential link to that fact.

Those are my main points, but I have one more.

In (i) I took BonJour to be rightly claiming that for a conclusion to be justified by an inference, the inference must be good, but I argued that he was wrongly claiming that our justification of its goodness must be *a priori*. This disagreement concerned that justification *whoever* provided it. However, BonJour's (1998) actual requirement for a justified conclusion was that *the very person making the inference* accompany it with an *a priori* insight into its goodness. Paul Boghossian (2001), following Lewis

Is There *a Priori* Knowledge?

Carroll, pointed out that this requirement that a proposition *about* the inference accompany the inference leads to an unstoppable regress. BonJour has responded to this point with a very curious move: "it is often and quite possibly always a mistake to construe [*a priori* insights] as *propositional* in form"; "the relevant logical insight must be construed as non-propositional in character, as a direct grasping of the way in which the conclusion is related to the premises and validly flows from them." BonJour's requirement, thus construed, has a role in his responses to both (i) and (ii).

This construal seems to commit BonJour to an "*a priori* knowing-how," something that surely makes no sense. The relations between propositions in an inference are not propositions, of course, but any insights *about* those relations are *essentially* propositional, having contents specified by "that"-clauses (e.g. "that *p* follows from *q*") like any other propositions.

BonJour's requirement was mistaken from the beginning. For an inference to justify a person's conclusion it simply has to *be* good. In an epistemological moment the person may indeed have the insight that the inference *is* good. Still, the justification of her conclusion does not depend on her having this insight. And, as I argued in (i), we should see such insights as empirical anyway.

Conclusion: BonJour's response to (i) does not undermine my argument that belief in the *a priori* is unmotivated. And his response to (ii) leaves the *a priori* as obscure as ever.

Last Rejoinder

Laurence BonJour

I have space only for three very quick points and two slightly more extended ones.

First, Devitt claims that I give no argument against the acceptability of rule-circular justification. But the passage that follows the phrase that he quotes was intended as such an argument and still seems to me to constitute a compelling one.

Second, Devitt tentatively suggests that a view of the sort he is defending might avoid rule-circularity by justifying each rule in terms of others. But if I understand what he is suggesting, such a justification would still be circular in the objectionable way: the justifications of at least some of the rules would ultimately depend, via a sequence of rules, on themselves.

Third, Devitt fails to understand the point about the atomistic character of *a priori* justification. As the rationalist conceives it, each individual instance of *a priori* justification depends only on the specific insight that is relevant to it, so that there is simply no need (and no use) for a general rule "yielding a priori insights."[1]

Fourth, Devitt asks how finding something to be intuitively necessary can constitute a reason for thinking that it is true. If the insight is genuine, then the answer is obvious. There is (obviously) no non-circular way to establish that such insights are genuine, but there is equally no cogent way to argue that they are not or that we could not have such a capacity which does not tacitly appeal to such insights.[2] To reject all such insights is to reject the capacity of human intelligence to have good reasons for believing anything beyond the narrow deliverances of direct experience. Appeal to "rules" into whose truth-conduciveness one has no such insight does nothing to address this issue. And to simply insist, as Devitt does, that any reason for thinking that any non-tautological claim about the world is true must be empirical is to back oneself into a corner from which there is no escape: to repeat, most of the claims that we think we have reasons to accept are not matters of direct experience, and experience alone cannot establish that they are connected to experience in a way that makes them likely to be true.

Fifth, Devitt denies that a person making an inference must have an insight into its correctness for his conclusion to be justified, claiming that all that is required is that the inference "be good." Perhaps there is some sense of the multifarious term "justification" for which this is correct. But a person who lacks such an insight has no *reason* for thinking that the resulting conclusion is true, and a person who infers in this way generally has no reason for thinking that any of his conclusions are true. (It seems to me obvious that there is a kind of insight into the cogency of such an inference that underlies and justifies the propositional claim that it is cogent: one sees how and why the conclusion follows, not simply that it follows. But I did not intend that this was a form of "knowing how" as that notion has ordinarily been understood.)

Notes

1 For more discussion, see BonJour (1998, pp. 142–7).
2 For some elaboration of this point, see BonJour (1998, pp. 153–6).

References for chapter 4

Boghossian, P. (2001) Inference and insight. *Philosophy and Phenomenological Research*, 63, 633–40.

BonJour, L. (1998) *In Defense of Pure Reason: A Rationalist Account of a Priori Justification*. Cambridge: Cambridge University Press.

BonJour, L. (2001a) Precis of *In Defense of Pure Reason*. *Philosophy and Phenomenological Research*, 63, 625–31.

BonJour, L. (2001b) Replies. *Philosophy and Phenomenological Research*, 63, 673–98.

Braithwaite, R. B. (1953) *Scientific Explanation*. Cambridge: Cambridge University Press.

Devitt, M. (1990) Meanings just ain't in the head. In G. Boolos (ed.), *Meaning and Method: Essays in Honor of Hilary Putnam*. New York: Cambridge University Press.

Devitt, M. (1996) *Coming to Our Senses: A Naturalistic Program for Semantic Localism*. New York: Cambridge University Press.

Devitt, M. (1997) *Realism and Truth*, 2nd edn with a new afterword. Princeton, NJ: Princeton University Press.

Devitt, M. (1998) Naturalism and the *a priori*. *Philosophical Studies*, 92, 45–65.

Devitt, M. (2001) A shocking idea about meaning. *Revue Internationale de Philosophie*, 208, 449–72.

Devitt, M. (2002) Underdetermination and realism. In E. Villanueva and E. Sosa (eds), *Realism and Relativism: Philosophical Issues, Volume 12*. Oxford: Blackwell.

Duhem, P. (1954) *The Aim and Structure of Physical Theory* (trans. P. Wiener). Princeton, NJ: Princeton University Press (originally published 1906).

Field, H. (1996) The a prioricity of logic. *Proceedings of the Aristotelian Society*, 96, 1–21.

Field, H. (1998) Epistemological nonfactualism and the a prioricity of logic. *Philosophical Studies*, 92, 1–24.

Kuhn, T. S. (1962) *The Structure of Scientific Revolutions*. Chicago: Chicago University Press.

Papineau, D. (1993) *Philosophical Naturalism*. Oxford: Blackwell.

Psillos, S. (1998) *Scientific Realism: How Science Tracks Truth*. New York: Routledge.

Quine, W. V. (1961) Two dogmas of empiricism. In *From a Logical Point of View*, 2nd edn. Cambridge, MA: Harvard University Press.

Quine, W. V. (1966) The scope and language of science. In *The Ways of Paradox and Other Essays*. New York: Random House.

Quine, W. V. (1969) Epistemology naturalized. In *Ontological Relativity and Other Essays*. New York: Random House.

Quine, W. V. (1975) The nature of natural knowledge. In S. Guttenplan (ed.), *Mind and Language*. Oxford: Clarendon Press.

Rey, G. (1998) A naturalistic a priori. *Philosophical Studies*, 92, 25–43.

Rey, G. (2001) Digging deeper for the a priori. *Philosophy and Phenomenological Research*, 63, 649–56.

Van Cleve, J. (1984) Reliability, justification, and the problem of induction. In P. A. French, T. E. Uehling Jr and H. K. Wettstein (eds), *Midwest Studies in Philosophy, Volume IX: Causation and Causal Theories*. Minneapolis: University of Minnesota Press.

Ideas for further reading

Boghossian, P. and Peacocke, C. (eds) (2000) *New Essays on the a Priori*. Oxford: Clarendon Press.

Butchvarov, P. (1970) *The Concept of Knowledge, Part I*. Evanston, IL: Northwestern University Press.

DePaul, M. R. and Ramsey, W. (eds) (1998) *Rethinking Intuition: the Psychology of Intuition and Its Role in Philosophical Inquiry*. Lanham, MD: Rowman and Littlefield.

Hanson, P. and Hunter, B. (eds) (1992) *Return of the a Priori*. Calgary, Alberta: University of Calgary Press.

Kitcher, P. (1980) A priori knowledge. *Philosophical Review*, 76, 3–23.

Kornblith, H. (ed.) (1994) *Naturalizing Epistemology*, 2nd edn. Cambridge MA: MIT Press.

Kornblith, H. (2000) The impurity of reason. *Pacific Philosophical Quarterly*, 81, 67–89.

Moser, P. (ed.) (1987) *A Priori Knowledge*. Oxford: Oxford University Press.

Pap, A. (1958) *Semantics and Necessary Truth*. New Haven, CT: Yale University Press.

Sleigh, R. C. (ed.) (1972) *Necessary Truth*. Englewood Cliffs, NJ: Prentice Hall.

Sumner, L. W. and Woods, J. (eds) (1969) *Necessary Truth*. New York: Random House.

PART II

FOUNDATIONAL KNOWLEDGE

Introduction

Matthias Steup

A building typically has two parts: a foundation and a superstructure. According to foundationalists, knowledge is structured just like a building. They hold that, without foundational knowledge on which non-foundational knowledge rests, there couldn't be any knowledge at all. Coherentists deny this. They claim that no part of our knowledge is firm enough to serve as a foundation, and no part of our knowledge is so weak as to require one. Rather, our knowledge forms a web in which all parts support each other.

If a belief is to count as an instance of foundational knowledge, exactly how would it have to be justified? The basic idea is that such a belief must be justified in a way that is independent of the subject's justification for any other beliefs. Suppose, for example, that my belief that I have a headache is justified by one and only one thing: my headache. This would be a kind of justification that is entirely independent of the justification I have for any other beliefs, and thus would be the kind of justification that could give me foundational knowledge of my headache. Or suppose, looking at a flower before you, you believe that it is red. You believe that it is red because it looks red to you. If what justifies your belief about the flower's color is its looking red to you, and nothing else is involved in justifying this belief, then you have foundational knowledge of the flower's color.

Coherentists claim that there are no beliefs whose justification is independent from the justification we have for any other of our beliefs, for they hold that the justification of any belief, B, is derived from the justification of either the whole belief system to which B belongs, or a certain subset of that system. When we apply this latter thought to the example of the red flower, we can think of coherentism as the view that your belief about the flower's color is justified because you are justified in believing various other things, such as that the flower looks red to you, that visual experiences are a reliable source of information for you, and that you have no reason to suspect that, under the present circumstances, your visual experience of the flower's color is misleading.

Philosophers who believe in the existence of foundational knowledge face the challenge of having to explain how such knowledge is possible. It is easy to see why the *beliefs* mentioned at the end of the previous paragraph might give you justification for believing that the flower is red. It is less easy to see how your belief about the flower's color could be justified by nothing but the *experience* of the flower's looking red to you. The task, then, is to give a plausible and detailed account of how foundational justification works. In addition, foundationalists need to explain exactly how foundational beliefs can confer justification onto non-foundational beliefs.

Coherentists face considerable challenges, too. One serious problem that arises for them is the avoidance of vicious circularity. Another one has to do with psychological facts about the way we normally form perceptual beliefs. Does an ordinary person's belief system really contain all of the beliefs from which, according to coherentism, a typical perceptual belief derives its justification? It would seem that the kind of belief system coherentists have in mind is rather sophisticated. If an ordinary subject's belief system does not contain beliefs as sophisticated as those that coherentists envision, coherentism would have the unfortunate consequence of rendering the perceptual beliefs of ordinary, unsophisticated subjects unjustified.

Chapter 5: Is Infinitism the Solution to the Regress Problem?

Why think that there is any foundational knowledge? According to an ancient argument proposed by Aristotle (*Posterior Analytics*), there must be foundational knowledge if there is any knowledge at all. Consider something you take yourself to know, say proposition p. Either you have a reason for p, or you do not. If you know p without having a reason for it, your knowledge of p is foundational. If you have a reason for p, say q, q must be something you know as well. Unless your knowledge of q is foundational, you need a reason, r, for q. But your knowledge of r is either foundational or based on a still further reason, and so forth. So either we admit the existence of foundational knowledge, or we end up in an infinite regress. In response to this problem, we might want to advocate

1 Skepticism: if you do not know p in the first place, there will not be a regress.
2 The benignity of circularity: knowledge of p is possible even if the regress loops back onto itself.
3 The benignity of infinity: knowledge of p is possible even if the regress goes on forever.
4 The possibility of foundational knowledge: the regress terminates in a kind of knowledge that obviates the need for further reasons.

According to the regress argument for foundationalism, options 1–3 are unacceptable. Whether one finds oneself in sympathy with this argument depends on whether one agrees that options 1–3 are indeed as grim as foundationalists claim they are.

In the first essay in part II of this volume, Peter Klein makes a case on behalf of option 3.

Klein's argument for the view he labels *infinitism* has two main targets: foundationalism and coherentism. To explain why these views ought to be rejected, he makes the following assumptions:

1 If either foundationalism or coherentism is correct, we should be able to use one of these theories to show how our beliefs are justified, without, in the process of doing so, slipping into an infinite regress.
2 When trying to show that a belief is justified, we must avoid both *arbitrariness* and *circularity*. We cannot claim a belief to be justified without giving a reason for it, but we must not give a reason to which we appealed already at an earlier point in the regress.
3 When a foundationalist or a coherentist claims that a belief is justified by a characteristic C, we can always *go meta*: we can always ask why we should think that a belief's having C makes it likely that the belief is true.

With these assumptions in place, Klein's argument against foundationalism proceeds as follows. At some suitable point, the foundationalist will claim that the regress ends in a belief whose justification is foundational by virtue of characteristic C. At that point, Klein will pose the meta-question: Why think that C is an indication of the belief's truth? If the foundationalist has no answer, she is guilty of arbitrariness. If she cites a reason that was already mentioned, she violates the stricture against circularity. If she accepts the need of having to respond to the meta-question, the regress will continue. So foundationalism should give way to infinitism because the only way for a foundationalist to avoid an infinite regress is to endorse either arbitrariness or circularity, either one of which is unacceptable.

Klein's argument against coherentism is structurally analogous. Whatever characteristic, C, the coherentist will cite when attempting to justify the target belief, Klein will go meta: Why think that C is indicative of truth? The coherentist will then face the same options as the foundationalist: she will be guilty of either arbitrariness or circularity, or else must admit that the regress continues.

One obvious objection to infinitism is that the mind is finite: we do not have the mental capacity to support our beliefs with infinite chains of reasons. Klein replies that what he requires is not that each justified belief be supported by an infinite number of beliefs, but merely that, when we justify a belief by giving reasons, there must be a new and different reason *available* for each of the reasons we give.

In his critical essay on infinitism, Carl Ginet suggests that we can find plausible examples of foundational knowledge in the area of perceptual and *a priori* justification. Ginet anticipates that, in response to such examples, Klein would of course go meta: Why think that perceptual and *a priori* beliefs of the kind in question are likely true? Ginet accepts the challenge of establishing a truth connection at that level. But, he asks, what reason is there for thinking that demand for the truth connection will generate an *infinite* number of reasons? What would the content of these reason be? Klein's response is that, whenever the meta-question is answered by citing a certain characteristic, C, we should ask what reason there is to think that C is true. Ginet questions, however, that the regress will actually continue once we have gone meta. The meta-question, Ginet suggests, can be adequately answered by citing epistemic principles that are knowable immediately and *a priori*. When the foundationalist cites such principles, the regress stops. Although Klein does not directly address this point, it may safely be assumed that he would go meta once again: if our belief in these principles is justified, this must be so because of a certain feature our belief has. Why think that that feature makes it likely that the belief is true?

Ginet's final objection is that justification is like value: unless some things are intrinsically valuable, nothing is instrumentally valuable. Likewise, unless some justification is generated without being inferred, no beliefs can be justified at all. In response, Klein denies the analogy. Justification need not be generated non-inferentially. Rather, it emerges when inferential chains are long enough.

Chapter 6: Can Beliefs Be Justified through Coherence Alone?

In the two essays on this question, Katherine Elgin and James van Cleve both answer it negatively. But whereas van Cleve advocates a moderate version of foundationalism, Elgin defends a broadly coherentist view. Justification is, according to Elgin, holistic. It is primarily the justification of a whole system of beliefs. The justification individual beliefs enjoy is derived from the coherence of the overall system. However, not just any coherent belief system confers justification on its members. Individual beliefs are justified by virtue of being members of a coherent system only when we have reason to think that their truth is the best explanation of why they cohere.

Elgin, then, holds that justification is primarily a matter of explanatory coherence. Nevertheless, she allows for a kind of justification that is of a foundational nature. *Deliverances*, in Elgin's theory, are representations that present themselves as true, such as perceptual or memorial inputs, other beliefs, or passing thoughts. Since they present themselves as true, deliverances are *initially tenable*. Alas, initial tenability is a weak and precarious epistemic status. We have only a slight reason for thinking that an initially tenable proposition is true.

Elgin allows as well for a certain degree of *epistemic priority*. Theories can be defeated by observations. But the epistemic status of observations arises only from the fact that we have reasons to trust them. Here, two central strands of Elgin's account becomes apparent. First, though perhaps not an advocate of a pure form of coherentism, Elgin rejects foundationalism. According to her, there is no foundational knowledge because, without receiving most of its justification from other beliefs, no belief enjoys the degree of justification necessary for knowledge. Second, she rejects externalism as well. Observational beliefs acquire their epistemic status because of not their reliability itself but rather our understanding of it.

It is uncontroversial that coherence is a source of justification, at least inasmuch as it can augment the justification a belief has to begin with, perhaps by being initially tenable, or perhaps simply because it is grounded in a perceptual or introspective experience. In his essay, van Cleve makes a case for the view that, although coherence is indeed a source of justification, it cannot *by itself* give a belief all the justification it needs to qualify as an instance of knowledge. No belief, according to van Cleve, could be justified unless it were possible for some beliefs to acquire complete justification – a degree of justification high enough for knowledge – without receiving support from any other beliefs. To make a case for this claim, van Cleve compares two formulas designed to calculate the probability that witnesses whose testimony agrees speak the truth. According to the Boole formula, it is probable that they speak the truth only if each witness enjoys an antecedent degree of credibility. According to the Huemer formula, it can be probable that their testimony is true even if none of the witnesses is credible individually. The Boole formula represents the foundationalist claim that without antecedent credibility, coherence cannot by itself generate any impressive degree of justification. The Huemer formula supports the coherentist thought that coherence can generate justification all by itself.

Van Cleve notes that the Huemer formula is more plausible than the Boole formula. But it would be a mistake to conclude from this that coherentism is vindicated. When we assign a high probability to the coherent testimony of several witnesses, none of whom is credible on her own, we assume that they really exist. If the combined force of their testimony suggests that p is true, we would have little reason to accept p if we didn't antecedently have good reason to believe that the witnesses really exist and give testimony in support of p. But that's analogous to what foundationalists have always claimed. The coherence of our experiences and beliefs provides us with a good reason for taking our beliefs to be true only if we have foundational knowledge of the fact that we have these experiences and beliefs. If one has foundational knowledge of that kind, then, according to van Cleve, one knows that p *solely* because one remembers, introspects, or perceives that p.

Chapter 7: Is There Immediate Justification?

Suppose you look at a book with a blue cover. What would it take for you to have immediate justification for the proposition:

B: The book is blue.

According to James Pryor, your justification for believing B would have to be such that it does not come from the justification you have for believing any other propositions. What might such other propositions be? They might, for example, be propositions about the reliability of B's origin. Let us explore that thought a bit further.

Suppose the book *looks* blue to you. Let's refer to this perceptual experience as evidential item E1. According to the proposal just mentioned, E1 is only part of your justification for B. In addition, you need an evidential item E2: evidence, perhaps in the form of suitable track record memories, for the proposition that E1 is an instance of a reliable kind of experience. On that view, your justification for B consists of the conjunction of E1 and E2. On the face of it, such a view looks coherentist. However, if E2 were comprised solely of memories of the reliability of your perceptual faculties, this view could be considered foundationalist. For in that case, E2 would not consist of any further *beliefs* from which B receives its justification. The view in question, then, would be coherentist at the evidential level, while allowing for foundational beliefs that are justified without receiving justification from any other beliefs.

Pryor's conception of immediate justification implies that, if your having justification for B indeed requires your being in possession of E1 and E2, your justification for B is *not* immediate. If your justification for B is immediate, then it must come from E1 alone. So Pryor's conception of immediate justification overlaps with Van Cleve's conception of basic beliefs. According to both authors, if your knowledge of B is foundational, it must be justified, not by a body of evidence that would support a coherent set of beliefs of which B is a member, but *solely* by E1.

Why think that there is such a thing as immediate justification? Pryor does not think that the Regress Argument provides us with the best reason in support of immediate justification. Rather, he suggests, the best reason is provided by the abundance of plausible examples of immediate justification. Obviously, we have many justified beliefs about our own mental states and their contents. It is plausible to assume that they are justified by the mental states they are about. For instance, it is plausible to assume that, when I believe that I have a headache, my belief is immediately justified by my headache itself.

Next, Pryor proceeds to discuss what he calls the "Master Argument for Coherentism." A rough and ready version of it goes as follows:

(1) Justifiers must have assertively represented propositional content.
(2) Only beliefs have such content.

Therefore:

(3) Only beliefs can be justifiers.

If this conclusion were true, immediate justification would be impossible, for in that case whenever a belief is justified it would be justified by virtue of receiving its justification from one or more other beliefs. To defend foundationalism against this argument, it is sufficient to deny (2), on the ground that experiences, perceptual and otherwise, can assertively represent propositional content. Pryor's preferred response to the Master Argument, however, is to deny both premises. (1), Pryor suggests, is motivated by what he calls the *Premise Principle*. According to this principle, justifiers must be such that they can be used as premises in an argument. In the concluding sections of his essay, Pryor argues that foundationalists should not endorse the Premise Principle.

According to Michael Williams, the search for foundations is bound to be frustrated. The need for immediate justification, he suggests, is of a theoretical nature, stemming from the Agrippan trilemma of having to choose between circular reasons (coherentism), infinitely many reasons (infinitism), and ultimate reasons (atomism). The dilemma arises when we are asked to justify a belief by giving reasons. When trying to respond to such a request, pressure is generated to achieve full epistemic self-awareness while eventually giving an ultimate reason that is free of any presupposition. So pressure is generated on behalf of internalism and atomism. The need for atomism could be met by beliefs that are justified solely because they are reliably produced. But this conflicts with the demand for internalism. The challenge is for the subject herself to understand why her belief is justified. If this challenge is to be met, the subject must recognize that her belief was reliably produced. But then the putatively ultimate reason is backed up by a further reason, and the regress continues.

What, then, can satisfy the twin demands of atomism and internalism? According to traditional foundationalism, the Given can: mental states immediately presented to consciousness. But how are we to conceive of the Given? If the Given has propositional content, the possibility of error arises, and thus the need for further justification. If, on the other hand, the Given does not have propositional content, one wonders how it can supply the subject with a reason. This, Williams reminds us, is the dilemma that, according to Sellars (1963), is the fundamental difficulty foundationalists face. Williams suggests that today we are still without an effective response to this dilemma.

Williams, then, doubts that the twin demands of atomism and internalism can be reconciled. Thus, at the end of his essay, he entertains the thought that the entire project of responding to the Agrippan dilemma is ill-conceived. Perhaps, he surmises, justification simply is not the kind of thing the nature of which can be captured by a systematic theory.

Chapter 8: Does Perceptual Experience Have Conceptual Content?

Suppose perceptual experiences are a source of justification. From the externalist point of view, there is a straightforward explanation of why this should be so: sense perception is a reliable process. That's why perceptual experiences can justify our perceptual beliefs. From the internalist point of view, however, it is not so easy to see how our perceptual beliefs can derive their justification from perceptual experiences themselves. Compare perceptual experiences with *beliefs* about perceptual experiences. There is less mystery in the assumption that the latter can serve as a source of justification. For example, if we wonder what might justify my belief that the book on the desk is blue, the following conjunctive belief is certainly a good candidate: "My belief originates in a visual experience of kind K, and such experiences are reliable." There is considerably more mystery, however, in the claim that my belief might be justified *solely* by the perceptual experience I have when the book looks blue to me.

One way of explaining why perceptual experience can justify perceptual beliefs is to conceive of them as having conceptual content: the same kind of content beliefs have. This would bring perceptual experiences into what Sellars called the *logical space of reasons* (Sellars, 1963), and thus would make them eligible as a source of justification. In his contribution to this section, Bill Brewer defends the claim that perceptual experiences do indeed have conceptual content. He derives this conclusion from two premises: (i) perceptual experiences are reasons for our perceptual beliefs; (ii) perceptual experiences cannot be reasons for perceptual beliefs without having conceptual content. Having defended the first premise elsewhere (Brewer, 1999),

Brewer focuses on defending the second. His defense, which rests on two main points, appeals to what Pryor referred to as the "Premise Principle." First, justifiers must be such that they can serve as premises in an argument. If an item x has the capacity of making it epistemically justified for S to believe that p, it has this capacity by virtue of being the sort of thing that can be used in an argument for p. This is the very thing that qualifies x, from the point of view of epistemic rationality, as a reason for p. Second, if an item x has the capacity to justify S in believing that p, then it must be a reason for S herself to believe that p. It must be a reason S possesses. But if x is a reason that S possesses, then x must have a content that can be expressed by the concepts S possesses. From these two claims, Brewer concludes that a subject's perceptual experiences cannot give her reasons for her perceptual beliefs without having conceptual content.

In his response to Brewer's essay, Alex Byrne provides some background to the debate over perceptual content, and then proceeds to discuss two arguments for the claim that perceptual content is not conceptual. The first of these is based on the premise that perceptual experiences have a degree of richness that outstrips the perceiver's conceptual resources. The second argument rests on the premise that non-linguistic animals – beings which do not possess any concepts – can perceive the same content humans can perceive. Byrne examines both arguments and concludes that neither succeeds.

Next, Byrne focuses on an argument by John McDowell in support of claim that perceptual content is conceptual. According to McDowell, perceptual reasons must be conceptual because reasons must be such that the subject can articulate them (McDowell, 1994). Upon examining this argument, Byrne finds that it does not establish its conclusion. Finally, Byrne turns to a similar argument of Brewer's, based on the premise that a subject's reasons must be recognizable by the subject as her reasons. Once again, Byrne arrives at the outcome that conceptualism has not been established.

In the essay's final section, Byrne points out that, if one holds that perceptual content is non-conceptual, one is in effect claiming the following: if what is perceived is p but p is not conceptual, then S cannot believe that p. But it is hard to understand why the content that we perceive should not also be content that we can believe. Byrne suggests, therefore, that the default position should be that perceptual content is conceptual.

References

Brewer, B. (1999) *Perception and Reason*. Oxford: Oxford University Press.
McDowell, J. (1994) *Mind and World*. Cambridge, MA: Harvard University Press.
Sellars, W. (1963) Empiricism and the philosophy of mind. In *Science, Perception and Reality*. London: Routledge and Kegan Paul.

Is Infinitism the Solution to the Regress Problem?

Infinitism Is the Solution to the Regress Problem

Peter Klein

The Regress Problem

The *locus classicus* of the regress problem is to be found in Sextus Empiricus's *Outlines of Pyrrhonism*:

> The later Skeptics hand down Five Modes leading to suspension, namely these: the first based on discrepancy, the second on the regress *ad infinitum*, the third on relativity, the fourth on hypothesis, the fifth on circular reasoning. That based on discrepancy leads us to find that with regard to the object presented there has arisen both amongst ordinary people and amongst the philosophers an interminable conflict because of which we are unable either to choose a thing or reject it, and so fall back on suspension. The Mode based upon regress *ad infinitum* is that whereby we assert that the thing adduced as a proof of the matter proposed needs a further proof, and this again another, and so on *ad infinitum*, so that the consequence is suspension [of assent], as we possess no starting-point for our argument. The Mode based upon relativity . . . is that whereby the object has such or such an appearance in relation to the subject judging and to the concomitant percepts, but as to its real nature we suspend judgment. We have the Mode based upon hypothesis when the Dogmatists, being forced to recede *ad infinitum*, take as their starting-point something which they do not establish but claim to assume as granted simply and without demonstration. The Mode of circular reasoning is the form used when the proof itself which ought to establish the matter of inquiry requires confirmation derived from the matter; in this case, being unable to assume either in order to establish the other, we suspend judgment about both.[1]

Although the three alternative strategies for solving the regress will be the focus of this essay, a brief discussion of the two other modes will be useful in understanding what initiates the regress.

The Modes were recipes for avoiding *dogmatism*, i.e. the disposition to assent to non-evident propositions when it is not settled whether they are true. One could locate such a non-evident proposition either by noting that there was credible disagreement about it or by merely recognizing that there could be credible disagreement. For in order to avoid epistemic hubris, the recognition that our epistemic peers could sincerely disagree with us about the truth of some proposition forces us to regard it as requiring reasons in order to rise to the desired level of credibility.

The Regress Problem can be put as follows: Which type of series of reasons and the account of warrant associated with it, if any, can increase the credibility of a non-evident proposition? Can a series with repeating propositions do so? Can one with a last member do so? Can one that is non-repeating and has no last member do so?

Foundationalists and coherentists typically address the trilemma in two steps. First, they cavalierly reject the infinitist option by alluding to our "finite mental capacity." Second, they argue for one of the remaining options by disjunctive elimination.[2] We will consider the "finite mind" objection in due course. My point here is only that infinitism has been given a short shrift, if any shrift, by epistemologists.

The argument in this paper has three essential steps: *first*, I will argue that neither foundationalism nor coherentism can solve the regress problem; *second*, I will present an infinitist account of warrant and explain how reasoning in accord with it can solve the regress problem; *third*, I will argue that the best objections to infinitism fail.[3]

Step 1: Neither Foundationalism nor Coherentism Can Solve the Regress Problem

The regress problem concerns the ability of reasoning to increase the rational credibility of a questioned proposition. It is not crucial what degree of credibility is at stake. The task is to produce an account of warrant, where "warrant" refers to the property possessed by propositions or beliefs such that (1) true beliefs with that property are known[4] and (2) reasoning in accordance with the dictates of that account increases our rational confidence in non-evident propositions.

My claim will be that neither foundationalism nor coherentism provides such an account of warrant. I will *not* be arguing that either account of warrant is incorrect. I will be arguing that neither account of warrant can provide a solution to the regress problem because neither account can be employed by a self-conscious practitioner to increase the rational credibility of a questioned proposition and, thus, a primary reason for adopting either foundationalism or coherentism has been eliminated.

Foundationalists and coherentists differ about the way in which warrant originates and is transferred. Varieties of foundationalism can be demarcated (i) by the features of basic propositions in which warrant arises, (ii) by the degree of warrant that arises initially, and (iii) by the rules of inference that transfer warrant. But all foundationalists think of warrant as arising autonomously in so-called basic propositions and being transferred to other propositions through permissible forms of inference.

Coherentists *could* think of warrant as transferring from one proposition to another. This form of coherentism, what I will call the "warrant-transfer" variety, holds that some proposition, p, transfers its warrant to another proposition which can, in turn, pass it to another proposition. Eventually the warrant is transferred back to p. This view endorses circular reasoning. Now, I don't think any epistemologist explicitly advocated this view – although the critics of coherentism occasionally characterize it in this way, as did the Pyrrhonians and Aristotle.[5]

The second variety of coherentism – the form that *has* been advocated – is what I will call the "warrant-emergent" form. Warrant emerges from the structure of the mutually supporting propositions.[6] Warrant is *not* a property of a particular proposition except in the trivial sense that a proposition is warranted *iff* it is a member of such a set of mutually supporting propositions. As the set of propositions becomes increasingly comprehensive and the mutual support intensifies, the degree of warrant for each increases. This view eschews incestuous circular reasoning in which warrant is transferred from some ancestor proposition to its descendants and then back again to the ancestor.

Our question is whether the account of warrant underlying foundationalism or either of the two forms of coherentism provides a basis for a solution to the regress problem. Let us begin with foundationalism and imagine a dialogue between Fred, the *F*oundationalist, and Doris, the *D*oubter. (Fred/Doris could be sub-persona if we are envisioning a Cartesian-style, *sotto voce* meditation). Fred asserts some proposition, say p. Doris says something – who knows what – that prompts Fred to believe that he had better have reason(s) for p in order to supply some missing credibility. So, Fred gives his reason, r_1, for p. (r_1 could be a conjunction.) Now, Doris asks why r_1 is true. Fred gives another reason, r_2. This goes on for a while until Fred (being a practicing foundationalist) arrives at what he takes to be a basic proposition, say b.

Doris will, of course, ask Fred for his reason for b. But Fred, being a self-conscious, circumspect foundationalist will tell Doris that b doesn't need a reason in order to possess the autonomous bit of warrant. He will say that her question "Why do you believe that x?" though appropriate up to this point is no longer appropriate when "b" is substituted for "x" because b is basic. There is no reason that supplies the *autonomous* warrant that b has.[7]

Grant that foundationalism is true; b has some autonomous bit of warrant that arises because b has some foundational property, F, such that any proposition having F is autonomously warranted, and every non-basic proposition that depends upon b for its warrant would lose some of its warrant were b not autonomously warranted.

Doris should say to Fred, "I grant that b has autonomous warrant. But what I want to know is whether autonomously warranted propositions are, in virtue of that fact, somewhat likely to be true." Her worry becomes a "meta" worry. But she went meta, so to speak, because Fred went meta first.[8]

Given that with regard to any proposition, once we consider whether it is true, we must hold it, deny it, or withhold it (i.e. neither hold nor deny it), Fred is now faced with a trilemma:[9]

1 He can hold that autonomously warranted propositions are somewhat likely to be true in virtue of the fact that they are autonomously warranted.
2 He can deny that autonomously warranted propositions are somewhat likely to be true in virtue of the fact that they are autonomously warranted.

Is Infinitism the Solution to the Regress Problem? | 133

3 He can withhold whether autonomously warranted propositions are somewhat likely to be true in virtue of the fact that they are autonomously warranted.

If he takes alternative 2, then using b as a reason for the first non-basic proposition in the series is arbitrary. Holding b is not arbitrary. Doris has granted that b is autonomously warranted and she could grant that it is not arbitrary to hold a proposition that has autonomous warrant. But if Fred believed that such propositions were not even somewhat likely to be true in virtue of being autonomously warranted, how could he think that b could provide a good reason for thinking that the penultimate proposition was likely to be true? Fred thinks that the warrant for all of his beliefs rests on basic propositions. If he thought that b's possession of F was not the least bit truth conducive, then why is he using b and all the other basic propositions on which the warrant for his non-basic beliefs rests?

The same applies to alternative 3. Doris has asked whether the fact that b is autonomously warranted makes it at all likely that b is true. Fred responds that he doesn't have an opinion one way or the other. Fred thinks b is true but he neither has a reason for thinking it is true nor does he think that basic propositions are somewhat likely to be true because they are autonomously warranted. So, from Fred's point of view and Doris's, Fred ought not to use b as the basis for further beliefs. The mere fact that he thinks b is true is not sufficient for him to use b as a reason, unless he thinks that his thinking that b is true somehow makes it likely that b is true.

If he takes alternative 1, then using b as his reason for the penultimate proposition is not arbitrary, *but that is because the regress has continued.* Fred has a very good reason for believing b, namely b has F and propositions with F are likely to be true. Fred, now, could be asked to produce his reasons for thinking that b has F and that basic propositions are somewhat likely to be true in virtue of possessing feature F.

Therefore: foundationalism cannot solve the regress problem, even if it were true. A practicing foundationalist cannot increase the rational credibility of a questioned proposition through reasoning.

Let us turn to coherentism. The first form, the warrant-transfer form, is easily seen to be unable to solve the regress problem because Carl, the Coherentist, cannot increase the credibility of some proposition, p, by citing p in its own evidential ancestry. If the reasoning is to increase the credibility of the questioned proposition for Carl, then that credibility will not already be cathected to the proposition. For if it were, then it is pointless to begin reasoning in the first place. Presumably that is what is wrong with circular reasoning. It cannot increase the credibility of a questioned proposition.

Indeed, the difficulty facing *all* warrant-transfer accounts (foundationalism and this type of coherentism) is more serious than that credibility will not be *added* to the questioned proposition by reasoning. There is a danger that credibility will actually diminish as the warrant is transferred.[10] If all of the inferences employed in the reasoning were deductive and if an appropriate form of closure holds, it would seem that credibility would not be lost. It could even increase. But if during the transfer of warrant some credibility were lost, as it would be, if the inference links were non-deductive, then, the longer the series or the larger the circle, the more credibility would be lost.

The only escape from this difficulty for a warrant-transfer theorist is to (i) limit the number of transfers allowed or (ii) require that there are sufficiently strong coherence relations to make up for the lost warrant or (iii) require that enough of the transfers are by way of deduction. Those stipulations seem entirely *ad hoc*.

The second form of coherentism, the warrant-emergent form, seems more promising because it eschews circular reasoning, and warrant for propositions could increase as the number of threads in the web of propositions increases and/or the web becomes more tightly woven. But there is one problem with this form of coherentism. As others have pointed out, it is nothing but a type of foundationalism – one step foundationalism.[11] In this case, the foundational property, F, which all warranted propositions have, is that each is a member of a set of coherent propositions. The Carl–Doris discussion would follow the same general pattern as the Fred–Doris discussion where the foundational property, F, is simply the proposition's membership in the set of coherent propositions.

Thus, Carl faces a trilemma similar to Fred's, discussed above. If he says either "no" or "I withhold" then vesting his credence in a coherent set of propositions is arbitrary. Why should he adopt a coherent set rather than an incoherent set? If he says that coherent propositions are likely to be true in virtue of the fact that they are coherent, then he faces the third horn.[12] For either the proposition "coherent sets are *ipso facto* likely to contain propositions that are true" is included in the initial coherent set or it isn't. If it is, then he has fallen back to the warrant-transfer, i.e. question-begging, form of coherentism. If it isn't, then he has just added a new proposition to the coherent set and the regress has continued.

Now, coherentists might suggest that mere coherence is not sufficient to demarcate a set of warranted propositions. They could require, for example, that the set contain some propositions that have some further feature, namely that they are spontaneously endorsed or that their content has certain phenomenal properties (for example, see BonJour, 1985). But that is just another specification of the foundational F-property and the trilemma would reappear.

Therefore: coherentism cannot solve the regress problem, even if it were true. A practicing coherentist cannot increase the credibility of a questioned proposition through reasoning.

Perhaps there is no solution to the regress problem – i.e. no way to add credibility to a proposition by reasoning. But before we come to that rather dismal conclusion, it would be appropriate to look at the third alternative.

Step 2: Infinitism

What is infinitism? Infinitism is like the warrant-emergent form of coherentism because it holds that warrant for a questioned proposition emerges as the proposition becomes embedded in a set of propositions. Infinitism is like foundationalism because it holds that some propositions are epistemically prior to others. But some caution is needed if we are to be able to account for the coherentist intuition that (some) propositions are mutually supporting. For example, "all humans are mortal" is a reason for believing that "this human is mortal," and the converse is true. Some have thought that the universal generalization is always epistemically prior to the particular, and others have thought that the particular is always epistemically prior to the generalization. Each view runs afoul of our reasoning practice. Sometimes we offer the generalization as a reason for the particular – when the particular is what is questioned. Sometimes we offer the particular as a reason for the generalization – when the generalization is questioned. But we cannot use the generalization as a reason for the particular and the particular as a reason for the generalization *in the course of one reasoning session.* That would be to fall into circular, question-begging reasoning.

What we seek is an account of warrant that is not a warrant-transfer view and is not warrant-emergent finite coherentism. There is only one option remaining. What we need is warrant-emergent infinitism. Such a view leads neither to the arbitrary employment of a so-called basic propositions nor to the endorsement of circular reasoning. It can solve the regress problem because it endorses a warrant-emergent form of reasoning in which warrant increases as the series of reasons lengthens.

Infinitism results from adopting the following two principles:[13]

> *Principle of Avoiding Circularity* (PAC): for all propositions, x, if x is warranted for a person, S, at t, then for all y, if y is in the reason-ancestry of x for S at t, then x is not in the reason-ancestry of y for S at t.

> *Principle of Avoiding Arbitrariness* (PAA): for all propositions, x, if x is warranted for a person, S, at t, then there is some reason, r_1, available to S for x at t; and there is some reason, r_2, available to S for r_1 at t, etc., and there is no last reason in the series.

PAC is readily understandable and requires no discussion. It simply recognizes that a warrant-transfer view cannot solve the regress problem by endorsing circular reasoning. PAA, on the other hand, introduces the notion of "available reasons" and some account of that is required.

There are two conditions that must be met in order for a proposition to be *available* to S as a *reason* for x at t. First, the proposition must be *available* to S at t; that is, it must be appropriately "hooked up" to S's beliefs and other mental contents at t. In order for a proposition to be available in this sense it need not be occurrently believed or endorsed by S at t. For example, the proposition "352 + 226 = 578" is available even though it might never be consciously entertained. Whether this is best understood as (a) a disposition to believe that 352 + 226 = 578 or (b) a second order disposition to form a disposition to believe that 352 + 226 = 578 is a matter of detail that can be put aside.

The second condition is that the proposition must be a *reason* for S at t. Now, what makes a proposition a reason need not be fleshed out here. That's a good thing because the issue is a difficult one and there are many alternative accounts that could be employed by the infinitist. It is here that infinitism can (but need not) make room for externalist accounts of justification and for a supervenience requirement in which the supervenience base is limited to non-normative facts.[14] For example, some proposition, say p, could be held to be a reason for q *iff*

1 p is true and it renders q probable; or
2 p would be accepted as a reason for q in the long run by the appropriate epistemic community; or
3 p would be offered as a reason for q by an epistemically virtuous individual; or
4 there is cognitive process available to S which reliably takes true beliefs that p into true beliefs that q.

There are other possible accounts. The point is that whatever the proper account of reasons is, coherentists, foundationalists, and infinitists will have to employ it because each view holds that there are reasons for at least some of our beliefs. So, this thorny issue can be set aside for the purposes of this essay.

Nevertheless, these two conditions make clear what infinitism is committed to and, more important, what it is *not* committed to. For example, the mere existence of an infinite set of propositions each of which entails the next in the series is not sufficient for there to be the appropriate series of reasons available which could provide the missing credibility. As has been pointed out by others, there will be an infinite series of propositions each entailed by a previous one in the series for *every* proposition. The point is that not just *any* infinite series of propositions will do. The propositions must be available and they must be reasons.[15]

Step 3: Replies to the Best Objections to Infinitism

It is now time examine what I think are the two best objections to infinitism, beginning with the oldest. Recall what Sextus said:

> The Mode based upon regress *ad infinitum* is that whereby we assert that the thing adduced as a proof of the matter proposed needs a further proof, and this again another, and so on *ad infinitum*, so that the consequence is suspension [of assent], as we possess no starting-point for our argument.

Now, if efficacious reasoning required that warrant originate in and be transferred from a basic proposition, this criticism would be just. But for the reasons given above, infinitism eschews such a view. The "starting point" of reasoning is, as Peirce says: doubt. A proposition becomes questionable and, consequently, it lacks the desired rational credibility. Reasoning scratches the itch. The infinitist holds that finding a reason for the questioned proposition, and then another for that reason, etc., places it at the beginning of a series of propositions each of which gains warrant and rational credibility by being part of the series. Warrant increases not because we are getting closer to a basic proposition but rather because we are getting further from the questioned proposition. But the Pyrrhonist is correct that the infinitist's conception of reasoning precludes assenting to a non-evident proposition. Dogmatism is incompatible with practicing infinitism. Warrant, and with it rational credibility, increases as the series lengthens; but the matter is never completely settled.

In conclusion let me turn to the finite mind objection. Here is what John Williams says:

> The [proposed] regress of justification of S's belief that p would certainly require that he holds an infinite number of beliefs. This is psychologically, if not logically, impossible. If a man can believe an infinite number of things, then there seems to be no reason why he cannot know an infinite number of things. Both possibilities contradict the common intuition that the human mind is finite. Only God could entertain an infinite number of beliefs. But surely God is not the only justified believer. (Williams, 1981, p. 85)

I hope that it is clear how to answer that objection. Infinitism does not require that we "hold" an infinite number of beliefs – if that means that there is some time at which an infinite number of beliefs are occurrent. Infinitism does require that there be an infinite non-repeating set of propositions each of which is an available reason for a preceding one.

But some philosophers have suggested that such a set cannot be available. Audi, for example, writes:

> Let me suggest one reason to doubt that human beings are even capable of having infinite sets of beliefs. Consider the claim that we can have an infinite set of arithmetical beliefs say the 2 is twice 1, the 4 is twice 2, etc. Surely for a finite mind there will be some point or other at which the relevant proposition cannot be grasped . . . and what we cannot grasp we cannot believe. I doubt that any other lines of argument show that we can have infinite sets of beliefs; nor, if we can, is it clear how infinite epistemic chains could account for any of our knowledge. (Audi, 1993, pp. 127–8)

Let us grant that such a set is not available to us. Of course, it does not follow that there could not be an infinite set of propositions available whose members do not increase in complexity. In fact, *contra* Audi, I think there is a simple argument to show that there is such a set.

Suppose we have a very limited set of concepts or vocabulary: {x is F, red, indexical "that"}. In other words, we can believe of an object: that is red. Now imagine that there are an infinite number of red objects. We could believe of each object that it is red. Those are different beliefs because the truth conditions of the propositions affirmed in the beliefs are distinct.

Are there an infinite number of red objects? I don't know. But that is not necessary for my argument. All I need to show is that a finite mind *can* have access to an infinite number of beliefs. And I have shown that.

Audi also claims that even if there were an infinite series of propositions each of which is available it is not "clear how infinite epistemic chains could account for any of our knowledge." Now, if knowledge required actually completing the series, knowledge would not be possible. But why suppose that knowledge requires the highest possible degree of warrant or absolutely credible belief? As the series lengthens, warrant and credibility increase. Nothing prevents it increasing to the degree required for knowledge.[16]

Notes

1 Sextus Empiricus, *Outlines of Pyrrhonism*, I, 166–9.

2 For a foundationalist employing this strategy, see Audi (1993, pp. 127–8); for a (former) coherentist employing it, see BonJour (1985, pp. 18–24).

3 Some of these objections, as well as others, are treated in more detail in Klein (1999, 2003, 2004).

4 For this use of "warrant," Plantinga (1993, p. 3).

5 Aristotle, *Posterior Analytics*, 73a1–5.

6 For a defense of warrant-emergent coherentism, see BonJour (1985).

7 Reasons might supply additional warrant, but these are or ultimately depend upon other basic propositions for their warrant. Doris could ask what reason(s) he has for believing the conjunction of the basic propositions. Fred's reply will be the same, "there is no reason for believing that conjunction other than each conjunct."

8 For a similar argument, see BonJour (1985, pp. 9–14). I have discussed this elsewhere (see Klein, 1999).

9 Ernest Sosa discusses a similar issue in his 1994 (p. 107) and in the forthcoming "False dichotomies" to be published by Oxford University Press in a volume of conference proceedings honoring Robert Fogelin, edited by Walter Sinnott-Armstrong. I have discussed Sosa's views in Klein (forthcoming).

10 Thus, infinitism cannot endorse a warrant-transfer view. This potential problem for infinitism was originally suggested to me by Troy Cross.

11 I do not think the expressions "warrant-transfer coherentism" or "warrant-emergent coherentism" are original with me. But I do not recall where I first ran across those terms. Laurence BonJour (1985) distinguishes the two types of coherentism, as does Ernest Sosa (1980). Sosa also points out that warrant-emergent coherentism is a form of what he calls "formal foundationalism." Thus, the claim that some forms of coherentism are actually forms of foundationalism is not original with me.

12 Ernest Sosa (1997) advocates seizing this horn of the trilemma in his 1997. I have discussed this in Klein (forthcoming).

13 Note that PAC and PAA are necessary conditions for warrant. They are not intended to be jointly sufficient. At least a "non-overrider" clause and a "non-defeasibility" clause would need to be added in order to have a sufficient set of conditions. For discussions of those issues see Klein (1971, 1981, 2003).

14 This is important because it provides the basis for an answer to the objection that infinitism cannot account for the supervenience of the normative on the non-normative discussed in Goldman (1979), Sosa (1980), and van Cleve (1992, especially pp. 350–1 and 356–7).

15 This objection to infinitism was developed in Post (1980, especially p. 34–5), and in Post (1987, pp. 84–92). For my reply, see Klein (1999, p. 312).

16 I am indebted to the paper "Infinitism and degrees of justification" by Jeremy Fantle for making this point so clearly. I wish to thank Anne Ashbaugh, Troy Cross, Jeremy Fantl, Alvin Goldman, Brian Mclaughlin and Ernest Sosa for their help with this essay. Ancestor versions were read at the New Jersey Regional Philosophical Association, University of Colorado-Boulder, Montclair State University, and Bryn Mawr College. The discussions at the time and follow-up conversations and e-mails were very valuable, especially those with George Bealer, David Benfield, Michael Huemer, Aryeh Kosman, Michael Krausz, and Kenneth Richman.

References

Audi, R. (1993) *The Structure of Justification*. New York: Cambridge University Press.

BonJour, L. (1985) *The Structure of Empirical Knowledge*. Cambridge, MA: Harvard University Press.

Goldman, A. (1979) What is justified belief? In G. S. Pappas (ed.), *Justification and Knowledge*. Dordrecht: D. Reidel.

Klein, P. (1971) A proposed definition of propositional knowledge. *Journal of Philosophy*, 67, 471–82.

Klein, P. (1981) *Certainty: A Refutation of Scepticism*. Minneapolis: University of Minnesota Press.

Klein, P. (1993) When infinite regresses are *not* vicious. *Philosophy and Phenomenological Research*, 63, 718–29.

Klein, P. (1999) Human knowledge and the infinite regress of reasons. *Philosophical Perspectives*, 13, 297–332.

Klein, P. (2003) Knowledge is true, non-defeated justified belief. In S. Luper (ed.), *Essential Knowledge*. Harlow: Longman.

Klein, P. (2004) What *is* wrong with foundationalism is that it cannot solve the epistemic regress problem. *Philosophy and Phenomenological Research*, 68, 166–71.

Klein, P. (forthcoming) Skepticism: ascent and assent. In J. Greco (ed.), *Philosophers and Their Critics*. Oxford: Blackwell.

Plantinga, A. (1993) *Warrant: The Current Debate*. New York: Oxford University Press.

Post, J. (1980) Infinite regresses of justification and of explanation. *Philosophical Studies*, 38, 31–52.

Post, J. (1987) *The Faces of Existence*. Ithaca, NY: Cornell University Press.

Sosa, E. (1980) The raft and the pyramid. *Midwest Studies in Philosophy*, 5, 3–25.

Sosa, E. (1994) Philosophical skepticism and epistemic circularity. *Proceedings of the Aristotelian Society*, 68, 263–90.

Sosa, E. (1997) Reflective knowledge in the best circles. *Journal of Philosophy*, 94, 410–30.

van Cleve, J. (1992) Semantic supervenience and referential indeterminacy. *Journal of Philosophy*, 89, 344–61.

Williams, J. (1981) Justified belief and the infinite regress argument. *American Philosophical Quarterly*, 18, 85–8.

Infinitism Is not the Solution to the Regress Problem

Carl Ginet

Many of our beliefs are justified beliefs: they are such that epistemic rationality would not forbid our holding them. And often what justifies a belief is the fact that the believer has (or has "available": more on this later) other justified beliefs from which the belief in question can be properly inferred. That is to say, the justification of many a justified belief is by inference from one or more other beliefs: it is *inferential justification*. For example, from my belief (based on observation) that our car is not in the driveway and my belief that my wife is the only one besides me who has a key to our car, I infer that my wife is not at home.

The premise beliefs must, of course, themselves be justified, if belief in what is inferred from them is to be thereby justified; and their justifications may be by inference from still other beliefs; and the justifications of those further beliefs may be inferential; and so on. Can this go on without end? If not, how can it end? Those questions are the regress problem.

I think that it cannot go on without end, that any ramifying structure of inferential justifications must end in justifications that are not inferential. Not so long ago I thought this truth so obvious as to need no argument. But Peter Klein has made me realize that it is not *that* obvious. (Besides his contribution to the present debate, see especially Klein, 1999. My page references will be to this latter paper.)

Klein holds that inferential justifications not only can ramify without end but *must* do so for any belief that is truly justified. He holds that every justification must be inferential: no other kind of justification is possible. (He also holds, and with this we must all agree, that no inferential justification can be circular, can be such that a belief is inferred ultimately from itself.) This is Klein's *infinitism*.

I on the other hand insist that inferential justification cannot ramify without end (or, rather, beginning), and that if justification is possible then non-inferential justification must be possible. Klein calls this view *foundationalism*. It might also be called *finitism*.

Examples of Non-inferential Justification

One reason I think that non-inferential justification is possible is that I think we can give clear examples of it. Let me give two, one *a priori* and one *a posteriori*.

A priori

Consider the following sentence:

A: Anything that lasts exactly one hour lasts exactly sixty minutes.

Someone who does not accept that what sentence A says is true – who doubts or denies that, or is uncertain whether, what it says is true – must be counted as one who does not understand what sentence A says (provided he has no specific reason to suspect that what it says, together with other equally evident-seeming propositions, entails a contradiction; this proviso is a complication I will hereafter usually omit to mention, as it is, for sentence A, always satisfied in actual cases).

Someone who does understand what sentence A says, and therefore believes it, is justified in believing it. The fact which constitutes his being justified in believing it is simply the fact that he understands what the sentence says. That he understands what it says entails that he believes what it says. So it cannot be that epistemic rationality requires that he ought not to believe it *even though* he understands it. Nor, surely, can it require that he ought not to understand what it says. If, as far as epistemic rationality is concerned, he cannot be criticized for understanding it, then he cannot be criticized for what his understanding it requires, his believing it. Therefore, given that he understands what it says, he is justified in believing it.

The fact that he understands it *is* his justification for believing it, because that fact entails his believing it. This sort of justification does not appear to involve any sort of inferential justification: it does not entail any (available) belief in any premise such that what the sentence says is properly inferable from that premise. Therefore, one who understands, hence believes, what sentence A says is one who has a non-inferentially justified belief.

This belief and a similarly non-inferentially justified belief that

> B: Anything that lasts sixty minutes lasts longer than anything that lasts just fifty-five minutes.

might provide the ultimate premises for an inferential justification for believing (what A and B obviously entail) that

> C: Anything that lasts one hour lasts longer than anything that lasts just fifty-five minutes.

In such a case the subject's justification for believing C originates in her understanding, hence believing, A and B: the regress ends there.

A posteriori

Suppose that my visual system is working properly and I see a blue smear on a white surface in good light a few feet in front of me. Suppose further that I believe that I see a blue smear on a white surface in good light a few feet in front of me and I am not aware of any reason to think that in this instance things may not be what they seem, to think that my visual system may not be working properly or that external circumstances may be conspiring to produce a visual illusion. Then I am justified in that belief.

What justifies my belief? The following two facts are sufficient: (1) my visual experience is as if (my visual experience represents that) I see a blue smear on a white surface in good light a few feet in front of me and (2) I am not aware of any reason to think that in this instance things may not be what they visually seem to me to be. Given those facts, there is no basis for faulting me for holding the belief. No good reason could be given for saying that, despite those facts, I ought not, I am unreasonable, to believe that I see a blue smear on a white surface.

If these facts do constitute a justification for that belief, that justification is obviously not inferential. It involves no further beliefs at all. Fact (1) is just the fact that I have a certain specific sort of visual experience, a fact which does not include or entail any particular belief on my part. My having this experience does not in itself include my believing that I have it (whether or not it is impossible for me to fail to believe that I have it if I do), nor does the visual experience include (or entail) my believing that what the experience represents as being there before me actually is there before me, that there is a blue smear on a white surface in good light a few feet in front of me. Fact (2) is completely negative. It is just the *absence* of any (available) belief that would be reason for me to suspect that, in this instance, things may not be what they visually seem to be; and this absence does not entail the *presence* of any particular (available) beliefs at all.

This non-inferentially justified belief, that I see a blue smear on a white surface, might be an ultimate premise of an (no doubt complex and extended, but finite) inferential justification for believing that my grandson was recently in the room with blue fingerpaint on his hands. Among the other ultimate premises in this justification would be memory beliefs non-inferentially justified in parallel fashion, by a combination of my seeming to remember that I came to know the propositions believed and my lacking any reason to think that in this instance my memory is not to be trusted.

Objections to These Examples

One objection is suggested in Klein's comments on his Principle of Avoiding Arbitrariness – which is the principle that "For all x, if a person, S, has a justification for x, then there is some reason, r_1, available to S for x; and there is some reason, r_2, available to S for r_1; etc." Klein (1999, p. 299) says:

> Note that there are two features of this principle. The first is that it is reasons (as opposed to something else like appropriate causal conditions responsible for a belief) that are required whenever there is a justification for a belief. The second is that the chain of reasons cannot end with an arbitrary reason – one for which there is no further reason. [Both features] are needed to capture the well-founded intuition that *arbitrary beliefs*, beliefs for which no reason is available, should be avoided.

These remarks suggest that the facts cited in my alleged non-inferential justifications do not justify the beliefs in question because they do not entail that the believer has a *reason* for the belief. The argument seems to be this:

1 One's belief is unjustified if one lacks a good reason for it.
2 Having a good reason for a belief *just means* having another belief from which the belief in question can be properly inferred, i.e. having an inferential justification for it.
∴ To have a justification for a belief is to have an inferential justification for it.

It must be granted (it is a tautology) that one's belief is unjustified if one lacks a reason for it in the sense of *some sort of justification* for it. But it should not be granted, and it does not follow, that one's belief is unjustified if one lacks a reason for it in the sense of an *inferential justification* for it. If premises 1 and 2 seem intuitively acceptable to us when we read them, this can only be because we shift from one sense of "having a reason" to the other in going from one premise to the other.

I find it quite intelligible to say that my *reason* for believing that I saw a blue smear on a white surface was the fact that my visual experience was as if that were so, together with the fact that I was aware of no reason to think that in this instance things were not as they visually seemed to be. Hence I am inclined to allow that "having a reason" can be broadly used to cover non-inferential justifications and, sticking with that broad sense throughout the argument above, to accept premise 1 and reject premise 2. But the crucial point is that, if premise 2 is urged on the basis of the ordinary use of "having a reason," then premise 1 cannot be taken as clear on the basis of ordinary usage; it needs to be argued that being justified in a belief requires having a reason in the (supposedly ordinary) sense of having an inferential justification.

Specifically, it needs to be shown why any putative example of non-inferential justification (such as the ones I have given) cannot really be such. Klein considers the suggestion that a belief might be justified by some property P it has that does not entail the believer's having an inferential justification for it and responds as follows:

> Pick your favorite account of the property, P. . . . Why is having P truth-conducive? Now, either there is an answer available to that question or there isn't. . . . If there is an answer, then the regress continues – at least one more step. . . . If there isn't an answer, the [belief] . . . is arbitrary. (Klein, 1999, p. 303)

> . . . arguing that such beliefs are likely to be true because they possess a certain property, P, will not avoid the problem faced by foundationalism. Either [this] . . . justification provides a reason for thinking the [believed] . . . proposition is true (and hence the regress does not end) or it does not (hence, accepting the base proposition is arbitrary). (Klein, 1999, p. 304)

These remarks suggest the following counter to my claim that the facts cited in each of my examples do provide non-inferential justification for the belief in question: those facts are relevant to justifying the belief only if the believer has (available), as a reason for the belief, a further belief that when such facts obtain the belief is likely to be true; they cannot all by themselves justify the belief but can provide only a part of an inferential justification for it.

Thus, with respect to my putative example of a non-inferential *a priori* justification, Klein would seem to want to say the following: you propose that the belief in question (that anything that lasts exactly one hour lasts exactly sixty minutes) is justified by its having the property of being such that (a) the subject understands the proposition believed and (b) that proposition is such that believing it is a requisite of understanding it; but the subject is not justified in that belief unless it is also the case that he has (available), as inferential support for it, the further belief that the belief's having that property makes it likely to be true. And with respect to my putative example of a non-inferential *a posteriori* justification, he would seem to want to say: you propose that the belief in question (that I see a blue smear on a white surface in good light a few feet in front of me) is justified by its having the property of being accompanied by its visually seeming to me as if I see a blue smear on a white surface in good light a few feet in front of me and by my lacking awareness of any reason to think that in this instance things may not be what they visually seem to be; but you are not justified in that belief unless it is also true that you have (available), as inferential support for it, the further belief that the belief's having that property makes it likely to be true.

I will discuss just this second response, concerning my claim about the *a posteriori* justification of the perceptual belief (and leave it as an exercise for the reader to infer what I would say about the first response, to my claim concerning the *a priori* justification). We should note first that plenty of people who are justified in such a perceptual belief when they satisfy the sort of condition I specified do not in fact have any such further belief (that the perceptual belief's being accompanied by the perceptual experience, etc., makes it likely to be true) – perhaps because they have never entertained any such proposition, perhaps they even lack the concepts (e.g. of subjective visual experience or of probability) needed to entertain it.

In response to this Klein will point out that he is not requiring the subject actually to have the further belief but only that it be *available* to him, in the sense that, if the subject were to have the concepts needed to entertain the proposition in question and were to entertain it, he would accept it. (That Klein is prepared in this way to count as available to a subject a belief in a proposition that the subject does not yet possess the concepts to entertain is clear from his response (1999, pp. 308–9) to the challenge "to show that there can be an infinite number of reasons given a finite vocabulary each of which can be entertained by a human being.")

Moreover, Klein might argue, this potential further belief is a *reason* for the perceptual belief in these circumstances because it would be unreasonable of the subject in these circumstances not to accept this further proposition (were he to entertain it) while continuing to hold the perceptual belief; and insofar as the believer acquires his perceptual belief because of the visual experience, he *acts as if* he had the further belief (that the perceptual belief's being accompanied by the perceptual experience, etc., makes it likely to be true), he acts as one would who was motivated by such a further belief.

Perhaps so, I say, but only if he actually is motivated by this potential further belief can it be counted among his reasons for acquiring the perceptual belief. That a potential belief is *available* in Klein's sense makes it perhaps a potential reason but it is not enough to make it among the believer's actual reasons. And only if it is among his actual reasons is it part of his actual justification. It is true that the subject must, if his perceptual belief is justified in these circumstances, have available (in Klein's weak sense) this other belief. But this is only because his just having that perceptual belief in these circumstances entails that he has available (in Klein's sense) that other belief; and from this it does not follow that its availability is any part of his actual justification. And the issue we are debating, I take it, is whether the *actual* justification for some beliefs can be non-inferential.

It is a trivial and uninteresting truth that, for any belief, the believer has a *potential* inferential justification. Consider a young child who has acquired enough understanding of elementary arithmetic to believe that $2 + 3 = 5$.

The proposition that

(*) The smallest even prime added to the cube root of 27 equals the square root of 25.

is such that, were the child to understand and entertain it, it would be unreasonable of him not to accept it while continuing to believe that $2 + 3 = 5$; so that in believing that $2 + 3 = 5$ he acts as would one who believed the proposition (*). Yet it is clear that the child's potential belief in (*) is not among his reasons for believing that $2 + 3 = 5$ and not part of the story as to why his so believing is justified.

For any proposition P that any subject believes, there is another proposition such that, were he to entertain it, it would be unreasonable of him not to accept it while continuing to believe P (and thus he acts as would one who believed this further proposition), namely, a proposition of the form "$P \vee (Q \wedge \neg Q)$" (where Q is any other proposition). It is clear that the subject's potential belief in this proposition is not among his reasons for believing P and not part of the story as to why he is justified in this belief (if he is).

If I tell you that in his present circumstances S would accept the following proposition were he to entertain it:

(L) It is likely to be true that one sees a blue smear on a white surface when one's visual experience is as if one were seeing a blue smear on a white surface.

I indirectly indicate to you what justifies S in believing that he sees a blue smear on a white surface – namely, the fact that his visual experience is as if he were seeing a blue smear on a white surface (and he is unaware of any reason to think that in this instance things are not what they visually seem): you can infer that he is disposed to believe (L) because his visual experience is of that sort. But of course reporting that fact about his potential belief in order to indirectly indicate his justification is not the same as reporting that that fact *is* (part of) his justification.

The notion of an available reason for a belief might be strengthened in such a way as to make it plausible that, if the belief that (L) is, in that stronger way, available to S as a reason for believing that he sees a blue smear, then it is a reason of his for so believing. An additional requirement that might do the trick is this: (L) is available to S as a reason for so believing only if S is disposed, upon entertaining and accepting (L), to believe that the fact that (L) was among his reasons for so believing. It would then, perhaps, be right to say that, if the belief that (L) is available to S as a reason in that stronger sense, then it is part of S's actual justification for believing that he sees a blue smear on a white surface that the belief that (L) is available to him. His *tacit* belief that (L), we might say, was a tacit reason of his for believing that he sees a blue smear on a white surface.

But of course it does not follow from this concession that the facts I cited earlier, of his having a certain sort of visual experience and lacking any reason to think that in this instance things are not what they seem, do not all by themselves provide S with a non-inferential justification. It does not follow, and I see no reason to concede, that if those facts obtained but the belief that (L) was *not* available to S in that stronger sense – surely a possible case – then S would not be justified in believing that he sees a blue smear on a white surface. We would still have no argument that a belief cannot be justified unless the believer has available (in the stronger sense) an inferential justification for it.

Two Problems for Infinitism

First problem

Let us suppose that the notion of availability is strengthened in some such way as I have suggested, so as to make it plausible that a belief B2 that is available as a reason for a belief B1 is, not merely a potential reason, but among the believer's actual reasons for B1. Given that stronger (less easily satisfied) notion of availability, infinitism – the doctrine that a belief is justified only if the believer has available an inferential justification for it – would face the following question.

What reason can be given for thinking that any of our beliefs is such that the believer *has available in that stronger sense* an infinitely ramifying structure of inferential justifications, for thinking that infinitism has not laid on justification of belief a requirement that is never (or seldom) actually met? With regard to many people who acquire a basic perceptual belief when they have appropriate perceptual experience, it may be plausible to suppose that, if they entertained the general proposition to the effect that when one has such experience the perceptual belief is likely to be true, they would not only believe it but also take this tacit general belief to be part of their reason for their perceptual belief. But is it equally plausible to suppose that they have available in that same strong sense still another belief which is their tacit reason for holding that tacit general belief? What would it be? And what would be their tacit reason for *that* tacit belief?

To argue that it is *in principle possible* for a human being to have available (in the stronger sense) an infinite number of beliefs would not be enough. To make it plausible that there actually occur justifications having the endlessly ramifying structure that infinitism says all justifications must have, the infinitist must provide representative examples of particular such structures possessed by cognitively normal human subjects – examples about which it would be credible that cases essentially like them actually occur. This would be none too easy to do.

It would, of course, be out of the question to specify individually all of the links in an endless chain. One can specify an infinite series only by providing a general way of (an algorithm for) finding a new member of the series no matter how (finitely) far the series has already been extended. Such an algorithm would have to tell us, with respect to a sort of belief we are sure is well justified – e.g. my belief as I look out the window at my driveway that there is a car there – how to construct an endless inferentially linked chain of specific premise beliefs, which is such that it is plausible to think that, in the ordinary sort of circumstance in which (as we think) such a belief is justified, that infinite series of beliefs is available (in the stronger sense) to the holder of the belief. Specifying such an algorithm would be a formidable task. In fact, I am at a loss to see how it could be done.

Second problem

A more important, deeper problem for infinitism is this: Inference cannot *originate* justification, it can only *transfer* it from premises to conclusion. And so it cannot be that, if there actually occurs justification, it is all inferential.

Inferential justification is analogous to instrumental value in this respect. Things have value as means to other things only if ultimately some things have value in themselves and not just as means to other things. The relation *x-is-a-means-to-y* can only transfer to *x* whatever value *y* has; it cannot *create* any value. But there can be no value to be transferred unless ultimately something else, something other than the means–end relation, does create value. Analogously, the relation *p-can-be-properly-inferred-from-q* can only transfer to p whatever justification q has; it cannot create any justification. But there can be no justification to be transferred unless ultimately something else, something other than the inferential relation, does create justification.

Jonathan Dancy (1985, p. 55) puts the point this way:

> Justification by inference is conditional justification only; [when A is inferred from B and C] A's justification is conditional upon the justification of B and C. But if all justification is conditional in this sense, then nothing can be shown to be actually non-conditionally justified.

Klein (1999, p. 313) replies to Dancy's remarks as follows: "The answer is simply that although every proposition is only provisionally justified, that is good enough if one does not insist that reasoning settle matters once and for all." But this reply misses the point. From the denial that reason (or justification) can ever settle matters once and for all it follows only that every justification is provisional in the sense of *defeasible* – where a justification is defeasible if it is compatible with the facts F1 constituting the justification that there be other facts F2 that defeat the justification, i.e. F2 and F1 combined would *not* justify what F1 alone does justify, so that facts F1 justify only provided that, only so long as, no defeating facts F2 turn up. That a justification is provisional in this sense does not entail that it is inferential. By conditional justification Dancy means not provisional, but inferential justification, where the fact that the premise beliefs are justified and have the inferential relation to the conclusion explains why the conclusion belief is justified. And the point of the objection is that an endless chain of inferential justifications can never ultimately explain why any link in the chain is justified.

Consider another analogy, between acceptable inference and justification on the one hand and deductively valid inference and truth on the other. Deductively valid inference preserves, but does not create, truth. If a set of premises are true then the property of truth will be "transferred" to any conclusion validly deducible from them. But, given a chain of propositions that are linked by the deductive relation, there is nothing in that relation itself that contributes to making any of those propositions true, no matter how extended the chain might be.

Analogously, acceptable inference preserves justification: if one has justification for believing the premises then one has justification for believing anything one recognizes as acceptably inferable from them. But, given a chain of beliefs linked by acceptable inference, there is nothing in the inferential relation itself that contributes to making any of those beliefs justified, nothing that explains why any of them is justified; and this is so no matter how extended the chain might be.

References

Dancy, J. (1985) *Introduction to Contemporary Epistemology*. Oxford: Blackwell.
Klein, P. (1999) Human knowledge and the infinite regress of reasons. In J. E. Tomberlin (ed.), *Philosophical Perspectives, 13 (Epistemology)*. Oxford: Blackwell.

Reply to Ginet

Peter Klein

Let me begin by thanking Carl Ginet. He has helped me to see more clearly where infinitism and finitism can agree, and where and why they diverge.

First, I will list the areas where finitists and infinitists can agree. Second, I will list an area where I believe agreement can be reached. Third, I will discuss some remaining areas of disagreement and attempt to defend infinitism. Finally, I will conclude with a brief remark about the basic difference between the two views.

Areas of Agreement between the Infinitist and the Finitist

A1 A belief is justified for S when epistemic rationality "would not forbid . . . holding" it (Ginet, p. 140).[1]

A2 There are some beliefs that require having reasons in order to be *actually justified* for S. Those reasons must be available to S, and at least some of the those reasons must "motivate" the belief (Ginet, p. 145).

A3 The process of giving reasons for a belief comes to an end in actual circumstances, and what's more, the cannons of epistemic rationality do not require that further reasons motivate the belief in order for it to be at least partially actually justified.

A4 In a slightly extended use of "reason" such things as perceptual states, memories, or understanding the meaning of an expression are reasons that can make a belief at least partially justified. In the case discussed by Ginet, "no good reason could be given for saying that . . . I am unreasonable to believe that I see a blue smear on a white surface" (Ginet, p. 142).

An Area of Potential Agreement

Terms like "reasonable" or "justified" are comparative. It might be more reasonable for S* to believe that p than it is for S to believe that p. Thus, in granting (in A4) that S is not unreasonable in believing p, it does not follow that S* could not be more reasonable in believing that p. For example, if S has reasons for believing that p and S* has those reasons plus some additional ones, then S* is more reasonable in believing that p than S is in believing that p.

Areas of Disagreement

Primary areas of disagreement concern the ability of finitism to solve the regress problem and the manner in which warrant originates and is transferred. The finitist holds that some belief, say the belief that there is a blue smear on a white surface, is autonomously warranted for me in virtue of (1) the visual experience of it being as if there is a blue smear on a white surface in good light a few feet in front of me and (2) the absence of any reason for believing that the visual experience is not veridical. The warrant that arises in such a fashion is transmitted to other beliefs by inference.

An infinitist should point out that even if warrant or justification could arise in that fashion and subsequently could be transferred by inference, such an account of warrant will not provide a basis for addressing the regress problem, i.e. to correctly describe how reasoning can increase the warrant for a proposition, say p. Why is p held to be true? A reason, say b, is provided. Simplifying matters, suppose b were autonomously warranted. The finitist claims that no further reason for b is required in order for S to be epistemically rational in holding p. The infinitist should respond in two ways:

(i) The infinitist is *not* denying that b is actually justified to some degree or that p is justified by b to some degree. The infinitist *is* claiming that S would be better justified in believing p on the basis of believing b, if S also had a further reason for holding b. Such a reason is that b-type propositions are likely to be true in virtue of, say, general truths about the causal history of beliefs with b-type contents.

(ii) If it is agreed that S is better off epistemically when S has a reason for believing that b-type propositions are likely to be true, then the infinitist will point out that the regress of warrant-producing reasons does not stop at b. Infinitism can explain how the warrant of b-type propositions, and hence p-type propositions, can be increased in ways that cannot be explained by the finitist. Further, were the finitist to concede that warrant can be augmented for "basic" propositions by further reasoning, then on what basis can the finitist deny that reasoning can produce warrant in the first place?

The finitist will probably demur here for two reasons. First, it will be claimed that for *any* proposition, p, there will always be another proposition such that if S failed to believe it and S* did believe it, S* would be better warranted than S in believing that p (Ginet, pp. 145–6). Thus, it is too easy to increase the warrant of a belief. Second, there comes a point in our reasoning where we cannot imagine what the next reason in the chain of beliefs could be (Ginet, p. 147).

There is some tension between these two claims for if one can give a general recipe for constructing a further reason in every case, then it is easily imaginable how the chain could continue. Nevertheless, the infinitist should reject both claims.

The first claim rests on providing a general recipe for constructing a further reason for any proposition, say p. I have discussed similar objections elsewhere and pointed out that it is not sufficient that there be such a proposition that can serve as a reason for p; it must also be "available" to S (see Klein, 1999, pp. 311–12). But Ginet's objection is not so easily handled. He asks us to consider any proposition, p, and correctly points out that there will be another proposition available (in the sense that it is appropriately hooked up with S's beliefs) that is such that if S were not to believe it, S would not be as well justified as S* would be were S* to believe it. That proposition is $[p \vee (q \ \& \ \sim q)]$. But it should be recalled that according to infinitism there are at least two necessary conditions of justification: (i) the Principle of Avoiding Arbitrariness (PAA), which generates an infinite series of propositions; and (ii) the Principle of Avoiding Circularity (PAC), which blocks circular reasoning. PAC was not the primary concern of Ginet's response, because he grants that coherentism is not the correct view of warrant. Nevertheless, it is that second principle which is of use here. PAC is: for all propositions, x, if x is warranted for a person, S, at t, then for all y, if y is in the reason-ancestry of x for S at t, then x is not in the reason-ancestry of y for S at t. Now, since $[p \vee (q \ \& \ \sim q)]$ is equivalent to p, a chain which included the former as an ancestor of the latter would violate PAC. Hence, S is not better justified in believing p were S also to believe that $[p \vee (q \ \& \ \sim q)]$; but were S not to believe $[p \vee (q \ \& \ \sim q)]$, then S would not be as well justified in believing that p. In other words, not believing an equivalent proposition can lower the degree of justification, but believing it cannot increase the justification.

Now to the second claim. Ginet suggests that there is a point in the reason giving process such that no further reasons could be given.

> With regard to many people who acquire a basic perceptual belief when they have appropriate perceptual experience, it may be plausible to suppose that, if they entertained the general proposition to the effect that when one has such experience the perceptual belief is likely to be true, they would not only believe it but also take this tacit general belief to be part of their reason for their perceptual belief. But is it equally plausible to suppose that they have available in that same strong sense still another belief which is their tacit reason for holding that tacit general belief? What would it be? And what would be their tacit reason for *that* tacit reason? (Ginet, p. 147)

Recall the *types* of tacit reasons that have been adduced for holding the tacit general belief. Descartes was faced with just this problem in the *Meditations*, namely: Do we have any reasons for thinking that our perceptual equipment typically yields the truth? We know his type of answer: there are *a priori* reasons available that show that the equipment is reliable. The currently more fashionable type of answer is based upon *a posteriori* reasoning involving mechanisms posited by evolutionary biology. Thus, I suggest it is easy to imagine how the reasoning could continue because we have good examples of such reasoning. Will reasoning in support of *that* tacit reason ultimately beg the question? I don't believe it need do so and have argued for that elsewhere (see Klein, forthcoming).

Basic Difference: Reasoning Can Originate Warrant

For Ginet, and many epistemologists, the primary reason for rejecting infinitism is that it is committed to the view that all warrant originates by inference (see Klein, 1999, pp. 310–11).

> A more important, deeper problem for infinitism is this: inference cannot originate justification, it can only transfer it from premises to conclusion. And so it cannot be that, if there actually occurs justification, it is all inferential. (Ginet, p. 148)

This objection would be conclusive if inferential justification were correctly construed (as Ginet suggests) as analogous to instrumental value. Just as there must be non-instrumentally valued objects, there must be non-inferentially justified beliefs.

But infinitism rejects (or ought to reject) this analogy.[2] Infinitism, like the plausible versions of coherentism, depicts justification as emerging when the set of propositions that are appropriately adduced as reasons expands. Of course, were the foundationalist to insist on thinking of warrant as originating in some propositions and then being transferred by inference to other propositions, he or she would be begging the question at hand. For it is that very concept of warrant that infinitism is challenging.[3]

Notes

1 All references to Ginet refer to his "Infinitism Is not the Solution to the Regress Problem," this volume.
2 Ginet rightly criticizes my response to Dancy's objection on this point. I did not see clearly at that stage in the development of infinitism that it must reject the analogy. I have tried to correct that in Klein (forthcoming).
3 I wish to thank Anne Ashbaugh, Alvin Goldman, and Ernest Sosa for their discussions about the issues in this essay.

References

Klein, P. (1999) Human knowledge and the infinite regress of reasons. *Philosophical Perspectives*, 13, 297–332.
Klein, P. (forthcoming) Skepticism: ascent and assent. In J. Greco (ed.), *Philosophers and Their Critics*. Oxford: Blackwell.

Reply to Klein

Carl Ginet

1 Fred and Doris

In Klein's dialogue between Fred and Doris, foundationalist Fred doesn't do as well as I think he should. Let me revisit the scene and try to give him some help.

Let the proposition that Fred has asserted be

Little Benny has been in the living room with blue paint on his hands.

Doris asks Fred why he thinks this is so and Fred answers:

There's a blue smear on the wall.

And Doris asks Fred why he thinks that is so and Fred replies by asserting, among other things (such as that he has just come into the living room), the following:

(P) I see a blue smear on a white surface right in front of me.

If Doris has the temerity to ask Fred why he thinks *that* is so, Fred could with some justice reply, "What do you mean? Didn't you hear me? I said I *see* it right in front of me." But Fred is a parent, as well as an epistemologist, and has learned to be patient with insatiable askers of "Why?" So he instead says, "I have no reason for thinking that I see a blue smear on a white surface, in the sense of a premise from which I infer it, but it is eminently reasonable of me, as it would be of anyone, to think that I see such a thing when, as is the case, I am prompted to do so by the fact that

(C) My visual experience is as if I see such a thing and I am aware of no reason to think that my visual experience might in this case be misleading me.

Doris now asks Fred whether, if he is indeed being reasonable in believing P in circumstance C, isn't he also obliged to believe both of the following two propositions (should he entertain them)?

(R1) When C obtains, it is likely to be true that I see a blue smear on a white surface.
(R2) C does obtain.

And isn't it only because these beliefs are available to him as (good) reasons for believing P that he is justified in believing P?

I would advise Fred to reply as follows. I do believe R1 and R2 (now that I consider them) and I see that their truth provides reason to believe P. And it would be unreasonable of me not to do this, while still believing P and thinking my doing so to be justified. An equally good reason for believing P would be constituted by R2 together with

> (R1*) When C obtains, it is reasonable for me to believe that I see a blue smear on a white surface.

I am not persuaded, however, that the availability of either of these reasons for believing P constitutes my actual reason for believing P. But let that pass. Let us suppose, for the sake of this discussion, that the availability of justified belief in, say, R1* and R2 was my reason for believing P and hence constituted (at least part of) my justification for believing it.

Doris now asks Fred whether, if he is justified in believing R1* and R2, he must not have available further beliefs as reasons for those beliefs. If he were to listen to me, Fred would respond as follows.

No, I need no premise from which to infer R1*. This is because R1* is a basic *a priori* principle constitutive of the concept of justification for belief in a perceptual proposition like P: it is a principle such that understanding it requires accepting it.

Nor do I need a premise from which to infer R2. This is because the following is a basic *a priori* principle constitutive of the concept of justification for a conscious-state proposition like R2:

> (R3) When C obtains and one is prompted by that fact to believe that C obtains, then that belief is justified.

It follows from this principle that, given that my belief that C obtains is prompted by the fact that C obtains, I am justified in that belief, whether or not I have available further beliefs that support it. It is clear that R3 could not serve as a premise in an inference justifying belief in R2 (that C obtains), because the other premise would have to be R2! R3 is not part of an inferential justification I have for believing that C obtains, but rather the basic principle of justification that entails that I am non-inferentially justified in believing that C obtains by the fact that my belief is prompted by C's obtaining.

So the lesson I draw from my version of the dialogue is that inferential justification of perceptual beliefs need not regress further than non-inferentially justified belief (or available belief) in conscious-state propositions like R2 and self-evident principles of justification like R1*.

2 Inferentialism Drives Out Infinitism?

In the last part of Klein's essay things take a startling turn. On p. 137 Klein says:

> The infinitist holds that finding a reason for the questioned proposition, and then another for that reason, etc. places it at the beginning of a series of propositions each of which gains warrant and rational credibility by being part of the series. Warrant increases not because we are getting closer to a basic proposition but rather because we are getting

further from the questioned proposition. . . . Warrant, and with it rational credibility, increases as the series lengthens.

And in his last paragraph, in response to Audi's remark that even if there were an infinite series of propositions each of which is available, it is not "clear how infinite epistemic chains could account for any of our knowledge," Klein says:

Now, if knowledge required actually completing the series, knowledge would not be possible. But why suppose that knowledge requires the highest possible degree of warrant or absolutely credible belief? As the series lengthens, warrant and credibility increase. Nothing prevents it increasing to the degree required for knowledge.

In my essay I said that the (to my mind) most severe difficulty with Klein's infinitism is that it is committed to the thesis that inference alone can create justification. Here Klein seems to embrace this commitment wholeheartedly, holding that the longer the chain of inferential justification for a given belief the greater the justification created, and that, if the chain is long enough (but still finite), the justification can "increase to the degree required for knowledge." This seems to give us the result that knowledge does not require infinitely long chains of inferential justification after all: infinitism gives way to inferentialism. Worse yet, given Klein's thesis that inferential justification is the only sort of justification there can be, we seem to get the result that one could start with a belief (or set of beliefs) that is totally unjustified, because it lacks any inferential justification, and by spinning out a long enough chain of inference from it reach a belief that has the degree of justification required for knowledge.

These results are so counterintuitive that I hesitate to attribute them to Klein. But how else are we to interpret the quoted remarks?

Can Beliefs Be Justified through Coherence Alone?

Non-foundationalist Epistemology: Holism, Coherence, and Tenability

Catherine Z. Elgin

Much epistemology assumes that cognitive success consists in knowledge, where knowledge is justified or reliable true belief. On this conception, since propositions are the contents of beliefs and the bearers of truth values, they are what is known. If this is right, the sort of justification of interest to epistemology seems to be the justification of individual propositions. A linear model of justification is almost inevitable. To justify a given proposition is either to infer it from already justified propositions or to show how belief in it emerges from reliable belief forming mechanisms. S is justified in believing p on the basis of q, and q on the basis of r, and so on. Holists contend that this picture is misleading. They maintain that epistemic acceptability is, in the first instance, acceptability of a fairly comprehensive system of thought, comprised of mutually supportive commitments. The priority in question is epistemological, not historical. There is no contention that people come to believe a theory before coming to believe the various claims that comprise it. The point is that regardless of the order in which they are acquired, claims are justified only when they coalesce to constitute a tenable system of thought. The acceptability of individual sentences, as well as methods and standards, is derivative, stemming from their role in a tenable system.

The challenge for such an epistemology is to explain how systematic interconnections give rise to justification, how the fact that deliverances dovetail affords reason to believe they are true. Some philosophers hold that the coherence of a sufficiently comprehensive constellation of claims makes them true (Blanshard, 1939; Rescher, 1973). This strikes me as implausible, but I will not argue against it here. The position I want to investigate is that coherence is the source of epistemic justification, not the ground of truth. But if truth is independent of what we believe, why should mutual accord among our beliefs be indicative of truth? What is the connection? To avoid begging questions, it is perhaps better to begin by focusing not on the justification of beliefs, but on the justification of deliverances, these being representations that present themselves as candidates for belief. If we are concerned with justification, we should not limit ourselves to assessing the status of what we actually believe, but ask which of the things that could in given circumstances be believed should in those circumstances be believed. Deliverances, as I use the term, include perceptual inputs, fixed or transient beliefs, passing thoughts, and so forth.

Perhaps things will become clearer if we consider a case. Yesterday Meg's Latin book was stolen from her locker. Three students may have witnessed the theft. None of them is very reliable. Anne is given to proving theorems in her head, and tends to be oblivious to her surroundings when preoccupied with a tricky proof. To compensate for her habitual distractedness, she draws plausible inferences about mundane events, and often does not notice whether her opinion is due to observation or to such an inference. Ben frequently forgets to wear his glasses. Like Anne, he draws plausible inferences about events around him, and tends not to remember having done so. Chauncy is simply a liar. Presumably he knows when he is speaking sincerely, but given the fluency and frequency of his lies, nothing he says is trustworthy. Not surprisingly, the social circles of the three students do not intersect; none would deign to speak to the others. When questioned about the theft, Anne and Ben report what they think they saw, but confess that they are not sure what they actually witnessed and what they inferred. Chauncy insists that his report is accurate, but in view of his record, his claim is suspect.

Individually, none of the reports would count for much. Had only one of the witnesses been present, the most we could reasonably conclude would be that the thief might fit the description. But all three reports agree, and agree in alleging that the thief had an unusual appearance: he had spiked green hair. This makes a difference. Even though individually each report is dubious, and the probability of a green haired textbook thief is low, the fact that the three reports provide the same antecedently improbable description inclines us to believe it. Their accord evidently enhances the epistemic standing of the individual reports (Lewis, 1946, p. 346). We seem to have more reason to believe each of them in light of the others than we have to believe them separately. The question is: why? How can multiple statements, none of which is tenable, conjoin to yield a tenable conclusion? How can their relation to other less than tenable claims enhance their tenability?

Given the unreliability of the witnesses, we might expect them to be wrong about the thief. But we would not expect them to all be wrong in the same way. The fact that they agree needs an explanation. If they were in cahoots, the explanation would be straightforward: they conspired to tell the same tale. But not being on speaking terms, they are probably not co-conspirators. If the description they provided fit a relevant stereotype, then a penchant for plausibility could explain their accord. But green spiked hair is far from any stereotype one might harbor for a textbook thief. So despite Anne's and Ben's propensity to draw inferences based on plausibility, their descriptions of the thief do not seem to result from such an inference. Evidently the best explanation of the agreement is that the reports are true.

It is not just our ability to exclude obvious alternatives that leads us to credit the allegation. A variety of collateral considerations support it. Some bear directly on the content of the claim. Dan dimly recalls seeing an odd looking stranger lurking in the hallway. The custodian thinks he saw a container of hair dye in the trash. Although the tentativeness of these reports makes them less than wholly credible, they are suggestive enough to buttress the eyewitness testimony. Other collateral considerations concern the witnesses and their circumstances. Book thefts are observable events, so there is nothing inherently dubious about a claim to have seen someone steal a book. The light and the sight lines were such that the witnesses could have seen what they report. The witnesses are adept at recognizing furtive adolescent behavior. None was subject to psychological experiments with implanted memories. None was on drugs. And so on. Separately, these factors count for little. Either their credibility is low or their bearing is slight. But they weave together to make a solid case. This suggests that the epistemic tenability of the several reports and the conclusion they sanction derives from their mutual supportiveness.

Although our focus is on the status of the allegation, it is the account as a whole that is or is not acceptable. Many of the relations of justification are reciprocal. The allegation is acceptable only if (at least most of) the rest of the constellation of supporting considerations is. But since the eyewitnesses are unreliable and the contentions of the collateral witnesses are tenuous, the acceptability of the testimony likewise depends on the acceptability of the allegation. The epistemic status of the allegation is inseparable from the status of the rest of the story. Some of the background information may be separately secured, but to a considerable extent, the various components of the story stand or fall together.

The thesis of the sort of epistemological holism that I want to consider is that epistemic justification is primarily a property of a suitably comprehensive, coherent account, when the best explanation of coherence is that the account is at least roughly true. The epistemic justification of individual claims derives from their membership in a justified account. There is no universally accepted criterion of coherence. But at least this is required: the components of a coherent account must be mutually consistent, cotenable and supportive. That is, the components must be reasonable in light of one another. Since both cotenability and supportiveness are matters of degree, coherence is too. So if it can be shown that epistemic justification is a matter of coherence, there remains the question of how coherent an account must be in order for it to be epistemically justified. Before facing that worry, though, other challenges need to be met. At least two worries immediately arise. The first is that coherence is too demanding an epistemic requirement. The second is that it is not demanding enough.

Even where we take ourselves to be on solid ground, contravening considerations are not uncommon. Mrs Abercrombie, the aging geometry teacher, says that during the relevant period she saw a young man sporting a green hat. A green hat is not green hair, so her report conflicts with the reports of the other witnesses. Ms Mintz, the hall monitor, insists no one was in the corridor at the time of the alleged theft. Mr Miller, the classics teacher, disputes the allegation on the grounds that students do not want Latin books enough to steal them. These reports are clearly relevant to and at odds with the account I gave. If we incorporate them into my account, we render it incoherent. But we seem to have no legitimate reason to exclude them. The problem is this: the discussion so far suggests that the credibility of the various claims comprising an account depends on how well they hang together. If so, the failure of other, equally relevant information to cohere threatens to discredit the account.

Although true, this is not so daunting as it appears. The immediate threat of incoherence comes from assuming that we must take seemingly contravening considerations at face value and incorporate them into an account as they stand. But we need do no such thing. Rather, we assess contravening considerations just as we do the rest of our evidence. Recall that we did not take the eyewitness reports at face value. We initially deemed them suspect because our background information indicated that the informants are unreliable. The credibility of the reports increased because of their agreement with one another and the support provided by collateral information. That agreement gave us reason to think that the general unreliability of the witnesses did not affect the standing of these particular reports. Contravening considerations are subject to similar assessments. Mrs Abercrombie, being near-sighted and woefully out of date, cannot even imagine that a green thatch on someone's head might be his hair. That being so, her characterization of the suspect as wearing a green hat seems close enough to count as supporting rather than undermining the original allegation. Although Ms Mintz flatly disputes what others have said, there are reasons to doubt that her claim is true. Since the three eyewitnesses saw each other in the corridor during the period when Ms Mintz denies that anyone was there, her contention is dubious on independent grounds. Since she occasionally goes AWOL to smoke a cigarette, there is reason to suspect that she was absent when the theft occurred. Mr Miller's argument cannot be so easily discredited. But the book is gone. Meg put it in her locker when she arrived at school. It was not there when she returned. Even if Latin books are not attractive targets for teenage thieves, the book's having been stolen may better explain its absence than any available alternative would. Just as other considerations compensate for the improbability of a green haired thief, other considerations compensate for the improbability of a Latin book thief. In determining the acceptability of a claim, we assess the considerations that afford evidence pertaining to its tenability. This is not always a simple yes/no matter. We may find that although an evidence statement is unacceptable or unsupportive as it stands, with suitable modifications, it would be. And we may find that the modifications themselves are acceptable. Coherence remains crucial. Sometimes it is achieved directly, sometimes by discrediting or disarming threats.

The coherence that affords epistemic justification is not just coherence among object-level deliverances. We have higher-order commitments about what sorts of object-level deliverances are trustworthy, about how much credibility to accord them, about how they ought to mesh, and about what to do when commitments clash. These higher-order commitments supply reasons to revise or reject some deliverances but not others when conflicts occur. The coherence that constitutes epistemic justification is something we achieve, not something that simply falls out of the relations in which our object-level deliverances happen to stand to one another.

The second worry is that coherence can readily be achieved through epistemically illicit means. A good nineteenth-century novel is highly coherent, but not credible on that account. Even though *Middlemarch* is far more coherent than our regrettably fragmentary and disjointed views about the book theft, the best explanation of its coherence lies in the novelist's craft, not in the truth (or approximate truth) of the story. The coherence of the story affords virtually no reason to think it is true. This is surely right. But rather than taking this objection to completely discredit the contention that coherence conduces to epistemic acceptability, I suggest that it indicates something different: coherence conduces to epistemic acceptability only when the best explanation of the coherence of a constellation of claims is that they are (at least roughly) true.

Although epistemology generally focuses on the beliefs of a single individual, I began with a public case because the otherwise unlikely agreement of independent witnesses clearly shows how the best explanation of the coherence of a given body of claims may be that they are (at least roughly) true. The case of a single individual can be trickier. Sometimes people confabulate. They compose a coherent narrative by ignoring, bracketing, or overlooking factors that detract from the story they seek to construct. The process may be unconscious. Obviously, when a subject is confabulating, the coherence of her beliefs is not explained by their truth. If it is hard to tell whether she is confabulating, it is hard to tell whether coherence confers epistemic standing on her beliefs. But to understand how, why, and when coherence engenders credibility, it is best to put this complication aside. Then we see that the story I have told could be told of a single epistemic agent as well. If the best explanation of the coherence of an agent's system of thought is that it is at least roughly true, and she has no overriding reason to think otherwise, she is justified. Anne is aware of what she thinks she saw, and what she thinks the other witnesses report. She is privy to the relevant background information about apparent sight lines and the like. Since her various relevant cognitive commitments mesh and the best explanation of their meshing is that they are at least roughly true, according to epistemological holists, she is justified in accepting them.

One might argue that even the best nineteenth-century novel does not pose as great a threat as we sometimes suppose. No matter how deeply immersed I am in the story, a single glance up from the page is enough to convince me that I am not in a drawing room in nineteenth-century England. The story, though internally coherent, manifestly fails to mesh with the rest of my experience. This is true, but the question is what to make of it. On the one hand, too restricted a cluster of mutually supportive claims seems inadequate to engender credibility. We can't make the story credible simply by ignoring everything else we believe. On the other hand, insisting that all our commitments need to cohere seems unduly demanding. If acceptability requires coherence with everything we accept (or with everything we accept for cognitive purposes; Lehrer, 1986), it is but a short step to skepticism. One wayward belief, however remote from current concerns, could discredit an entire constellation of beliefs. Theories that ground justification in coherence then face a problem of scope.

Worries about scope, however, seem not to do justice to the problem that confronts us here. Faced with a clash between the deliverances of the novel and those of my glance, it is obvious which I should accept. There is no temptation to resolve the tension by dismissing perceptual deliverances or taking *them* to be the fiction. They seem to possess an epistemic privilege that prevents considerations of coherence from overriding them. The capacity of perceptual deliverances to trump the claims of a tightly knit novel may seem conclusively to demonstrate that epistemological justification cannot consist in coherence.

The matter deserves further consideration though. Until the source of perception's epistemic privilege is clear, it is premature to rule coherence out. A variety of reasons have been offered. Foundationalists argue on *a priori* grounds that knowledge requires that there be some independently credible beliefs. They hold that perceptual deliverances are among the independently credible beliefs because perceptual deliverances derive at least some of their warrant from the circumstances in which they occur, not their relation to other deliverances. Exactly how credible they are is a matter of dispute (BonJour, 1985, pp. 26–30). But they must, foundationalists contend, have some measure of credibility that does not derive from their accord with other convictions. Reliabilists argue that a deliverance is epistemically acceptable if produced by a reliable mechanism. Some perceptual mechanisms are reliable, hence some perceptual deliverances are acceptable. Since the reliability of perceptual mechanisms is independent of the relations of their deliverances to other deliverances, perceptual deliverances are independently credible.

There are at least two separate insights here. The reliabilist argument targets the need for a link to the world. The reason for crediting the casual glance while dismissing the deliverances of the novel is that we take it that perception provides the link. The way the world is constrains our perceptual deliverances more immediately and directly than it does our other beliefs. Insofar as the contents of knowledge claims concern the way the world is, it makes sense that the constraints the world supplies should override other considerations. The foundationalist position underscores the idea that some deliverances – in particular, those of perception – seem at least prima facie credible independently of their connections to other beliefs.

What the objections show is that if perception is to provide the sort of check on theorizing that we think it should, egalitarianism *vis-à-vis* object-level deliverances will not do. An egalitarian theory would hold that each deliverance has an equal claim on our epistemic allegiance. On the principle of one man, one vote, there is no basis for privileging some deliverances over others. If a perceptual deliverance fails to cohere with an otherwise coherent theory, the perceptual deliverance ought to be rejected then, since the claims of the many outweigh the claims of the one. But no matter how comprehensive and integrated an empirical account is, no matter how many other beliefs the account manages to incorporate, observations should have the capacity to discredit it. They have that capacity only if the epistemic claims of perceptual deliverances at least sometimes outweigh those of theory. But it does not follow that perceptual deliverances must be utterly immune to revision or rejection on the basis of considerations of coherence. Nor does it follow that the epistemic privilege granted to perceptual deliverances is independent of coherence considerations.

If we think about our situation when we glance away from the novel, we recognize that we draw on more than the sentences comprising the novel and our current perceptual deliverances. We tacitly rely on a fairly extensive and epistemologically informed understanding of novels and perception. We know enough about underlying mechanisms to have reason to credit some perceptual deliverances. We know enough about literature to realize that novels are typically literally false. That constitutes sufficient reason for even casual perceptual deliverances to override the claims of the novel.

Can Beliefs Be Justified through Coherence Alone?

Juxtaposing the novel with perception might seem to make the problem too easy, though. Regardless of what we think about perception, if we recognize that a novel is a work of fiction, we have reason to discount any direct claims it may seem to make on our epistemic allegiance. (I say direct claims because I believe that novels play a significant, albeit indirect, role in the advancement of understanding. But how they do so is not germane to this discussion (Elgin, 1996, pp. 183–200).) The serious challenge comes from a coherent factual account that conflicts with perceptual deliverances. If holism holds that such an account always overrides perceptual deliverances, it seems plainly unacceptable. However tightly woven an empirical account may be, we would be epistemically irresponsible to ignore recalcitrant evidence. Foundationalists take this latter point to be decisive: if observation can show a theory to be unjustified, then coherence cannot be the locus of justification.

This would be so, if observation worked in isolation. For then, owing to its epistemic privilege, one perceptual deliverance would have the capacity to discredit an entire system of thought. But this is a myth. Only observations we have reason to trust have the power to unseat theories. So it is not an observation in isolation, but an observation backed by reasons that actually discredits the theory.

The holist response to the challenge presented by observation is this: *a priori*, perceptual deliverances have no special weight. They are just deliverances jockeying for inclusion in coherent bodies of thought. But over time, as we attend to the fates of our various deliverances, we learn that the incorporation of some, but not others, yields accounts which are borne out by further experience, hence which retain their coherence over time. This gives us grounds for discrimination. We realize that the deliverances we take to be perceptual are more likely to be confirmed than spontaneous deliverances that just leap to mind. So we assign greater weight to perceptual deliverances than to passing thoughts. Moreover, we learn that not all perceptual deliverances are on a par. Those that are credible tend to come in mutually reinforcing streams, so isolated perceptual deliverances count for little. We begin to draw distinctions among perceptual deliverances. For example, we discover that peripheral vision is less trustworthy than central vision. So we have reason to discount what we see out of the corner of the eye. This is not to say that we dismiss the deliverances of peripheral vision out of hand, but that we demand more in the way of corroboration. Some of us discover that we are color blind or tone deaf or myopic. That is, we learn that our perceptions of colors, tones, or the dimensions of distant objects are not to be trusted. And so on. We come to assign different weights to perceptual deliverances depending on how well they accord with other things we take ourselves to have reason to credit – other appearances of the same object, the reports of other observers, the implications of our best theories about the visible properties of items of the kind in question, and so forth.

The issue is not simply how well a given content meshes with other things we believe, but how well a given content from a given source in given circumstances does. The weight we attach to perceptual deliverances derives from our understanding of the world and our access to it. Initially, perhaps, this is just a matter of track records. Some perceptual deliverances seem to integrate better into acceptable systems of thought than spontaneous thoughts that just leap to mind. Later, as we develop physiological and psychological accounts of ourselves, which explain our perceptual mechanisms, we gain additional reasons to take some perceptual deliverances to be credible. The epistemic privilege that some perceptual deliverances enjoy then derives from an understanding of ourselves as perceiving organisms. That is, the reason for assigning those deliverances significant epistemic weight derives from the coherent account of perception that backs the assignment. Contrary to what foundationalists contend, the justification for privileging perception derives from the relation of perceptual judgments to the rest of our theory of ourselves as cognitive agents interacting with a mind-independent world.

The reliabilist account seems to fare slightly better. What justifies assigning my visual inputs significant epistemic weight seems to be that vision is a reliable perceptual mechanism. What justifies dismissing my forebodings is that premonition is not. This is not quite right though. It is not the brute reliability or unreliabilty of a source that supplies the justification, but an understanding of that reliability or unreliability. Even if my forebodings are accurate, so long as we have no reason to trust them, they bear little weight.

This argument explains both why some perceptual deliverances have the capacity to unsettle theory, and why those deliverances are not intrinsically privileged. They owe their epistemic status to their place in our evolving understanding of the world and our modes of access to it. This has two welcome consequences. The first is that the privilege they enjoy is revocable. When I learn that I am color blind, I need to revise my views about which of my visual deliverances are acceptable. The second is that non-perceptual deliverances can in principle be equally weighty. This is an advantage in accounting for the epistemic status of scientific evidence and of testimony.

A look at modern science shows that it is not just (or perhaps even mainly) bare perceptual deliverances that have the capacity to discredit theory. The outputs of measuring devices do too. In an effort to retain a tie to classical empiricism, some philosophers of science argue that measuring devices are simply extensions of our senses. Just as eyeglasses enable near-sighted people to see what otherwise they could not, telescopes and microscopes enable everyone to see what otherwise we could not. So if seeing something in suitable circumstances has sufficient weight to undermine a coherent cluster of claims, seeing something through a telescope or microscope should be able to do so too. This idea is not unreasonable so long as we restrict ourselves to devices like optical telescopes and microscopes. But it stretches the bounds of plausibility to contend that radio telescopes, electron microscopes, MRIs, and the like are also mere extenders of the sense of sight. It seems better to forgo the strained analogy and simply characterize such devices as detectors. Then an understanding of what they detect, how they detect, and why they should be trusted supplies reason to accord their outputs considerable weight. Even without the strained analogy, the argument for crediting the outputs of scientific instruments thus parallels the argument for crediting perceptual deliverances. For although they are not perceptual mechanisms, the devices are among our modes of access to the world.

Testimony poses a similar problem. We acquire many of our beliefs from the testimony of others, and consider those beliefs justified. Some philosophers say that the justification for accepting testimony is *a priori*. *Ceteris paribus*, we are justified in accepting what people tell us. Others say it is inductive. We should believe only those who have shown themselves to be relevantly reliable in the past. The former seem to endorse gullibility, the latter to unduly limit acceptability. Something more sensitive is wanted. Evidently the question is not whether testimony *per se* is or is not prima facie acceptable. Some testimony is frankly incredible; some requires a good deal of corroboration; some is straightforwardly acceptable. The acceptability of a bit of testimony depends on how well its content coheres with other relevant deliverances, how well the belief that the testifier is competent with respect to her allegation coheres, and how well the belief that she is sincere coheres. Because of its mesh with our background beliefs, straightforwardly acceptable testimony scores high on all of these measures. Just as different perceptual deliverances are accorded different weights, so are different testimonial deliverances. Testimony with sufficiently strong backing can discredit a hitherto coherent cluster of beliefs.

Even though the deliverances of perception, testimony, and instrumental readings have no special standing *a priori*, in light of our developing theories of the world and our modes of access to it, some of them turn out to have considerable epistemic weight. This satisfies the demand that acceptable beliefs be appropriately constrained by the way the world is. It also reveals that holism has the resources to recognize that deliverances can differ in weight, some being more credible than others. The claims of the few can in suitable circumstances outweigh the claims of the many.

Achieving coherence is not just a matter of excluding untoward deliverances though. In the interests of systematicity, we may incorporate considerations we have no antecedent reason to believe. For example, although there is no direct evidence of positrons, symmetry considerations show that a physical theory that eschewed them would be significantly less coherent than one that acknowledged them. So physics' commitment to positrons is epistemically appropriate. Considerations we have no independent reason to believe can acquire tenability then because they strengthen the coherence of the systems they belong to.

The issue of scope remains. The totality of a person's beliefs and/or deliverances is not particularly coherent. Not only are there outliers and inconsistencies among beliefs, there are also clusters of beliefs that are relatively isolated from one another. Meg's cluster of beliefs about the pituitary gland, the evidence that bears on the acceptability of these beliefs, the trustworthiness of bits of testimony on the subject, and the proper methods for assessing such things has few and loose connections to her cluster of views about parliamentary procedure, the evidence that bears on these views, the trustworthiness of testimony about the subject, and the proper methods for assessing them. It seems that she could easily be badly wrong about the former without her error having any significant effect on the tenability of her views about the latter. Outliers and inconsistencies among beliefs are in principle relatively unproblematic. According to a holism, outliers lack justification. Because they lack suitable connections to other things we believe, we have no reason to credit them. Inconsistencies among beliefs conclusively demonstrate that some of the beliefs are false. But it is not obvious that mutual indifference of belief clusters is objectionable. It is not clear that we should consider Meg epistemically defective because of the lack of close ties between the two clusters. On the other hand, if the clusters of beliefs are too small and too numerous, complacency over their mutual indifference seems problematic.

We do not want to license ignoring inconvenient tensions among beliefs by consigning them to mutually irrelevant clusters.

The problem neither has nor needs an *a priori* resolution. Our evolving theories of the world and our access to it provide us with an appreciation of the relations in which our various clusters of beliefs should stand to one another and the requirements they should satisfy. Such a *laissez-faire* attitude might seem to allow for the acceptability of crazy constellations of views. If we leave it to our evolving theories to decide what range of considerations acceptable accounts must answer to, we may be forced to endorse isolated islands of claptrap. The worry is more apparent than real. We have theories about theories, which enable us to assess the reasons, methods, standards, and evidence that our various object-level theories appeal to. Some requirements, such as logical consistency, apply globally. Regardless of how far apart Meg's views about politics and endocrinology are, unless they can be conjoined without contradiction they are not all acceptable. Other requirements, like the need to respect judicial precedents or to accord with biochemical findings, are more limited in range. But even these do not enable us to isolate belief clusters entirely. Even if Meg's views about endocrinology and politics have few points of contact, her views about endocrinology and hematology have many.

Consistency requirements do more than rule out express contradictions. The requirement that like cases be treated alike demands that if a consideration has weight in one area but not in another, there be an acceptable reason for the difference. In order to be tenable, a system of mutually reinforcing claims must either answer to the logical and evidential standards to which other theories are subject or be backed by a tenable account of why those standards do not apply. Some theories have such backing. There are, for example, cogent reasons why mathematics is not subject to empirical testing. So infinitary mathematics is not threatened by the absence of empirical evidence for its findings. In epistemically objectionable cases, no such reasons are available. The claims of astrology, although mutually reinforcing, are epistemically unacceptable because they yield predictions that are either too vague to be tested or are not borne out when tested. Since astrology makes empirical claims, there are considerations to which it ought to be responsive which it fails to accommodate. To say that something cannot be ruled out *a priori* is not to say that it cannot be definitely and decisively ruled out.

Epistemological positions that construe knowledge as justified true belief generally treat being justified, being true, and being believed as three separate features of a propositional content. The standard objection to coherentism is that coherence among propositional contents is so easily achieved that it affords no reason to believe that the contents are true, hence no justification for them. This overlooks the fact that the contents in question are not just any propositional contents, they are belief contents or deliverance contents. That is, they are contents that present themselves as true. This makes a difference. For the fact that they present themselves as true gives us some slight reason to think that they are true. The word "slight" is crucial. I do not contend that we have sufficient reason to credit such contents. But at least two considerations speak in favor of granting them a slight measure of credibility. Beliefs form the basis for action, so the success of our actions affords evidence of the truth of the corresponding beliefs. Moreover, we learn from experience. Once we come to recognize that premonitions tend not to be borne out, we cease to credit them. We may continue to experience feelings of foreboding, for example, but they cease to qualify as deliverances.

Manifestly these considerations are far too weak to demonstrate that beliefs or deliverances are epistemically justified. They do, however, give us reason to think that beliefs and deliverances have some claim on our epistemic allegiance. They have an epistemic edge. We have better reason to incorporate them into our systems of thought than to incorporate contents we are neutral about. Beliefs and deliverances are, I suggest, initially tenable. But initial tenability is a weak and precarious epistemic status. Considerations of overall coherence often require revision or rejection of initially tenable commitments. Initially tenable commitments can conflict. They may be mutually incompatible or non-cotenable. Or they may be sufficiently isolated that they are incapable of giving support to or gaining support from other things we believe. Then they cannot be incorporated into an epistemically acceptable system.

Epistemical acceptability, I contend, requires reflective equilibrium (Elgin, 1996; Rawls, 1971). A system of thought is in equilibrium if its elements are reasonable in light of one another. This is a matter of coherence. An equilibrium is reflective if the system is as reasonable as any available alternative in light of our initially tenable commitments. Such a system is not required to incorporate as many initially tenable commitments as possible. As we have seen, there are weighting factors that favor some incorporations over others. Moreover, rather than incorporating commitments, a system may show why we were misled into accepting them, or may include modifications of them.

The standards of reasonableness are second-order commitments, and are subject to the same sorts of considerations as our first-order deliverances. The fact that we accept them indicates that they are prima facie acceptable. But they can conflict, or fail to yield verdicts in cases where they should, or yield verdicts that we find unacceptable. Then they too are subject to revision or rejection in order to yield a comprehensive system of first- and second-order commitments that is on reflection something we can endorse.

Whether the sort of holism that results is a coherence theory is not clear. Using BonJour's (1985) categories, it might be classified as a very weak foundationalism or as a coherence theory. Deliverances derive their initial tenability from their status as deliverances. That suggests that something other than coherence is involved. But initially tenable commitments display at least two features that are not characteristic of standard foundational beliefs. First, there are no intrinsically privileged kinds of deliverances. The account does not insist that there is something epistemically special about perception or introspection or analyticity. It simply says that the fact that a consideration presents itself as true gives it a modest measure of tenability. Second, even that small measure of tenability is easily lost. Tenable theories are justified in part by reference to initially tenable deliverances, but they need not incorporate the deliverances by reference to which they are justified.

Whether we call such an epistemology a coherence theory does not in the end matter. The virtues of the theory are as follows. (1) It does not privilege any sorts of beliefs or representations *a priori*. What beliefs and representations are worthy of acceptance is something we learn by developing increasingly comprehensive, coherent accounts of the world and our access to it. (2) It enables us to start from whatever deliverances we happen to have. But because it insists that we subject those deliverances to rigorous assessment, such a starting point is not question begging. (3) The standards of assessment are themselves the fruits of epistemic activity, and can change in response to feedback (Goodman, 1984, p. 69). (4) Hence, everything is subject to revision. A system of thought that we can on reflection accept today may be one that we cannot on reflection accept tomorrow. But so long as a system is in reflective equilibrium and the best of explanation of its being so is that it is at least roughly true, it and its components are justified. What results is neither certainty nor skepticism but a fallible, provisional, but reasonable epistemological stance.

References

Blanshard, B. (1939) *The Nature of Thought*. London: George Allen & Unwin.
BonJour, L. (1985) *The Structure of Empirical Knowledge*. Cambridge, MA: Harvard University Press.
Elgin, C. (1996) *Considered Judgment*. Princeton, NJ: Princeton University Press.
Goodman, N. (1984) *Fact, Fiction, and Forecast*. Cambridge, MA: Harvard University Press.
Lehrer, K. (1986) The coherence theory of knowledge. *Philosophical Topics*, 14, 5–25.
Lewis, C. I. (1946) *An Analysis of Knowledge and Valuation*. La Salle, IL: Open Court.
Rawls, J. (1971) *A Theory of Justice*. Cambridge, MA: Harvard University Press.
Rescher, N. (1973) *The Coherence Theory of Truth*. Oxford: Clarendon Press.

Further reading

Adler, J. (1986) Knowing, betting, and cohering. *Philosophical Topics*, 14, 243–57.
Bender, J. (ed.) (1989) *The Current State of the Coherence Theory*. Dordrecht: Kluwer.
Goodman, N. and Elgin, C. (1988) *Reconceptions*. Indianapolis: Hackett.
Harman, G. (1973) *Thought*. Princeton, NJ: Princeton University Press.
Lehrer, K. (1974) *Knowledge*. Oxford: Clarendon Press.
Sellars, W. (1968) *Science and Metaphysics*. London: Routledge & Kegan Paul.
Sellars, W. (1963) *Science, Perception and Reality*. London: Routledge & Kegan Paul.
Sosa, E. (1985) The coherence of virtue and the virtue of coherence. *Synthese*, 64, 3–28.
Sosa, E. (1980) The raft and the pyramid. *Midwest Studies in Philosophy*, 5, 3–26.
Williams, M. (1980) Coherence, justification, and truth. *Review of Metaphysics*, 37, 243–72.

Why Coherence Is not Enough: A Defense of Moderate Foundationalism

James van Cleve

I

Foundationalism has been characterized as the view that "the knowledge which a person has at any time is a structure or edifice, many parts and stages of which help to support each other, but which as a whole is supported by its own foundation" (Chisholm, 1964). To unpack the metaphor, we may say that the foundation consists of *basic beliefs* – beliefs that a subject is justified in holding even in the absence of any justifying reason for them – and all other justified beliefs derive their justification at least in part from such basic beliefs.

The classical argument for foundationalism is an infinite regress argument going back to Aristotle: unless there were basic beliefs, every justified belief would rest on further justified beliefs, and so on without end. An infinite regress is not in fact the only alternative to basic beliefs, but the other alternatives are equally problematic, or so foundationalists maintain. To canvass all the options, let us set down four propositions that jointly imply the existence of an infinite regress of justified beliefs:

1 Some beliefs are justified.
2 No belief is justified unless some other belief serves as a reason for it.
3 One belief cannot serve as a reason justifying another unless the first is itself justified.
4 If A serves as a reason justifying B, then B cannot serve (directly or indirectly) as a reason justifying B. B? or A?

These four propositions jointly entail the existence of an infinite regress of justified propositions. We are therefore faced with five alternatives: accept the infinite regress or reject one of the four assumptions.

Skeptics (of the universal ilk) deny 1, maintaining that no beliefs whatever are justified. *Foundationalists* deny 2, maintaining that some beliefs are justified in the absence of reasons. *Positists* (not to be confused with positivists) deny 3, maintaining that chains of justifying reasons can terminate in reasons that are not justified themselves, but are simply individual or societal posits.[1] *Coherentists* deny 4, maintaining that beliefs can be justified in virtue of relations of mutual support. *Infinitists* accept all four assumptions and the resulting infinite regress.

All five options have their takers. Skepticism and infinitism are both defended elsewhere in this volume (see the essays by Fumerton and Klein). Positism finds advocacy in Wittgenstein's *On Certainty* and in assorted postmodern thinkers (Wittgenstein, 1969). But I think it is fair to say that the leading contenders among the five options are foundationalism and coherentism.

Coherentism is sometimes characterized as a view that sanctions circular reasoning, but that is an oversimplified construal of it. Coherentists do not typically endorse simple loops in which A justifies B, B justifies C, and C justifies A; rather, they envision vast webs of belief in which everything is supported by some significant portion of the remaining beliefs: A by B and C, B by A, D, J, and K, and so on.

For their part, foundationalists do not typically deny the power of coherence to contribute to the overall epistemic status of a body of belief. They simply insist that coherence cannot do all the work on its own – there must be at least a modicum of intrinsic credibility or non-inferential warrant possessed by basic beliefs before coherence can have its amplifying effect.

Laurence BonJour distinguishes three grades of foundationalism (BonJour, 1985, pp. 26–30). According to *strong* foundationalism, basic beliefs are "not just adequately justified, but also *infallible, certain, indubitable,* or *incorrigible*" (BonJour, 1985, pp. 26-7). According to *moderate* foundationalism, the non-inferential warrant possessed by basic beliefs need not amount to absolute certainty or any of the other privileged statuses just mentioned, but it must be "sufficient by itself to satisfy the adequate-justification condition for knowledge" (BonJour, 1985, p. 26). Finally, according to *weak* foundationalism,

> basic beliefs possess only a very low degree of epistemic justification on their own, a degree of justification insufficient by itself either to satisfy the adequate-justification condition for knowledge or to qualify them as acceptable justifying premises for further beliefs. Such beliefs are only "initially credible," rather than fully justified. (BonJour, 1985, p. 28)

We must rely on coherence among such initially credible beliefs to amplify their level of warrant up to the point where it is adequate for knowledge.

As BonJour notes, weak foundationalism could be regarded as a hybrid view, mixing together foundational and coherentist elements. In fact, Susan Haack prefers to call it "foundherentism," which she illustrates with the example of a crossword puzzle. Experience corresponds to the clues, which give an initial presumption in favor of certain beliefs or entries in the puzzle; the initial beliefs are then confirmed by the way in which they interlock with other entries (or sometimes discarded because they do not fit in). Thus does coherence amplify (or its absence erode) the initial warrant possessed by basic beliefs (Haack, 1993).[2]

But if coherence can elevate the epistemic status of a set of beliefs in this way, what prevents it from generating warrant entirely on its own, without any need for basic beliefs? This is a question that has been asked by several authors, including BonJour:

> The basic idea is that an initially low degree of justification can somehow be magnified or amplified by coherence, to a degree adequate for knowledge. But how is this magnification or amplification supposed to work? How can coherence, not itself an independent source of justification on a foundationalist view, justify the rejection of some initially credible beliefs and enhance the justification of others? (BonJour, 1985, p. 29)

Can Beliefs Be Justified through Coherence Alone?

The implied suggestion is that if coherence can do what the weak foundationalist allows, it can also do what the thoroughgoing coherentist says it can do.

In the next section, I address this challenge. I argue that there is indeed a good rationale for the weak foundationalist's insistence that before coherence can do its work, there must be initially credible inputs for it to work upon. But I also argue that the level of initial credibility cannot be as low as that envisioned by weak foundationalists, who should therefore upgrade their position to moderate foundationalism. Finally, in section III, I offer some critical reflections on the coherentist alternative defended by Catherine Elgin.

II

An excellent example of a weak foundationalist theory is provided by C. I. Lewis's theory of memory knowledge. It has two elements:

> First; whatever is remembered, whether as explicit recollection or merely in the form of our sense of the past, is *prima facie* credible because so remembered. And second; when the whole range of empirical beliefs is taken into account, all of them more or less dependent upon memorial knowledge, we find that those which are most credible can be assured by their mutual support, or as we shall put it, by their *congruence*. (Lewis, 1946, p. 334)[3]

Lewis defines a congruent set as one in which any member is more probable given the rest than it is on its own:

> A set of statements, or a set of supposed facts asserted, will be said to be congruent if and only if they are so related that the antecedent probability of any one of them will be increased if the remainder of the set can be assumed as premises. (AKV, p. 338)

A point on which Lewis repeatedly insists is that congruence alone cannot generate probability or warrant. Rather, some of the statements must have initial credibility, which congruence can then amplify:

> The feature of such corroboration through congruence that should impress us, is the requirement that the items exhibiting these congruent relationships must – some of them at least – be *independently given facts* or have a probability which is antecedent. (AKV, p. 352)

How *much* probability must the congruent items have? Only a "slight" amount, Lewis tells us, illustrating his point with the example of individually unreliable witnesses who tell the same story:

> Our previous example [AKV, p. 239] of the relatively unreliable witnesses who independently tell the same circumstantial story, is another illustration of the logic of congruence; and one which is more closely typical of the importance of relations of congruence for determination of empirical truth in general. For any of these reports,

taken singly, the extent to which it confirms what is reported may be slight. And antecedently, the probability of what is reported may also be small. But congruence of the reports establishes a high probability of what they agree upon, by principles of probability determination which are familiar: on any other hypothesis than that of truthtelling, this agreement is highly unlikely. (AKV, p. 346)

But how much probability is a "slight" amount? In one place Lewis says, "Anything sensed as past is just a little more probable than that which is incompatible with what is remembered and that with respect to which memory is blank" (AKV, p. 358). He thereby implies that a remembered piece of information has a probability greater than 0.5, given that it is remembered. (This is because it is an axiom of the probability calculus that $P(\sim h,e) = 1 - P(h,e)$; thus a proposition has greater probability than its negation if and only if it has probability greater than 0.5.) Thus according to Lewis's version of weak foundationalism, the congruence of a set of remembered items can raise their level of justification arbitrarily high, but only if the items have initial credibility amounting to a probability (given that we seem to remember them) greater than 0.5.

To this latter aspect of Lewis's theory BonJour has raised an objection. There is no need, he says, for Lewis's requirement that memory reports or other cognitive deliverances have initial credibility:

> What Lewis does not see, however, is that his own example shows quite convincingly that no antecedent degree of warrant or credibility is required. For as long as we are confident that the reports of the various witnesses are genuinely independent of each other, a high enough degree of coherence among them will eventually dictate the hypothesis of truth telling as the only available explanation of their agreement – even, indeed, if those individually reports initially have a high degree of *negative* credibility, that is, are much more likely to be false than true (for example, in the case where all of the witnesses are known to be habitual liars). (BonJour, 1985, pp. 147–8)

We are now presented with a clear-cut issue to investigate: in order for the congruence of a set of items to raise their credibility to near 1, what level of antecedent credibility is required? Must it be greater than that of their negations and thus greater than 0.5, as Lewis maintains? Or may it be less than 0.5, as BonJour implies when he says that the reports of the witnesses (or of our memory) may be more likely false than true?

For light on this question, we may look to discussion of a traditional topic in probability theory: how to assess the probability that independent witnesses who agree in their testimony are telling the truth. This is a problem to which a number of classical authors have proposed answers. One of the standard answers is due to George Boole (1952, p. 364):[4]

> Let p be the general probability that A speaks the truth, q the general probability that B speaks the truth; it is required to find the probability that, if they agree in a statement, they both speak the truth. Now agreement in the same statement implies that they either both speak truth, the probability of which beforehand is pq, or that they both speak falsehood, the probability of which beforehand is $(1 - p)(1 - q)$. Hence the probability

beforehand that they will agree is pq + (1 − p)(1 − q) and the probability that if they agree, they will agree in speaking the truth is accordingly expressed by the formula

$$w[= P(A \text{ and } B \text{ speak truly, they agree})] = \frac{pq}{pq + (1 - p)(1 - q)}$$

For an explanation of the rationale behind Boole's formula, I must refer the reader to what I have said elsewhere.[5] Here there is space only to note the bearing of his formula on the issue separating Lewis and BonJour. Suppose that A and B each tell the truth 60 percent of the time; that is, suppose that p and q are each equal to 0.6. The reader may verify that in this case, w = 0.69. That is, setting A's credibility and B's each equal to 0.6, the probability that X is true given that they each testify to it is 0.69. More generally, if we plug in any numbers greater than 0.5 as p and q, w will be greater than the mean of p and q. So far we have an illustration of the point, common ground for Lewis and BonJour, that congruence can boost credibility.

But what if we plug in values of p and q equal to or less than 0.5? If 0.5 goes in, 0.5 comes out; and if p and q are each less than 0.5, the output value will be less than their mean. For example, if p and q are each 0.1, w is approximately 0.01. In other words, if the witnesses have what BonJour calls "negative credibility" (credibility less than 0.5), the probability of a statement given that they both testify to it is not enhanced but diminished! So if Boole's formula is correct, Lewis is vindicated and BonJour refuted: with initial credibilities less than 0.5, coherence makes things worse rather than better.

There is reason to be suspicious of Boole's formula, however. In deriving it, he tacitly assumes that there are only two possible answers to the questions put to the witnesses – true or false. That is why he can equate agreement with "both speak truly or both speak falsely." In a more realistic scenario, the witnesses would be asked multiple-choice questions, and if they agreed in giving the same answer out of ten possible choices (let us say), their agreement would be much more impressive.

A formula allowing for an arbitrary number of possible answers to questions has been devised by Michael Huemer (1997).[6] For simplicity's sake, Huemer assumes that the witnesses have the same level of credibility, so p = q. If n is the number of possible answers and X is the answer on which independent witnesses A and B agree, then Huemer's formula may be written as follows (omitting details of the derivation):

$$P(X, A \text{ says } X \ \& \ B \text{ says } X)[= W] = \frac{np^2 - p^2}{np^2 - p^2 + 1}$$

This formula agrees with Boole's in the special case where n = 2, but gives dramatically different results in the cases not covered by Boole's. Specifically, it enables coherence to have its amplifying affect even when the credibility level of the witnesses is below 0.5, just so long as it is greater than the chance or random guessing level of 1/n. For example, if p is only 0.3, but there are ten possible answers (say, ten possible last digits in a glimpsed license plate number), then w = 0.62. If p = 0.3 and n = 100 , then w = 0.86. For any value of p, just so long as it is greater than zero, we can bring the final probability of X (i.e. its probability given that the witnesses

Chapter Six

agree on it) as close as we like to certainty by making n high enough. With a more complex version of the formula, we can also make w higher by increasing the number of witnesses.

If Huemer's formula is correct, then, BonJour is vindicated and Lewis refuted. Initial credibilities need not be greater than 0.5; they need only be greater than the chance level of $1/n$ (where n = the number of possible answers). If enough witnesses agree without collusion in giving the same answer from among a large enough number of choices, it becomes overwhelmingly likely that they are correct, even if their initial level of credibility was scarcely above zero.

Is BonJour right, then? Can coherence alone be a source of warrant without need of inputs with initial credibility? An answer of yes would be too hasty, for there is another requirement of initial credibility we have yet to consider. The requirement at which we have so far demurred is the requirement that what is reported must be more probable than not (and thus have probability greater than 0.5) given that a witness (or an ostensible memory) attests to it. If several individually unreliable reporters agree without collusion, then the fact to which they bear common witness may have high probability in the end. But in attaching a high final probability to the fact attested, we are of course taking for granted that the various witnesses *do* testify to it. If we had reason to think that the courtroom and all its proceedings were happening only in a dream or a novel, the fact that the ostensible reports hang together would count for little. And so it is with the reports of memory, the senses, and cognitive systems more generally: coherence among them lends high final credibility only on the assumption that the reports genuinely occur.

How, then, do we know *these* things: that witness A does say X, that I do ostensibly remember Y, that I do seem to see Z? Many foundationalists would say that these are the grounds on which the rest of our knowledge rests, and that they must themselves be matters of basic knowledge.[7] Lewis himself famously maintained that nothing can be probable unless something is certain, and among the certainties he placed the facts that I do have this or that presentation of sense or memory. His insistence on certainty is controversial,[8] but it seems to me that a good case can be made that there must at least be high intrinsic credibility – perhaps high enough to constitute knowledge – attaching to the facts that such-and-such cognitive states (be they experiences, ostensible memories, or beliefs at large) are actually taking place. If this is right, we must not only abjure pure coherentism: we must also adopt a moderate rather than a weak foundationalism.

I see only one plausible alternative to an assumption of high initial credibility or knowledge-sufficient warrant at the foundational level, and that is the view that the promptings of sense or memory function as *external* conditions of knowledge. An external condition of knowledge is a condition that makes knowledge possible regardless of whether it is itself known to obtain. For example, in Goldman's reliability theory, if a subject comes to believe p as the result of a reliable process, his belief is knowledge regardless of whether the subject knows anything about the reliability of the process (Goldman, 1979). Perhaps the facts that I have such-and-such ostensible perceptions or memories could function in this external way, contributing to my knowledge even if not themselves known. The idea would be that my ostensible perceivings and rememberings are not pieces of evidence on which I conditionalize when their epistemic status is high enough;[9] instead, they are facts whose mere obtaining confers credibility on their contents.

I turn now to another point at which I think a theory of knowledge that invokes coherence must make a concession to either foundationalism or externalism.

The example of the witnesses who agree is in one respect a drastically oversimplified case of coherence. The agreement of the witnesses is literal identity, or at least logical equivalence, of content: witness 1 says X and so does witness 2. But the coherence that figures in epistemology is typically a much looser sort of hanging together. The coherence of ostensible memories is not their all being memories that p, for the same p or something logically equivalent. Nor is the coherence of beliefs or cognitions generally like that. Rather, it is a type of coherence that is exemplified by the following items:

I seem to remember seeing a skunk last night;
I seem to remember smelling a skunk last night;
I seem to remember that the lid was on the garbage can when I went to bed;
I now see that the can has been knocked over and trash strewn about;
There was a skunk here last night;

and so on. In other words, it is not identity or even equivalence of content, but rather something like the relation Lewis calls congruence: a matter of each item being more probable given the rest than it is on its own.

What are these coherence-constituting relations of probability founded upon, and how do we know that they obtain?

One answer has been given by Russell: "It is only by assuming laws that one fact can make another probable or improbable" (Russell, 1948, p. 188). Perhaps Russell goes too far in requiring strict laws in order for one fact to make another probable, but it is plausible that we at least require rough empirical generalizations. Where do these generalizations come from? Presumably, they are inferred inductively from particular facts gathered by memory. And now the following difficulty emerges: ostensible memories give rise to knowledge only with the help of coherence; coherence depends on laws or empirical generalizations; and such generalizations can be known only with the help of memory. In short, we cannot get coherence without the help of laws, and if memory does not suffice on its own to give knowledge of particular facts from which the laws are inferred, we cannot get laws without the help of coherence. It appears to follow that we cannot have any knowledge from memory unless the occurrence of ostensible memories is prima facie sufficient for knowledge. Such was Russell's own conclusion:

> memory is a premise of knowledge. . . . When I say memory is a premise, I mean that among the facts upon which scientific laws are based, some are admitted solely because they are remembered. (Russell, 1948, pp. 188–9).

Note the word "solely." Russell is saying that individual memories must be capable of giving rise to knowledge on their own, without benefit of coherence. This is compatible, of course, with allowing that the warrant provided by memory is defeasible, as Russell did allow. But the resulting view is nonetheless a foundationalism of memory knowledge stronger than that of Lewis, who required only an initial "slight" presumption in favor of the truth of any ostensible memory. Russell's view accords to memory greater epistemic powers than that: ostensibly remembering that p is a source of prima facie warrant that, if undefeated (and if p is true) is strong enough for knowing that p. In BonJour's terms, we have again advanced from weak to moderate foundationalism, this time as regards the contents of ostensible memories rather than the occurrences of them as mental events.

Russell's argument assumes that coherence and the laws that underlie it contribute to our knowledge only if they are themselves known. As in the case of the occurrences of our ostensible memories, one could challenge this assumption by going external, holding that coherence does its work regardless of whether the subject knows it obtains. This is the second point at which I believe coherentism can avoid a concession to foundationalism only by making a concession to externalism. The fact that p, q, and r do cohere with one another, as well as the facts that they are deliverances of our cognitive systems to begin with, are facts that must either function externally or be known foundationally.

III

As the debate between foundationalists and coherentists has progressed, each side has moved in the direction of the other. Contemporary foundationalists are seldom foundationalists of the strong Cartesian variety: they do not insist that basic beliefs be absolutely certain. They also typically allow that the elements in a system of belief can acquire enhanced justification through their coherence. On the other side, many coherentists admit that coherence alone is not the sole source of justification – there must be some initially credible inputs before coherence can work its wonders. Is there anything more to disagree about, or do foundationalists and coherentists now meet in the middle?

There are indeed still points of difference. To highlight several of them, I shall discuss the broadly coherentist views of Catherine Elgin as developed in her book *Considered Judgment* (1996; cited as CJ hereafter) and in her contribution to this volume.

Elgin characterizes herself as a proponent of reflective equilibrium.[10] As she conceives of it, reflective equilibrium has two chief requirements: "The components of a system in reflective equilibrium must be reasonable in light of one another, and the system as a whole reasonable in light of our initially tenable commitments." (CJ, p. 107; see also pp. ix, 13, and 127–8). It is by the second requirement that Elgin distinguishes her view from a pure coherentism: the components of a system in equilibrium must be answerable not just to one another, but also to our initially tenable commitments.[11]

The second requirement puts a "tether" on permissible systems (CJ, pp. 10, 107, 128), thereby enabling Elgin to avoid some of the objections to pure coherentism. For example, one of the standard objections to coherentism is that the contents of a consistent fairy tale would be a body of warranted propositions (see Schlick, 1973,

p. 419). Not so for Elgin, since the propositions in the story may be reasonable in light of each other without being reasonable in light of our initially tenable commitments.

Of the various things we believe, which have initial tenability? In Elgin's view, they *all* do, if we genuinely believe them: anything actually held has some initial tenability or presumption in its favor (CJ, pp. 101–2). The presumption may only be slight and it may be lost in the end, but it is there in the beginning.

What about the various principles of logic, evidence, and method whereby some things are reasonable in light of others? In Elgin's view, these have the same status as everything else: they are initially tenable if held, and they may gain or lose in tenability depending on how they fit in with everything else (CJ, p. 104).

Why is Elgin's view as so far set forth not simply a form of weak foundationalism, in which initially tenable claims function as basic beliefs? She cites two differences: unlike the justification that attaches to foundationalism's basic claims, initial tenability can be lost; it can also be augmented through coherence (CJ, p. 110).

It is not clear to me, however, that either of these features should be regarded as a prerogative of coherentists alone. In a typology of possible foundationalisms, Roderick Firth has suggested that the minimal tenet of foundationalism is simply this: basic beliefs have some measure of initial warrant that is not derived from coherence. This level of warrant may be increased by coherence with other statements or diminished, even to the vanishing point, by lack of coherence with other statements.[12] Firth's minimal view thus incorporates both of the features Elgin sees as antithetical to foundationalism.[13]

Nonetheless, I see two other questions on which foundationalists are apt to disagree with Elgin. First, are all commitments initially tenable, or only those in some specially marked out class? Second, are all commitments likewise revisable, or are some immune from subsequent rejection? On each question, Elgin takes the more egalitarian stand (CJ, pp. 101–2 and 121).

Using terminology from Michael Huemer, we may say that the first issue is the issue of phenomenal conservatism versus a more general doxastic conservatism (Huemer, 2001, pp. 99–115). Phenomenal conservatism is the view that if anything seems to be the case, one is prima facie justified in accepting it. The seemings can include perceptual seemings (it looks to me as if there is a red object over there), memorial seemings (I seem to remember being chased by a dog one day on my way to kindergarten), and intellectual seemings (it strikes me as self-evident that the relation of equality is transitive). Doxastic conservatism is the more sweepingly democratic view that anything the subject believes has some presumption in its favor – the products of wishful thinking and superstition no less than the deliverances of perception and memory. Foundationalists are typically phenomenal conservatives, while Elgin (in her book) is a doxastic conservative.

In her contribution to this volume, Elgin no longer espouses doxastic conservatism, or at any rate holds that coherentists need not be committed to it. She says that perceptual deliverances may be assigned special weight, provided they do not have it *a priori*. They have it only in virtue of coherence considerations: by accepting the deliverances of perception, we get systems that remain coherent over time (that is, they continue to jibe with new deliverances of perception). But might it not likewise be true that by accepting fantasies, we get systems that remain coherent with future contents of fantasy – especially if the fantasizer has a one-track mind? So it seems to me that there is a privileging of perception presupposed and not explained by this coherentist underpinning for it.

I turn now to the second point: are all commitments on a par as regards the possibility of revision? Elgin holds, with Quine, that in the quest for reflective equilibrium, anything may be revised. There is no commitment that may not be sacrificed in order to maximize the tenability of the entire system. Here I would like to protest that there are certain principles of logic, at least, that cannot be given up, because they are framework principles without which coherence could scarcely be defined. What would happen if we gave up the law of non-contradiction? It is not clear that there could any longer be such a thing as what Quine calls a recalcitrant experience, forcing changes elsewhere in the system. If a new deliverance stood in contradiction to things we already accepted, we could simply accept it with a "What – me worry?" shrug.

Here is another difficulty for a coherentism that holds everything revisable, at least if we understand this as "anything could be justifiably rejected," symbolized as "(p)possibly J ~ p." Suppose there is some proposition q (the law of non-contradiction, perhaps?) whose truth is necessary for anything to belong to a coherent system and therefore necessary for anything to be justified. Since ~q entails that nothing is justified, we now have *possibly J (nothing is justified)*, which is absurd.[14]

A related question about the status of the rules and principles of logic and evidence is whether they have force only because a subject is committed to them. I gather Elgin would say yes, but I say no. Consider a system of beliefs containing the elements p, q, and p → ~q. Suppose it is not a sheer fact of logic, independent of anything the subject believes, that the system is inconsistent and in need of revision. Could we make the system intolerably inconsistent by adding the principle: if any two of {p, q, and p → ~q} are true, then the third must be false? No, for anyone who could live comfortably with the original system could live comfortably with the expanded system. Such is the lesson the tortoise taught Achilles (Carroll, 1895).

I wish to raise one more question about the role of logical and evidential relations in Elgin's coherentism. Elgin defines both coherence and equilibrium in terms of the relation "p is reasonable in light of q, r, and s." What is the required epistemic status of this relation (or of the logical and other relations on which it supervenes)? Must such relations be known to hold among the propositions in a system before the propositions are warranted for the subject? And if so, how does such knowledge arise?

I see three possibilities to consider in answer to these questions. First, the holding of coherence-constituting relations might be regarded as an external condition of knowledge, making knowledge possible regardless of whether the subject knows that such relations hold. Although this seems to me a good way for a coherentist to go, I gather that Elgin would not find it congenial. On more than one occasion, she expresses her dissatisfaction with externalist stratagems in epistemology (CJ, pp. 22, 46, 51; this volume, p. 163). Second, it might be held that logical relations and other relations of support are known to hold because they are necessary relations, apprehendable *a priori*. But this, too, is an option Elgin would reject. In the first place, it would be a concession to foundationalism; in the second place, she has Quinean qualms about there being any propositions at all that are true necessarily and known *a priori* (CJ, pp. 40–6 and 53–7). Third, it might be held that coherence-constituting relations are known to hold because the propositions saying that they hold are part of the best overall coherent system that is reasonable in light of our antecedent commitments.[15] But that way lies an infinite regress. A proposition p affirming a relation of coherence would be justified only because the subject is justified in believing that p belongs to a coherent system. That belief in turn would be justified only because the subject is justified in believing that *p belongs to a coherent system* belongs to a coherent system, and so on. Even if it is the same system every step of the way, we still get a regress in which ever more complicated propositions must be believed with justification to belong to the system. The untenability of such a regress suggests to me that we should go instead with one of the first two options, agreeing with the externalist that coherence propositions need not be known at all or with the foundationalist that they are known because they are either basic propositions or propositions inferrable from basic propositions.

IV

I have not lived up to the title of this essay, for I have not offered a complete defense of moderate foundationalism. I hope nonetheless to have shown that an internalist coherentism cannot be a satisfactory theory of justification. We must be either externalists or foundationalists, and if we are foundationalists, our foundationalism must be of the moderate rather than the weak variety.

Notes

1 The distinction between positism and foundationalism is lost on those who cannot hear the word "justified" as anything but a past participle, implying that some act or relation of justifying has occurred whereby a belief is justified by something else that serves as a reason for it. For foundationalists, "justified" simply connotes a favorable epistemic status, which a belief may have even though the subject has no reason for it. In this connection, another term, such as "evident" or "credible," might be less misleading than "justified."

2 Haack summarizes her theory in Haack (2000). She does not classify foundherentism as weak foundationalism, believing it essential to foundationalism that the foundations not receive support from other elements in the structure.

3 Hereafter I shall cite this work in the text as AKV.

4 This paper was first published in 1857.

5 James Van Cleve, "Can coherence generate warrant?" (in preparation).

6 I discuss Huemer's work at some length in "Can coherence generate warrant?"

7 For foundationalists who hold that propositions about the physical world are always derived, not basic, that A says X would not be basic after all. It would rest, however, on deliverances that are basic.

8 For further discussion of Lewis's view, see Van Cleve (1977). For a method of assigning probabilities in relation to evidence without assuming that the evidence is certain (in the sense of having probability 1), see Jeffrey (1983).

9 By "conditionalizing" I mean drawing the inference "h has probability n given evidence e, and e is certainly true; therefore, h has probability n."

10 The term was coined by John Rawls (1971, pp. 20f). It refers to a state of affairs in which specific judgments and general principles have been brought into agreement with each other through a process of mutual adjustment.

11 Elsewhere Elgin adds other requirements. One is that there must not be a competing system that is more tenable overall (Elgin, 1996, p. 107). Another is that the best explanation of the system's coherence must be that it is at least roughly true ("Non-foundationalist epistemology: holism, coherence, and tenability," this volume).

12 See Firth (1964, pp. 466–7) for his progressively weaker foundationalisms.

13 Even so staunch a foundationalist as Roderick Chisholm incorporates Elgin's two allegedly distinctive features to some extent. Although the warrant belonging to Chisholmian "self-presenting" propositions can be neither increased nor diminished by their relations to other propositions, the same is not true of the warrant possessed by "indirectly evident" propositions. Their epistemic status is defeasible, and it may be raised by concurrence (Chisholm's term for coherence). See Chisholm (1977, chapters 2 and 4).

14 In fairness to Elgin, I note that she may give special status to the law of non-contradiction. She says that tenable systems must at least be logically consistent, or else be all-entailing (CJ, p. 136). Against this rationale, however, I note that in revisionary relevance logic, contradictions do not entail everything.

15 Perhaps this is what coherentists should say in response to Russell's question about how the laws underlying coherence are known.

References

BonJour, L. (1985) *The Structure of Empirical Knowledge.* Cambridge, MA: Harvard University Press.

Boole, G. (1952) On the application of the theory of probabilities to the question of the combination of testimonies or judgments. In *Studies in Logic and Probability.* London: C. A. Watts.

Carroll, L. (1895) What the Tortoise said to Achilles. *Mind*, 4, 275–80.

Chisholm, R. M. (1964) The myth of the given. In R. M. Chisholm et al., *Philosophy.* Englewood Cliffs, NJ: Prentice Hall.

Chisholm, R. M. (1977) *Theory of Knowledge*, 2nd edn. Englewood Cliffs, NJ: Prentice Hall.

Elgin, C. (1996) *Considered Judgment.* Princeton, NJ: Princeton University Press.

Firth, R. (1964) Coherence, certainty, and epistemic priority. *Journal of Philosophy*, 61, 545–57. Reprinted in R. Chisholm and R. J. Swartz (eds, 1973) *Empirical Knowledge.* Englewood Cliffs, NJ: Prentice Hall.

Goldman, A. (1979) What is justified belief? In G. Pappas (ed.), *Justification and Knowledge.* Dordrecht: D. Reidel.

Haack, S. (1993) *Evidence and Inquiry.* Oxford: Blackwell.

Haack, S. (2000) A foundherentist theory of empirical justification. In E. Sosa and J. Kim (eds), *Epistemology.* Oxford: Blackwell.

Huemer, M. (1997) Probability and coherence justification. *Southern Journal of Philosophy*, 35, 463–72.

Huemer, M. (2001) *Skepticism and the Veil of Perception.* Lanham, MD: Rowman & Littlefield.

Jeffrey, R. (1983) *The Logic of Decision*, 2nd edn. Chicago: University of Chicago Press.

Lewis, C. I. (1946) *An Analysis of Knowledge and Valuation.* LaSalle, IL: Open Court.

Rawls, J. (1971) *A Theory of Justice.* Cambridge, MA: Harvard University Press.

Russell, B. (1948) *Human Knowledge: Its Scope and Limits.* New York: Simon & Schuster.

Schlick, M. (1973) The foundation of knowledge. In R. Chisholm and R. J. Swartz (eds), *Empirical Knowledge*. Englewood Cliffs, NJ: Prentice Hall.

van Cleve, J. (1977) Probability and certainty: a re-examination of the Lewis–Reichenbach debate. *Philosophical Studies*, 32, 323–34.

Wittgenstein, L. (1969) *On Certainty*. Oxford: Blackwell.

Chapter Six

Is There Immediate Justification?

There Is Immediate Justification

James Pryor

1 Justification

I want to talk about a certain epistemic quality that I call "justification," and inquire whether that quality can ever be had "immediately" or "non-inferentially." Before we get into substantive issues, we need first to agree about what epistemic quality it is we'll be talking about, and then we need to clarify what it is to have that quality immediately or non-inferentially.

When I say I call this epistemic quality "justification," you are liable to think, "Oh I know what that is." You may. But experience has taught me that different philosophers use and understand the term "justification" differently, even *before* they start spinning substantive theories about what "justification" amounts to. So we should proceed cautiously. You *may* use the term "justification" to describe the same epistemic quality as I do; or you may use it to describe some different status or quality. You may use some *other* term, or no term at all, to describe the quality I call "justification."

I say that *you have justification to believe P* iff you are in a position where it would be epistemically appropriate for you to believe P, a position where P is epistemically likely for you to be true. I intend this to be a very inclusive epistemic status.[1] Some philosophers say you can know P without "having any justification" for your belief. We can assume that whenever a subject knows P, she will be in a position where it would be epistemically appropriate to believe P. So on my usage, whoever knows P has justification to believe P. (Perhaps she has that justification *because* she knows.) The philosophers who say otherwise are using "having justification" to mean something different, or more specific, than the epistemic status I am using it to mean. The same goes for philosophers who say a belief can be epistemically appropriate, and so play a role in justifying other beliefs, though you do not "have any justification" for

[handwritten margin notes: People often talk past one another. Trying to prevent this ✓]

[handwritten margin notes: Justification defined]

it. On my usage, *all it means* to have justification to believe something is that it is appropriate for you to believe it, and to rely on that belief in forming other beliefs. Some philosophers call this epistemic status "entitlement" or "warrant," rather than "justification." For the sake of a shared discussion, though, we need to fix on a single terminology.

If there is some state or condition you are in *in virtue of which* you have justification to believe P, I'll call it a "justification-making condition," or a *justification-maker* for short. This is a condition that *makes it* epistemically appropriate (or more appropriate) for you to believe P, rather than disbelieve P or suspend judgment. It is a truth-maker for your having justification to believe P. (Firth, 1964, called these conditions "warrant-increasing properties.") We can say that conditions of this sort *justify* you in believing P. They are *justifiers*. (We will encounter a different way to understand talk of "justifiers" in section 6 below.)

In what follows, it will be useful for us to distinguish between *having justification* to *believe* P, and actually *appropriately holding* a belief in P. To have justification *to* believe P, it is not important whether you *actually do* believe P (nor, if you do, why you do); there just have to be things that make believing P an appropriate attitude for you *to* have. To *appropriately believe* P more is required. You need to believe P; you need to have justification *to* believe P; and you also need to believe P *on the right grounds*. You need to believe it *for* reasons that make you have justification to believe it; you can't believe it for other, bad reasons, or on a whim.[2] There are further conditions as well: for instance, you need to be taking proper account of any evidence you have that tells against or undercuts your grounds for believing P. I describe another further condition in Pryor (forthcoming). Only when all such conditions are met will your belief in P be appropriately held.

2 Immediate Justification

Now that we have a grip on the notion of "justification," let's clarify what it means to talk about "immediate justification."

For some propositions, you have justification to believe them because *other* propositions you have justification to believe epistemically support them. For instance, suppose you look at the gas gauge of your car, and it appears to read "E." So you have justification to believe:

(Gauge) The gas gauge reads "E."

That, together with other things you justifiedly believe about your car, gives you justification to believe:

(Gas) Your car is out of gas.

(It is not important for our purposes whether you *actually do* believe (Gauge) or (Gas). Given your evidence, you *ought* to believe them.) In this example, your justification to believe (Gas) *comes* in part from the fact that you have justification to believe

(Gauge). That is, having justification to believe the latter is part of *what makes you* have justification to believe the former. The justification you have in this example to believe (Gauge) does *not* in the same way come from your having justification to believe (Gas). (One mark of this is that evidence that undercut your justification to believe (Gauge) would *ipso facto* undercut your justification to believe (Gas); but not vice versa.) When your justification to believe P comes in part from your having justification to believe other, supporting propositions, I will say that those latter propositions *mediate* your justification to believe P. (This kind of justification is sometimes called "inferential" justification. We will encounter a second way in which justification can be "inferential" later.) When your justification to believe P does *not* come from your justification to believe other propositions, I will call it *immediate.*

Some clarifications.[3] First, the question whether your justification to believe P is mediate or immediate is a question about *what kind* of epistemic support you have for P. It is not a question about *how much* support you have: nothing in our definition requires immediately justified beliefs to be infallible or indefeasible. Nor is it a question about what psychological processes you have undergone. The support you have to believe P can be mediate (or "inferential") even if you didn't *arrive at* P by deriving or inferring it from other beliefs.

Second, in order for you to have immediate justification to believe P, it is not required that your justification *comes from nowhere,* that there is nothing that *makes you* so justified. It is only required that what makes you justified doesn't include having justification for other beliefs.[4] There are various proposals about what can make one have immediate justification. For example, perhaps you are immediately justified in believing you feel tired because *you do* feel tired. Perhaps you are immediately justified in believing that tiredness is a mental state because *you understand* what tiredness is. And so on. It may be that there is no single correct account. Different propositions may be justified by different kinds of things.

Third, the fact that you have immediate justification to believe P does not entail that no other beliefs are required for you to be able *to form or entertain* the belief that P. Having the concepts involved in the belief that P may require believing certain other propositions; it does not follow that any justification you have to believe P must be mediated by those other propositions.[5]

Fourth, justification is usually defeasible. What a justification-maker for P gives you is provisional or prima facie justification to believe P; and *that* is what I am saying can be mediate or immediate. Whether it is *all things considered* appropriate for you to believe P will depend on what *other* evidence you possess, and whether it *defeats* the prima facie justification you have to believe P.

Fifth, beliefs can be epistemically overdetermined. You can have immediate justification and independent mediate justification to believe the same thing. In some cases, your belief will be grounded on the facts that make you have immediate justification; in other cases it might be grounded on the facts that make you have mediate justification, or on both sets of facts. This shows that we should try to explain the notion of "grounding" in a way that permits beliefs to be both grounded and immediately justified – if that is possible. (In section 7 we will consider an argument that it is not possible.)

3 Why Believe in Immediate Justification?

Now that we have achieved some clarity about what immediate justification *is*, let's ask why we should believe in it.

The most famous argument for immediate justification is called the *Regress Argument*. Really this is not one argument but several; because philosophers do not always have the same regress in mind. Sometimes they have in mind a *dialectical* regress: to defend your belief that P in argument, you need to appeal to other beliefs, but then how do you defend those other beliefs? Sometimes they have in mind a *grounding* regress: your belief in P is grounded in such-and-such other beliefs, but then what grounds those other beliefs? Sometimes they have in mind a *justification-making* regress: what makes you have justification to believe P is, in part, your having justification to believe such-and-such other propositions, but then what makes you justified in believing those other propositions?

Let's focus on this third, justification-making regress. There are four possible ways for the regress to play out:

(i)   The regress never ends. The justificatory chain goes on forever.
(ii) What makes you justified in believing P is your having justification to believe other things, and . . . what makes you justified in believing some of them is your having justification to believe P. That is, the justificatory chain includes some closed loops.
(iii) Eventually we get to a proposition you believe inappropriately, *without* having any justification for it. Though this belief is not itself justified, it is somehow able to justify you in believing further propositions.
(iv) Eventually we get to a proposition you have justification to believe, but that justification does not come from your believing, or having justification to believe, any further propositions.[6]

The foundationalist argues that options (i) and (ii) are untenable; so we have to accept (iii) or (iv). On either of those options, a subject can have justification to believe some propositions, that does not come from her having justification to believe any other propositions.[7]

Though this Regress Argument is the *most famous* argument for immediate justification, I do not think it is the *best* argument. It has the same weakness as any argument by elimination: everything turns on whether the rejected options really are untenable. That is not a matter that can be quickly decided. In addition, the Regress Argument assumes that justificatory relations always have a linear, asymmetric nature; and some epistemologists deny that that is so.

So I do not think the best argument for immediate justification is this Regress Argument. I think the best argument comes from *considering examples*.

Suppose I feel tired, or have a headache. I am justified in believing I feel those ways. And there do not *seem* to be any other propositions that mediate my justification for believing it. What would the other propositions be?

Suppose I raise my arm. I am justified in believing that I'm doing this in order to scare a fly. That is *my reason for* trying to raise my arm. Sometimes my reasons for acting are opaque to me and have to be carefully reconstructed. But not always. In cases like this one, my reasons can be immediately evident to me. There doesn't seem to be *anything else* I am justified in believing, that *makes me* justified in believing my reason for trying to raise my arm is to scare a fly. What would the other beliefs be?

I am imagining my grandmother. The way I am imagining her is sitting in her kitchen. Or at least, I believe it is. And it seems I could be *justified* in that belief. Again, it is hard to see what other propositions might mediate this justification.

I think about a domino and a chessboard. It is obvious to me that the only way to wholly cover two spaces on the board is to place the domino horizontally or vertically. That is something I *could* have derived from geometric premises. But in this case I didn't. I just immediately saw that it was true. In this case, too, my justification does not seem to be mediated by any further propositions.[8]

These and many other examples provide us with good candidates to be immediate justification. What we need to do is see whether such examples stand up to critical reflection.

4 The Master Argument for Coherentism

The main argument against immediate justification was historically directed at the Given Theory. That was a theory that offered a specific account of what some immediate justification-makers looked like. The precise details of the Given Theory aren't important for our inquiry.[9] What is important is that the Given Theory is just one possible account among many of what gives us immediate justification. Fans of immediate justification are also free to give different accounts. The following map may be helpful:

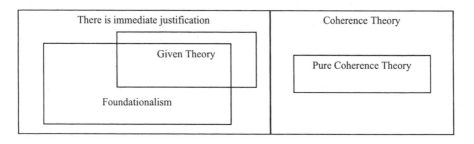

I make foundationalism a proper subclass of the view that there is immediate justification, because foundationalists also hold additional theses about the structure of your justification. One does not need to accept those additional theses, merely to believe that *some* beliefs are immediately justified. Coherentists deny that it is possible for any beliefs to be immediately justified. They say that justification always comes, *at least in part*, from your justification for other beliefs. I distinguish between pure and impure versions of coherentism. Pure coherentists claim that a belief can only be justified by its relations to other beliefs. Impure coherentists are willing to give some non-beliefs, such as perceptual experiences, a justifying role. They will just deny that those states are able to justify a belief *all by themselves*. They can only do so in cooperation with other justified beliefs. For instance, an impure coherentist might say that when it looks to you as if you have hands, *and* you have justification to believe that your visual experiences are reliable, *those facts together* can make you justified in believing that you have hands.[10]

Now, as I said, the main argument against immediate justification was historically directed at the Given Theory. This argument alleged that in order to be a justifier, you need to have certain characteristics, and that having those characteristics makes you be the sort of thing that itself needs justification. Here is a sample presentation, from BonJour:

> The basic idea of givenness . . . is to distinguish two aspects of ordinary cognitive states, their capacity to justify other cognitive states and their own need for justification, and then to try to find a kind of state which possesses only the former aspect and not the latter – a state of immediate apprehension or intuition. But we can now see plainly that any such attempt is fundamentally misguided and intrinsically hopeless. For it is clear on reflection that it is one and the same feature of a cognitive state, namely, its assertive or at least representational content, which both enables it to confer justification on other states and also creates the need for it to be itself justified – thus making it impossible in principle to separate these two aspects. (BonJour, 1985, p. 78)

The characteristics BonJour cites are having "assertive" or representational content. (Sometimes it is claimed, in addition, that a justifier has to have *conceptual* content. We will return to that idea later.) In order to have these characteristics, the coherentist argues, a state would itself have to be a belief – or at least be sufficiently like a belief that it in turn needs justifying. So we aren't going to find any immediate justifiers: conditions that are able to justify though they don't themselves need justifying. That is the core of the familiar argument against the Given Theory.

Notice that this argument really doesn't have anything specifically to do with the Given Theory. If it works, it should work against *any* account of immediate justification. In fact, if it works, then the only things which can play *any* justifying role will be other beliefs (or belief-like states). So the argument threatens impure coherence theories no less than it does views that countenance immediate justification. It is not really an argument *against the Given Theory*, then. It is more an argument *for pure coherentism*. I think of this argument as the *Master Argument for coherentism*.[11]

One step in this Master Argument insists that only states with propositional content can be justifiers. Let's call this:

The Content Requirement
In order to be a justifier, you need to have propositional content.

Why should we accept that requirement? Well, if a state doesn't have propositional content, then it can't stand in logical relations to beliefs. Davidson once complained:

> The relation between a sensation and a belief cannot be logical, since sensations are not beliefs or other propositional attitudes. What then is the relation? The answer is, I think, obvious: the relation is causal. Sensations cause some beliefs and in *this* sense are the

basis or ground of those beliefs. But a causal explanation of a belief does not show how or why the belief is justified. (Davidson, 1986, p. 311)

Of course Davidson is right that merely learning that some sensation S caused belief B does not *show* that B is justified, or that S is what makes it justified. However, it would be compatible with that that S *does* make B justified. Davidson wants to rule that possibility out. He thinks that sensation S *cannot* be what justifies B. So he must think that it is *only* by standing in logical relations to a belief that a state can justify the belief. He may be thinking: if a state doesn't stand in logical relations to a belief, then why should it justify that belief *as opposed to others*? For example, let's assume that headaches don't have propositional content. (Some philosophers argue that all mental states have propositional content. For the sake of discussion, we will assume with Davidson that they are wrong.) Why then should a headache justify me in believing *I have a headache*, as opposed to *I don't have a headache* or *I am a headache* or *There are no such things as headaches*? My headache itself wouldn't logically support *any* of those propositions; so it is not clear why it should justify some of them but not the others.

There is then some initial plausibility to the idea that in order to play the role of a justifier, a state has to be able to stand in logical relations; which it can only do if it has propositional content. (Objection: What about *a lack of defeating evidence*? That is not naturally thought of as a state with propositional content; but it does seem relevant to your justification. Reply: The Content Requirement should be understood as stating a necessary condition to be a prima facie justifier. The role defeating evidence plays is in settling a further question: When does prima facie justification get to become all things considered justification?)

The other step in the Master Argument insists that if a state has propositional content, then it will be a belief or epistemically like a belief:

Only Beliefs
Only beliefs (or other states that are epistemically like beliefs, and also require epistemic justification) have propositional content.

But wait a minute! *Desires* have propositional content, and they are not the sort of thing which *could* be, nor do they *need to be* justified – at least, not *epistemically* justified.[12]

The coherentist will respond: "That's true, desires have propositional content and don't need any epistemic justification. So the Only Beliefs premise as it stands is false. But desires aren't *capable* of justifying beliefs, either! So they're not a counter-example to *the conclusion* we want: that only beliefs can be justifiers. They just force us to be more specific about what features it is that enable a state to be a justifier. It takes more than just having propositional content. There are some ways of representing the proposition that P that *purport to be saying how the world is*, and other ways that don't. When a state represents that P in the first way, we can say that the state *assertively* represents that P. Desires may represent that P in some sense, but they do not represent it assertively. Neither do states like imagining and entertaining. When you desire that P, or imagine that P, or entertain the thought that P, your mental state does not purport to be saying that P is (already) true. What our Master Argument *should* say is that, to be a justifier, a state needs to have propositional content, *and* it needs to represent that proposition *assertively*. States that don't do that aren't even *purporting* to say how the world is, so how could they play the role of justifiers? And in order to represent a proposition assertively, a state will have to be a belief, or else sufficiently like a belief that it needs justifying too."

Let's revise the Master Argument as the coherentist proposes:

The Content Requirement (Revised)
In order to be a justifier, you need to have propositional content, and you need to represent that proposition assertively.

Only Beliefs (Revised)
Only beliefs (or other states that are epistemically like beliefs) represent propositions assertively.

∴ Only beliefs (or other states that are epistemically like beliefs) can be justifiers.

I want to mention two quick worries about this argument, and then dwell at length upon a third.

First, even if this argument were sound, it is not clear that it would establish coherentism. The argument says that the only things that could justify are states like belief, that "require" justification. A foundationalist might agree that beliefs in some sense always "require" justification, but argue that they are still sometimes *able to justify* other beliefs even when *they are not* themselves justified. (This was option (iii) in the Regress Argument.) The other beliefs that got justified in this way would count as "immediately justified," as I have defined it.

Second, we might worry whether the coherentist is himself in a position to accept the Master Argument. After all, doesn't the coherentist want facts about *coherence* to play a justifying role? Yet coherence is not itself a belief or a belief-like state. Here I think the coherentist can reply, "Notice that coherence is a property of *the contents* of your beliefs. Any set of beliefs having the same contents would be just as coherent. So it is OK to say that it is always your beliefs that are doing the justifying. It is just that certain sets of beliefs (those whose contents cohere well) justify more than others. Talk about the justifying role of *coherence* is shorthand for talk about which sets of beliefs justify and which don't." This seems to me a plausible line for the coherentist to take.

There is a third worry that the coherentist cannot so easily finesse, however. This worry once again concerns the Only Beliefs premise. The problem is that many philosophers of mind these days think of *experiences* as having propositional content. To say that experiences have propositional content is not to say that experiences are beliefs. It can look to you as if P without your believing that P. Experiences and beliefs just have it in common that they both represent propositions.[13] And both seem to represent propositions *assertively*; when they represent that P, they do so in a way that purports to say how the world is. So the Master Argument as we have it gives us no reason to exclude experiences from the ranks of justifiers.[14]

Yet, unlike beliefs, experiences aren't the sort of thing which *could be*, nor do they *need to be* justified. Sure, *beliefs about* what experiences you have may need to be justified. But *the experiences themselves* do not. (If someone comes up to you and demands, "*How dare you* have that experience? What gives you the right?" what should you say?) So we see that, contrary to the Only Beliefs premise, states that assertively represent a proposition *won't* always themselves require justification.

Where does this leave things between foundationalists (or fans of immediate justification more generally) and proponents of the Master Argument? A foundationalist *can* just stop here. He can say, "Well, we've seen that experiences are a counter-example to the Only Beliefs premise; so even if we accept the Content Requirement, that poses no obstacle to letting experiences play the role of justifiers. They might play that role in cooperation with other beliefs, as the impure coherentist allows, or they might do it all by themselves. We have seen no good reason yet to think they can't" (see, for example, Martin, 1993; Steup, 2001).

Some foundationalists do stop there. They are happy to accept the Content Requirement. But that is a pretty demanding constraint to put on what can be a justifier. And in fact, if you think about it, the Content Requirement will be well motivated only if an *even more demanding* constraint is. Let me explain.

The coherentist denies that the mere presence of a headache or a desire can justify you in believing anything, because these states don't assertively represent anything. They can't even justify you in believing that you have those states. But then neither should the mere presence of a belief or an experience justify you in believing you have *them*, either. For although beliefs and experiences do have propositional contents that they assertively represent, those contents are playing no role in the justificatory relation here envisaged. It seems just an unfair prejudice to allow states that assertively represent propositions to justify the belief that *you are in* those states, but deny the same ability to other states. We should either allow this justifying relation in every case, or prohibit it in every case.

The coherentist will try to prohibit it. They will say, "Look it's not just that the justifying state needs *to have* a content. The content needs to be in some sense *what does the justifying*." What that means, I guess, is that the content of the justifying state needs to *imply*, or *inductively* or *abductively support*, or stand in some other suitable evidential relation to the content it justifies. Let's give this idea a name: *abductive?*

Premise Principle
The only things that can justify a belief that P are other states that assertively represent propositions, and those propositions have to be ones that *could be used as premises* in an argument for P. They have to stand in some kind of inferential relation to P: they have to imply it or inductively support it or something like that.

Premise Principle

The contents of your beliefs and experiences will ordinarily not imply that *you are in* those states; so this principle will prevent your beliefs and experiences from directly justifying the belief that you are in them.[15]

I think this Premise Principle is the real intuitive force behind the coherentist's Content Requirement. Recall the Davidson quote from earlier. He was saying that to be a justifier, you have to stand in logical relations to the beliefs you justify. I think this is what he really had in mind. Here are some other authors also giving voice to the Premise Principle.

We cannot really understand the relations in virtue of which a judgment is warranted except as relations within the space of concepts: relations such as implication or probabilification, which hold between potential exercises of conceptual capacities (McDowell, 1994, p. 7).

> [A reason for S's believing that P is] a fact about that person which makes her believing that thing intelligible from the point of view of rationality. If this is to happen then the selected fact about S must be somehow related to (her) believing that P. And since this relation is to make her believing that P intelligible *from the point of view of rationality*, it is necessarily a relation which obtains in virtue of the correctness of some kind of reasoning. That is to say, successfully giving such a reason makes essential reference to the premise of an inference of some kind, whose conclusion is appropriately related, most likely by identity, to the content of the belief for which the reason is being given. (Brewer, 1999, p. 154; see also pp. 150–1)

The Premise Principle says that all justifying relations between states hold in virtue of "inferential relations" between their contents. We have to be sure we understand this properly.

First, the Premise Principle states a constraint on what can give you justification *to believe* things; it does not concern your actual beliefs or reasoning processes. It can allow that we often form beliefs that are *supported by* "inferential relations" without *engaging in* any inference.

It can also respect the difference that Harman (1986) emphasized between logic and reasoning. Harman said that just because you believe some premises that together imply P, it doesn't follow that it would be reasonable for you to infer P. It might, for example, be more reasonable to give up your belief in some of the premises. The Premise Principle can allow this. It is only trying to explicate the nature of prima facie justificatory relations. According to the Premise Principle, those always consist in "inferential relations" between contents. If your beliefs in some premises together imply P, and you have prima facie justification for those beliefs, then you have prima facie justification to believe P. But it might be unreasonable for you to *infer* P on those grounds, e.g. if you also have *other* evidence that tells against P, or that undercuts some of your prima facie justification for the premises.

Although there is *a sense* in which the Premise Principle claims all prima facie justificatory relations are "inferential," this is not the same as saying that all justification is "inferential" in the sense of being *mediated*. The coherentists would like to *argue from* the Premise Principle to that conclusion. But the Premise Principle by itself doesn't say it. Without supplementation, the Premise Principle would allow experiences to justify beliefs. For instance, an experience as of your having hands could justify the belief that you have hands. And justification of this sort would count as immediate. It is just that, according to the Premise Principle, the experience is able to justify that belief because of the "inferential relations" its content stands in to the content of the belief. (In this case, the "inferential relation" is straightforward: the

Chapter Seven

experience's content is the same as the content of the belief.) So the Premise Principle doesn't imply what people usually have in mind when they say that our perceptual justification is "inferential" or mediated. That is a view according to which we are in the first place justified in believing we have certain experiences, and then that justification for beliefs about our experiences is an essential part of what justifies our beliefs about the external world. The Premise Principle doesn't imply that; it would allow *our merely having* experiences with the right sorts of contents to justify beliefs about the external world.

Nor is the Premise Principle *implied by* the view that perceptual justification is mediated. For the latter view says nothing about what justifies our beliefs about our experiences. Perhaps, *contra* the Premise Principle, we are justified in those beliefs merely *by virtue of having* the experiences.

So there is no straightforward relation between the Premise Principle and the question whether perceptual justification is mediated or immediate. The relation between the Premise Principle and foundationalism more generally is also complicated. As I said before, some Foundationalists are happy to accept the coherentist's Content Requirement, and the Premise Principle that motivates it. They just argue that there can be justifiers that satisfy the Premise Principle but aren't beliefs.

Those arguments interact in interesting ways with the question whether experiences have "conceptual content." Some philosophers combine the Premise Principle with the view that you can only have the required type of "inferential relation" when both *relata* have conceptual content. That seems to be the view of Sellars (1963), McDowell (1994, lectures 1 and 3; 1998),[16] and Brewer (1999, chapter 5). The coherentists will go on to argue that experiences don't have conceptual content and so cannot be justifiers. McDowell and Brewer, on the other hand, think that experiences *are* justifiers; so they argue that experiences do have conceptual content after all. Others have argued that experiences can stand in the "inferential relations" the Premise Principle requires even if their content is not conceptual (see e.g. Heck, 2000; Peacocke, 2001).[17] Personally, I am not really sure what "conceptual content" is; so I won't enter into this debate. I just wanted to call attention to the role the Premise Principle plays in it.

We have been looking at the Master Argument for coherentism, and considering whether it succeeds in ruling out the possibility of immediate justification. I said that even if the Master Argument were sound, it might still be possible for unjustified beliefs to do some justifying; and that would be a kind of immediate justification. We have also seen that one can accept the Premise Principle and still say that experiences justify; that will be another kind of immediate justification. So one does not need to reject the Premise Principle, to believe in immediate justification.

Nonetheless, many foundationalists will want to reject the Premise Principle. It doesn't exclude *the very possibility* of immediate justification; but it does impose *quite a demanding constraint* on what can be an immediate justifier. Many foundationalists believe in justification-making facts that violate that constraint. For instance, many Foundationalists want to allow *facts about what sensations you are having*, or *facts about what mental activities you are engaging in*, to count as justifiers. Some want to allow *facts about what is required to possess certain concepts* to play a justifying role. Some say *facts about how reliable you are*, or *facts about whether your cognitive faculties are functioning properly*, or *facts about what beliefs are irresistible*, can play a justifying role. And so on. Each of these facts concerns matters that go beyond what assertive states you are in; so the Premise Principle would exclude them all from being justifiers.

I think, then, that it would be valuable to consider whether the Premise Principle is really well motivated. The rest of this essay will consider some arguments on its behalf.

There is one type of argument that I won't consider. Those are "arguments from the trenches": arguments of the form "Theory So-and-So gives the correct substantive account of justification; and that theory only postulates justifiers of the sort the Premise Principle permits." Assessing any argument of that type would require examining the pros and cons of different theories of justification, and determining whether Theory So-and-So really is an adequate theory. That is well beyond the scope of this essay. Instead, I will look at arguments that try to establish the Premise Principle "from on high," *before* we have decided upon a substantive theory of justification. I am going to argue that *no argument of that sort* succeeds. Hence, I think we have no reason to give the Premise Principle any authority when we are choosing among competing theories of justification. If I am right, that will clear the way for the many foundationalist theories that postulate immediate justifiers that violate the Premise Principle.[18]

5 Avoiding Arbitrariness

Our first argument for the Premise Principle is one that I have already mentioned. Consider a state without propositional content, like your headache. Since it has no propositional content, this state can't stand in logical relations to any beliefs. So why should it justify *any one* belief as opposed to others? Why should it justify the belief *I have a headache*, as opposed to *I don't have a headache*, or any other belief? What can the foundationalist say to make the justifying relations he postulates non-arbitrary?

Chisholm provides a nice example of what is being objected to here. His view was that having an experience would give one prima facie justification for (or "tend to make evident") certain beliefs (see e.g. Chisholm, 1989). The justifying relations Chisholm postulated struck many philosophers as *ad hoc*. That impression was particularly forceful because of the model of experience Chisholm worked with. When we describe an experience as one of sensing or being-appeared-to *squarely*, that is supposed to be a description of the experience's intrinsic phenomenal quality. We might naturally *take* such an experience to be one in which we are perceiving an external square; but "being-appeared-to squarely" isn't a description of what external objects we seem to be perceiving. It doesn't mean "having an experience *that represents that there is a square*." Chisholm didn't think experiences had representational content. Hence, the justifying relations he postulated seemed to lack any principled motivation. Why should sensing squarely justify beliefs about squares, rather than beliefs about squirrels? Many think Chisholm had no adequate answer to this question; so his position seems arbitrary and unsatisfying.

I certainly agree that epistemologists should give principled, non-arbitrary rationales for the justifying relations they postulate. However, I see no reason to think that they will *have to* appeal to propositional contents to do it. A foundationalist might attribute other kinds of structure to some of his justifiers. On certain theories of events, for example, events have something like a logical structure. The event of my having a headache has a logical structure akin to the structure of the proposition that I have a headache. Wouldn't these structures be enough to enable the foundationalist to avoid the charge of arbitrariness?[19] This is just one option for a foundationalist to pursue. It is hard to draw any general assessment, until we see how the details work out. But the idea that only the Premise Principle can save us from arbitrariness seems unwarranted to me.

6 Evidence and Reasons

Where I have been talking about "justification-makers" or "justifiers," some other philosophers will talk about "evidence" or "reasons"; and there are several arguments that the latter notions have to conform to the Premise Principle. This might be thought to show that justification-makers *also* have to conform to the Premise Principle.

Recall that a "justification-maker" is defined to be whatever makes it epistemic appropriate for you to believe some propositions rather than others. We should be open to the possibility that terms like "evidence" and "reasons" do not express exactly that notion. They may express different, or more specific, notions.

For instance, some philosophers argue that "reasons" and "evidence" have to be the sort of thing that can *probabilify* a hypothesis, and hence, that the hypothesis can have a *probability conditional on*. Hypotheses also have to be able to *explain* our evidence, be *inconsistent with* our evidence, and so on. All of these roles require evidence to have propositional content. So how could states without propositional content justify or be evidence? (See Williamson, 2000, pp. 194–7; Plantinga, 2001, p. 62.)

In response, I say: let's not assume too quickly that "evidence" and "justifier" are perfect synonyms. Consider that we sometimes use the terms "belief" and "desire" to refer to *propositions that* one believes and desires, rather than to *one's states* of believing or desiring them. Similarly, I think, sometimes we use "evidence" to refer to *propositions that are* evident to one, rather than to the states that make them evident. In other words, we use "evidence" to refer not to our justification-makers, but rather to the propositions that they (most directly) justify. We call those propositions "our evidence" because they can serve as evidence for further reasoning. This diagnosis would permit things like headaches, that do not *themselves* have propositional content, to be justification-makers – so long as *what* they give one justification *to* believe *is* a proposition.

A second argument says that we ordinarily understand "justifications" for a belief to be *arguments* that support the belief. If you have *reasons* for your belief, they should be considerations you could in principle *cite*, or *give*, to someone who doubted or challenged the belief. You can't give someone else a non-propositional state like a headache (at least, not in the relevant sense); you can only give them *premises* and *arguments* that inferentially support your belief. This seems to show that justifications and reasons *are* limited to things permitted by the Premise Principle. (See, for example, McDowell, 1994, pp. 165-6.)

There may be a notion of "a reason" that these remarks properly articulate. We can call it the *dialectical* notion of a reason. I want to emphasize, though, that that notion is *different* from the notion of a justification-maker that I have been employing in this paper, and that the Premise Principle is meant to be formulated in terms of.

It is useful here to distinguish two construals of the verb "justify." On the first construal, "justifying" a belief in P is a matter of proving or showing the belief to be just (or reasonable or credible). This is something that *a person* does, by giving some argument in support of that belief. (Here we can include both arguments whose conclusion is P, and arguments whose conclusion is that your belief in P is epistemically appropriate, or is likely to be true.) By extension, we can also talk about *things* justifying beliefs; in this extended sense, a thing counts as justifying a belief if it is something *you are in a position to use* to prove or show your belief to be just. Such things would be "reasons" in the dialectical sense articulated above. To be explicit, let's call these things *justification-showers*.

There is also a second way to construe the verb "justify," which sees it as akin to the verbs "beautify" and "electrify." When a combination of light and color beautifies a room, it is not *proving* that the room is beautiful; rather, it is *making* the room beautiful. Similarly, on this understanding, justifying a belief is a matter of *making* a belief just or reasonable, rather than a matter of *showing* the belief to be just. That is how I understand the notion of a justification-maker.[20]

No doubt there are some interesting connections between justification-making and justification-showing. But they are two different notions; so we should not assume that their extensions will coincide. It *needs argument* to show that nothing is eligible to be a justification-maker unless it can also be a justification-shower. Until we have such an argument, the fact that justification-showers always conform to the Premise Principle should not persuade us that justification-makers must do so as well.

Even if we manage to separate the notion of a justification-maker from the dialectical notion of "a reason," I expect proponents of the Premise Principle will still insist there is enough of a connection between justification and "reasons" for constraints on the latter to support some restrictions on the former.

For instance, they can observe that there is a difference between *reasons there are* to believe P – where these include reasons not now available to you – and *reasons you have* to believe P. For example, one reason *there is* to believe you will soon be sick is the fact that you just drank poison. But if you are unaware of that fact, then it is not a reason you have. For something to be a reason you have, for it to justify *you* in believing P, it has to be in some sense *epistemically available* to you. It has to be the sort of thing you could *take as* a reason. When it is not available to you – e.g. when you are not in a state that assertively represents it, and so not in a position to appeal to it in arguing for P – then it may be *a* reason to believe P, but it won't be a reason you have. For anyone with "internalist" sympathies, these reflections should apply to justifiers just as much as they do to reasons.[21]

I think it is right to distinguish between things such that *you would* be justified in believing P, if you were aware of them, and things that *do* justify you in believing P.

I think it is also right that if something justifies you, then it has to be in some sense "available" to you. But I think it would be wrong to assume that this kind of "availability" requires you to be in representational states. As I understand the notion of "availability," it is correlative to the notion of a ground. A justifier is available to you at a given time – it will be something you can "take as" a reason – if it is something that could then *ground* a belief of yours. If the foundationalist can make sense of beliefs being *grounded on* non-representational justifiers like headaches, then he can make sense of those justifiers being sufficiently available to you.

Our next argument for the Premise Principle will question whether the foundationalist *can* make sense of the grounding relation, without appeal to beliefs or other representational states.

7 Grounding and Being Guided by Norms

We introduced the notion of *a ground* to distinguish between cases where you believe P *for* good reasons, or on grounds that justify you in believing P, and cases where you believe P on bad grounds, ones that do not justify that belief. What does it take for your belief to be *grounded on* some fact or condition C that you are in? A natural thought is that your belief counts as so grounded iff it is formed (or sustained) in a way that is guided by the epistemic norm "When in C, believe P." If that is right, then the best way to understand the grounding relation is by inquiring into what it takes to be guided by such a norm.

I understand an *epistemic norm* to be a claim about how we should be, in epistemic matters. Some norms merely evaluate the quality of a static epistemic situation, e.g. *You should not (it is inappropriate to) have inconsistent beliefs.* Others instruct us how to *change or improve* our situation, e.g. *If you believe that A is F, then you should believe that B is F too*; or *You should gather as much evidence as possible.* Only some epistemic norms tell us what to believe or to refrain from believing. Those are the norms that we need to consider here. We can take them to be of the form: *When you are in conditions C, you should believe (or refrain from believing) P.* Putting it in the imperative: *When you are in C, believe P.* Norms like these will be correct just in case being in C does make it the case that you should believe P. In other words, just in case being in C is a justification-maker for the proposition that P.

For any norm, there will be a difference between acting in a way that merely *happens to accord* with the norm, on the one hand, and *being guided by* the norm, or *complying with it, on the other.* You act in accordance with a norm "When in C, do φ" just in case you always φ when in C. You need not be *trying* to follow that norm. You may have φed for reasons that have nothing to do with C. You may even regard being in C as decisive reason *to refrain from* φing – but just never have noticed that you were in C. In order to comply with the norm, on the other hand, the fact that you are in C *does* in some sense need to guide or be your reason for φing. We need to know what this relation amounts to, when φing consists in forming (or sustaining) a belief.

One account of this will portray you as *deliberately following* the norm, in the way that one can deliberately follow a cooking recipe. I mean three things by this. First, on this account your belief will be voluntarily chosen. Forming it will be a genuine action of yours. Second, your belief will be chosen for a reason (a practical reason). In forming the belief that P, you will have been guided by a norm "When in C, believe P" only if the fact (or apparent fact) that you are in C is among your reasons for actively forming that belief. Third, this account says that to be acting for the reason that you are in C, you have to *represent* that reason to yourself. You have to be in a position to employ the proposition that you are in C as a premise in your practical reasoning. The upshot of these three assumptions is that your belief can be guided by the norm "When in C, believe P" only when you represent to yourself that you are in C, and can employ that proposition as a premise in reasoning. This may be thought to lend some support to the Premise Principle.[22]

Some replies. First, even if this account of belief-formation were right, it is not clear that it would really support *the Premise Principle.* It seems only to support the claim that, for C to be a justifier that grounds your belief, you need to be in some state that assertively represents you as being in C. This doesn't imply that C *itself* is a representational state. Still, this account will imply that representational states are present whenever your belief is properly grounded. And that may be of some use to a defender of the Premise Principle. He may urge that it is really the state that *represents you* as being in C, and not the condition C itself, that is doing the justifying.[23]

Second, this account of belief-formation seems to rely on too reflective and deliberate a picture of what it takes to act for a reason, or in compliance with a norm. Consider activities like playing a musical instrument, figuring out why your car or computer isn't working, or making judgments of grammaticality. These are practical skills whose exercise seems to be governed by rules. But we don't think subjects need to think about or deliberately apply any rules when they are performing those activities. They don't even need to be *aware of why* they are acting in the precise ways they do. Many philosophers would regard their actions as guided by rules, for all that. So, prima facie, it seems possible to act in a way that is guided by rules without representing to yourself that you are in conditions C so now you should do so and so.[24]

Finally, I think the present account of belief-formation misrepresents *how active* we are with respect to our beliefs. Many justified beliefs aren't formed in the deliberate way it describes, because forming those beliefs *isn't an action of ours,* in the first place. We do exercise voluntary control over some aspects of our epistemic lives: what evidence we gather, what sources we consult, and so on. But when it comes to our here-and-now doxastic choices, these are usually involuntary and unreflective. Our beliefs usually just *result from* our other epistemic efforts. They just *happen,* in the way that sneezing or digesting happen. Ordinarily we make no intentional choices about what to believe. One *can* choose to believe something, and then seek ways *to get* oneself to believe it – just as we can seek ways *to get* ourselves to sneeze or digest. But that is not the way we usually form justified beliefs.[25]

Some philosophers argue for the strong thesis that it is impossible for justified beliefs *ever* to be formed by deliberate choice. Perhaps that is right. But here I need only the following, much weaker thesis: some beliefs are appropriately held, and so properly grounded, even though they *aren't* formed by deliberate choice. So it can't in general be required for grounding a belief that one have formed the belief in the deliberate way that the account we are considering describes.

Here a proponent of the Premise Principle might say: "True, we don't always *ourselves* deliberately choose our beliefs. But that is how an ideal reasoner would form beliefs. And it is a constraint on any condition that purports to justify our beliefs that it could ground the belief of an ideal reasoner who did choose his beliefs deliberately."

I am not sure that the fully reflective and deliberate reasoner envisaged here is a coherent ideal for us to aim at. Such a reasoner would never form or change beliefs, except by deliberately following an epistemic norm. But deliberately following a norm requires *already* having beliefs about (or at least, some representation of) whether its antecedent conditions are fulfilled. From where is the ideal reasoner supposed to get *those* beliefs? Since she is an ideal reasoner, she would have to have formed *them* by deliberately following norms, too. But then she would need further beliefs, about whether the antecedent conditions of *those* norms are fulfilled.... There is a real threat that this reasoner would never be able to get started. She would never *be able to* deliberately follow a norm for forming beliefs. So she would be doxastically paralyzed. Or, if she were able to get started, it would only be by virtue of believing an infinite hierarchy of propositions. Neither option gives us a very promising model to aspire to.[26]

If your belief's being grounded on condition C isn't a matter of your *deliberately following* a norm when you form that belief, then what is it a matter of? This is a difficult question. I can't guarantee that when we work out the details, they won't turn out to be inhospitable to views that violate the Premise Principle. But I think we *can* be assured that there is no argument here for the Premise Principle "from on high," no argument that will settle the question before we work out those details.[27]

Notes

1 Though it doesn't include everything. I think it is possible for subjects to believe P inappropriately, and so without justification, though be non-culpable for doing so. (Perhaps the epistemic faults that led to the belief are too subtle and well entrenched for those subjects to recognize.) So there is one kind of positive epistemic status, being *epistemically blameless* in believing P, that does not entail that one has justification to believe P. See Pryor (2001, section 4) for discussion and references.

2 The relation of believing something *for* such-and-such a reason is sometimes called "the basing relation." However, I think that terminology encourages too voluntaristic and reflective a picture of the phenomenon; I prefer to call it "the grounding relation" instead. We will talk more about this relation in section 7. For further discussion, see Korcz (1997) and Audi (1993, chapters 3, 7, and 8).

3 For more about immediate justification and what it does and does not require, see Alston (1989, chapter 3), Audi (1993, chapter 3), and Pryor (2000).

4 We have to be careful here: I expect that what makes you justified in believing one proposition may often make you justified in believing several. Suppose being in state S makes you justified in believing $P_1, \ldots, P_n$. As I understand talk of "making it true" that you have justification, being in S can make it true that you have justification to believe $P_2, \ldots, P_n$ (let S^* be the state of having this justification), and also make it true that you

have justification to believe P_1, without its following that being in S^* is part of what makes you justified in believing P_1. Hence, your justification to believe P_1 can be immediate, even if what makes you justified in believing P_1 also makes you justified in believing other propositions, too.

5   Consider: in order to have the concept of a unicorn I may need to believe (i) that unicorns have hooves, and (ii) that unicorns have horns. Now suppose I acquire evidence that a virus has killed all hoofed creatures. Since I believe unicorns to be hoofed creatures, I form the belief (iii) that no unicorns currently exist. It is clear that (ii) plays no role in justifying this belief. This shows that there can be propositions *you need to believe* in order to have certain concepts (you need to believe (ii) in order to have the concept of a unicorn), without those propositions *mediating your justification* for every belief involving the concepts. Now, (iii) is not an immediately justified belief. But it serves to make my point. We can see the same phenomenon with beliefs that *are* good candidates to be immediately justified, like (iv) *If any unicorn exists, it is identical with itself.* (ii) plays no more role in justifying that belief than it plays in justifying (iii).

6   On some presentations of the Regress Argument, the regress stops with your last justified belief (or, as I say, with the last proposition you have justification *to* believe). On others, the regress stops with what justifies your last justified belief: the states or conditions that *make you* justified in believing it. These are just different ways of talking; there is no real philosophical disagreement here.

7   Many foundationalists shun option (iii), but structurally it also qualifies as a foundationalist option. For example, a foundationalist might claim that *merely having* a belief that P – even without justification – makes you justified in believing that *you do* have that belief.

8   I owe this example to Tim Maudlin.

9   Briefly, and I as I understand it, that theory invoked a mode of awareness that (i) had a success-grammar, (ii) was a cognitive relation to things or events, rather than to propositions, and (iii) wasn't mediated by your awareness of anything else. This mode of awareness went under various names: direct apprehension, acquaintance, etc. It was usually claimed that what we are so aware of are sense-data. However, as I understand the Given Theory, it neither entails, nor is it entailed by, belief in sense-data. The Given Theory is undergoing something of a revival these days: see Fales (1996) and DePaul (2001).

10   Davidson and BonJour (when he was a coherentist) are pure coherentists; Cohen (2002) is a recent example of impure coherentism.

11   The argument dates back to a debate between Schlick and Hempel. Schlick said we can sometimes "compare propositions to facts," and thereby acquire justification for believing those propositions. Hempel argued that the only way to acquire justification for believing a proposition is to "compare" it to things that stand in logical relations to it, namely *other propositions*. See Schlick (1932/3), Hempel (1934/5a), Schlick (1934/5), and Hempel (1934/5b). Wittgenstein voices a view akin to Hempel's in *Philosophical Investigations*, section 486. The Master Argument has been given many times since (for example, Sellars, 1963, sections 3–7; Williams, 1977, chapter 2; BonJour, 1978, section 4, 1985, chapter 4; Davidson, 1986). (In more recent writings, BonJour rejects the Master Argument. See note 18, below.)

12   Some might want to count *instrumental* desires as epistemically justified when the means–end beliefs that motivate them are justified. I wouldn't. But in any case, we can set instrumental desires aside and just consider cases where you desire that P for its own sake. Those desires have propositional content, and *they* don't need to be epistemically justified.

13 One finds this view in Sellars (1963), Hintikka (1969), Dretske (1981, chapter 4 and 6), Evans (1982, chapter 5–7), Peacocke (1983, chapter 1), Searle (1983, chapter 2), Burge (1986), Lewis (1986), and in many places since. It is disputed whether experiences also have *additional* introspectible properties, beyond their propositional content; but there is broad agreement these days among philosophers of mind that they *at least* have propositional content.

14 John Broome suggested that we might also count *intentions* as assertively representing propositions; propositions about how we will act in the future. If so, then the Master Argument would give us no reason to exclude intentions from the ranks of justifiers, either.

15 They may be able to justify those beliefs *indirectly*, if their content is such that you can infer from its truth that you are likely to have certain beliefs or experiences. But the coherentist should have no objection to that.

16 What McDowell (1994) calls "The Myth of the Given" is the view that things without conceptual content can play a justification-making role. Curiously, McDowell (1994, p. 144) seems to allow that *the fact that you are having a certain sensation* or impression might, together with justified beliefs about how such sensations are reliably caused, justify you in beliefs about the external world. McDowell thinks this kind of epistemic role is too "indirect" to be fully satisfactory; but he does seem prepared to count it as a justifying relation. This sits ill with his otherwise thoroughgoing commitment to the Premise Principle.

17 Two caveats about Peacocke. First, he would put his point like this: experiences can stand in the kinds of *rational relations* cited in the Premise Principle even if their content is non-conceptual. He is reluctant to call those relations "inferential relations" except when both *relata* are conceptual. Second, Peacocke does not himself accept the Premise Principle. He thinks that non-representational states like pains can also justify beliefs (see pp. 254–5).

18 Although many foundationalists' theories commit them to rejecting the Content Requirement and the Premise Principle, it is rare to find much explicit and sustained discussion of these principles. BonJour is one author who does discuss them. In BonJour (1978, 1985, chapter 4), he endorsed the Master Argument; but he has changed his mind and now rejects the Premise Principle. He thinks there can be "descriptive relations" between a belief and a non-propositional state that make the belief justified when one is in the non-propositional state. See BonJour (2001, pp. 29ff). Other authors who discuss the Premise Principle are: Millar (1991, chapter 4), Reynolds (1991), and Fales (1996, chapter 5–6). Fales's terminology can mislead, but in essence his view is this: experiences do not themselves have propositional contents, and so can't stand in the kind of "inferential relations" required by the Premise Principle. However, their phenomenal qualities do have a proposition-*like* structure, and we have a way to non-propositionally "apprehend" this structure. Fales thinks that is all that is needed to justify our perceptual beliefs. Millar *does* allow that experiences have propositional contents, but he thinks experiences are individuated by their phenomenal types rather than by their contents. He also thinks it is these phenomenal types that are epistemologically important. He says there are "quasi-inferential" links between phenomenal types and beliefs that experiences of those types make appropriate. These links, not the experiences' content, explain why experiences justify the beliefs they do.

19 I am indebted to Mark Johnston for discussions of this possibility.

20 The noun "justification" has both a count use and a mass use. The count use ("He has a justification for that belief") is most naturally read as referring to arguments or justification-showers. The mass use ("He has some justification to believe that"; "She has more

justification than he does"; etc.) is more naturally read as referring to the presence of justification-makers.

21 I am indebted to Mark Schroeder for discussions of this objection. See also Unger (1975, chapter 5). BonJour (1985, chapters 2 and 3) and Brewer (1999, pp. 19, 49, and esp. 163ff) claim that nothing can be a reason for you unless you are in a position to recognize it *as* a reason. McDowell (1994, pp. 52–3) insists that anything that is going to count as a reason-giving relation "must be able to come under the self-scrutiny of active thinking." I think this means that your reasons must be available for you to think about and critically assess.

22 See, for example, Brewer (1999, pp. 165–9). Pollock considers, and criticizes, a similar argument on behalf of what he calls "the doxastic assumption" that only beliefs can be justification-makers (Pollock, 2001, p. 41; see also Pollock and Cruz, 1999).

23 Brewer (1999, pp. 168–9) takes this line.

24 Other philosophers have also argued against overly deliberate and reflective accounts of being guided by an epistemic norm. See Pollock and Cruz (1999, pp. 124–30 and 136–7), Millar (1991, esp. p. 121), and Reynolds (1991).

25 For some recent discussion of the question whether belief is voluntary, see Alston (1989, chapter 5), Steup (2000), Feldman (2001), Audi (2001), and Ginet (2001).

26 See also van Cleve (1979), Pollock and Cruz (1999, p. 125), and Pollock (2001, pp. 44–5).

27 I would like to thank Tony Brueckner, Rich Feldman, Mark Greenberg, Ram Neta, Christian Piller, Mark Schroeder, Matthias Steup, and audiences at NYU, UNC-Chapel Hill, Princeton, Kansas, Oxford, and York, for conversations and feedback that helped me write this essay.

References

Alston, W. (1989) *Epistemic Justification*. Ithaca, NY: Cornell University Press.

Audi, R. (1993) *The Structure of Justification*. Cambridge: Cambridge University Press.

Audi, R. (2001) Doxastic voluntarism and the ethics of belief. In M. Steup (ed.), *Knowledge, Truth and Duty: Essays on Epistemic Justification, Responsibility, and Virtue*. Oxford: Oxford University Press.

BonJour, L. (1978) Can empirical knowledge have a foundation? *American Philosophical Quarterly*, 15, 1–13.

BonJour, L. (1985) *The Structure of Empirical Knowledge*. Cambridge, MA: Harvard University Press.

BonJour, L. (2001) Toward a defense of empirical foundationalism. In M. R. DePaul (ed.), *Resurrecting Old-fashioned Foundationalism*. Lanham, MD: Rowman and Littlefield.

Brewer, B. (1999) *Perception and Reason*. Oxford: Oxford University Press.

Burge, T. (1986) Cartesian error and the objectivity of perception. In P. Pettit and J. McDowell (eds), *Subject, Thought and Context*. Oxford: Oxford University Press.

Chisholm, R. M. (1989) *Theory of Knowledge*, 3rd edn. Englewood Cliffs, NJ: Prentice Hall.

Cohen, S. (2002) Basic knowledge and the problem of easy knowledge. *Philosophy and Phenomenological Research*, 65, 309–29.

Davidson, D. (1986) A coherence theory of truth and knowledge. In E. LePore (ed.), *Truth and Interpretation: Perspectives on the Philosophy of Donald Davidson*. Oxford: Blackwell.

DePaul, M. R. (2001) *Resurrecting Old-fashioned Foundationalism*. Lanham, MD: Rowman and Littlefield.

Dretske, F. (1981) *Knowledge and the Flow of Information*. Cambridge, MA: MIT Press.

Evans, G. (1982) *The Varieties of Reference*. Oxford: Oxford University Press.

Fales, E. (1996) *A Defense of the Given*. Lanham, MD: Rowman and Littlefield.

Feldman, R. (2001) Voluntary belief and epistemic evaluation. In M. Steup (ed.), *Knowledge, Truth and Duty: Essays on Epistemic Justification, Responsibility, and Virtue*. Oxford: Oxford University Press.

Firth, R. (1964) Coherence, certainty, and epistemic priority. *Journal of Philosophy*, 61, 545–57.

Ginet, C. (2001) Deciding to believe. In M. Steup (ed.), *Knowledge, Truth and Duty: Essays on Epistemic Justification, Responsibility, and Virtue*. Oxford: Oxford University Press.

Harman, G. (1986) *Change in View*. Cambridge, MA: MIT Press.

Heck, R. G. Jr (2000) Non-conceptual content and the "space of reasons." *Philosophical Review*, 109, 483–523.

Hempel, C. G. (1934/5a) On the logical positivists' theory of truth. *Analysis*, 2, 49–59.

Hempel, C. G. (1934/5b) Some remarks on "facts" and propositions. *Analysis*, 2, 93–6. Reprinted in O. Hanfling (ed., 1981), *Essential Readings in Logical Positivism*. Oxford: Blackwell.

Hintikka, J. (1969) On the logic of perception. In *Models for Modalities*. Dordrecht: Reidel.

Korcz, K. A. (1997) Recent work on the Basing relation. *American Philosophical Quarterly*, 34, 171–89.

Lewis, D. (1986) Veridical hallucination and prosthetic vision. In *Philosophical Papers, Volume 2*. New York: Oxford University Press.

McDowell, J. (1994) *Mind and World*. Cambridge, MA: Harvard University Press.

McDowell, J. (1998) One strand in the private language argument. In *Mind, Value, and Reality*. Cambridge, MA: Harvard University Press.

Martin, M. (1993) The rational role of experience. *Proceedings of the Aristotelian Society*, 93, 71–88.

Millar, A. (1991) *Reasons and Experience*. Oxford: Clarendon Press.

Peacocke, C. (1983) *Sense and Content*. Oxford: Oxford University Press.

Peacocke, C. (2001) Does perception have a non-conceptual content? *Journal of Philosophy*, 98, 239–64.

Plantinga, A. (2001) Direct acquaintance? In M. R. DePaul (ed.), *Resurrecting Old-fashioned Foundationalism*. Lanham, MD: Rowman and Littlefield.

Pollock, J. (2001) Nondoxastic foundationalism. In M. R. DePaul (ed.), *Resurrecting Old-Fashioned Foundationalism*. Lanham, MD: Rowman and Littlefield.

Pollock, J. and Cruz, J. (1999) *Contemporary Theories of Knowledge*, 2nd edn. Lanham, MD: Rowman and Littlefield.

Pryor, J. (2000) The skeptic and the dogmatist. *Noûs*, 34, 517–49.

Pryor, J. (2001) Highlights of recent epistemology. *British Journal for the Philosophy of Science*, 52, 1–30.

Pryor, J. (forthcoming) Is Moore's argument an example of transmission-failure? (http://www.princeton.edu/~jimpryor/papers/#transmission).

Reynolds, S. L. (1991) Knowing how to believe with justification. *Philosophical Studies*, 64, 273–92.

Schlick, M. (1932/3) Über das Fundament der Erkenntnis. Reprinted as On the foundation of knowledge. In O. Hanfling (ed, 1981), *Essential Readings in Logical Positivism*. Oxford: Blackwell.

Schlick, M. (1934/5) Facts and propositions. *Analysis*, 2, 65–70. Reprinted in O. Hanfling (ed., 1981), *Essential Readings in Logical Positivism*. Oxford: Blackwell.

Searle, J. (1983) *Intentionality*. Cambridge: Cambridge University Press.

Sellars, W. (1963) Empiricism and the philosophy of mind. In *Science, Perception and Reality*. London: Routledge & Kegan Paul.

Steup, M. (2000) Doxastic voluntarism and epistemic deontology. *Acta Analytica*, 15, 25–56.

Steup, M. (2001) Foundationalism, sense-experiential content, and Sellars's dilemma (http://web.stcloudstate.edu/msteup/SellDilem.html).

Unger, P. (1975) *Ignorance: A Case for Skepticism.* Oxford: Oxford University Press.

van Cleve, J. (1979) Foundationalism, epistemic principles, and the Cartesian circle. *Philosophical Review,* 88, 55–91.

Williams, M. (1977) *Groundless Belief.* Oxford: Blackwell.

Williamson, T. (2000) *Knowledge and Its Limits.* Oxford: Oxford University Press.

Doing without Immediate Justification

Michael Williams

1 What Are Basic Beliefs?

The question of whether there are basic beliefs is usually said to concern whether there are beliefs that are *justified* "immediately" or "non-inferentially." The question has also often been discussed in terms of the possibility of immediate or non-inferential *knowledge*, though generally on the assumption that knowledge is some kind of justified true belief. However, such simple formulations of the question can be misleading. The question of whether there are basic beliefs is better understood as concerning whether there are beliefs that are "immediately justified" or "immediately known" according to a special and extremely demanding conception of immediate justification.

As I shall understand justification, to be justified in believing that P (where P stands for some proposition or other) is to be *epistemically entitled* to believe that P. James Pryor (this volume) speaks of a justified belief as one that it is "epistemically appropriate" to hold. I take these to be two ways of expressing the same idea. Like Pryor, I intend "having justification to believe that P" to be an inclusive epistemic status. So, for example, anyone who knows that P has justification to believe that P, no matter how knowledge is understood.

Now in a sense, you are entitled to believe whatever you like: it's a free country. Epistemically, however, you aren't. Explaining justification in terms of entitlement, or appropriateness, indicates that justification is a *normative* notion. Justification has to do with whether one's beliefs meet certain epistemic standards, hence with what one may (and perhaps in some cases ought to) do in the way of regulating one's beliefs.

We have an obvious interest in having *true* beliefs, for without lots of correct information, we have little or no chance of achieving our goals, whatever they happen to be. But why are we interested in having *justified* beliefs? A partial answer is that we do not come into the world equipped with the information we need. Epistemic norms govern the acquisition and retention of beliefs, with special reference to our interest in their truth. Epistemically appropriate believing is our route to holding beliefs that are (we hope) for the most part true.

Epistemic entitlement to believe that P can be acquired in various ways. One way is to possess and make proper use of good evidence that P. Justification acquired this way is *inferential*. It depends on – and is thus mediated by – other justified beliefs, i.e. those that constitute my evidence. But it does not seem that all (or even most) entitlement arises like this. When I have a headache, I don't have to find reasons to suppose that I have one. I "just know" that I do: my knowledge is "direct" or "immediate." Or again, I may carefully investigate the murder and, having assembled the evidence, be able to prove that the butler did it. But I might have *seen* him shoot the colonel (with my own eyes, in plain daylight), in which case my knowledge would have been direct. And surely there must be such knowledge. What else could provide the evidence on which inferential justification depends?

Now if the thesis that there are basic beliefs amounted to no more than the claim that there are things that (in some sense) we "just know," or that there is some important difference between *concluding* that something is so and *seeing* that it is, there would be no dispute about whether there are basic beliefs, and probably not much dispute about what sorts of beliefs are basic. But in fact both issues are controversial. Serious philosophers have denied that *any* knowledge is, strictly speaking, immediate or non-inferential. Moreover, most of those who have accepted the idea of immediate knowledge have argued that common-sense examples of non-inferential knowing, such as seeing the butler shoot the colonel, are not genuine, authentic examples, being more modest in their contents.

Basic beliefs are the stock in trade of epistemological *foundationalists*. For some time now, foundationalism has been out of favor, though for much of the twentieth century – indeed for much of the history of philosophy – foundationalism (of one sort or another) was in the ascendant. But there are signs that it is making a comeback (DePaul, 2001; Bonjour, 2003).

According to foundationalism, all justification starts with basic beliefs and flows "upward" from them. However, there is more to foundationalism than this. If foundationalism were no more than a structural-descriptive account of everyday knowledge, it is hard to see why anyone would not be a foundationalist. Didn't we just agree that there are lots of things we "just know"? So aren't we all foundationalists? The answer is "No." The theoretical commitments of traditional foundationalists are extensive. I mention four.

(TF1) Traditional foundationalism is *substantive*, rather than merely formal. According to substantive foundationalism, the class of basic beliefs is *theoretically tractable*. In particular, there are non-trivially specifiable kinds of beliefs, individuated by broad aspects of their content, that are fitted to play the role of terminating points for chains of justification. The distinction between basic and non-basic beliefs is thus ontological rather than merely methodological.

(TF2) Traditional foundationalism is *strong*. Basic beliefs, or terminating judgments, are *indubitable* or (a slightly weaker notion) *incorrigible*. Basic beliefs are always basic knowledge.

(TF3) Traditional foundationalism is *atomistic*. Basic beliefs provide absolute terminating points for justificatory chains. To do so, basic beliefs must be independent both *epistemically* and *semantically* of other justified beliefs. Since basic beliefs constitute *encapsulated* items of knowledge, there is no objection in principle to the idea of a first justified belief.

(TF4) Traditional foundationalism is *radically internalist*. The justification-making factors for beliefs, basic and otherwise, are all open to view, and perhaps even actual objects of awareness. At the base level, when I know that P, I am always in a position to know that I know that P, and perhaps even always *do* know that I know that P.

Clearly, the sorts of things that, commonsensically speaking, we take ourselves to be capable of "just knowing" do not typically meet all these conditions, or even any of them. Specifically:

(CS1) Ordinary examples of non-inferential beliefs come in a bewildering variety, displaying no obvious theoretical integrity.

(CS2) Ordinary non-inferential beliefs seem often to be only prima facie justified, hence corrigible.

(CS3) Mastery of the concepts involved in many ordinary non-inferential beliefs seems to presuppose background knowledge. For example, having the concept of a car involves knowing about roads, driving, and a good deal more besides. Thus ordinary non-inferential beliefs do not seem to be semantically free-standing.

(CS4) Many ordinary non-inferential beliefs derive from the unselfconscious exercise of generally reliable faculties or recognitional abilities. It is not clear that being justified in holding such beliefs always requires being in a position to assess the reliability of those faculties or abilities. We can *be* justified without justifiedly believing that we are justified.

Even if, at some level of abstraction, ordinary justification appears to accord with formal foundationalism, this is no reason to suppose that we ought to be foundationalists of the traditional kind.

All this leads up to my first and most fundamental point. The question of whether there are basic beliefs cannot be decided by appeal to common-sense examples. This is because "basic belief" is a theoretical concept, subject to stringent theoretical requirements. These do not derive straightforwardly from the desire to understand everyday justification. Rather, they are set by certain explanatory goals that are distinctively philosophical. We need to know what these are, and whether we are under any obligation to fulfil them.

2 The Agrippan Argument

Foundationalists typically hold that, if we deny that there are basic beliefs, we commit ourselves to some version of the coherence theory of justification, the traditional alternative to foundationalism. Since they think that the coherence theory is open to fatal objections, they conclude that foundationalism must be correct. Coherence theorists return the compliment. They argue that no beliefs could be basic, in the demanding sense required by foundationalism, and that, therefore, some version of the coherence theory must be workable. But why must we choose between foundationalism and the coherence theory? Come to that, why do we need *any* theory of knowledge?

Traditionally minded epistemologists think that we need a theory of knowledge (or justification) to explain how knowledge is *possible*. The possibility of knowledge needs explaining because there are powerful and seemingly intuitive arguments – skeptical arguments – to the effect that knowledge is *im*possible. A central problem of epistemology – perhaps the central problem – is to see how such arguments go wrong, thereby learning important lessons about knowledge and justification.

The skeptical argument that generates the apparent need to choose between foundationalism and the coherence theory is the Regress Argument, or as I like to call it "the Agrippan Argument" (after the philosopher who seems to have been the first to give it a skeptical spin). The argument presents us with an apparently devastating trilemma: Agrippa's trilemma.

Consider some belief that is (supposedly) justified inferentially: that is, my justification for holding it consists in my having justification to believe some other propositions (propositions that constitute my reasons for believing that P). The question arises: what makes me justified in believing them? If the answer is that I have justification for believing yet further propositions, the question can be renewed. And so on. If we agree to play along, pressing questions about justification the way the skeptic suggests, there seem to be three possible outcomes:

(i)   The justificatory chain goes on for ever.
(ii) The justificatory chain stops with a proposition for which I have no justification.
(iii) In tracing my justification for justification for justification . . . to believe that P, we are led back to reasons that include my belief that P.

However, according to the skeptic, all three outcomes are bad. If the justificatory chain goes on for ever, we are trapped in a vicious infinite regress: we are not justified in holding any one belief unless, *per impossibile*, we are already justified in holding an infinite number of prior beliefs. If the chain stops with a belief for which I have no justification, it stops with a brute *assumption*, and justification cannot result from making an assumption. And if the justificatory chain loops back on itself, my justification involves *circular reasoning*, which cannot provide justification for anything, since no belief can justify itself. Regress, assumption, circularity: Agrippa's Trilemma. If we cannot wriggle out, the result is skepticism.

Most epistemologists accept the skeptic's three options, but think that we can put a better face on one of them. If this is right, the space of epistemological theories divides into three regions:

Infinitism. The justificatory chain goes on for ever, but the "regress" is not vicious.
Foundationalism. The justificatory chain terminates, but not with a brute assumption.
Coherentism. There are closed inferential loops, but their presence does not imply justificatory circularity.

Because the regress strikes most theorists as obviously vicious, they have dismissed the infinitist option out of hand. If they are right, the menu reduces to two items: foundationalism and the coherence theory. This is how we get our dilemma. And at least at first glance, foundationalism and the coherence theory offer very different responses to the Agrippan problem.

According to foundationalism, the Agrippan skeptic is correct in claiming that there are limits to my ability to *give reasons* for my beliefs, but wrong in concluding that this shows the impossibility of my ever being justified in holding them. Far from being mere assumptions, basic beliefs are irreproachable, because presuppositionless, instances of knowledge. For such "intrinsically credible" beliefs, the question of what reasons there are for holding them does not arise.

From the standpoint of the coherence theory, the Agrippan Argument fails because it presupposes a "linear" conception of justifying inference (BonJour, 1985). On the linear conception, a belief derives its justification by receiving support from other justified beliefs. Given this conception, it will seem that the only way to avoid skepticism is to postulate beliefs that are justified independently of our holding any further justified beliefs. However, the coherence theory offers an alternative conception of the structure of justification. According to the coherence theory, a belief is justified in virtue of belonging to a suitably coherent total belief-system. Of course, beliefs in a system will be connected by various kinds of "inferential" connection: some beliefs will entail others; some will inductively confirm others; some will explain others. However, such inferential connections are not in and of themselves justificatory. They are relevant to justification in virtue of their contribution to the coherence of the system considered as a whole. Whereas, for foundationalism, justification is *atomistic* and "bottom up," for coherentism it is *holistic* and "top down."

Taking foundationalism and the coherence theory in their traditional forms, the theoretical dilemma presented by the supposed need to choose between them hardly seems compelling. Nevertheless, the polar opposites represented by foundationalism and the coherence theory exert a powerful attraction. To see why, we need to look more closely at the Agrippan Argument. For reasons of space, I will confine detailed discussion to foundationalism, though I think that the factors that have shaped traditional foundationalism shape the coherence theory too.

3 Skepticism and Philosophical Understanding

The essential feature of Agrippan skepticism is that it is universal. The Agrippan Argument applies to any arbitrary belief or claim. This is why it is available for indefinite reiteration. The skeptic's challenge is to explain how it is possible for us to know (or be justified in believing) *anything whatsoever* (Stroud, 1989).

The skeptic's question is peculiar. If I tell a child about dinosaurs, she may ask me how it is possible to know anything whatsoever about them. After all, they went extinct thousands of years ago, so no one has ever seen a dinosaur. I will reply by telling her about the fossil record and how it gives us clues to what different kinds of dinosaur there were, their different structures in turn giving clues to how they lived. But of course, in giving an explanation like this, I am only explaining how it is possible to know some things on the basis of others. What the skeptic wants – and what the traditional epistemologist means to provide – is an explanation of the possibility of knowledge in general. An explanation of the possibility of knowledge that takes certain facts for granted – treats them as if they were known – will lack the requisite generality. The skeptic imposes – and the traditional epistemologist accepts – a *Totality Condition* on a properly philosophical understanding of knowledge and justification (Williams, 1992).

The Totality Condition creates pressure to accept a further constraint: *internalism*, or full epistemic self-awareness. Internalism is the view that, to be justified in holding a belief, we must have "cognitive access" to its "justification-makers." So-called "externalist" theories of knowledge and justification, by contrast, allow epistemically appropriate believing to result from factors of which we are not aware. For example, an externalist may say that a belief of mine is epistemically appropriate if it is formed by a method that is *in fact* highly reliable, whether or not I *know about* the reliability of the method I used. For externalists, such reliability-knowledge is relevant to the quite different question of whether I know, or am justified in believing, that my original belief is justified. One can have beliefs that *are* epistemically appropriate without understanding *why*. Presumably, the "knowledge" we attribute to animals is like this. According to externalists, human knowledge is not *essentially* different (Kornblith, 2002).

Prima facie, internalism is not particularly plausible, at least if it is taken as a fully general view of ordinary justification (Goldman, 2001). Everyday justification often seems to work as externalists say it does, as, for example, when it flows from the unselfconscious exercise of dependable recognitional abilities (Fogelin, 1994, chapter 3). We do not always require people to have reflected systematically on their abilities at large, or even on their performance in the situation at hand.[1] However, *in the peculiar context of the skeptical challenge*, it is easy to persuade oneself that externalism is not an option.

An explanation of how knowledge or justification is possible has to do more than show that knowledge or justification is *logically* possible: that there is a way of thinking about knowledge that does not involve a contradiction. Externalists can surely manage this. They can sketch a consistent picture of the world in which we credit ourselves with reliable faculties and so, by externalist lights, with epistemically appropriate beliefs. But are we justified in believing that our faculties are reliable? Is that belief epistemically appropriate? If not, then for all we know, we have no justified beliefs. This is a significant concession to skepticism. We want a reply not just to the claim that we know nothing, but also to the meta-skeptical claim that for all we know, we know nothing. We want to know that we know. This too pushes us towards internalism.

Admittedly, committed externalists can resist this line of thought. They can say that our epistemic beliefs (meta-beliefs about the reliability of our faculties) may indeed be epistemically appropriate – by externalist standards! But how do they know that? Well, they believe it: appropriately, too, if this meta-epistemic belief is formed in some suitably reliable way. And so on. But that is the problem. More traditionally minded theorists will surely feel that externalists who go down this route are either accepting infinitism or simply turning their backs on the sceptical problem. The traditionalist thought is that the epistemic self-understanding we seek can be attained only if the epistemic appropriateness of our beliefs at large can be made in some way *evident*. This is an internalist demand.

This pressure to adopt internalism gets further reinforcement from the thought that the context of philosophical inquiry is inherently reflective. In doing philosophy, we step back from all particular practical engagements in order to make explicit presuppositions that we normally take for granted without formulating in a precise way. But once such presuppositions are made explicit, the question of their epistemic appropriateness cannot be avoided. In philosophy, we want to get clear about what, at the deepest level, we are committed to and whether we are entitled to those commitments.

To understand philosophical reflection this way is to link such reflection with a particular ideal of *self*-understanding. It is because it adopts this ideal that traditional epistemological reflection is conducted from a *first-person* standpoint. By contrast, externalist approaches to knowledge and justification are elaborated from a third-person point of view. Accordingly, to the traditionalist, externalist epistemologies embody an attitude that we might take to someone else: we see that he is a reliable informant about this or that, and so we take his beliefs in that area to be epistemically appropriate, not worrying about what, if anything, *he* knows about his own reliability. But it is not clear what would even be meant by proposing to take such an attitude towards oneself. Again, the very character of traditional epistemology, as a quest for total epistemic self-understanding, pushes us to adopt internalism.

Externalist epistemologies seem plausible, the skeptic will suggest, because they accord with what we already believe. Our common-sense–scientific picture of the world suggests that, within limits, our basic cognitive faculties – perception, memory, and so on – are fairly reliable, so that beliefs formed with the aid of those faculties tend to be epistemically appropriate. But in taking the common-sense picture of the world for granted, we are not explaining how it is possible to know *anything whatsoever*.

I argued at the very outset that the traditional conception of a basic belief is much richer than – and even at odds with – common-sense ideas about "non-inferential" justification. Traditional foundationalism is substantive, strong, atomistic, and radically internalist. Once we recognize the extreme generality of the traditional quest for epistemological self-understanding, these otherwise puzzling features of traditional foundationalism fall into place.

We have already seen how the Totality Condition on philosophical understanding of knowledge and justification creates pressure to adopt internalism. In just the same way, it pushes us towards atomism. If basic beliefs are to bring a definitive halt to the regress of justification, thereby explaining how it is possible for us to know or justifiably believe anything whatsoever, they must be absolutely presuppositionless. The quest for total self-understanding leads to a demand for encapsulated knowledge.

It might appear that there is less reason to suppose that foundationalism has to be strong. Why do basic beliefs have to be indubitable? Couldn't they be only prima facie justified? It is not obvious how. Suppose that basic beliefs are only true for the most part, and that there is no intrinsic feature by which to distinguish those that are true from those that are false: it seems that when I adopt such a belief, its being true is just a matter of luck. But one of the distinguishing features of justified beliefs is that they enable us to get things right in ways that are not just matters of luck.

Someone might reply that, if basic beliefs are reliable on the whole, the true ones result from good policy, not luck. But does justification result only from good policy mindfully followed, or is *de facto* reliability sufficient? If we take the first option, we need knowledge (or at least justified beliefs) concerning the reliability of basic beliefs; and this looks like the coherence theory. But if we take the second, we have gone back to externalism, which has already been rejected.

We might hope to escape this dilemma by arguing that basic beliefs are evidently probable. But it is not obvious what this suggestion comes to. Basic beliefs cannot be probable on (further) evidence. This is why traditional foundationalists have argued that, if any beliefs are to be probable (i.e. probable on one's evidence), some must be certain. In any case, it is no small task to explain, under the constraint of internalism, how basic beliefs can be both justified and presuppositionless. The most promising strategy involves arguing that attentively forming a basic belief ensures its truth. Again, we are pushed towards strong foundationalism.

Obviously, basic beliefs are very special. Only beliefs with a special kind of content have any hope of being basic. Traditional foundationalism is therefore bound to be substantive. This completes the traditional picture. But could any beliefs live up to the demands just scouted? That is the next question.

4 The Appeal to the Given

Wilfrid Sellars coined the phrase "the Myth of the Given" to refer to the doctrine that some things are "immediately" known: that some justified beliefs are basic (Sellars, 1997). In my view, Sellars's objections to the Myth have never been successfully rebutted. Recent would-be resurrections of traditional foundationalism are just attempts to square the same old circles. The repetitiveness of the debate reflects constraints on a solution to skepticism that are built into the way foundationalists understand the problem.

Although basic beliefs are sometimes said to be "self-justifying" or "self-evident," it does not seem that they could be self-evident in the same way that simple judgments involving necessary truths are sometimes thought to be (BonJour, 2003). In the case of a proposition such as "2 + 3 = 5," its truth is guaranteed by its content, so that understanding the proposition is a sufficient condition for recognizing its truth. But according to most foundationalists, basic empirical judgments are made true by *experience*, not by content alone. Foundationalists meet this difficulty with a certain account of how basic judgments get their meaning. An influential version of this account can be found in a classic paper by Moritz Schlick (1959), though the ideas Schlick calls on turn up in all traditional foundationalists (of the empiricist type).[2]

According to Schlick, *a priori* judgments are *analytic*: true by virtue of meaning. Basic empirical statements, while obviously not analytic, *resemble* analytic statements in that you cannot understand them without recognizing that they are true. To see how this can be, we must recognize that language is based on *two* sorts of meaning-constituting rules. There are *discursive* definitions, which link words to words and thus generate analytic truths. But there are also *ostensive* definitions, which link certain words (observation-terms) to observable things (or properties). Without ostensive definitions, language would lack empirical content.

Schlick adds two further ideas. First, basic observational judgments essentially involve demonstrative (indexical) terms : "this," "here," and "now." Such terms are always understood in the context of a "gesture" (perhaps only a mental focusing of attention) that singles out some item present to consciousness, so that one does not understand an indexical term, on a particular occasion of use, unless one manages to focus on the relevant item. Second, observation-terms – "red," for example – can be understood "phenomenally," i.e. to apply to how things are experienced or appear to me. Thus the thought expressed by "This is red" need not be taken to imply that some "material thing" is red, but only that redness is presented in my experience.

With these points in mind, consider "This here now is red," with "red" taken phenomenally. Understanding the indexical component in this judgment requires me to focus my attention on some particular item currently presented in my experience. Understanding the predicative component " . . . is red" requires me to have learned (via ostension) what things are properly called "red" (in virtue of how they look). In a case like this, to judge falsely I would either have to focus on the wrong item (thus misunderstanding the indexical component) or misapply the rule for "red" (thus misunderstanding the predicative component). At this level, then, I cannot mindfully judge falsely: a mistake would at most be "verbal," not factual. Nevertheless, since it is an empirical fact that something red is presented to me here and now, my judgment is genuinely informative.[3]

Now, since we are trying to explain the *ultimate* authority of basic judgments, we cannot rely on presuppositions concerning the reliability of our recognitional capacities. However, to characterize something as "red" is to put it in a class with other things. So in taking myself to understand "red," am I not presupposing that I am consistent in my usage: for example, that if the item I am focusing on had been green, I would not have thought of it as red? In other words, don't various reliability-presuppositions turn up to haunt us via the possession-conditions for observational concepts, even when those concepts are taken phenomenally?

The standard reaction to this question is to insist that purely phenomenal concepts must not just cancel any implications of extra-experiential existence: they must also be "non-comparative." But how does "This is (non-comparatively) F" differ from "This is what it is"? Basic judgments threaten to buy their immunity from error at the cost of being drained of descriptive content altogether. Judgments that were supposed to be the most particularized and concrete turn out to be the thinnest and most abstract, hence useless as foundations for knowledge, a point that goes back to Hegel's discussion of "sense certainty" (Hegel, 1977).

Turning from the judgments themselves to their experiential basis, traditional foundationalists hold that the contents of sensory experience are the objects of "direct apprehension" (Schlick's ostensive rules depend on this idea). The contents of experience are simply "present to consciousness." That is what it is to be "given," and it is in virtue of these given contents that basic empirical beliefs are justified. The picture thus contains three elements: the sensory experience, the basic belief or judgment that the experience is of such and such a character, and some kind of relation between the experience and the judgment which underwrites the judgment's epistemic appropriateness. The crucial question is: what kind of relation?

The standard term for the contexts of experience used to be "sense-data." Traditionally, sense-data have been treated as particulars: a sense-datum might be a red patch in my "visual field." Russell called this kind of awareness, in which a sensory particular is directly present to the mind, "knowledge by acquaintance" (Russell, 1969, pp. 113ff). It is important to see that acquaintance with sense-data is "direct" or "immediate" in two senses. Not only is it independent of any further beliefs, it is *pre-conceptual*. It makes propositional knowledge (involving conceptualization) possible. Thus Russell contrasts knowledge by acquaintance with knowledge by description. Knowledge by acquaintance is non-propositional knowledge.

This idea is very hard to understand. How can something be knowledge but at the same time non-propositional? What is the *content* of this knowledge, if not conceptual content? Sellars puts the point in the form of a dilemma (Sellars, 1963, pp. 129ff). If our acquaintance with sense-data is non-conceptual. this kind of "awareness" cannot function as a reason for a basic belief. But if it is a form of propositional knowledge, we are just replicating the kind of foundational knowing we were supposed to be accounting for. We have no explanation of its epistemic authority.

Fans of the given sometime recoil at the idea that the existence of items given to consciousness must be *argued* for (or can be argued against). After all, the contents of the given are *given* (Fales, 1996, p. 1; Williams, 1999, pp. 43ff). Our "acquaintance" with our own "sense-data" is something that we can all verify introspectively: we are, so to say, acquainted with acquaintance. In fact, the idea of the given is theoretically driven, arising entirely from the need to respond to the Agrippan problem. As we have seen, that problem demands an internalist solution. The foundations of knowledge must be sought in some kind of awareness: some kind of ultimate knowledge. But propositional knowledge seems fraught with reliability-presuppositions, threatening ultimacy. The result is the "discovery" of *non*-propositional knowledge.

Russell chose the term "acquaintance" for our relation to the sensory given to insinuate a connection with our pre-theoretical distinction between knowing a fact and knowing a person or place. But my "acquaintance" with sense-data is nothing like my knowing New York. Where knowing a place is a vague mixture of know-how (being able to get around) and factual knowledge (what are the major attractions, where to find a reasonably priced restaurant), Russellian acquaintance is supposed to be *sui generis*, distinct from both knowing how and knowing that. We have no pre-theoretical understanding of the appeal to the given and, if the argument of the previous paragraph is correct, no theoretical understanding either. Talk of the given, or knowledge by acquaintance, is a *deus ex machina*, introduced to do the job epistemologists think that they need to get done. It has no other justification. This is why the loss of content at the level of acquaintance with the sensory given recapitulates the earlier loss of content at the level of basic beliefs (which threatened to shrink to a kind of inarticulate pointing): the theoretical constraints are the same, thus always pushing in the same direction.

For this reason, we cannot escape Sellars's dilemma by claiming that we are acquainted with facts rather than with particulars (Fumerton, 1995, p. 76). Such understanding as we have of talk of acquaintance with facts is *derived from* our common-sense conception of seeing that things are thus and so. Lacking surplus value, talk of "acquaintance" is just a piece of stipulatively introduced terminology masquerading as a theory (Sellars, 1963, pp. 129–30).

By way of showing how little has changed, let me turn briefly to a recent attempt by BonJour to resuscitate traditional foundationalism (BonJour, 2003). BonJour's fundamental notion is that of "constitutive awareness." Consider consciously entertaining a belief: say, the belief that foundationalism is more defensible than most philosophers think. What sort of awareness is involved? One possibility is apperception: a higher-order state of awareness that takes the first-order belief as its object. But according to BonJour, it would be a mistake to think that his primary awareness of his first-order belief is apperceptive. Rather, he claims, "an essential and intrinsic aspect of having any occurrent belief just is being consciously aware of the two correlative aspects of its content: its propositional content . . . and . . . the assertory rather than e.g. questioning or doubting character of one's entertaining of that content" (ibid., p. 62). There is no question about how one knows what one thinks, since to (consciously) think anything is to be aware of what one is thinking. BonJour suggests treating sensory awareness in a parallel fashion, as "essentially involving "a constitutive, or "built-in," non-apperceptive awareness of its distinctive sort of content, namely sensory content" (ibid., p. 70).

What is sensory content? BonJour makes no bones about it: sensory content is *not* "propositional or conceptual in character" (ibid., p. 70, n. 6). How, then, does it justify basic beliefs? This question is posed in a particularly sharp way by Davidson. Davidson writes:

> The relation between a sensation and a belief cannot be logical, since sensations are not beliefs or other propositional attitudes. What then is the relation? The answer is, I think, obvious: the relation is causal. Sensations cause beliefs and in *this* sense are the basis or ground of those beliefs. But a causal explanation of a belief does not show how or why the belief is justified. (Davidson, 2001, p. 143)

If this is right, the appeal to constitutive awareness is no help. Even if essentially characterized by such awareness, sensory experience will have no epistemological significance.

BonJour's answer to Davidson is that the relation between experience and judgment is neither logical nor causal. It is *descriptive*, "having to do with the accuracy or inaccuracy of fit between a conceptual description and a non-conceptual object that the description purports to describe" (BonJour, 2003, p. 70). But now, what is the appeal to "constitutive awareness" doing? BonJour writes as though the intrinsic must-appear-to-be-what-it-is character of "sensory awareness" could somehow transfer itself to judgments (which can be accurate or inaccurate) about its contents. How does this happen? Here is what he has to say about why judgments about the contents of experience are so special:

> In the most familiar sorts of cases, e.g. where it is some physical object or situation that is being described, one could apparently have an awareness that is independent of the description in question and otherwise unproblematic from an epistemological standpoint only via some second conceptual state that embodies a second, perhaps more specific description, and this second description would of course itself equally require justification, so that no foundational justification would result. But in the very special case we are concerned with, where the non-conceptual item being described is itself a *conscious* state, one can be aware of its character via the constitutive or "built-in" awareness of content without the need for a further conceptual description and thereby be in a position to recognize directly that a conceptually formulated belief about that state is correct. (Ibid., p. 73)

Here we have the appeal to the given in full flower. A fact about an external object can never be directly known, because we have no access to such an object except via the conceptual awareness (the perceptual judgment, explicit or implicit) we want to validate. This problem does not arise for experiential judgments because, in the case of experience, we have a non-conceptual awareness of its character. This is just the *deus ex machina* we met a short while ago.

Even allowing BonJour the notion of constitutive awareness, he has not solved the epistemological problem, since he has not explained why experiential judgments are intrinsically *justified*. The fact that experiential contents cannot appear to be other than as they are, as far as sensory awareness goes, does not imply that we cannot misdescribe them. Indeed, as Sosa points out in a trenchant reply to BonJour (Sosa, 2003, pp. 117ff), they are *easily* misdescribed. Sosa reminds us of Chisholm's "speckled hen" problem (Chisholm, 1942). Chisholm argues that our sensory awareness of a speckled hen may involve the sensory presence of a determinate number of speckles. But we can't *see that* there are exactly (say) forty-two speckles on the hen's chest, a disability that is not remedied by retreating from the hen to what BonJour would call our "visual image" of the hen. The non-conceptual awareness that BonJour finds in sensory *experience* does not guarantee accuracy or even reliability in our experiential *judgments*. What BonJour needs is exactly what Schlick tries to provide: an account of how, in the case of certain very special empirical judgments, understanding them is a sufficient condition for seeing that they are true. This is where we came in.

Bonjour makes a further move that I find deeply revealing. In appealing to our "direct" grasp of the match between the contents of experience, Bonjour is trying to close off another potential regress. Although both experience and thought-contents are the objects of constitutive awareness, we might still wonder whether seeing that a particular thought-content matches the experiential content it purports to describe involves a second-order judgment, itself requiring justification. But BonJour simply *dismisses* this question.[4] He finds himself inclined, he writes,

> to regard the suggestion that a direct comparison of two conscious states need involve an independent judgment that must in turn be justified by something other than the

conscious contents of the states themselves as a clear case of objectionable over-intellectualization. If any intellectual comparison or assessment can ever be direct and unmediated by further judgment, surely this one can. And to deny that this is ever possible is to guarantee vicious regresses in all directions, rendering the operation of the intellect inherently futile. (BonJour, 2003, p. 65)

Since internalists are often accused by externalists of "over-intellectualizing" our epistemic procedures, this is something of a *tu quoque*. However, by common-sense, pre-theoretical standards, this regress is no more obviously artificial than the one that got us started in the first place. Indeed, externalists treat *that* regress in much the way BonJour treats this one. They think that epistemically appropriate beliefs often arise from the unselfconscious use of basic cognitive abilities: no reflective awareness is required. And they rely on intuition in just the way BonJour does: if such knowledge is possible anywhere, then it is surely possible in a case like this. BonJour finds such attempts to short-circuit the Agrippan problem wholly unsatisfactory. He wants to take the skeptical strategy of threatening us with regresses seriously enough to raise the question of whether to opt for foundationalism or the coherence theory, but not so seriously as to render responding to skepticism impossible in principle. This is completely *ad hoc*. But I find BonJour's maneuver significant, for it suggests that there is something artificial about the very idea of showing how knowledge is possible.

Conclusion

Since we can't have basic beliefs, we must learn to live without them. If, as foundationalists argue, the coherence theory is also fatally flawed, we will have to learn to live without the kind of philosophical self-understanding that epistemologists have traditionally sought. We can do this, if there is nothing to understand.

I cannot explore this thought in detail, but here is a hint. Justification involves epistemically appropriate believing. So by way of analogy, consider fair play, which involves ludically appropriate conduct. We can say something about fair play. It requires playing by the rules. It may also require respecting certain informal understandings. In baseball, you don't try to hit the man with the bat; in a card game, you don't try to peek at someone else's cards: things like that. But the idea of a systematic theory of fair play – a theory that goes beyond bromides like "Do not cheat," "Do not try to take unfair advantage of an opponent" – seems implausible. Maybe justification is like this. Perhaps there are various constraints on justification, depending on the subject in hand, the situation in which a question of justification arises, and so on. If so, the skeptic's hyper-general questions may be *deeply* flawed.

I think that this is a promising line of inquiry (Williams, 1992; though see Stroud, 1996). But its implications for our conception of epistemology, and for a detailed diagnosis of skepticism, are topics for another occasion.[5]

Notes

1 This is not to say that the possibility of our having justified beliefs is *in general* independent of our having the ability to give reasons: it isn't (Brandom, 1998).

2 Abundant internal evidence suggests that Sellars (1997) takes Schlick as his paradigm empiricist foundationalist.

3 Sellars's critique of Schlick (Sellars, 1997, section VIII) centers on the internalist demand that such semantic rules, by virtue of being normative rules, must be followed self-consciously. This raises important issues about rule-following that, unfortunately, I cannot follow up here.

4 But see his reply to Sosa (BonJour and Sosa, 2003). Responding to Sosa's claim that attending to one's experience is not sufficient to make beliefs about its content justified, BonJour suggests the only additional requirement is that "the person must apprehend or recognize the agreement or fit between the aspect of experience being attended to and the conceptual and the conceptual description given by the belief" (p. 193). Of course, if a person judges correctly, he may be said to "apprehend the fit" between his experience and his belief. But there is nothing in this except some inelegant terminology of no obvious utility. What BonJour is claiming is that there is a kind of non-judgmental apprehension that *explains* correct judgment and which is intelligible independently of it. He has nothing to justify this claim beyond the fact that his kind of foundationalism requires such non-propositional knowledge.

5 I want to thank Matthias Steup for his helpful comments on an earlier draft of this essay.

References

BonJour, L. (1985) *The Structure of Empirical Knowledge*. Cambridge, MA: Harvard University Press.

BonJour, L. (2003) A version of internalist foundationalism. In L. Bonjour and E. Sosa, *Epistemic Justification*. Oxford: Blackwell.

BonJour, L. and Sosa, E. (2003) *Epistemic Justification*. Oxford: Blackwell.

Brandom, R. (1998) Insights and blindspots of reliabilism. *The Monist*, 81, 371–92. Reprinted in Brandom, R. (2000) *Articulating Reasons*. Cambridge, MA: Harvard University Press.

Chisholm, R. (1942) The problem of the speckled hen. *Mind*, 51, 368–73

Davidson, D. (2001) A coherence theory of truth and knowledge. In *Subjective, Objective, Intersubjective*. Oxford: Oxford University Press.

DePaul, M. (ed.) (2001) *Resurrecting Old-fashioned Foundationalism*. Lanham, MD: Rowman and Littlefield.

Fales, E. (1996) *A Defense of the Given*. Lanham, MD: Rowman and Littlefield.

Fogelin, R. (1994) *Pyrrhonian Reflections on Knowledge and Justification*. Oxford: Oxford University Press.

Fumerton, R. (1995) *Metaepistemology and Skepticism*. Lanham, MD: Rowman and Littlefield.

Goldman, A. (2001) The internalist conception of justification. In H. Kornblith (ed.), *Epistemology: Internalism and Externalism*. Oxford: Blackwell.

Hegel, G. W. F. (1977) *The Phenomenology of Spirit* (trans. A. V. Miller. Oxford: Oxford University Press (chapter on "sense-certainty").

Kornblith, H. (2002) *Knowledge and Its Place in Nature*. Oxford: Oxford University Press.

Russell, B. (1969) *The Problems of Philosophy*. Oxford: Oxford University Press (first published 1912).

Schlick, M. (1959) The foundations of knowledge. In A. J. Ayer (ed.), *Logical Positivism*. New York: Free Press. First published as Über das Fundament der Erkenntnis. *Erkenntnis*, 4 (1943).

Sellars, W. (1963) Empiricism and the philosophy of mind. In *Science, Perception and Reality*. London: Routledge (a reprint with corrections, first published 1956)

Sellars, W. (1997) *Empiricism and the Philosophy of Mind. With a Study Guide by Robert Brandom*. Cambridge, MA: Harvard University Press.

Sosa, E. (2003) Beyond internal foundations to external virtues. In L. Bonjour and E. Sosa, *Epistemic Justification*. Oxford: Blackwell.

Stroud, B. (1989) Understanding human knowledge in general. In M. Clay and K. Lehrer (eds), *Knowledge and Skepticism*. Boulder, CO: Westview. Reprinted in Stroud (2000).

Stroud, B. (1996) Epistemological reflection on knowledge of the external world. *Philosophy and Phenomenological Research*. Reprinted in Stroud (2000).

Stroud, B. (2000) *Understanding Human Knowledge*. Oxford: Oxford University Press.

Williams, M. (1992) *Unnatural Doubts*. Oxford: Blackwell.

Williams, M. (1999) *Groundless Belief*. Princeton, NJ: Princeton University Press (first published 1977).

CHAPTER
EIGHT

Does Perceptual Experience Have Conceptual Content?

Perceptual Experience Has Conceptual Content

Bill Brewer

My thesis in this essay is:

(CC) Sense experiential states have conceptual content.

I take it for granted that sense experiential states provide reasons for empirical beliefs; indeed, this claim forms the first premise of my central argument for (CC).[1] The subsequent stages of the argument are intended to establish that a person has such a reason for believing something about the way things are in the world around him only if he is in some mental state or other with a conceptual content: a conceptual state. Thus, given that sense experiential states do provide reasons for empirical beliefs, they must have conceptual content.

The plan of the essay is this. After characterizing as precisely as possible *conceptual content* itself, I offer an argument for the claim that sense experiential states provide reasons for empirical beliefs only if they have conceptual content.[2] As I say, I assume without argument that sense experiential states do indeed provide such reasons. So this constitutes my prima facie argument for (CC) (section I). Then (in sections II and III), I consider a number of recent critical discussions of (CC).[3]

I

As I am using it, a *conceptual state* – that is to say, a mental state with *conceptual content* – is one whose content is the content of a possible *judgment by the subject*. So, a mental state is *conceptual*, in this sense, if and only if it has a representational content which is characterizable only in terms of concepts which the subject himself possesses, and which is of a form which enables it to serve as a premise or the conclusion of a deductive argument, or of an inference of some other kind (e.g. inductive or abductive).[4] The requirement that the content has a form which enables it to serve as the premise or conclusion of an inference captures the idea that conceptual contents are the contents of *judgments* – those mental acts which are the source of, and are themselves susceptible to, rational inferential justification in the light of their essential concern with the truth, their norm of correctly registering how things are. The requirement that the component concepts, which articulate inferential premises and conclusions in a way which makes explicit this inferential justificational power, should, in the case of a conceptual state, actually be possessed by the subject captures the idea that this should be a possible judgment *by that very subject.*[5]

My central argument for (CC) has the following overall form.

(1) Sense experiential states provide reasons for empirical beliefs.
(2) Sense experiential states provide reasons for empirical beliefs only if they have conceptual content.
∴ (CC) Sense experiential states have conceptual content.

I assume (1) without argument here. My argument for (2) proceeds in two stages, which mirror the two components of the notion of conceptual content identified above. The first stage makes explicit the connection between reasons and inference, and hence between giving reasons and identifying contents of a form which enables them to serve as the premises and conclusions of inferences. The second establishes a constraint upon genuine reasons – reasons *for the subject* – imposed by the way in which his own conceptual resources are available for the configuration of his mental states. Recalling the definition of conceptual mental states given above, as those with a representational content which is characterizable only in terms of concepts which the subject himself possesses and which is of a form which enables it to serve as a premise or the conclusion of a deductive argument or of an inference of some other kind, this yields the required conclusion, that having reasons in general consists in being in a conceptual mental state, and hence, in particular, that sense experiential states provide reasons for empirical beliefs only if they have conceptual content. I take each of the two stages in turn.

A reason is necessarily a reason *for* something. In the current context, sense experiential states are to provide reasons for the subject's making a particular judgment, or holding a certain belief, about how things are in the world around her. To give the subject's reason in this context is to identify some feature of her situation which makes the relevant judgment or belief appropriate, or intelligible, from the point of view of rationality. It is, paraphrasing McDowell (1985, p. 389), to mention considerations which reveal the judgment or belief as at least approximating to what rationally ought to happen in those circumstances. Now, making something intelligible from the point of view of rationality in this way necessarily involves identifying a valid deductive argument, or inference of some other kind, which articulates the source of the rational obligation (or permission) in question. This constitutes an explicit reconstruction of the reasoning in virtue of whose correctness this obligation (or permission) is sustained. For *rational* intelligibility, or appropriateness of the kind revealed by giving reasons, just is that mode of approbation which is made explicit by the reconstruction of *valid reasoning* of some such kind to a conclusion which is suitably related to the judgment or belief for which the reasons are being given.[6] Hence, in making essential reference to the relevant valid inference, giving a reason involves making essential reference to its premises and conclusion, and so, trivially, to the kinds of things which can serve as the premises or conclusion of some kind of inference. In keeping with the standard usage, I call such contents *propositions*. This, then, is the first premise of my argument for (2): giving reasons involves identifying certain relevant propositions – those contents which figure as the premises and conclusions of inferences explicitly articulating the reasoning involved. In particular, sense experiential states provide reasons for empirical beliefs only in virtue of their appropriate relations with propositions suitably inferentially related to the contents of the beliefs in question.

Second, we are interested here not just in any old reasons which there may be for making judgments or holding beliefs – such as their simply happening to be true, or beneficial in some mysterious way to the subject's overall well-being – but only in reasons *for the subject* to do these things, to take things actually to be the way she believes them to be. These must be the subject's *own* reasons, which figure as such *from her point of view*, in virtue of her being in the sense experiential states which provide such reasons. It follows from this that the premise propositions, suitably inferentially related to the contents of the beliefs in question, cannot be related to the relevant sense experiential states merely *indirectly*, as some kind of extrinsic characterization on the part of the theorist. Rather, they must actually *be* the contents of these experiential states, in a sense which requires that the subject has all of their constituent concepts. Otherwise, even though being in such states may make it advisable, relative to a certain external end or need, for her to make the judgment or hold the belief in question, it cannot provide *her own* reason for doing so. Thus, sense experiential states provide reasons for empirical beliefs only if they have conceptual content: this is (2) above.

The two stages of this argument for (2) can be illustrated by consideration of an apparently alternative conception of the rational role of sense experience. It is agreed on this conception both that this role is to be characterized by the association between the sense experiences involved and some form of reasoning, and that conceptual contents are identified by their role in deductive and other inferential reasoning. The key difference, it is claimed, between the rational role of sense experience and that of thought or judgment is that the relevant background reasoning capacities in the former case are essentially imagistic. So, crudely, just as the rational role of the thought that [p & q] in sustaining the judgment that p depends upon the deductive validity of the inference from [p & q] to p, the rational role of a perception of two figures in sustaining the judgment that they are identical in size and shape depends upon the correctness of a certain imagistic rotation and translation of the one figure into the other in connection with this judgment. Thus, a person sees the two figures in question, A and B, say; and she arrives at the judgment that they are identical in size and shape by imaginatively transforming A into B by a certain rotation and translation. She has a reason for her resultant belief that A and B are identical in size and shape. Her sense experience of A and B provides her reason for this empirical belief.

Yet there is, according to the proponent of this alternative conception, no need to regard the content of this sense experience as *conceptual*. For the reasoning in which it is involved, in virtue of which it provides the subject's reason for belief, is neither deductive nor strictly inferential of any other kind. So we do not even need to postulate the involvement of conceptual contents in this process of reasoning at all, except at the final stage of judgment, of course, never mind identify such propositions with the contents of the experiences in question.

This account faces at least the following two questions. First, what sustains the "correctness" of this imagistic reasoning? Second, how does its correctness in this sense provide the subject with *her* reason for belief?

In connection with the first, I claim that the "correctness" of the reasoning in question, with respect to the target judgment that A and B are identical in size and shape, is due to the deductive validity of the following argument.

> (a) If two figures can be moved one onto the other by translation and rotation, then they are identical in size and shape.
> (b) That$_A$ figure can be transformed into that$_B$ one by translating and rotating thus.[7]
> ∴ (c) A and B are identical in size and shape.

Clearly, not any old experiential manipulation counts as genuine imagistic *reasoning*, in the sense in which such reasoning is what backs the rational role of sense experience, according to the proposal under consideration. In order to serve this role, the manipulation in question must make the subject's belief in the proposition that A and B are identical in size and shape rationally appropriate. Insofar as it succeeds in doing so, I can see no alternative to the deductive argument above as the ultimate source of this rational appropriateness. It is precisely because this argument is valid that the manipulation which she performs in transforming A into B by translation and rotation makes her judgment that A and B are identical in size appropriate, or intelligible, from the point of view of rationality; and this is what it is for her experience to provide her with a reason for her belief.

More is required than simply the abstract existence, as it were, of this rational appropriateness, if her sense experience is to provide *her reason* for the empirical belief in question, if it is to make her believing that A and B are identical in size and shape actually reasonable *for her*. It would be no good, for example, if she were simply manipulating the experienced figures at random in her imagination, and found herself believing that they are identical in size and shape as the first thing which came into her head. The correctness of the imagistic reasoning which she performs in connection with the judgment that A and B are identical in size provides her reason for this belief only if she has some recognition of its correctness in this regard. I contend that it is a necessary condition upon her recognizing her reason for belief *as a reason*, in this sense, that her grasp of (a) and (b) should be in some way operative in her transition from her imagistic manipulation to her belief in (c). Of course, (a) is most likely to be a standing piece of background knowledge on her part, informing her move from (b) to (c). The key point for present purposes is that she actually endorses (b), and effectively deduces (c) from it in the context of background knowledge of (a). This, I claim, is precisely what her performance of the relevant piece of imagistic rea-

soning consists in. It is no idle experiential manipulation, but the directed endorsement of (b) as a ground for (c), in the light of (a). What makes this a piece of *imagistic* reasoning is the point noted earlier, that grasp of (b) is essentially experiential. For "that$_A$," "that$_B$," and "thus," as they occur in this premise, are all perceptual demonstratives, which depend for their correct understanding both upon the subject's actually standing in the relevant experiential relations with A and B, and upon her actually making the translational rotational transformation of A into B which she makes in imagination on this basis. The sense experience which provides her reason for belief therefore has precisely the content of premise (b), which is by definition conceptual: it constitutes the premise of a deductive argument, and has to be grasped by the subject in a sense which requires that she possess all of its constituent concepts. Contrary to initial appearances, then, the proposed alternative conception of the rational role of sense experience as grounded in peculiarly imagistic reasoning serves rather to illustrate and further reinforce the two-stage argument set out above for premise (2) of my central argument for (CC). I therefore take (2) to be established: sense experiential states provide reasons for empirical beliefs only if they have conceptual content.

Given my standing assumption of premise (1), this completes the prima facie case for (CC). In what follows, I attempt to provide further support for the conceptualist claim, and to round out my initial argument, by considering a series of recent critical discussions of this idea that the content of sense experiential states is conceptual.

II

Richard Heck (2000) presents a number of considerations, both against the conceptualist claim itself, and against premise (2) of my argument for (CC). I begin, in this section, with the former.

An initial objection to the conceptualist account of perceptual content is that this fails to capture the richness, or fineness of grain, in our sense experience. For surely a person can discriminate more shades of red in visual perception, say, than he has concepts of such shades, like "scarlet," for example. The standard conceptualist response to this initial objection is to exploit the availability of demonstrative concepts of color shades, like "that$_R$ shade," said or thought while attending to a particular sample, R.[8] Now, Heck agrees both that such demonstrative phrases do express genuine *concepts* of determinate color shades, and that these are actually available for use in thought by a subject attending appropriately to the sample in normal viewing conditions; but he insists that the conceptualist claim that such concepts capture the way in which the color of R is presented *in sense experience* is incompatible with a strong intuition that it is the way in which colors are so presented which *explains* how the subject had access to such demonstrative color-shade concepts in thought.

The conceptualist claims that sense experiential states have conceptual content, in particular that fine-grained color shades are experientially presented as falling under *demonstrative* concepts. Heck objects that this is incompatible with the idea that it is a person's experience of particular color samples which *explains* his possession of such demonstrative concepts. His argument must be this.

> (a) A person's sense experience of color samples *explains* his possession of the demonstrative color concepts under which they fall.
> (b) If experience is to *explain* a person's possession of a concept, C, then its content cannot involve C as a constituent.
> ∴ (c) Experiences of color samples do not have demonstrative color concepts as constituents.
> ∴ (d) The conceptualist's response to the Richness Argument fails.

Although Heck himself admits that he finds this argument compelling, he also grants explicitly that the conceptualist may, and indeed is likely to, resist it, by denying (b). The idea would be that, in the sense in which experience *explains* demonstrative concept possession, the explanation is constitutive rather than causal. On the conceptualist view, experience of a color sample, R, just is a matter of entertaining a content in which the demonstrative concept "that$_R$ shade" figures as a constituent. Thus, it is, in a perfectly natural sense, *because* he has the experience which he has that the subject is able to employ that concept in thought. In virtue of his entertaining the concept in experience, it is available for further use in judgment and belief.[9] Still, Heck pushes the anti-conceptualist argument further. For there are two consequences of the conceptualist account as it is now set up which he finds unacceptable. First, it is incompatible with any substantive account of what fixes the semantic value of the demonstrative color concepts involved. Second, it rules out the possibility of certain types of perceptual error, which evidently arise. I consider these in turn.

(CC) is indeed incompatible with an *Evansian* account of what fixes the semantic value of demonstrative concepts, on which "that$_R$ shade" is a concept of the fine-grained color of R in virtue of the fact that the subject's attitudes towards contents containing it are suitably sensitive to information about that color delivered mainly in perception (Evans, 1982, pp. 145ff; Heck, 2000, p. 493). For this account is rendered viciously circular by the claim that possession of such perceptual information is a matter of entertaining that very concept. It is not the only possible substantive account of what fixes the semantic value of demonstrative color concepts, though. For example, the conceptualist may well be inclined to develop the following closely related proposal. "That$_R$ shade" is a concept of the fine-grained color of R in virtue of the fact that the subject's attitudes towards contents containing it are suitably sensitive *that color itself*, where this sensitivity in large part depends upon his normal neurophysiological perceptual processing. So Heck's first further consequence is no consequence at all of the conceptualist account as it now stands.

Nor, I argue now, is his second. He asks us to consider the perceptual judgment expressed by a person's utterance of "*that* part of my desk is *that* color," pointing twice at the same part of her desk. This judgment is bound to be true. For the demonstrative "that color" refers to the color which the relevant part of her desk actually has. Yet her perceptual experience may be mistaken in the color it presents that part of her desk as being. So the content of her experience cannot be that of the perceptual demonstrative judgment, as the conceptualist account proposes. More generally, the present version of conceptualism is incompatible with the evident possibility of perceptual misrepresentation.

Evans's own work on demonstrative thought suggests a response to this line of objection (Evans, 1982, chapter 6, 1984). Demonstrative reference to a particular object depends, in Evans's view, on the subject's capacity to *keep track* of the object in question over time, appropriately modifying her attitudes and responses to its movement or her changing position in relation to it (Evans, 1982, chapter 6). Failure to exercise this capacity results in a failed attempt at a demonstrative thought about that thing, although the subject may of course instead be capable of entertaining various other kinds of thoughts, some of which may be true, some false. Similarly, then, the conceptualist might insist that there are tracking conditions upon success-ful demonstrative reference to the fine-grained colors of the things within her view. In particular, she must have some ability to keep track of the shade in question over certain variations in viewing conditions: some changes of perspective, lighting, the presence or absence of shadows, and so on. Given that she is tracking the color of something which she is looking at in this way, then her experience of it consists in her entertaining the conceptual content "that is colored thus," which is indeed bound to be true. Errors in color perception are perfectly possible on this account, though, when the required tracking fails, and the relevant demonstrative color concept "colored thus" is not available for the subject. Her experience in the relevant respect consists in a failed attempt to grasp that concept, a failed attempt at demonstrative reference to the specific shade in question, and is therefore, and in that sense, mis-taken. So perceptual error is perfectly possible on the conceptualist account as it is now set up, and Heck's second accusation is also mistaken.

Thus, I conclude that Heck's first wave of arguments, targeted directly against the conceptualist thesis (CC) itself, fail.[10]

Christopher Peacocke (2001) offers a number of additional arguments in favor of the claim that a level of non-conceptual content is essential to a proper understand-ing of the relations between sense experiential states and full blown thoughts about the world presented in experience, and so against the conceptualist account of sense experiential content, (CC). I focus in this section on his treatment of two such issues: the roles of non-conceptual experiential content in, first, a philosophical account of perceptual demonstrative concept possession, and, second, a causal developmental account of observational concept acquisition. In each case, he argues that an account of sense experiential content as involving demonstrative concepts of colors and other properties fails properly to capture the relevant role of experience in relation to thought.[11]

An initial problem for the conceptualist is the apparent insistence that all color experience depends upon possession of the general concept of a color *shade*. For the canonical expression of the demonstrative concepts purportedly involved in color experience is "that$_R$ shade," grasp of which clearly depends upon possession of this general concept. Yet the idea that a person must have the general concept in order to perceive objects as having various specific shades is quite implausible. Peacocke (2001, p. 245) also claims that the conceptualist's assumption that any "good, suc-cessfully referring perceptual demonstrative contain some general concept" is inde-pendently objectionable. For there are "cases in which a wholly unsupplemented perceptual demonstrative 'that' still secures reference in a suitable perceptual context" (ibid., p. 246). This looks, at first sight, like a point conducive to the conceptualist, as it provides a way of avoiding the implausible suggestion that all color experience depends upon possession of the general concept of a color *shade*. Peacocke goes on to develop a natural treatment of these cases of conceptually unsupplemented perceptual demonstrative reference, though, which is incompatible with (CC). This is the first point mentioned above, against the conceptualist account of sense experiential content. The basic idea is that determinacy of reference is secured by the supplementation of the bare demonstrative element, "that," by a non-conceptual *way* in which the relevant shade, shape, movement, or whatever, is presented in experience. He goes on to develop this idea with great subtlety and sophistication. It suffices for my purposes here, though, simply to remark once again upon the availability of an alternative treatment which is consistent with (CC). On this view, determinacy of reference is secured by the supplementation of the bare demonstrative "that," by the subject's actual attention to the *color* of the object in question, as opposed to its shape or movement, say, where this is a neurophysiologically enabled relation between the subject and *that property*, as opposed to any other, of the object which he is perceiving.

Second, Peacocke argues that the conceptualist cannot satisfactorily account for the phenomenon of learning a new observational concept, such as *pyramid*. For the subject's sense experience, on presentation with a positive instance in a teaching context, must be sufficient for her rationally to apply the concept. Yet this experience cannot have a content which includes the concept *pyramid* itself, if it is to serve as a means to her *acquisition* of it. "The natural solution to this . . . quandary," Peacocke (2001, p. 252) continues,

> is to acknowledge that there is such a thing as having an experience of something as being pyramid shaped that does not involve already having the concept of being pyramid shaped. What such an experience will have is a non-conceptual content which, if correct, is sufficient for something's falling under the observational concept *pyramid*.

I agree entirely with the first sentence of this passage; but reject the implication of the second that the conceptualist cannot make the required acknowledgment. Surely we may continue instead as follows. "What such an experience will have is a conceptual content involving the demonstrative concept, 'that (shape),' referring to the pyramid shape of the object in question." Of course, the same cannot be said in explanation of her acquisition of the concept "that (shape)" itself; but the conceptualist will claim that her appropriately attending to, and tracking, the shape of the object in question just is her entertaining that concept in experience. That is, she acquires it precisely in virtue of standing in these attentional and tracking relations with the actual shape of the object in the world.

Sean Kelley (2001) argues that color perception fails to satisfy a plausible condition upon the possession of demonstrative color concepts, and therefore that (CC) fails properly to capture the way in which colors are presented in experience. The condition which he cites is this: "in order to possess a demonstrative concept for x, a subject must be able consistently to re-identify a given object or property as falling under the concept if it does" (ibid., p. 403, italics removed). He calls it the *re-identification condition.* I agree that the conceptualist should accept this as a necessary condition upon the subject's possession of demonstrative color concepts of the kind which are invoked in the present development of (CC). Kelley then presents us with the following case, in which a person is able to distinguish between colors on the basis of his experience, yet is incapable consistently of re-identifying one of them later. First, the subject is presented a number of times with samples of two similar shades of green, which he is consistently right in asserting are distinct. Second, his answers are at chance in response to the question, of one of these samples, whether it is the shade which was previously presented on the left. Generalizing, Kelley insists that "there's nothing in the nature of *perception* to keep it from being true, that our capacity to discriminate colors exceeds our capacity to re-identify the colors discriminated" (ibid., p. 411). He therefore concludes that the conceptualist account of color experience is mistaken.

I entirely agree with Kelley that the conceptualist cannot simply deny the possibility of the case as described. I also acknowledge that a second response which he offers, of denying that the subject actually *experiences* either shade in the first phase, is desperate and quite *ad hoc.* There *are* cases where something along these lines may be correct, in which a person's successful behavior is controlled by a perceptually mediated sensitivity to a given feature of, or quantity in, the world, even though it is intuitively wrong to say that she actually experiences that feature, or quantity, as such. Still, I grant quite freely that Kelley's case is not to be assimilated to these: the subject's initial shade discrimination is genuinely experiential.

There are two points which can be made on the conceptualist's behalf, though. Both urge that *an* appropriate re-identification condition may still be met in Kelley's case, so as to reinstate the claim that the subject's initial experiential discrimination is conceptual.

First, consider the re-identification condition as it applies to possession of demonstrative concepts of particular individuals. This cannot require that a person be capable consistently of recognizing or re-identifying the particular in question after a complete break in experience. For nobody is capable under those conditions of distinguishing two qualitatively identical but numerically distinct such things, and any particular object *could* have such a twin; yet this does not make demonstrative reference to such individuals impossible. The right way to think of re-identification in this case, it seems to me, is in terms of the subject's capacity, first, to keep track of the thing in question over its movement or her changing position in relation to; and, second, to make sense at least of the *possibility*, under certain specific conditions, of its numerical identity with an object encountered after a break in experience. In parallel with this observation, then, the conceptualist may hold that what re-identification requires, insofar as this really is a necessary condition upon demonstrative color concept possession, is rather the following two abilities on the subject's part: first, to keep track of the same shade over various changing viewing conditions – such as a gradual brightening/dimming of the light, the movement of shadows across the relevant colored object, and so on – during a single extended period of observation;

second, to make sense at least of the *possibility*, under certain specific conditions, that things encountered in the future, after a break in experience, are genuinely identical in shade with the initial sample.

Now, nothing in Kelley's case, as described so far, rules out the subject's ability to keep track of both shades of green in just this sense. Still, he may be inclined to modify the case in order stipulatively to rule this out, and continue to claim that nothing in the nature of *perception* makes the modified case impossible. A conceptualist *might*, with more plausibility than earlier in my view, bite the bullet at this point, and rely on the force of the argument *for* (CC) to insist that this new case must in fact be impossible; but there is a second point which may be more compelling.

This would be to claim that the initial, discriminating sense experience is irreducibly relational in content, presenting the two samples as "colored *thus-in-relation-to-that*." This is a complex demonstrative color concept, which picks out both of the shades of green presented, but in a way which is essentially context-dependent. It identifies them *in relation to each other*. Still, I contend, this complex demonstrative will display sufficient context-independence to meet the relevant re-identification requirement in Kelley's case. The subject will be able consistently to re-identify both shades in relation to each other for some time at least after the initial encounter. Indeed, the case of the paint color chips serves to my mind to reinforce this claim. Looking at a series of such chips together, suppose that you arrive at the view that one of them is the best color for the room you are about to paint. Having dropped them, it may well be very difficult to re-identify that shade by picking them up and looking at them individually one by one. You can normally pick it out by looking at a few of them together, thereby recognizing it as "that-shade-in-relation-to-these." This is precisely what is involved in meeting the relevant re-identification requirement for the complex, relational demonstrative color concept concerned.

This response is similar in spirit to one which Kelley considers explicitly, according to which the conceptual content of the subject's initial discriminating experience is "that there is that difference between the two samples" (Kelley, 2001, p. 417, italics removed). He replies, first, that it is not at all clear how the conceptualist could argue that this *must* be the right analysis of the situation; and, second, that this notion of a demonstrative identification of a color shade difference needs to be worked out in detail before the suggestion is fully satisfactory. Both replies may equally be offered against my own proposal of invoking relational demonstrative color concepts. The latter is perfectly apt in that context; but I see no good reason to believe that the required detail cannot possibly be provided. I would counter the former by putting weight on my initial argument for (CC). In the light of that argument, the subject's initial discrimination must be made on the basis of a sense experiential state with *some* conceptual content. Given his failure in connection with the associated re-identification requirements, this cannot involve the simple demonstrative concepts of the two shades of green, "that$_1$ shade" and "that$_2$ shade," say. Further reflection on re-identifying paint color samples, though, suggests an alternative candidate conceptual content, employing relational demonstratives. This is not in any obvious way objectionable, and indeed has in my view considerable independent plausibility. So there is good reason, provisionally at least, to accept that account of the case.

I conclude that the recent direct objections to (CC) which I have considered are unconvincing. The initial argument for (CC) has also attracted criticisms, though; and, especially given the additional weight which I just placed upon this in defending the conceptualist against direct attack, it is appropriate at this point to turn to these.

III

As I mentioned above, both Heck and Peacocke offer objections to the second premise of my argument for (CC): (2) sense experiential states provide reasons for empirical beliefs only if they have conceptual content. They focus on the second stage of the argument, which moves from the claim that the reasons in question are *the subject's* reasons for believing what she does to the conclusion that the sense experiential states which provide those reasons should actually have as their contents the conceptually articulated propositions figuring in the background argument which makes explicit their rational bearing on the beliefs in question. That move rests upon the requirement that reasons for the subject must be recognizable as such, and susceptible to rational scrutiny and evaluation *by her*. Heck and Peacocke each accept the requirement; but they go on to argue, along somewhat similar lines, that the move is a non-sequitur. I begin by discussing Peacocke's proposal by which he contends that the non-conceptualist is capable of meeting the *recognition requirement*.

His key idea is that the required recognition, scrutiny, and evaluation of the status of the reasons provided by sense experiential states for empirical beliefs may be achieved by invoking the subject's capacity for demonstrative reference to the, nevertheless *non-conceptual*, ways in which things are presented in experience:

> a thinker can ask "Is something's looking that way a reason for judging that it's square?," for instance. On the approach I advocate, "that way," in this particular occurrence, refers demonstratively to a way in which something can be perceived. The reference itself is made *by* something conceptual: demonstrative concepts can enter conceptual contents. There is no requirement that the reference *of* the demonstrative be conceptualized.... So thought can scrutinize and evaluate the relations between non-conceptual and conceptual contents and obtain a comprehensive view of both. (Peacocke, 2001, pp. 255–6)

I am not confident that I properly understand Peacocke's proposal here. For I find it difficult to interpret it other than as a variant of the second-order approach, which he grants is unacceptable. The suggestion certainly *seems* to be that a person's recognition of her experientially based reason for believing that something she sees is square, say, consists in her appreciation both that her experience presents that thing in the world in *that way*$_w$, and that something's looking that way$_w$ is a reason to believe that it is square. Thus, she derives the conclusion that she has a reason for believing that it is square. Yet this suggestion has all the serious difficulties familiar from discussions of classical foundationalism, both in accounting for the subject's knowledge of the nature of her experience, as presenting the object in question in that way$_w$, and in explaining her reasons for believing that something's looking that way$_w$ is a reason to believe that it is square.[12]

The only alternative which I can see would be to interpret the subject's *appreciation* both that her experience presents the relevant object in that way$_W$, and that something's looking that way$_W$ is a reason to believe that it is square, simply in terms of her standing inclination, in conditions of perception which are not evidently abnormal in some relevant respect, to judge that something which is experientially presented to her in that way$_W$ is square. Yet this is effectively to deny that she has any real recognition of her reason *as a reason*, or engages in any reflective scrutiny or evaluation of it as such.

On the conceptualist account, on the other hand, this dilemma is avoidable. For entertaining a conceptual content is a matter of grasping its truth condition on the basis of the way in which this is systematically determined by the semantic values of its components and their mode of combination, which are in turn precisely what determine its inferential relations with other such contents. Thus, a person's actually *being in* a sense experiential state with a conceptual content requires her grasp of that content in just the way which grounds its reason-giving status. Hence she automatically recognizes its status as such.

So, I contend that Peacocke's proposal, as I understand it at least, does not provide a satisfactory account of how the non-conceptualist is capable of meeting the recognition requirement upon the reason-giving role of sense experience.

Heck begins, along similar lines to Peacocke, by claiming that the conceptualist argument for (2) depends upon a mistaken assumption that any accurate reflective thought about sense experiential content must share, or at least embed, the actual content of the experience itself. More precisely, the assumption he uncovers is as follows. "The content of a judgment about how things appear to me, when such a judgment is correctly made, is the same as the content of one of my perceptual states" (Heck, 2000, p. 513). This assumption is clearly illegitimate, as it entails conceptualism directly, with the addition only of the uncontroversial claim that correct judgments about how things appear to me in perception are possible. For the contents of any such judgments are themselves conceptual by definition. Like Peacocke, Heck continues by offering a positive account of how it is possible to engage in effective reflective recognition, scrutiny, and evaluation, at the conceptual level, of the reason-giving status of *non-conceptual* sense experiential states. My complaint against this is, likewise, not that conceptual thought about non-conceptual contents is simply impossible – the assumption which Heck uncovers is not essential to the conceptualist case – but rather that it is bound to involve an unacceptable second-order account of how the recognition requirement is met for the reasons provided by sense experiential states.

Suppose that a person is in a sense experiential state with non-conceptual content. Evans offers the following description of how he may arrive at a correct conceptual judgment which captures how things appear to him in that experience.

[A] subject can gain knowledge of his internal informational [e.g. perceptual] states in a very simple way: by re-using precisely those skills of conceptualization that he uses to make judgments about the world. Here is how he can do it. He goes through exactly the same procedure as he would go through if he were trying to make a judgment about how it is at this place now, but excluding any knowledge he has *of an extraneous kind.*

(That is, he seeks to determine what he would judge if he did not have such extraneous information.) The result will necessarily be closely correlated with the content of the informational state which he is in at that time. . . . This is a way of producing in himself . . . a cognitive state [e.g. a judgment of appearance] whose content is *systematically* dependent upon the content of the informational state. (Evans, 1982, pp. 227–8, quoted by Heck, 2000, at p. 515)

Even if this Evansian description is entirely unobjectionable, the consequent account of how the recognition requirement is me in perception, presumably, still has the following, second-order, form.

(a) It appears to me that p.
(b) Its appearing to me that p gives me a reason to believe that p.
∴ (c) I have a reason to believe that p.

It is therefore subject to all the familiar difficulties facing classical foundationalism, of providing satisfactory reasons, meeting, as they must, the recognition requirement, in connection with the subject's beliefs at both (a) and (b) of this argument.[13]

There is strong prima facie motivation for the conceptualist account of sense experiential content in my initial central argument for (CC). Objections to (CC) itself are unconvincing; and criticisms of the second premise of that central argument are also wanting. I therefore conclude that:

(CC) Sense experiential states have conceptual content.

Notes

1 See Brewer (1999, esp. chapters 2 and 3), for extended argument in support of this assumption.
2 This draws heavily on (Brewer, 1999, section 5.1). It receives further elucidation and defense in sections 5.2 and 5.3; and I engage with a number of important criticisms in Brewer (2001a, b).
3 In particular, I discuss Heck (2000), Peacocke (2001), and Kelly (2001).
4 Note that such contents may be ineliminably *demonstrative*, the component concepts of which can only be grasped by a person actually standing in certain perceptual-attentional relations with their semantic values, or by someone who has done so within the range of his capacity to retain the relevant demonstrative concepts in memory. This inclusion is extremely important to my own account of how it is that sense experiential states provide the reasons which they do for empirical beliefs. See Brewer (1999, esp. chapter 6).
5 Note that this way of understanding "conceptual content" is incompatible with a constraint upon the notion which Heck (2000, p. 486) ascribes to Evans (1982), and himself intends to respect, namely, that the claim that even the content of belief is conceptual should be substantive rather than trivially definitional. If, as I take is the case, belief is the upshot of judgment by the subject in question, then belief content is conceptual by definition on my understanding. Stalnaker (1998) clearly respects Heck's constraint in arguing that *all* content is non-conceptual. As he means it, this is certainly an interesting and substantive thesis; but it is not properly put in these terms as I use them here. My concern is with the

extent to which perception is to be assimilated to judgment, in respect of the nature and type of its content. In the context of an understanding of conceptual states as those whose content is the content of a possible judgment by the subject, this raises precisely the question of my title: do sense experiential states have conceptual content?

6 Note here that I intend "validity" to be interpreted very widely, to capture the correctness or acceptability of inductive and abductive reasoning as well as formal deductive validity.

7 Note that this second premise is only available to be thought by the subject in virtue of her actual experiential relations with A and B, and of the imaginative manipulation which she performs on the basis of these relations. For "that$_A$," "that$_B$," and "thus" are all essentially experiential perceptual demonstratives. Still, (b) is none the worse for that. Indeed, this fact helps to explain the sense in which the reasoning in question is *imagistic*.

8 For more detailed presentation of both the initial objection and the demonstrative response, along with supporting references, see McDowell (1994, lecture III, and afterword, part II) and Brewer (1999, section 5.3.1).

9 See Brewer (2001a, in discussion with Eilan) for further development of the objection and reply here.

10 I consider below, in section III, his further arguments against premise (2) of my argument for (CC).

11 I return, in section III, to a discussion of his further claim, *pace* my premise (2) above, that a non-conceptualist account of the content of sense experiential states is capable of explaining their role in providing reasons for empirical beliefs.

12 See Brewer (1999, chapter 4) for extended criticism of any second-order account of how the recognition requirement is met in perceptual knowledge.

13 Again, see Brewer (1999, chapter 4) for far more on this.

References

Brewer, B. (1999) *Perception and Reason*. Oxford: Oxford University Press.

Brewer, B. (2001a) Précis of *Perception and Reason*, and response to commentators (Naomi Eilan, Richard Fumerton, Susan Hurley, and Michael Martin). *Philosophy and Phenomenological Research*, 63, 405–64.

Brewer, B. (2001b) Précis of *Perception and Reason*, and response to commentator (Michael Ayers). *Philosophical Books*, 43, 1–22.

Evans, G. (1982) *The Varieties of Reference*. Oxford: Oxford University Press.

Evans, G. (1985) Understanding demonstratives. In *Collected Papers*. Oxford: Oxford University Press.

Heck, R. G. (2000) Non-conceptual content and the "space of reasons." *Philosophical Review*, 109, 483–523.

Kelly, S. D. (2001) Demonstrative concepts and experience. *Philosophical Review*, 110, 397–420.

McDowell, J. (1985) Functionalism and anomalous monism. In E. LePore and B. McLaughlin (eds), *Actions and Events*. Oxford: Blackwell.

McDowell, J. (1994) *Mind and World*. Cambridge, MA: Harvard University Press.

Peacocke, C. (2001) Does perception have a nonconceptual content? *Journal of Philosophy*, 98, 239–64.

Stalnaker, R. (1998) What might non-conceptual content be? *Philosophical Issues*, 9, 339–52.

Perception and Conceptual Content

Alex Byrne

Perceptual experiences justify beliefs – that much seems obvious. As Brewer puts it, "sense experiential states provide reasons for empirical beliefs" (this volume). In *Mind and World* McDowell (1994, p. 162) argues that we can get from this apparent platitude to the controversial claim that perceptual experiences have conceptual content: "we can coherently credit experiences with rational relations to *judgment* and belief, but only if we take it that spontaneity is already implicated in receptivity; that is, only if we take it that experiences have conceptual content." Brewer agrees. Their view is sometimes called *conceptualism*; *non-conceptualism* is the rival position, that experiences have non-conceptual content. One initial obstacle is understanding what the issue is. What is conceptual content, and how is it different from non-conceptual content?

Section 1 of this essay explains two versions of each of the rival positions: *state* (non-)conceptualism and *content* (non-)conceptualism; the latter pair is the locus of the relevant dispute. Two prominent arguments for content *non*-conceptualism – the richness argument and the continuity argument – both fail (section 2). McDowell's and Brewer's epistemological defenses of content conceptualism are also faulty (section 3). Section 4 gives a more simple-minded case for conceptualism; finally, some reasons are given for rejecting the claim – on one natural interpretation – that experiences justify beliefs.

1 Two Conceptions of Conceptual and Non-conceptual Content

1.1 Concepts

Start with "concepts." What are they, and what is it to "possess" one? The "concept" terminology in the philosophical literature is at least three ways ambiguous, and often writers do not explicitly say which sense they have in mind. In the *psychological* sense, a concept is a mental representation of a category: something that is (literally) in the head, perhaps a (semantically interpreted) word in a language of thought. Thus, the mentalese word that applies to all and only horses, if there is such a thing, is the concept *horse*, or (in the more usual notation) HORSE. Someone possesses HORSE just in case this mental representation is part of her cognitive machinery.

In the *Fregean* sense (pun intended), concepts are certain kinds of Fregean senses, specifically Fregean senses of predicates (e.g. "is a horse"). They are supposed to be constituents, together with other kinds of senses (e.g. senses of singular terms like "Seabiscuit") of the senses of sentences (e.g. "Seabiscuit is a horse"), otherwise known as Fregean Thoughts. In the Fregean sense, to possess the concept *horse* is to grasp a Thought with the concept *horse* as a constituent. "Grasping" such a Thought may be glossed thus: believing that p, where "p" is replaced by any sentence whose sense has the concept *horse* as a constituent.[1]

In the *pleonastic* sense of "concept," the primary locution is "possessing a concept." Someone possesses the concept F iff she believes that . . . F . . . (for some filling of the dots). So, for example, someone who believes that Seabiscuit is a horse, or that horses are birds, or that all horses are horses, possesses the concept *horse*. Note that in the pleonastic sense, one might regard apparent reference to "the concept *horse*," "the concept *round*," etc., as a mere *façon de parler*, to be paraphrased away. If an entity is needed to serve as the concept *horse*, then the semantic value (whatever it might be) of the predicate "is a horse" is the obvious choice.[2]

These three senses of "concept" are very different. In the pleonastic sense, it is uncontroversial that there are concepts (at least if scare quotes are inserted around "there are"); in any event, it is uncontroversial that people possess concepts. But Fregeanism is controversial, and there are many controversies surrounding concepts in the psychological sense. Indeed, a behavioristically inclined philosopher might accept Fregeanism and deny that there are any concepts in the psychological sense. And of course one might accept that there are concepts in the psychological sense while rejecting Fregeanism.

The prominent participants in the debate over conceptual and non-conceptual content are Fregeans, and accordingly they use "concept" in the Fregean sense. This should be borne in mind when reading various quotations. But, as will become apparent, the main considerations are independent of this assumption. For this reason (see also section 1.4), "concept" is used here in the pleonastic sense unless explicitly noted otherwise; it is never used in the psychological sense.

1.2 Content

Next, "content." Some mental states have content: the belief that Seabiscuit is a horse has the content that Seabiscuit is a horse; the hope that Seabiscuit will win has the content that Seabiscuit will win. Contents are *propositions*: abstract objects that determine possible-worlds truth conditions. Three leading candidates for such abstract objects are Fregean Thoughts, Russellian propositions (structured entities with objects and properties as constituents), and Lewisian/Stalnakerian propositions (sets of possible worlds). Sometimes "proposition" is reserved exclusively for the contents of the traditional propositional attitudes like belief and hope; in this usage, if these contents are Thoughts (for example), then Russellian "propositions" are not propositions. In the terminology of this essay, "proposition" is used more inclusively: in this usage, Russellian propositions might not be the contents of the traditional attitudes.

On one common view that forms the background to the conceptual/non-conceptual content debate, perceptual experiences, like beliefs and hopes, are representational mental states with content. A typical introduction of the idea is this:

> A visual perceptual experience enjoyed by someone sitting at a desk may represent various writing implements and items of furniture as having particular spatial relations to one another and to the experiencer, and as themselves as having various qualities. . . . The representational content of a perceptual experience has to be given by a propo-

sition, or set of propositions, which specifies the way the experience represents the world to be. (Peacocke, 1983, p. 5)[3]

A visual illusion (e.g. an apparently bent stick in water) is, on this account of perception, much like a false belief. One's experience has the content that the stick is bent, but this content is false: the stick is straight. (As we will see in section 1.5, the preceding sentence will be qualified by a proponent of non-conceptual content.)

1.3 State conceptualism

Sometimes the notion of non-conceptual content is introduced along the following lines:

> Mental state M has non-conceptual content p iff it is possible to be in M without possessing all the concepts that characterize p,

where the concept *F characterizes* the proposition p iff p = that ... F ...[4] If M does not have non-conceptual content, then it has *conceptual* content: anyone who is in M must possess all the concepts that characterize p (compare Crane, 1992, p. 143; Martin, 1992, p. 238; Tye, 1995, p. 139).

This way of talking is misleading. If M has "non-conceptual content" in the present sense, this does not imply that M has a *special kind* of content. In particular, if perceptual states have "non-conceptual content," these contents might be the sort that are also the contents of belief (see section 1.5 below).

If the conceptual/non-conceptual distinction is explained in this fashion, it is much better to take it as applying to *states*, not to *contents*.[5] Putting the distinction more hygienically: state M with content p is a *non-conceptual state* iff it is possible to be in M without possessing all the concepts that characterize p.

1.4 Content conceptualism[6]

On another way of explaining the conceptual/non-conceptual distinction, the phrase "non-conceptual content" isn't at all misleading, because non-conceptual content really is a special kind of content. In the first instance it is explained negatively: non-conceptual content is *not* conceptual content, where the latter is characterized either as belief content, or as content with concepts in the Fregean sense as constituents.[7]

Content conceptualists assert, while content non-conceptualists deny, that the content of perceptual experience is conceptual:

> According to the picture I have been recommending, the content of a perceptual experience is already conceptual. A judgment of experience does not introduce a new kind of content, but simply endorses the conceptual content, or some of it, that is already possessed by the experience on which it is grounded. (McDowell 1994, pp. 48–9, note omitted)

As noted, the main players in the debate hold that the contents of belief are Fregean Thoughts. So for them, the characterization of conceptual content as belief content, and the characterization of it as Fregean content, are equivalent. But since it is not assumed here that belief content is Fregean, we need to choose one of these characterizations. Section 1.1 announced that "concept" will be used in the pleonastic sense, and this was partly in anticipation of Brewer's stipulation (this volume, p. 229–30, n. 5) that conceptual content is *belief content*; given this stipulation, it is a substantive question whether conceptual content is also Fregean. Sometimes the stipulation is the reverse. Stalnaker (1998a) defends the view that the content of both belief and perception is "non-conceptual," by which he means (at least) that it is not composed of Fregean concepts; in the (perhaps not ideal) terminology of this essay, Stalnaker's view is content *conceptualism*.

Since everyone agrees that propositions expressed by sentences are of a kind that can be believed, *linguistic* content is automatically conceptual. Suppose that when one looks at a stick in water, the content of one's experience is a certain proposition p. A non-conceptualist will deny that p is the proposition that the stick is bent. It is not an entirely unrelated proposition: perhaps p strictly implies that the stick is bent. But p is not a proposition that can be expressed by a sentence (e.g. "the stick is bent"), or named by a that-clause (e.g. "that the stick is bent"). Of course, this does not imply that p cannot be referred to at all; indeed, we have already referred to it (see also section 3.2).

According to *total* content non-conceptualism, the content of experience is exclusively non-conceptual; Evans seems to hold this view. According to *partial* content non-conceptualism, *every* perceptual state has some non-conceptual content – but at least occasionally a conceptual proposition will be one of the propositions t hat together comprise a perceptual state's overall content. This is Peacocke's (1992, p. 88) position. Conceptualists typically hold that the content of experience is exclusively conceptual, so "partial content conceptualism" is rarely (if ever) an occupied position. In order to simplify the discussion, the focus will be on *total* content (non-)conceptualism.

1.5 The relation between state and content conceptualism

State and content conceptualism (or non-conceptualism) are sometimes conflated; at any rate they are frequently not properly distinguished.[8] What is the relation between the two views?

Suppose that (total) *content non*-conceptualism is true: if perceptual state M has content p, p is non-conceptual. So p ≠ that s (for any sentence replacing "s"), and hence p is not characterized by *any* concepts. It trivially follows that anyone who is in M must possess all the concepts that characterize p, and thus (according to the explanation in section 1.3) that M is *conceptual*. So content non-conceptualism implies state conceptualism. But it is more natural to amend the account of section 1.3 by stipulating that as stated it only applies when p *is* characterized by some concepts, and adding that if M has *non*-conceptual content q, then M is a *non*-conceptual state. With this amendment adopted, content non-conceptualism entails state non-conceptualism; equivalently, state conceptualism entails content conceptualism. (This is of course not an exciting result, merely the consequence of a somewhat arbitrary stipulation.)

Suppose, on the other hand, that *state non*-conceptualism is true. One may be in perceptual state M with content p, even though one does not possess the concepts that characterize p – *a fortiori*, one does not believe p or doubt p. Still, p might be a perfectly ordinary proposition (e.g. that there is a purple octagon before one) of the sort that is the content of belief. So state non-conceptualism does not entail content non-conceptualism; equivalently, content conceptualism does not entail state conceptualism.

Since McDowell and Brewer's epistemological arguments are primarily intended to establish *content* conceptualism ("conceptualism," for short), this is our main topic.

2 The Richness Argument and the Continuity Argument

Why think conceptualism is false? This section briefly discusses two of the best known arguments.

2.1 The richness argument

The richness argument is present in embryo form in *The Varieties of Reference.*[9] Heck elaborates it in this way:

> Consider your current perceptual state – and now imagine what a complete description of the way the world appears to you at this moment might be like. Surely a thousand words would hardly begin to do the job. . . . Before me now, for example, are arranged various objects with various shapes and colors, of which, it might seem, I have no concept. My desk exhibits a whole host of shades of brown, for which I have no names. . . . Yet my experience of these things represents them far more precisely than that, far more distinctively, it would seem, than any other characterization I could hope to formulate, for myself or for others, in terms of the concepts I presently possess. The problem is not lack of time, but lack of descriptive resources, that is, lack of the appropriate concepts. (Heck, 2000, pp. 489–90)

The conclusion of this argument is non-conceptualism: "the content of perceptual states is different in kind from that of cognitive states like belief" (ibid., p. 485).

This argument departs from the claim that a visual experience can represent shades of color (among other properties) "of which, it might seem, I have no concept." Specifically, one can have a visual experience that represents that an object has a certain determinate shade of brown ($brown_{17}$, say) without possessing the concept $brown_{17}$. Let us set out the argument using Heck's particular example.

Argument H
P1 Heck has a visual experience with content p; p is true at a possible world w iff the desk is $brown_{17}$ in w; Heck does not believe that . . . $brown_{17}$ . . . (for any filling of the dots).

Hence:

C1 p is not *conceptual*; in particular, it is not the proposition that the desk is brown$_{17}$. That is, non-conceptualism is true.

But C1 does not follow from P1. Assume, as Heck does, that the contents of beliefs are Thoughts. Then *one* possibility consistent with P1 is that p is (say) the possible worlds proposition that is modally equivalent to (but distinct from) the Thought that the desk is brown$_{17}$. But *another* possibility consistent with P1 is that p is simply the Thought that the desk is brown$_{17}$.[10]

2.2 The continuity argument

The continuity argument is also present in embryo form in *Varieties* (Evans, 1982, p. 124). Here is Peacocke's version:

> Nonconceptual content has been recruited for many purposes. In my view the most fundamental reason – the one on which other reasons must rely if the conceptualist presses hard – lies in the need to describe correctly the overlap between human perception and that of some of the nonlinguistic animals. While being reluctant to attribute concepts to the lower animals, many of us would also want to insist that the property of (say) representing a flat brown surface as being at a certain distance from one can be common to the perceptions of humans and of lower animals. The overlap of content is not just a matter of analogy, of mere quasi-subjectivity in the animal case. It is literally the same representational property that the two experiences possess, even if the human experience also has richer representational contents in addition. If the lower animals do not have states with conceptual content, but some of their perceptual states have contents in common with human perceptions, it follows that some perceptual representational content is nonconceptual. (Peacocke, 2001b, pp. 613–14)[11]

This argument may be set out as follows:

Argument P
P1 Humans do, and the lower animals do not, possess concepts.

Hence:

C1 Humans are in states (e.g. beliefs) with conceptual content, and the lower animals are not in states with conceptual content.
P2 Some of the perceptual states of lower animals have contents in common with human perceptual states.[12]

Hence (from C1, P2):

C2 Human perceptual states have a kind of content that is not conceptual. That is, non-conceptualism is true.

P1 may be restated like this:

P1(restated) Humans have beliefs, and the lower animals do not.

With this clarification of P1 made, it is unclear how it can support C1. On the face of it, one might reasonably hold P1 together with the view that perceptual content, in humans and lower animals, is the same kind of content that can be believed – thus denying C1. Further, P1 is quite disputable. The least unpromising line of argument for the claim that the lower animals lack beliefs attempts to link having beliefs with speaking a language. But, first, existing attempts to argue in this fashion are unconvincing and, second, Peacocke himself emphasizes the relative independence of language and thought.

An additional problem with the argument is the tension between P1 and P2. According to P1, the lower animals are radically unlike us cognitively: they neither know, think, nor believe that this surface is brown. According to P2, the lower animals are importantly like us perceptually: the surface can appear to some of them *exactly* as it appears to some of us. Now Peacocke does not deny that the lower animals are in states *somewhat* like beliefs – "proto-beliefs," say. And if proto-beliefs are available to the theorist of animal minds, presumably so are "proto-perceptions," which do not overlap in content with genuine perceptions. If the lower animals merely proto-believe, why don't they merely proto-perceive?

3 Epistemological Defenses of Conceptualism

According to one traditional account of perception, it consists in the passive receipt of sensations (the Given), which then justify certain judgments – that an orange triangle is before one, for instance. In *Mind and World*, McDowell (1994, p. 7) distills the idea of the Given thus: "the space of reason, the space of justification or warrants, extends more widely than the conceptual sphere." This is unacceptable, according to McDowell, because it cannot explain how "experience [can] count as a reason for holding a belief" (ibid., p. 14). "We cannot really understand the relations in virtue of which a *judgment* is warranted except as relations within the space of concepts: relations such as implication or probabilification" (ibid., p. 7).[13] Non-conceptualism is a version of "the Myth of the Given" (ibid., p. 51).

Brewer's *Perception and Reason* develops and extends McDowell's epistemic complaint against non-conceptualism. Brewer's basic argument is succinctly stated:

1   Sense experiential states provide reasons for empirical beliefs.
2   Sense experiential states provide reasons for empirical beliefs only if they have conceptual content.
(CC) Sense experiential states have conceptual content (this volume, p. 218).

McDowell's argument can be similarly outlined.

McDowell and Brewer make extensive use of the related notions of a subject's having a reason, a perceptual state's providing (or being) a reason, and so forth. Before we proceed further, talk of reasons need to be clarified.

3.1 Reasons

Someone might have a reason to believe that it will rain soon, for example. What sort of things *are* reasons (for belief)?[14] One common and well motivated answer is "propositions": that there are storm clouds on the horizon could be someone's reason to believe that it will rain soon, and so on (see Unger, 1975, pp. 200–6; Williamson, 2000, pp. 194–200; Thomson, 2001, pp. 22–6). McDowell uses the terminology of "reasons" informally, Brewer less so. Although Brewer never explictly says that reasons are propositions, he comes close enough: "giving reasons involves identifying certain relevant propositions – those contents which figure as the premises and conclusions of inferences explicitly articulating the reasoning involved" (this volume, p. 219). Reasons, we may say, are propositions. (Perhaps some propositions – the false ones, for instance – are not reasons.) A subject S *has* various reasons $p_1, p_2, \ldots$; if S has reason p, then that is a reason for S to believe some proposition q. Typically different reasons are reasons to believe different propositions: S might have reason p_1 to believe q_1, and reason p_2 to believe q_2, yet not have reason p_1 to believe q_2.

If p is one of S's reasons, must S believe p? Suppose S is planting his tomatoes, and there are storm clouds approaching, although they are so far away that S does not notice them. One might say that S has a reason – namely, that there are storm clouds approaching – to believe that it will rain soon, even though he does not believe that there are storm clouds approaching. On the other hand, there is certainly an important epistemological difference between believing and not believing one's reasons.

Some regimentation of terminology is required. Let us distinguish:

(a) p is a reason *for* S to believe q;
(b) p is a reason S *has* to believe q;
(c) S's reason *for believing* q is p.

(Compare Thomson, 2001, pp. 23–4.) On the proposed regimentation, (c) implies (b) which implies (a), and no converse implication holds.

Only (b) and (c) imply that S believes p. Suppose p = the proposition that there are storm clouds approaching, and that p is true but not believed by S. Then p is a reason *for* S to believe that it will rain soon (or so we may suppose), but p is not a reason S *has* to believe that it will rain soon.

Only (c) implies that S believes q; moreover, it implies (when q ≠ p) that S's belief q is, in the usual terminology, "based on" his belief p (see e.g. Pollock and Cruz, 1999, pp. 35–6). Suppose S has two reasons to believe that it will rain soon: that storm clouds are approaching, and that the barometer is falling. S might come to believe that it will rain soon *because* of the former reason, not the latter. If so, then the proposition that the barometer is falling is a reason S has to believe that it will rain soon, but is not S's reason for believing that it will rain soon. For completeness, we may stipulate that if q is a reason S *has*, then (one of) S's reasons for believing q is q itself.

One other piece of jargon needs explaining:

(d) S's mental state M supplies reason p for S to believe q.

When M is a perceptual state, the explanation of (d) should approximate the intended interpretation of Brewer's slogan that "sense experiential states provide reasons for empirical beliefs." Requiring (d) to entail that S *has* reason p to believe q would be too strong; merely requiring (d) to entail that p is a reason *for* S to believe q would be too weak. Splitting the difference, (d) may be (vaguely) explained thus: S's being in M puts S in a position to have a reason, namely p, to believe q. In other words: S's being in M makes reason p to believe q readily accessible to S.

A final point. Whether or not reasons are believed, they *can* be believed. So, although "proposition" is used here widely, to include non-conceptual contents, this account of reasons as propositions makes them all conceptual.

As we will see, this regimented terminology does not exactly match either Brewer's or McDowell's usage; still, it ought to be adequate for formulating and evaluating their arguments.

3.2 An example

It will help to have a simple example of the sort of view that McDowell's and Brewer's arguments are intended to rule out. Pretend (solely for the sake of illustration) that the content of belief is Russellian, and imagine a non-conceptualist who holds in addition that the content of perception is Lewisian/Stalnakerian. Suppose a certain blue book *o* looks blue to S. According to our non-conceptualist, the content of S's experience is the possible worlds proposition that is true at a world w just in case *o* is blue in w, which we can take to be the set of worlds {w | *o* is blue in w}. If S endorses the content of his experience, he will make a judgment with the content that *o* is blue, which we can take to be the ordered pair ⟨*o*, blueness⟩. As Evans (1982, p. 227) says, this "process of conceptualization or *judgment* takes the subject from his being in one kind of informational state (with content of a certain kind, namely non-conceptual content) to his being in another kind of cognitive state (with a content of a different kind, namely, conceptual content)." The Russellian singular proposition ⟨*o*, blueness⟩ is, of course, modally equivalent to the possible worlds proposition {w | *o* is blue in w} that the non-conceptualist claims is the content of S's experience. We may suppose that our non-conceptualist agrees with Brewer's first premise ("Sense experiential states provide reasons for empirical beliefs"): she holds that perceptual states, although they have non-conceptual content, supply (conceptual) reasons for belief. Further suppose – in what amounts to a concession to Brewer and McDowell – that our non-conceptualist endorses a very strong reading of Brewer's first premise. She holds that perceptual states are *intrinsic* suppliers of reasons – they do not supply reasons only when other contingent conditions obtain. In particular, our non-conceptualist affirms:

(*) Necessarily, if *o* looks blue to S, then S is in a position to have a reason to believe that *o* is blue.[15]

Let us now examine whether our non-conceptualist can fend off McDowell's and Brewer's arguments.

3.3 McDowell

Mind and World contains a number of rather compressed objections against non-conceptualism.[16] One is this:

> In the reflective tradition we belong to, there is a time-honoured connection between reason and discourse. . . . Peacocke [a representative non-conceptualist] cannot respect this tradition. He has to sever the tie between reasons for which a subject thinks as she does and reasons she can give for thinking that way. Reasons the subject can give, in so far as they are articulable, must be within the space of concepts. (McDowell, 1994, p. 165)

This suggests that if S has a reason p to believe q (or, perhaps, if S's reason for believing q is p) then S must be able to give – that is, *state* – the reason. This immediately implies that S's reason is conceptual – if S can utter some sentence that expresses the proposition that is his reason, then since propositions expressed by sentences are conceptual contents, S's reason is conceptual.

But *our* non-conceptualist accepts that *all* reasons, whether articulable or not, are within the space of concepts. So, whatever McDowell's complaint is, it cannot be put in the terminology of this essay by saying that, according to the non-conceptualist, reasons are not conceptual.

One premise of McDowell's argument is evidently that reasons must be "articulated." We might therefore begin to set out the argument as follows:

Argument M1

    P1 If someone's reason for believing p is q, she is in a position knowingly to assert that she has reason q to believe p.

P1 is probably a stronger formulation of the "articulation" requirement than McDowell intends; in any case it is hardly obvious. But we can postpone the issue of whether P1 is true: as will be argued shortly, the main problem with Argument M1 is elsewhere.

Suppose that S in the example of section 3.2 goes on to form the belief that *o* is blue. What is S's reason for believing this? McDowell (1994, p. 165) continues:

> I do not mean to suggest any special degree of articulateness. . . . But suppose one asks an ordinary subject why she holds some observational belief, say that an object within her field of view is square. An unsurprising reply might be "Because it looks that way." That is easily recognized as giving a reason for holding the belief. Just because she gives expression to it in discourse, there is no problem about the reason's being for which . . . and not just part of the reason why.

This suggests that S's reason to believe that *o* is blue is the psychological proposition that *o looks* blue (to S).[17] And of course this is superficially attractive. So this gives us the second premise:

    P2 S's reason for believing that *o* is blue is that *o* looks blue.

Hence (from P1, P2):

> C1 S is in a position knowingly to assert that S's reason for believing that *o* is blue is that *o* looks blue.

Now the task is to get from C1 to the falsity of non-conceptualism. If C1 is true, S is in a position to know what his reasons are, and that his belief that *o* is blue is "based on" his belief that *o* looks blue. But why can't the non-conceptualist accommodate these pieces of self-knowledge as well (or as badly) as the conceptualist? Once it is clear that the non-conceptualist agrees (or should agree) that *reasons* are conceptual, the articulation requirement seems beside the point. Argument M1 is going nowhere.

A paragraph later McDowell apparently introduces a new consideration:

> The routine point is really no more than that there can be rational relations between its being the case that P and its being the case that Q (in a limiting case what replaces "Q" can simply be what replaces "P"). It does not follow that something whose content is given by the fact that it has correctness condition that P can *eo ipso* be someone's reason for, say, judging that Q, independently of whether the content is conceptual or not. We can bring into view the rational relations between the contents . . . only by comprehending the putatively grounding content in conceptual terms, even if our theory is that the item that has that content does not do its representing in a conceptual way. A theory like Peacocke's does not credit ordinary subjects with this comprehensive view of the two contents, and I think that leaves it unintelligible how an item with the non-conceptual content that P can be someone's reason for judging that Q. (Ibid., p. 166, note omitted)[18]

One argument suggested by this passage does not appeal to the claim that reasons must be articulated, or that S's reason is a psychological proposition. In our terminology, the crucial idea is to link *supplying reason* p with *having content* p.

Argument M2
> P1 S's perceptual state supplies a reason for S to believe that *o* is blue.
> P2 If S's perceptual state supplies a reason for S to believe that *o* is blue, then this reason is the content of S's perceptual state.

Hence (from P1, P2, given that reasons are conceptual):

> C1 S's perceptual state has conceptual content.

Our non-conceptualist is about as well placed as the conceptualist to accommodate P1. If S's perceptual state is a "mere sensation," then it certainly seems puzzling how it might supply a reason to believe that *o* is blue, as opposed to, say, that *o* is red, or that some other object *o** is square, or whatever (see Steup, 2001; Pryor, this volume). However, our non-conceptualist, like the conceptualist, denies that S's perceptual state is a mere sensation: it has content, and moreover content that *strictly implies* that *o* is blue. So the non-conceptualist's position that S's perceptual state supplies a reason that is *not* the content of the state seems perfectly defensible, which is to say that P2 is quite doubtful.

3.4 Brewer

We have assumed that McDowell is a *content* conceptualist (see the quotation above in section 1.4). In fact, this attribution is somewhat problematic, because content conceptualism does not appear to be equivalent to McDowell's other characterizations of his view.[19] Matters are clearer with Brewer: "[A] *conceptual state* – that is to say, a mental state with *conceptual content* – is one whose content is the content of a possible *judgment by the subject*" (this volume, p. 217). So Brewer's slogan that "sense experiential states have conceptual content" implies that they have content of the sort that can be believed (or judged), and so implies content conceptualism. Hence, whatever else Brewer wants to add (see the sentence in his essay immediately following the one just quoted), for present purposes we can take this to be the conclusion of his argument.

Return to the example of section 3.2. What, according to Brewer, is S's reason for believing that *o* is blue?

As we saw in the previous section, there is some indication that McDowell takes it to be the proposition that *o* looks blue (to S). Brewer, however, thinks otherwise. Generalized, the view that S's reason for believing that *o* is blue is that *o* looks blue (to S) amounts to this: one's perception-based knowledge of one's environment rests on a foundational layer of reasons concerning one's psychology. As Brewer argues at length in *Perception and Reason* (chapter 4; see also this volume, pp. 227–8), this "second-order view" is a disastrous model of perceptual knowledge, not least because it tacitly presumes a dubious account of self-knowledge. Of course, Brewer does not deny that that propositions about how things appear are sometimes among one's reasons for believing propositions about one's environment: for instance, if a certain book looks dark blue, that might be a reason for believing that the illuminant is a tungsten bulb, rather than a fluorescent one. And presumably the proposition that an object looks blue is often *among* the reasons one has to believe that it is blue. But this reason is not particularly important – typically one does not need to have it in order to know that an object is blue.[20]

The proposition that *o* looks blue to S having been excluded, there is only one remaining candidate for the proposition that is S's reason (or, at least, S's important reason): the proposition that *o* is blue. So we may take Brewer to hold that this proposition is S's reason for believing that *o* is blue. How do we get from this to the desired conclusion, namely that the non-conceptualist is mistaken, because the content of S's experience is the proposition that *o* is blue?

> These must be the subject's *own* reasons, which figure as such *from his point of view*. It follows from this, first, that the subject's having such a reason consists in his being in some mental state or other, although this may be essentially factive. For any actually motivating reason *for the subject* must at the very least register at the personal level in this way. Second, it also follows that it cannot be the case that the proposition, reference to which is required . . . in characterizing the reason in question, can merely be

related to the mental state of the subject's *indirectly*, by the theorist in some way. Rather, it must actually be the content of his mental state in a sense which requires that the subject has all of its constituent concepts. Otherwise ... it cannot constitute his *own reason*. [Thus, sense experiential states provide reasons for empirical beliefs only if they have conceptual content]. (Brewer, 1999, p. 152, note omitted; square bracketed quotation from this volume, p. 219)

Concentrating on our subject S, one version of Brewer's argument is this:

Argument B1
P1 S has a reason (namely: that *o* is blue) to believe that *o* is blue. (Added for emphasis: this is S's *own reason*, etc.)
P2 S's having a reason consists in S's being in some mental state.

Hence (from P1, P2):

C1 S's having a reason (namely: that *o* is blue) to believe that *o* is blue consists in S's being in some mental state M.
P3 This mental state M has the proposition that *o* is blue as its content. ("It must actually be the content of his mental state. ... Otherwise ... it cannot constitute his *own reason*").

Now this mental state M must be S's perceptual state, so:

C2 S's perceptual state has the content that *o* is blue, and hence has conceptual content.

P2 might be questioned, but the main problem with the argument is the last step. Suppose we grant that there is a mental state M, being in which *constitutes* S's having a reason to believe that *o* is blue. What could M be? To have a reason p is (at least) to believe p, so S's being in M has to entail that S believes that *o* is blue. An obvious candidate for M is simply the state of believing that *o* is blue; another less obvious but more plausible candidate is the state of knowing that *o* is blue, neither of which is S's perceptual state. (Recall Brewer's remark that the state may be "essentially factive," and see Unger, 1975, pp. 206–11; Williamson, 2000, chapter 9.)

Perhaps, though, we should concentrate on a case where S does not endorse the content of his experience. He does not *believe* that *o* is blue, and hence does not *have* a reason to believe that *o* is blue, but (we are supposing) nonetheless is *in a position* to have a reason. This leads to another version of the argument:

Argument B2
P1 S is in a position to have a reason (namely: that *o* is blue) to believe that *o* is blue.
P2 If S is in a position to have a reason to believe that *o* is blue, this is because one of S's mental states M supplies this reason.

Hence (from P1, P2):

C1 S's mental state M supplies a reason (namely: that *o* is blue) for S to believe that *o* is blue.

Does Perceptual Experience Have Conceptual Content?   243

P3 If S's mental state M supplies a reason, that reason is the content of M.

From C1 and P3, it follows that M, whatever it is, has the content that o is blue. Further, M must be S's *perceptual* state (because S does not *believe* that o is blue, etc.). So:

C2 S's perceptual state has the content that o is blue, and hence has conceptual content.

Here the weakest link is P3. If the only alternative is that M has *no* content, then P3 might be attractive. But another alternative is that M has the non-conceptual content {w | o is blue in w} (recall the previous section's discussion of Argument M2).

So far we have assumed that Brewer's insistence that "sense experiential states provide reasons ... [that are] the subject's *own* reasons, which figure as such *from her point of view*" (this volume, p. 219) is accommodated by the claim (in our terminology) that perception *supplies* reasons. That is (again in our terminology), perception puts the subject in a position to *have* reasons. Unfortunately that is not quite right.

One reason for suspecting that Brewer has something more in mind is the presence in the above quotation of the phrase "as such." And later he writes that his argument "rests upon the requirement that reasons for the subject, must be recognizable as such, and susceptible to rational scrutiny and evaluation *by her*" (this volume, p. 227). Brewer labels this the "recognition requirement" (see also Brewer, 1999, p. 19, n. 2). It should bring to mind McDowell's demand that a subject should be able to "articulate" her reasons, and indeed Brewer views the recognition requirement as one way of developing McDowell's point (ibid., p. 163).

The just-quoted statement of the recognition requirement suggests that if a subject has reason p to believe q, she must be able to recognize this fact. If so, the recognition requirement is basically a non-linguistic version of P1 in Argument M1 (to get something approximating to the recognition requirement, replace P1's "to knowingly assert" with "to recognize").[21]

However, we have already seen that McDowell's "articulation requirement" seems to be of little help in deriving conceptualism. If the recognition requirement is just a weaker version of the articulation requirement, then it will be no more helpful. And, in any case, this version of the recognition requirement is very implausible.[22]

However, on closer examination the recognition requirement appears to be something quite different. In *Perception and Reason* Brewer notes the distinction between "a person's simply making a transition [in thought] in a way which happens to accord with the relevant norms and her being guided by such norms in what she does" (ibid., p. 165). In our terminology this is more-or-less the distinction between: (a) believing q, *having* reason p to believe q, but not believing q *for* the reason p; and (b) believing q *for* the reason p. A specific example of each was given in section 3.1.

Starting from this distinction, Brewer then argues for the recognition requirement:

it is central to this distinction, between action in accord with a rule and genuine rule-following, that in the latter case [the subject] is guided in making the transition by recognition of her reason *as a reason for doing so*. ... In other words the condition which forms the starting point of the present line of argument does indeed obtain [i.e. the recognition requirement is true]: genuinely reason-giving explanations cite reasons which in some sense are necessarily recognized as such by the subject. (Ibid., p. 166)

Here it appears that terminology of "recognizing reasons as such," "in some sense," is supposed to be a notational variant of the terminology of "being guided by" reasons. If so, then the recognition requirement can be stated as follows: any genuine reason-giving explanation (where the explanandum is that S believed p and q is the reason) implies that S believed p *for* the reason q. We may grant that this is true; but it seems much too weak to do any heavy lifting in an argument for conceptualism.

4 Do Experiences Have Conceptual Content?

So far we have not come across any persuasive considerations in favor of either conceptualism or non-conceptualism. Is the pessimistic conclusion that the issue is at a standoff?

One initial reason for optimism is that conceptualism should be the default position. All parties agree, in effect, that perceiving is very much like a traditional propositional attitude, such as believing or intending; the issue is whether the contents or propositions that perceiving is a relation to are conceptual. When it is put like that, non-conceptualism is decidedly puzzling. When one has a perceptual experience, one bears the perception relation to a certain proposition p. The non-conceptualist claims that it is impossible to bear the *belief* relation to p – but why ever not? Absent some argument, the natural position to take is that the contents of perception can be believed. (This unappetizing feature of non-conceptualism is somewhat obscured because participants in the debate typically reserve "proposition" for *conceptual* contents.)

A second consideration is this. As noted in section 3, McDowell disparages non-conceptualism as another version of the Myth of the Given, and the comparison is particularly apt. The traditional Given is ineffable, a feature shared by non-conceptual content. The non-conceptual content of experience is not *thinkable* – and it cannot be whistled either. Reflecting on one's experience, one might have some inchoate suspicion that there is something special about its content, and often this seems to motivate non-conceptualism. Yet any such motivation is doubtfully coherent. Distinguish between thinking *about* a proposition (e.g. "⟨o, blueness⟩ is a singular proposition," "The proposition Bill asserted is controversial") from (merely) thinking *with* a proposition (e.g. "o is blue," "Experience has conceptual content"). When one thinks *with* p, one's thought has p as its content (or as part of its content). According to the non-conceptualist one can only think *about* the content of one's experience – "The content of my present experience is true iff *o* is blue" is not a thought *with* the content of one's experience. But then it is very hard to see how reflection on experience could possibly lead one reasonably to suspect that its content is non-conceptual. One starts with a thought like "It appears to me that my environment is thus-and-so," and ends with something like "So I suppose the content of my experience is rich/perspectival/phenomenal/non-conceptual . . ." If the premise is to have any bearing on the conclusion, the content one ends up thinking *about* must be the content one started thinking *with*, in which case no sensible conclusion can be that the content is non-conceptual.

For one more objection, recall the distinction made in section 1.4 between *total* and *partial* non-conceptualism. To simplify matters, the discussion so far assumed that the dispute was between the total conceptualist and the total non-conceptualist. But is total *non*-conceptualism at all plausible? Imagine some very basic case of seeing that *p*, where one would say without any reservation that the proposition that *p* specifies, at least in part, how things visually strike one: seeing that *o* is blue, for example. Given the rather abbreviated way in which the notion of perceptual content is usually introduced, we lack any grip on what it would mean to *deny* that the proposition that *o* is blue is part of the content of one's experience.[23]

Is the *partial* non-conceptualist any better off? She might well agree that when one *sees that o* is blue, that proposition is always part of the content of one's experience (cf. Peacocke, 1992, p. 88). But she must hold that *some* experiences have exclusively non-conceptual content (say, in the example of section 3.2, the possible worlds proposition {w | *o* is blue in w}). We may suppose the partial non-conceptualist claims that when *o* looks blue to S, but he does not see that *o* is blue (perhaps because *o* isn't blue), the content of S's experience is exclusively non-conceptual. However, the retreat to partial non-conceptualism does not help. We are told that: (a) the content of experience captures the way things perceptually appear to the subject; (b) when S sees that *o* is blue the content of his experience includes the proposition that *o* is blue; and (c) when *o* looks blue to S this proposition is not part of the content of his experience. But, surely, in case (b) and (c) things appear the same way to S, which conflicts with (a).[24]

Finally, let us briefly revisit the strong interpretation of Brewer's first premise which was foisted on the non-conceptualist. Restricted to the specific example of section 3.2, this interpretation was:

(*) Necessarily, if *o* looks blue to S, then S is in a position to have a reason to believe that *o* is blue.

The idea behind (*) is this: there is an *intrinsically rational* transition (akin to a rational inference) between S's visual experience as of *o*'s being blue, and S's judgment that *o* is blue. Non-conceptualists often seem to endorse something along these lines.

(*) is a rather perplexing thesis. If *o merely* looks blue, why should that put one in a position to have *any* reason to believe that it is blue? Is testifying that *o* is blue a positive consideration all by itself? Shouldn't the witness have some other qualifications? Granted, S's state represents that *o* is blue, so the accusation that the state is just arbitrarily connected with the proposition that *o* is blue is misplaced. Nonetheless, fending off the arbitrariness charge does not amount to a positive defense of (*).

One might try to support (*) by contemplating a counterfactual situation in which absolutely nothing has any color, and yet objects look colored to S; in particular, *o* looks blue to S. It is often claimed that in any such situation S is in a position to have a reason to believe that *o* is blue. However, this is arguably an overreaction to the fact that it would be perfectly understandable for S to believe that *o* is blue – S would be *epistemically blameless* for having this belief. (For some relevant discussion, see Pryor, 2001, pp. 114–18; Sutton, forthcoming.)

Let us widen the issue by considering a schematic and more general version of (*):

(**) Necessarily, if *o* looks blue to S and condition C obtains, then S is in a position to have a reason to believe that *o* is blue.

Uncontroversially true instances of (**) are obtained by replacing "condition C obtains" with "S sees that *o* is blue," "S knows that *o* is blue," "S has a reason to believe that *o* is blue," etc. Is there an instance of (**) that is: (a) an expression of the intuitive idea that experiences justify belief; (b) controversial; (c) true? For short, does (**) have *interesting* instances? Yes, according to the proponent of (*); they will say C is the vacuous condition. Yes, according to some reliabilists; they will explain C in terms of causal or counterfactual dependencies between *o*'s color and the way *o* looks to S.

But it is not clear why interesting instances of (**) are needed, in which case the search to find one may be called off. Suppose we take on board Brewer's point that perception can deliver knowledge of the colors of objects (say) without the support of reasons concerning how things appear. If one is sufficiently sophisticated, one can also know how things appear; combining the two, one can come to know that blue objects typically look blue. Hence, when one next recognizes that an object looks blue, one has a reason to believe that it is blue – even if it is *not* blue. Thus, simply assuming innocuous instances of (**), we can explain the contingent fact that when an object looks blue, one's perceptual state supplies one with a reason (perhaps not a very strong reason) to believe that the object is blue. What more needs explaining?

It must be emphasized that interesting instances of (**) are not being attributed to either Brewer or McDowell.[25] But if none is correct, then there is no true and exciting interpretation of the slogan that started this essay. In fact, it is more economical to reserve the slogan for a substantive epistemological claim. And if we do, the moral is this: experiences have conceptual content; yet, while we often know things by perception, experiences do not justify beliefs.[26]

Notes

1   This account of possessing the concept *horse* in the Fregean sense will do for present purposes, but it would not be acceptable to some Fregeans. According to Peacocke (1992), in order to possess a concept one must meet the concept's "possession condition," which "states what is required for full mastery of [the] concept" (ibid., p. 29). It turns out that one may believe that Seabiscuit is a horse (for example), without having "full mastery" of the concept *horse*, and so without possessing it (ibid., p. 27–33). Since "having full mastery of the concept *horse*" and "possessing the concept *horse*" are equivalent bits of jargon which cannot be explained in terms of belief, Peacocke in effect takes the notion of concept possession as primitive. A better proxy for this notion (although not an explanation of it) is this: someone possesses the concept *horse* (e.g.) iff it is *clearly true* that she believes the Thought that ... horse ... (for some filling of the dots).

2   Because concepts are supposed to correspond to categories, the allowable substituends for "F" are always restricted, although the restriction is rarely made explicit. The nature of the restriction can be left open here.

3   Peacocke (1983) assumes that the content of experience is conceptual. In later work defending the opposite view, Peacocke does not describe the content of experience as propositional (see the first paragraph in this section).

4   The allowable substituends for "F" should be taken from Enriched English, containing all concept expressions that *could be* introduced into English (including, for example, possible adjectives for highly determinate shades of color like "brown$_{26}$," "brown$_{17}$," etc.). Similarly for "s" in section 1.5 below.

5   Note that as applied to contents, the distinction is not even guaranteed to be exclusive. Suppose M has non-conceptual content p, and that the content p could be believed (that is, there is such a mental state as the belief p). Then, because the belief p automatically "has conceptual content p," p will be both "conceptual" and "non-conceptual."

6   The useful "state/content" terminology is borrowed from Heck (2000, pp. 484–5).

7   Some theorists, notably Peacocke, go on to give a positive characterization. According to Peacocke, the non-conceptual content of experience is a combination of "scenario content" and "protopropositional content." These abstract objects are built to Russellian specifications: a protopropositional content *is* a simple sort of Russellian proposition, while a scenario content is something more complicated, but likewise constructed from materials at the level of reference (Peacocke, 1992, chapter 3). See also Evans (1982, pp. 124–9).

8   As Stalnaker (1998a, b) points out, examples of conflations between state and content (non-)conceptualism are neatly dissected in Speaks (2003).

9   See Evans (1982, pp. 229 and 125, n. 9). A related argument is in Dretske (1981, chapter 6); however, plainly Dretske is arguing for something like *state* non-conceptualism.

10 See Byrne (1996, p. 264, n. 6). The richness argument is opposed by McDowell (1994, pp. 56–60, 1998) and Brewer (1999, pp. 170–4) on the ground that demonstratives like "that shade" can capture the content of color experience (see also Kelly, 2001). However, McDowell and Brewer appear to concede that the argument provides a prima facie consideration in favor of (content) non-conceptualism.

11 Cf. Bermúdez (1998, chapters 3 and 4), McGinn (1989, p. 62). McDowell (1994, p. 64) in effect denies P2; see also Brewer (1999, pp. 177–9).

12 The "lower animals" include cats and dogs, and perhaps monkeys and apes (Peacocke, 2001a, p. 260).

13 An appropriate ending for this sentence would be "which hold between conceptual contents." In fact, the sentence ends: "which hold between potential exercises of conceptual capacities." See note 19 below.

14 Brewer (e.g. 1999, p. 150) sensibly holds that reasons for belief and reasons for action are similar sorts of thing. The latter will not be discussed here.

15 Perhaps S would not be "in a position to . . . " unless he possessed the concept *blue*; if so, add that he does.

16 Apart from Brewer (1999), other important discussions of McDowell's arguments include Heck (2000, pp. 511–20) and Peacocke (2001a, pp. 255–6).

17 As McDowell exegesis, this is wrong (see note 19 below); but it is instructive to proceed as if it were right.

18 This quotation is rather loosely expressed, which might be partly responsible for McDowell's allegation of unintelligibility. McDowell's "P" and "Q" are schematic *sentence* letters. Any instance of McDowell's last schematic sentence will have a declarative sentence in place of "P." For instance: ". . . that leaves it unintelligible how an item with the non-conceptual content that *o* is blue can be someone's reason . . . " But, as noted earlier

in section 1.4, sentences (e.g. "the book is blue") express conceptual contents. In other words, there is no such thing as "the non-conceptual content that o is blue." A more precise reworking of McDowell's last sentence would be: " ... leaves it unintelligible how an item with the non-conceptual content p can be someone's reason for judging q." Here the schematic letter "p" may be replaced by a singular term (perhaps a description) refering to a particular nonconceptual content – for instance, in our simple example, "{w | o is blue in w}" – and "q" may be replaced by a "that-clause" – for instance, "that o is blue."

19 His more usual style of explanation in terms of "capacities": "It is essential to conceptual capacities, in the demanding sense, that they can be exploited in active thinking. ... When I say the content of experience is conceptual, that is what I mean by 'conceptual'" (McDowell, 1994, p. 47). But the connection between capacities and content is unclear (cf. Stalnaker, 1998a, pp. 105–6).

20 And McDowell (1995) agrees; see also Heck (2000, pp. 516–19). The answer "Because it looks blue" to the question "How do you know it is blue?" is appropriate because it gives the *source* of one's reasons, rather than a statement of them (see Byrne, 2004).

21 See also this volume, pp. 228–9, where a non-conceptualist attempts to meet the recognition requirement by formulating an argument with the conclusion "I have a reason to believe that p."

22 In the first place, both everyday life and empirical psychology indicate that subjects are often poor at recognizing their reasons. In the second place, the recognition requirement as stated is objectionable on more philosophical grounds (see especially Williamson, 2000, chapter 8).

23 One example of an explanation of perceptual content is the quotation from Peacocke in section 1.2; another is in Harman (1990, p. 264).

24 Stalnaker (1998a) and Speaks (2003) provide other reasons for content conceptualism (although they wouldn't put the conclusion that way).

25 For Brewer's sophisticated and complex account of the sense in which experiences justify beliefs, see Brewer (1999, chapter 6), and the helpful discussion in Martin (2001).

26 Many thanks to Jim Pryor, Susanna Siegel, Robert Stalnaker, and Matthias Steup; portions of sections 1 and 2 are adapted from Byrne (2002/3).

References

Bermúdez, J. L. (1998) *The Paradox of Self-consciousness*. Cambridge, MA: MIT Press.

Brewer, B. (1999) *Perception and Reason*. Oxford: Oxford University Press.

Byrne, A. (1996) Spin control: comment on John McDowell's *Mind and World*. In E. Villanueva (ed.), *Philosophical Issues 7*. Atascadero, CA: Ridgeview.

Byrne, A. (2002/3) DON'T PANIC: Tye's intentionalist theory of consciousness. In *A Field Guide to the Philosophy of Mind*. Symposium on Michael Tye, *Consciousness, Color, and Content* (http://host.uniroma3.it/progetti/kant/field/tyesymp_byrne.htm).

Byrne, A. (2004) How hard are the skeptical paradoxes? *Noûs*, 38, 299–325.

Crane, T. (1992) The nonconceptual content of experience. In T. Crane (ed.), *The Contents of Experience*. Cambridge: Cambridge University Press.

Dretske, F. (1981) *Knowledge and the Flow of Information*. Oxford: Blackwell.

Evans, G. (1982) *The Varieties of Reference*. Oxford: Oxford University Press.

Gunther, Y. (ed.) (2003) *Essays on Nonconceptual Content*. Cambridge, MA: MIT Press.

Harman, G. (1990) The intrinsic quality of experience. *Philosophical Perspectives*, 4, 31–52. Reference is made to the reprint in G. Harman (1999) *Reasoning, Meaning and Mind*. Oxford: Oxford University Press.

Heck, R. (2000) Nonconceptual content and the "space of reasons." *Philosophical Review*, 109, 483–523.

Kelly, S. (2001) The non-conceptual content of perceptual experience: situation dependence and fineness of grain. *Philosophy and Phenomenological Research*, 62, 601–8. Reprinted in Gunther (2003).

Martin, M. (1992) Perception, concepts, and memory. *Philosophical Review*, 101, 745–64. Reference is made to the reprint in Gunther (2003).

Martin, M. (2001) Epistemic openness and perceptual defeasibility. *Philosophy and Phenomenological Research*, 63, 441–8.

McDowell, J. (1995) Knowledge and the internal. *Philosophy and Phenomenological Research*, 55, 877–93. Reference is made to the reprint in J. McDowell, *Meaning, Knowledge, and Reality*. Cambridge, MA: Harvard University Press.

McDowell, J. (1994) *Mind and World*. Cambridge, MA: Harvard University Press.

McDowell, J. (1998) Reply to commentators. *Philosophy and Phenomenological Research*, 58, 403–31.

McGinn, C. (1989) *Mental Content*. Oxford: Basil Blackwell.

Peacocke, C. (1983) *Sense and Content*. Oxford: Oxford University Press.

Peacocke, C. (1992) *A Study of Concepts*. Cambridge, MA: MIT Press.

Peacocke, C. (2001a) Does perception have a nonconceptual content? *Journal of Philosophy*, 98, 239–64.

Peacocke, C. (2001b) Phenomenology and nonconceptual content. *Philosophy and Phenomenological Research*, 62, 609–15.

Pollock, J. and Cruz, J. (1999) *Contemporary Theories of Knowledge*. Lanham, MD: Rowman and Littlefield.

Pryor, J. (2001) Highlights of recent epistemology. *British Journal for the Philosophy of Science*, 52, 95–124.

Speaks, J. (2003) Is there a problem about nonconceptual content? Manuscript (http://www.artsweb.mcgill.ca/programs/philo/speaks/papers/nonconceptual-content.pdf).

Stalnaker, R. (1998a) What might nonconceptual content be? In E. Villanueva (ed.), *Philosophical Issues* 9. Atascadero, CA: Ridgeview. Reference is made to the reprint in Gunther (2003).

Stalnaker, R. (1998b) Replies to comments. In E. Villanueva (ed.), *Philosophical Issues* 9. Atascadero, CA: Ridgeview.

Steup, M. (2001) Foundationalism, sense-experiential content, and Sellars's dilemma. Manuscript (http://web.stcloudstate.edu/msteup/SellDilem.html).

Sutton, J. (forthcoming) Stick to what you know. *Noûs*.

Thomson, J. J. (2001) *Goodness and Advice*. Princeton, NJ: Princeton University Press.

Tye, M. (1995) *Ten Problems of Consciousness*. Cambridge, MA: MIT Press.

Unger, P. (1975) *Ignorance*. Oxford: Oxford University Press.

Williamson, T. (2000) *Knowledge and Its Limits*. Oxford: Oxford University Press.

PART III

JUSTIFICATION

Introduction

Matthias Steup

According to internalists, the things that make beliefs justified or unjustified – call them "J-factors" – must be internal to the mind. How is such internality to be understood? According to one way of answering this question, J-factors must enjoy an epistemically privileged status: they must be recognizable on reflection. According to an alternative answer, only mental states can be J-factors. Externalists deny that J-factors must meet any such constraint.

Why think that internalism is correct? Some epistemologists have argued for internalism on the following two grounds: (i) epistemic justification is matter of meeting one's epistemic duties; (ii) the things that determine whether a subject has or has not met her duty are internal. However, many epistemologists find at least one of these premises implausible. Alternative arguments for internalism focus on proposed externalist accounts of justification. Such accounts typically conceive of justification in terms of conclusive reasons (Dretske, 1971), reliability (Goldman, 1979), or truth-tracking (Nozick, 1981). Let's refer to an externalist theory of justification, whatever its details may be, as "ETJ." Internalists argue that there are plausible counter-examples showing that the implications of ETJ simply do not square with what we intuitively think justification is all about. To begin with, evil demon victims and brains-in-a-vat have justified beliefs. According to ETJ, they don't (Cohen, 1984: Ginet, 1985). Second, there are examples of subjects with beliefs that, though intuitively unjustified, are justified according to ETJ (BonJour, 1985, chapter 3).

Why think that externalism is correct? The fundamental externalist thought is that justification should either turn a true belief into, or at least carry it a good distance towards being, an instance of knowledge. Justification, thus understood, must confer objective probability. But objective probability is an external matter. It is not the kind of thing that is recognizable on reflection.

Furthermore, externalists claim that there is knowledge without internal justification. For example, animals and little children have knowledge, but they are not sophisticated enough to have justification of the kind internalists have in mind. Therefore, the sort of property that transforms, or tends to transform, a true belief into an instance of knowledge is an external property: one that is to be identified (in one way or another) with being grounded in a reliable origin.

To the first of these arguments for externalism, internalists will reply that the kind of justification they have in mind is necessary for knowledge even though such justification fails to make beliefs objectively probable. As far as animals and little children are concerned, internalists have two options. First, they could deny that animals and little children have knowledge. Second, they could argue that there are two kinds of knowledge: the kind that dogs, cats, and even mice can have, and a higher kind available only to beings sophisticated enough to have good reasons for what they believe. According to this reply, externalism is right about the former and internalism about the latter kind of knowledge.

Chapter 9: Is Justification Internal?

Some externalists, then, challenge the assumption that knowledge requires the possession of good reasons. A different objection to internalism questions the claim that having good reasons is an internal matter. In his essay in defense of externalism, John Greco articulates just such an objection. He distinguishes between two modes of epistemic evaluation: objective and subjective. The former is uncontroversially externalist. The latter is concerned with epistemic appropriateness, or responsibility. According to internalists, that is precisely the kind of evaluation that is subject to the internality constraint. Greco argues, however, that whether a belief is responsibly held is at least in part a function of its etiology (its causal history), and thus partially an external matter. For example, if a belief has its origin in an unreliable source, then it is not responsibly held even if the subject cannot remember the belief's unreliable origin. Consequently, Greco rejects the following, internalist principle: subjects whose mental states are alike must be alike with regard to the justificational status of their beliefs.

Furthermore, Greco rejects an objection to externalism due to Richard Fumerton. According to Fumerton, what is most problematic about externalism is that it makes the rejection of skepticism too easy. Greco's reply is that the project of refuting skepticism does not diminish but instead increases the plausibility of externalism, since internalism engenders regress problems and thus makes it impossible to advance an effective antiskeptical argument.

In the last section of his essay, Greco argues that all interesting concepts of epistemic evaluation make etiology relevant. But etiology is necessarily an external matter. Therefore, Greco concludes, there are no interesting epistemic concepts that are internalist.

In his essay in defense of internalism, Richard Feldman proposes that, if we identify the property of epistemic justification with the property of having good reasons, then it follows that epistemic justification is an internal matter, on the ground that what reasons a subject has are solely a function of what mental states the subject is in. In response to Greco's claim that there are no interesting concepts of justification that can be classified as internalist, Feldman observes that there are at least two interesting epistemic concepts that are clearly internalist: consistency among a subject's beliefs, and a belief's being supported by good reasons.

Feldman agrees with Greco that we should distinguish between a belief's being held *for* the good reasons the subject has in its support (well foundedness, in Feldman's terminology) and the subject's merely *having* good reasons for her belief, whether or not the belief is based on these reasons. Feldman does not object to Greco's claim that the former kind of epistemic status is sensitive to etiology. Nor does Greco make the claim that the latter kind of status *is* sensitive to etiology. But, Feldman argues, if having good reasons is part of well foundedness, and well foundedness is necessary for knowledge, then having good reasons is necessary for knowledge, and therefore qualifies as epistemically interesting.

Feldman also addresses cases of the following kind:

(i)   S has good reasons for her belief that p;
(ii) S's belief originates from an unreliable source;
(iii) S does not remember the origin of her belief.

Feldman argues that, in cases like that, S's belief is justified. In light of S's good reasons, neither disbelieving nor withholding p would be appropriate attitudes for her. Since it cannot be that belief, disbelief, and suspension of judgment are all inappropriate, it follows that believing that p is the attitude towards p that is appropriate for S. So S is justified in believing that p even though her belief originated in an unreliable source.

Chapter 10: Is Truth the Primary Epistemic Goal?

There is broad agreement that knowledge is more than just true belief. What, though, must be added to true belief to get knowledge? According to traditional, internalist epistemology, two more ingredients are necessary: justification understood as having good reasons, plus whatever is needed to preclude Gettier cases. According to this view, S knows that p only if S is justified in believing that p. But a person can be justified in believing that p in various ways. If believing that p is pleasant for S, or likely to help S succeed with an endeavor she cares about, S may have *prudential* justification for believing that p. It is also possible that considerations of loyalty, the pursuit of the good, or perhaps a given promise give S justification for believing that p. In that case, S might have *moral* justification for believing that p. Clearly, neither of these kinds of justification is required for knowledge. How, then, are we to distinguish between *epistemic* justification, the kind required for knowledge, and *other* kinds of justification, which are not required for knowledge? The standard answer is that epistemic justification is linked to *truth* in a way in which moral and prudential justification are not. One way of fleshing out exactly how epistemic justification is linked to truth is to view truth as a *goal*: we aim at believing what is true and not believing what is false. Whereas epistemic justification is instrumental in achieving this goal, moral and prudential justification are not.

But do we really have any such goal? And if we have such a goal, exactly what kind of a goal is it? Among the epistemic goals we can identify, is the truth goal the primary one? In his essay on this topic, Marian David begins by contrasting the truth goal with the knowledge goal. He identifies various candidates for each of these goals, and discusses which of them may plausibly be ascribed to us. Next, he turns to the relationship between the goal of having true beliefs, and the goal of having justified beliefs. His basic point is that the relationship between these goals is more plausibly captured by

(1) we want justified beliefs because we want true beliefs

rather than

(2) we want true beliefs because we want justified beliefs.

This point, David argues, gives us a reason for thinking that the true belief goal is more basic than the justified belief goal. He cautions, however, that we should not conceive of the relationship between truth and justification as a means relationship, or as one that is grounded in the causal consequences of having justified beliefs. Rather, he suggests that the greater plausibility of (1) is grounded in the fact that justified beliefs are likely to be true.

When it comes to the relation between the knowledge goal and the truth goal, the opposite relation seems to obtain. It would appear that we want our beliefs to be true because we want knowledge, not that we want knowledge because we want our beliefs to be true. David suggests, however, that we can reconceive the truth goal as the goal of having beliefs that are nonaccidentally true. This would allows us to view the truth goal as the ultimate epistemic goal.

In the last section of his essay, David examines the question of why we value knowledge more highly than mere true belief. He discusses monism and pluralism about epistemic values, and explores a way of defending the view that we want knowledge because we want true beliefs.

In his opposing essay, Jonathan Kvanvig defends the view that truth is not the primary epistemic value. In addition to truth, there are many other epistemic values: for example, knowledge, understanding, wisdom, justification, and making sense of something. Among these, truth is not primary, but just one goal among others. Truth, according to Kvanvig, becomes the primary candidate only when we adopt a conception of epistemology as the analysis of knowledge, as David does. From Kvanvig's point of view, this is unduly reductive. Epistemology, Kvanvig suggests, is more than that: it is the study of successful cognition. Thus he objects to and rejects David's account of truth as the primary epistemic goal, touching upon such topics as the Gettier problem, supervenience, and reliabilism. In the end, however, he endorses an account that is not altogether different from David's. The fundamental function of cognition, Kvanvig proposes, is that of determining, for any p, whether p. Nevertheless, Kvanvig insists, there are epistemic goals which are not subservient to the goal of having true beliefs. One such goal is that of epistemic responsibility, a goal that, according to Kvanvig, we can conceive of without invoking truth.

Chapter 11: Is Justified Belief Responsible Belief?

Richard Foley and Nicholas Wolterstorff both answer this question affirmatively. They also agree on de-emphasizing the connection between knowledge and justification. But they disagree on how justification is to be analyzed.

Foley conceives of rationality in terms of the effective pursuit of goals. Roughly, the general formula of rationality goes as follows: a decision is rational if the subject is rational in believing that the decision will satisfy her goals. For the assessment of belief rationality, the relevant goal is the epistemic goal: that of now having true and comprehensive beliefs. Accordingly, whether a belief, B, is rational depends on whether it is rational for the subject to believe that B satisfies the epistemic goal. On the surface, this account appears to be circular. Foley suggests that when supplemented with a substantive theory – such as foundationalism, coherentism, or reliabilism – the appeal to epistemic rationality can be cashed out in non-epistemic terms.

Epistemic rationality, according to Foley, is an idealized notion, and thus not well suited for the evaluative purposes of daily life. For when we wish to evaluate beliefs, what matters is the full set of a person's goals, not just the epistemic goal. In every-day evaluations, getting the truth on a certain topic remains an important goal, but it also matters how much time one wishes to allocate to an investigation of that topic. Consequently, Foley introduces two further notions: justified belief and non-negligent belief. In both cases, a belief's evaluation is sensitive to the subject's full range of goals.

There are two ways in which rational and justified belief can come apart. First, suppose S's evidence indicates to S that believing that p would not be rational for S. If S's total set of goals does not warrant spending the time needed to sift through the evidence, S's belief that p would be justified but not rational for S. Second, suppose that S's evidence is sufficient to make believing that p rational (without making it certain). Suppose further that, since other people's lives hang in the balance, S's total set of goals demands certainty. In that case, believing that p would be rational but not justified for S.

According to Wolterstorff, the evaluation of beliefs in terms of an epistemic "ought" is in fact an ongoing practice. The challenge is to understand it. When we believe as we ought, then, according to Wolterstorff's terminology, we are *entitled* to our beliefs. But how can a belief's epistemic status be a matter of entitlement when beliefs are not intentionally undertaken actions? According to Wolterstorff, the involuntary nature of belief is irrelevant to its epistemic evaluation, for the epistemic "ought" applies to belief-forming dispositions that we exercise or fail to exercise.

In his critical response to Foley's theory, Wolterstorff raises two main objections. First, he argues that there is no exit from the circle of deontological concepts. We cannot analyze the epistemic "ought" using some further, non-deontological concept. In response, Foley denies that this negative verdict is warranted. Second, Wolterstorff argues that Foley's account of epistemic justification or entitlement, as well as his account of epistemic rationality, fails because of the possibility that the subject's relevant meta-belief was formed sloppily. Suppose S believes that believing that p will satisfy the relevant goal. Since in forming this meta-belief S was epistemically irresponsible, S is not entitled to this meta-belief. Wolterstorff claims that, as a result, S's belief that p is not entitled either, nor, for that matter, epistemically rational – contrary to what Foley's account implies about such cases.

Responding to this objection, Foley argues that it is one thing for a belief to be held responsibly, and another for it to have been acquired responsibly. Whether a belief that was irresponsibly acquired in the past is, in the present, irresponsibly held depends on whether the subject has, in the present, evidence indicating that she was irresponsible in the past when she acquired the belief. If she does not have such present-time evidence, then the belief is responsibly held although it was irresponsibly acquired. So from the fact that the relevant meta-belief was acquired irresponsibly, it does not necessarily follow that the relevant first-order belief is epistemically defective.

To this reply, Wolterstorff responds that we are still left with the possibility of the kind of cases he has in mind – cases in which the subject's evidence in the present undermines her entitlement to the relevant meta-belief. Such cases show, according to Wolterstorff, that a belief is entitled or responsibly held only if the relevant meta-belief is itself entitled, and thus show that epistemic responsibility is indeed deontological all the way down.[1]

Note

1 I wish to thank Mylan Engel for his helpful comments on all three introductions.

References

BonJour, L. (1985) *The Structure of Empirical Knowledge*. Cambridge, MA: Harvard University Press.

Cohen, S. (1984) Justification and truth. *Philosophical Studies*, 46, 279–95.

Dretske, F. (1971) Conclusive reasons. *Australasian Journal of Philosophy*, 49, 1–22.

Ginet, C. (1985) Contra reliabilism. *Monist*, 68, 175–87.

Goldman, A. (1979) What is justified belief? In G. Pappas (ed.), *Justification and Knowledge*. Dordrecht: Reidel.

Nozick, R. (1981) *Philosophical Explanations*. Cambridge, MA: Harvard University Press.

Pappas, G. (ed.) (1979) *Justification and Knowledge*. Dordrecht: Reidel.

Is Justification Internal?

Justification Is not Internal

John Greco

1 The Internalism–Externalism Debate in Epistemology

When we say that someone knows something we are making a value judgment – we are saying that there is something intellectually good or right about the person's belief, or about the way she believes it, or perhaps about her. We are saying, for example, that her belief is intellectually better than someone else's mere opinion. Notice that we might make this sort of value judgment even if the two persons agree. Suppose that two people agree that the earth is the third planet from the sun. Nevertheless, we might think that one person knows this while the other person merely believes it. If so, we are making a value judgment – we are saying that there is something intellectually better going on in the case of knowledge. Another way to put the point is to say that knowledge is a normative notion. There is something normatively better about the case of knowledge, as opposed to the case of mere opinion, or even the case of true opinion. Finally, saying that someone knows something is not the only sort of value judgment we can make about her belief. Even if we agree that some belief falls short of knowledge, we might nevertheless judge that it is justified, or rational, or reasonable, or responsible. In each such case, we are saying that there is something normatively better about the case in question, as opposed to the case of mere opinion, or even the case of true opinion.

Internalism in epistemology is a thesis about the nature of this sort of normativity. More precisely, it is a thesis about what sorts of factors determine the epistemically normative (or evaluative) status of belief. Internalists claim that the epistemic status of a belief is entirely determined by factors that are relevantly "internal" to the believer's perspective on things. That is, when a person S has some belief b, whether b is justified (or rational, or reasonable, or responsible) for S is entirely a function of factors that are relevantly internal to S's perspective. By contrast, the "externalist" in epistemology denies this. The externalist says that the epistemic status of a belief is *not* entirely determined by factors that are internal to the believer's perspective. When internalism and externalism are characterized this way, a number of things become apparent.

First, internalism is a rather strong thesis, in the sense that it says that epistemic status is *entirely* a function of internal factors. By contrast, the denial of internalism is a relatively weak thesis. Externalism in epistemology holds that *some* factors that are relevant to epistemic status are not internal to the believer's perspective. Second, it is apparent that there are a number of kinds of epistemically normative status, corresponding to a number of kinds of epistemic evaluation. As already noted, we can say that a belief is justified, or rational, or reasonable, or intellectually responsible, and these need not mean the same thing. It is possible, then, to be an internalist about some kinds of epistemic status and an externalist about others. Hence there are a variety of internalisms and a corresponding variety of externalisms.

Third, we get different understandings of internalism (and externalism) depending on different ways that we understand "internal to S's perspective." The most common way to understand the phrase is as follows. Some factor F is internal to S's perspective just in case S has some sort of privileged access to whether F obtains. For example, a factor F is relevantly internal to S's perspective if S can know by reflection alone whether F obtains.[1] A related, though not equivalent, understanding of "internal to S's perspective" is as follows. Some factor F is internal to S's perspective just in case F constitutes part of S's mental life.[2] For example, a person's perceptual experience counts as internal on this understanding, since how things appear perceptually to S is part of S's mental life in the relevant sense. Also, any belief or any representation that S has about how things are would be internal on this understanding, since a person's beliefs and other representations are also part of her mental life. These two understandings are related because it is plausible to think that one has privileged access to what goes on in one's mental life, and perhaps *only* to what goes on in one's mental life. In that case, the two understandings would amount to the same thing for practical purposes. Internalism would then be the thesis that epistemic status (of some specified sort) is entirely a function of factors that are part of one's mental life, and to which one therefore has privileged access.

Finally, it is apparent that some varieties of internalism are initially more plausible than others. That is, some sorts of epistemic evaluation are obviously externalist on the above understandings. Most importantly, and perhaps most obviously, whether a belief counts as *knowledge* is an external matter, if only because a belief counts as knowledge only if it is true, and whether a belief is true is typically an external matter.

There is another reason why knowledge and many other sorts of epistemic evaluation must be understood as externalist, however. Consider that we can evaluate both persons and their beliefs in two very different ways. Broadly speaking, we can evaluate persons and their beliefs either from an "objective" point of view or from a "subjective" point of view. From the objective point of view, we can ask whether there is a "good fit" between the person's cognitive powers and the world. For example, we can ask whether the person has a sound understanding of the world around her, or whether she has a good memory, or accurate vision. Also from this point of view, we can ask whether a person's methods of investigation are "reliable," in the sense that they are likely to produce accurate results. Notice that when a person gets positive evaluations along these dimensions, her relevant beliefs will as well: her beliefs will be largely true, or objectively probable, or objectively well formed, or reliably formed. On the other hand, there is a second broad category of epistemic evaluation. This sort concerns not whether a belief is objectively well formed, but whether it is subjectively well formed. It asks not about objective fitness, but about subjective appropriateness.

Common sense tells us that these two sorts of evaluation can come apart. For example, suppose that someone learns the history of his country from unreliable testimony. Although the person has every reason to believe the books that he reads and the people that teach him, his understanding of history is in fact the result of systematic lies and other sorts of deception. How should we evaluate this person's beliefs epistemically? By hypothesis, they are not well formed, objectively speaking: they are based on lies and deceptions. Nevertheless, there are clear senses in which the person's beliefs might be subjectively well formed. If the person has been deceived through no fault of his own, we might fairly say that his beliefs are intellectually responsible, or perhaps epistemically rational. We are inclined to say similar things about the victim of a convincing hallucination. Suppose that Descartes believes there is a fire before him, and that he believes this on the basis of vivid sensory experience embedded in a broad and coherent set of background beliefs. But suppose also that Descartes is the victim of a massive and systematic illusion. The illusion, we can imagine, is undetectable and occurs through no fault of his own. Again, any epistemic evaluation of Descartes's belief will fall into one of two broad categories, or some combination of these. The belief can be evaluated in terms of its objective fit (in which case it fares poorly), or it can be evaluated in terms of its subjective appropriateness (in which case it fares well).

And now to the point: internalism is pretty much a non-starter with respect to evaluations of the first category. Evaluations from an objective point of view involve factors such as accuracy, reliability, and appropriate causal relations to one's environment. And these are paradigmatically external factors. That is, they are factors that cannot be understood as internal to our cognitive perspective, whether we understand "internal" in terms of privileged access or in terms of what goes on in one's mental life. This is why there are no internalist theories of knowledge. Knowledge, it would seem, requires both objective and subjective factors. Put another way, a belief counts as knowledge only if it is *both* objectively well formed and subjectively appropriate. But since the former sort of status involves external factors, knowledge itself is external. Internalism, therefore, is best understood as a thesis about the second broad category of epistemic evaluation: it is a thesis about what factors determine subjective appropriateness.

We have now arrived at the following understanding of internalism:

(I) Whether a belief b is subjectively appropriate for a person S is entirely a matter of factors that are internal to S's perspective.[3]

Suppose we use the term "epistemic justification" to name the sort of subjective appropriateness that is required for knowledge. A standard form of internalism says that (I) holds with regard to epistemic justification (for example, see Ginet, 1975; Chisholm,

1977; Conee and Feldman, 2001). Alternatively, one might think that (I) holds for other kinds of subjective appropriateness, independently of their connection to knowledge. For example, one might think that rationality is an important and independent normative property, and that whether a belief is rational is entirely a matter of factors that are internal to S's perspective.

I will argue that internalism is false in all of its varieties. More exactly, I will argue that internalism is false in all of its *interesting* varieties – it is false as a thesis about any interesting or important sort of normative epistemic status. Most importantly, internalism is false as a thesis about epistemic justification, or the kind of subjective appropriateness that is required for knowledge. That is bad enough, but in fact the situation for internalism is much worse. Internalism is false as a thesis about any interesting or important sort of epistemic evaluation, and any corresponding sort of epistemic normativity. In section 2 I will look at three considerations that are commonly put forward in favor of internalism as a thesis about epistemic justification, and I will argue that none of these adequately motivates the position. In fact, all three considerations motivate externalism about epistemic justification. In section 3 I will give a general argument against internalism in all its (interesting) varieties.

2 Three Motivations for Internalism

Three considerations are commonly put forward in favor of internalism, where internalism is understood as a thesis about epistemic justification, or the sort of justification that is required for knowledge. I will consider these in turn.

2.1 Epistemic justification as epistemic responsibility

The first consideration begins with an assumption about the nature of epistemic justification. Namely, a belief b is epistemically justified for a person S just in case S's belief b is epistemically responsible. However, the argument continues, epistemic responsibility is entirely a matter of factors that are internal to S's perspective. Therefore, epistemic justification is entirely a matter of factors that are internal to S's perspective.[4]

The essentials of the argument can be stated this way:

1 A belief b is epistemically justified for a person S just in case S's believing b is epistemically responsible.
2 Epistemic responsibility is entirely a matter of factors that are internal to S's perspective.

Therefore,

3 Epistemic justification is entirely a matter of factors that are internal to S's perspective. (1, 2)

Let us grant for the sake of argument that epistemic justification is a matter of epistemic responsibility. In other words, let us grant premise 1 of the argument. Nevertheless, premise 2 of the argument is false. Specifically, it is not true that epistemic responsibility is entirely a matter of factors that are internal to S's perspective. Two sorts of considerations establish this point.

First, the notion of responsibility is closely tied to the notions of blame and praise. For example, judgments concerning whether a person is *morally* responsible with respect to some action or event are often equivalent to judgments about whether the person is morally blameworthy with respect to the action or event. Similarly, judgments concerning whether a person is *epistemically* responsible with respect to some belief b are often equivalent to judgments about whether the person is epistemically blameworthy with respect to b. And now the point is this: whether a person is epistemically blameworthy for holding some belief is partly a function of the person's prior behavior: if S's reasons for believing b are the result of prior negligence, then S is not now blameless in believing b. An example will illustrate the point.

> Example 1. Maria believes that Dean Martin is Italian. She believes this because she seems to remember clearly that it is so, and she presently has no reason for doubting her belief. But suppose also that Maria first came to this belief carelessly and irresponsibly (although she has now forgotten this). Many years ago, she formed her belief on the basis of testimony from her mother, who believes that all good singers are Italian. At the time Maria knew that her mother was an unreliable source in these matters, and she realized that it was not rational to accept her mother's testimony.

Clearly, Maria is not now blameless in believing that Dean Martin is Italian. Again, prior negligence is a factor determining present responsibility, and even if that negligence is not internal to S's perspective. Therefore, premise 2 of the argument above is false.

A second consideration also establishes that premise 2 is false. First, we can make a distinction between (a) *having* good reasons for what one believes, and (b) believing *for* good reasons. Anyone who knows the axioms of arithmetic *has* good reasons for believing a theorem in the system. But unless one puts two and two together, so to speak, one does not believe the theorem in question *for* the right reasons.[5] And now the point is this: a belief is epistemically praiseworthy only if it is believed for the right reasons. Two examples illustrate the point.

> Example 2. A math student knows all the relevant axioms but doesn't see how the axioms support a theorem that must be proven on the exam. Eventually he reasons fallaciously to the theorem, and believes it on the basis of his fallacious reasoning.

> Example 3. Charlie is a wishful thinker and believes that he is about to arrive at his destination on time. He has good reasons for believing this, including his memory of train schedules, maps, the correct time at departure and at various stops, etc. However, none of these things is behind his belief – he does not believe what he does *because* he has these reasons. Rather, it is his wishful thinking that causes his belief. Accordingly, he would believe that he is about to arrive on time even if he were not.

Is Justification Internal?

Clearly, the math student's belief about the theorem is not praiseworthy. Likewise, Charlie is not praiseworthy in believing that he will arrive on time.

The moral to draw from both examples is that "etiology matters" for epistemic responsibility. In other words, whether a belief counts as epistemically responsible depends, in part, on how the belief was formed. Since these beliefs were formed on the basis of bad reasons rather than good reasons, they are not epistemically praiseworthy. In fact, the same moral can be applied to example 1. Prior negligence also figures into the etiology of a belief, and is a factor in determining whether a belief is epistemically responsible. And of course, the etiology of a belief concerns factors that are external to the believer's perspective. Putting all this together, we may conclude that epistemic responsibility is not entirely a matter of factors that are internal to S's perspective. Accordingly, understanding epistemic justification in terms of epistemic responsibility does not motivate internalism about epistemic justification. In fact, it motivates externalism about epistemic justification (see Greco, 1990).

2.2 Like believers have like justification

A second consideration that is sometimes put forward in favor of internalism invokes a strong intuition about epistemic justification. Namely, in many cases it seems that believers who are alike in terms of internal perspective must also be alike in terms of epistemic justification. The point is often illustrated by considering Descartes's victim of an evil deceiver. Suppose that the victim is exactly like you in terms of internal perspective. Even if the victim lacks knowledge, the argument goes, surely his beliefs are as well justified as yours are. If you are justified in believing that there is a table before you, and if the victim's perspective is exactly as yours, then he must be justified in believing that there is a table before him.[6]

The considerations about epistemic responsibility above suffice to counter this line of reasoning, however. The problem is that two believers might be alike internally, and yet different regarding the causal genesis of their beliefs. And once again, etiology matters. Suppose that two persons arrive at the same internal perspective, but that one does so in a way that is epistemically responsible, whereas the other does so on the basis of carelessness, thick-headedness and stupidity. The two persons will not be alike in epistemic justification, although they share the same internal perspective.

2.3 Replying to skepticism

A third consideration invoked in favor of internalism is that externalism makes an answer to skepticism too easy. Philosophical problems are supposed to be difficult. If the externalist has an easy answer to the problem of skepticism, this argument goes, then that is good reason to think that externalism is false. At the very least, it is good reason to think that the externalist has changed the subject, that he is no longer talking about our traditional notions of justification and knowledge.[7]

How does externalism make an answer to skepticism too easy? The idea is roughly as follows. According to the skeptic, one can know via sense perception only if one knows that sense perception is reliable. Similarly, one can know by inductive reasoning only if one knows that inductive reasoning is reliable. This creates problems for the internalist, because it is hard to see how one can mount a non-circular argument to the desired conclusions about the reliability of one's cognitive powers. There is no such problem for the externalist, however, since the externalist can deny the initial assumption of the skeptical argument. For example, an externalist can insist that sense perception gives rise to knowledge so long as sense perception *is* reliable. There need be no requirement, on an externalist account, that one *know* that one's perception is reliable. What is more, on an externalist account one seemingly *can* know that one's cognitive powers are reliable, and easily so. For example, one can use reliable perception to check up on perception, and then reason from there that perception is reliable. Similarly, one can use reliable induction to check up on induction, and then reason from there that induction is reliable.

In this context Richard Fumerton writes,

> All of this will, of course, drive the skeptic crazy. You cannot *use* perception to justify the reliability of perception! . . . You cannot *use* induction to justify the reliability of induction! Such attempts to respond to the skeptic's concerns involve blatant, indeed pathetic, circularity. (Fumerton, 1995, p. 177)

> The fundamental objection to externalism can be easily summarized. If we understand epistemic concepts as the externalist suggests we do, then there would be no objection in principle to using perception to justify reliance on perception . . . and induction to justify reliance on induction. But there is no philosophically interesting concept of justification or knowledge that would allow us to use a kind of reasoning to justify the legitimacy of using that reasoning. Therefore, the externalist has failed to analyze a philosophically interesting concept of justification or knowledge. (Fumerton, 1995, p. 180)

The problem with this argument against externalism is that it is self-defeating. In effect, the argument claims that only internalism can give a satisfying reply to traditional skeptical concerns. On the contrary, I want to argue, if one concedes internalism then it is *impossible* to give a satisfying reply to traditional skeptical concerns. Specifically, if one concedes that epistemic justification is internalist, then the skeptic has all he needs to construct skeptical arguments that are otherwise sound. Put simply, internalism about epistemic justification guarantees skepticism about epistemic justification.

We may see the point if we consider non-basic knowledge, or knowledge based on evidential grounds.[8] Presumably, S knows p on the basis of evidence E only if E is a reliable indication that p is true. For example, consider the case where S believes that there is a bird in the tree on the basis of her sensory evidence. Presumably, S *knows* that there is a bird in the tree only if the sensory evidence that S has is indeed a *reliable* indication that there is a bird in the tree. That seems to be something that anyone should concede. But now something important follows from this. Namely, the reliability of S's evidence is one factor that determines whether S's belief has epistemic justification. On the assumption of internalism, then, S knows p on the basis of E only if E's reliability is something that is within S's perspective.

But now what does *that* mean? In what sense could the reliability of one's evidence be within one's perspective? Presumably, the internalist will have to accept something like this: in cases of knowledge, S's belief that "E is a reliable indication that p" is itself epistemically justified. But now how could that be? How could S have epistemic justification for this belief about her evidence? On the assumption of internalism, it is hard to see how she could.

Consider propositions of the form "E is a reliable indication that p." For example, consider the belief that such and such sensory evidence is a reliable indication that there is a bird in the tree. Clearly, this is itself a belief about the world. That is, it is a belief about the character of one's sensory appearances, and about the relationship between those sorts of appearances and real birds and trees. Now this sort of belief will not be knowable *a priori*. Rather, it is the sort of belief that is known, if at all, on the basis of empirical evidence. And therefore we are threatened with a regress or a circle. That is, if S can know that there is a bird in the tree only if she knows that her evidence for this is reliable, and if she can know that her evidence is reliable only if both (a) she has evidence for *this*, and (b) she has evidence that this new evidence is reliable, then there would seem to be no end to this sort of problem. For presumably S's belief that her new evidence is reliable will require further evidence, and it will now be necessary that S know that *this* evidence is reliable, and so on.

This problem was illustrated by the example of knowing that there is a bird in the tree on the basis of sensory appearances. But it is really a very general problem, which arises in any case where a belief about the world is based on empirical evidence. For in any such case, the belief that one's evidence is reliable will itself be a belief about the world based on empirical evidence, and so we will be off and running. For example, consider the belief that all crows are black, which is based on inductive evidence involving past observations of crows. If internalism is true, then one is justified in believing that all crows are black only if one is justified in believing that one's past observations are a reliable indication of one's present belief about crows. But this belief about one's evidence is itself a belief about the world, and will itself require empirical evidence.

One strategy for avoiding this sort of problem is to attempt an *a priori* argument to the effect that one's evidence is reliable. That is, one might try to show that one's evidence is reliable, but without using further empirical evidence to do so. That would stop the regress in its tracks. But this strategy is a dead end. In principle, it would require showing that our sensory evidence *must* be a reliable indication of our perceptual beliefs, and that our inductive evidence *must* be a reliable indication of our inductive beliefs. But neither of these things is true. Rather, it is at most a contingent fact about us and our world, not a necessary fact about our evidence, that sensory appearances are a reliable indication of perceptual beliefs. Likewise, it is at most a contingent fact about us and our world, not a necessary fact about our evidence, that past observations are a reliable indication of unobserved cases.

The line of reasoning set out above is closely analogous to Hume's skeptical reasoning. Just like our internalist, Hume believed that one's empirical evidence gives rise to knowledge only if one knows that one's evidence is reliable. For example, Hume thought one must know that, in general, sensory appearances are a reliable guide to reality. Likewise, he thought one must know that, in general, observed cases are a reliable indication of unobserved cases. But there is no way to know such things,

Hume argued, without reasoning in a circle. And so there is no way to know such things at all. The present point is this: if one adopts an internalist account of epistemic justification, then Hume has all the premises he needs to mount his skeptical argument. Put another way, there will be nothing else to challenge in Hume's reasoning. Here is that reasoning, set out more formally:

Skepticism about perception

1 All our perceptual beliefs depend for their evidence on (a) sensory appearances, and (b) the assumption (R) that sensory appearances are a reliable indication of how things are in the world.
2 But (R) is itself an assumption about how things are in the world, and so ultimately depends for its evidence on perceptual beliefs involving sensory appearances.
3 Therefore, assumption (R) depends for its evidence on (R). (1, 2)
4 Circular reasoning cannot give rise to knowledge.
5 Therefore, (R) is not known. (3, 4)
6 All our perceptual beliefs depend for their evidence on an assumption that is not known. (1, 5)
7 Beliefs that depend for their evidence on an unknown assumption are themselves not known.
8 Therefore, no one has perceptual knowledge. (6, 7)

Skepticism about induction

1 All our inductive beliefs depend for their evidence on (a) past and/or present observations, and (b) the assumption (R′) that observed cases are a reliable indication of unobserved cases.
2 But (R′) is itself an assumption about something unobserved, and so ultimately depends for its evidence on induction from past and/or present observations.
3 Therefore, belief (R′) depends for its evidence on (R′). (1, 2)
4 Circular reasoning cannot give rise to knowledge.
5 Therefore, (R′) is not known. (3, 4)
6 All our beliefs about unobserved matters of fact depend for their evidence on an assumption that is not known. (1, 5)
7 Beliefs that depend for their evidence on an unknown assumption are themselves not known.
8 Therefore, no one knows anything about unobserved matters of fact. (6, 7)

What is wrong with Hume's arguments? In each case, the independent premises of the argument are 1, 2, 4, and 7. Also in each case, 2, 4, and 7 seem uncontroversial. That leaves premise 1 as the only thing left to challenge. But if internalism is true, then in each case premise 1 is true.

Once again, a closer look at a motivation for internalism ends up providing a motivation for externalism. Internalism, we have seen, makes it impossible to reply to Hume's skeptical arguments. On the contrary, we can hope to avoid Hume's skeptical conclusions only by adopting externalism.[9]

3 The General Argument against Internalism

The arguments in section 2 are directed against internalism about epistemic justification, or the sort of subjective justification that is required for knowledge. We have noted, however, that it is possible to be an internalist about other kinds of normative epistemic status. More specifically, one might think that there are other sorts of subjective appropriateness, which are independent of knowledge and epistemic justification, but which nevertheless correspond to interesting and important kinds of epistemic evaluation. Perhaps this sort of normativity is at issue when we evaluate the beliefs of Descartes's demon victim. There is no question about whether the victim has knowledge, and we might even agree that he lacks epistemic justification. Still, we might insist, there is *some* sense in which the victim's beliefs are intellectually respectable, or up to par, or at least not objectionable. In this section I will argue that there is no important or interesting normative property that is also internalist. To be clear, I do not mean to deny that there are important epistemic properties that are independent of knowledge and justification. I think there are. My point is rather that no such property is internalist.[10]

The argument begins by recalling the two broad kinds of evaluation noted above. We said that, broadly speaking, we can evaluate persons and their beliefs either from an "objective" point of view or from a "subjective" point of view. The objective point of view concerns (roughly) whether a belief has good objective fit with the world. From this point of view, we ask such questions as whether a belief is accurate, or reliably formed, or appropriately causally related to the facts. The subjective point of view concerns (roughly) what is subjectively appropriate to believe. From this point of view, we ask such questions as whether a belief is subjectively plausible, or responsibly formed, or well motivated. The argument then proceeds as follows. First, evaluations from the objective point of view are obviously externalist. Considerations concerning accuracy, reliability, and causal relations involve factors that are paradigmatically externalist. But, second, evaluations from the subjective point of view are also externalist. For example, the considerations in section 2 show that epistemic responsibility, no less than reliability, is a function of etiology. But the etiology of a belief is an external matter – it concerns such things as the history of the belief and the reasons why it is held, and these are things that are typically external to one's perspective. And now for the final premise of the argument: there is no interesting or important kind of epistemic evaluation that does not concern either objective fit or subjective appropriateness. Therefore, no interesting or important kind of epistemic evaluation, and no corresponding sort of epistemic normativity, is internalist.

A corollary of this argument is that all interesting kinds of epistemic normativity depend on factors related to accuracy and/or etiology. Of course, one can *stipulate* a kind of evaluation that abstracts away from these entirely. For example, we can stipulate that Mary's belief about Dean Martin is "weakly blameless" in the following sense: S's belief b is weakly blameless just in case S is no more blameworthy at the moment for believing b than she was a moment before. The present point is that this sort of normativity will not be interesting.

One way to see why is to look at the purpose of epistemic evaluation. It has often been noted that knowledge is a social product with a practical value. We are social, highly interdependent, information-using, information-sharing beings. As such, it is essential to our form of life that we are able to identify good information and good sources of information. In this context, it is not surprising that we make evaluations concerning how beliefs are formed, their history in relation to other beliefs, why they are believed, etc. In other words, it is not surprising that we make evaluations concerning whether beliefs are reliably and responsibly formed. But evaluations of these sorts involve considerations about accuracy and etiology. And, therefore, evaluations of these sorts are externalist evaluations.

This context also shows why judgments that abstract entirely away from external factors will be uninteresting. For example, why should we care that Mary is no more blameworthy for her belief at the moment than she was the moment before? We care about whether Mary is, in general, a responsible and reliable cognitive agent. We also care about whether, in this instance, Mary arrived at her belief in a reliable and responsible way. We also care, of course, about whether Mary's belief is true. These are important considerations about Mary and about her belief – considerations that are important from the point of view of information-using, information-sharing beings such as ourselves. On the other hand, "time-slice" evaluations that abstract away entirely from the formation of beliefs, their relation to the world, and the character of believers will not be very important. Of course, we often want to abstract away from *some* external factors – we often want to abstract away from some or others. The point here is that we never want to abstract away from *all of them at once*. In other words, we have no interest in epistemic evaluations that are (entirely) internalist.

Consider the analogy to moral evaluation. We care about which people are good and which actions are right. That is, we care whether, in general, a person is a reliable and responsible moral agent. And we care about whether, in a particular instance, a person acted in a responsible and reliable way. What we don't care about is artificial, time-slice evaluations such as that S is not more blameworthy at the moment for bringing about some state of affairs than she was the moment before. Neither do we care whether some action A is right relative to S's own moral norms, in abstraction from questions about how S did A, or why S did A, or whether S's norms are themselves any good. Of course, we often want to abstract away from *some* external considerations – we want to abstract away from some or others. The point is that we never want to abstract away from *all of them at once*. In other words, we have no interest in moral evaluations that are (entirely) internalist.

These last points can be illustrated by applying them to a particular version of internalism. A number of philosophers have wedded internalism to evidentialism (for example, see BonJour, 1985; Conee and Feldman, 2001). The main idea behind evidentialism is that a belief has positive epistemic status (of some sort or another) if and only if it is appropriately related to good evidence. Put another way, S's belief b has positive epistemic status just in case b "fits" S's evidence. The internalist adds to this that notions such as "good evidence" and "fit" are to be understood along internalist lines (for example, see Conee and Feldman, 2001, 1985).

Consider a case where S has a belief b and evidence E. For example, let E be a set of observations together with relevant background beliefs, and let b be the belief that all crows are black. There are many dimensions along which S's belief can be evaluated. For example, we can ask (a) whether E is true, (b) whether E is objectively probable, (c) whether E was reliably formed, (d) whether E was responsibly formed, (e) whether E leaves important information out, (f) whether E is a reliable indication that b is true, (g) whether b is objectively probable on E, and (h) whether S believes b because S believes E. All of these are external matters, involving factors that are neither part of S's mental life nor something to which S has privileged access in the typical case. Now certainly, in some situations we want to abstract from some of these matters. For example, we might be interested to know whether S's evidence is responsibly formed, whether or not S's evidence is true. Alternatively, we might be interested to know whether S's evidence makes her belief probable, whether or not her evidence was responsibly formed. But is there any situation in which we are interested to abstract away from *all* these factors at once? In other words, is there any situation in which we are interested to abstract away from *all* external factors? It is hard to imagine that there is.

Let us consider what is perhaps the most plausible possibility along these lines. We are sometimes interested to know, it might be suggested, whether S's belief is justified in the following sense: S believes b and S has E, and believing b on the basis of E would be licensed by the norms of evidence that S accepts. Remember, however, that we are supposed to be abstracting away from all external considerations. There is no question, therefore, whether S's norms of evidence are in fact reliable, or whether E is itself probable, or whether E was arrived at through prior negligence, or whether S believes b because S believes E, etc. Abstracting away from all of this, why would we be interested to know whether b is licensed by norms of evidence that S accepts? Why would this be an important evaluation to make? It would be analogous to asking whether S's action A is licensed by the *moral* norms that S accepts, but independently of any questions about the adequacy of S's moral norms, or prior negligence by S, or the probable or actual consequences of A, or S's motives in performing A. As in the epistemic case, it is hard to imagine a situation in which that sort of moral evaluation would be interesting or important. Both moral and epistemic evaluations, we may conclude, are more closely tied to the world than that. They concern not just what is internal to one's perspective, but how that perspective is related to things outside it.

One apparent drawback of this argument is that it is difficult to fight over what is "important" or "interesting." However, in my mind the dispute between internalists and externalists comes down largely to just this issue. Accordingly, I have tried to put the ball in the internalist court by (a) focusing the argument right there and (b) making it explicit that internalist evaluations abstract away from *all* externalist considerations. When we focus the dispute in this way, I think many will agree that the sorts of evaluations left over – the sorts that count as internalist – are not very interesting. Not in life, because they do not serve the purposes of information-using, information-sharing cognitive agents. Not in philosophy, because an internalist reply to traditional skeptical arguments is impossible, and so cannot serve that philosophical purpose.

4 Conclusion

We may now take stock of the arguments presented against internalism and in favor of externalism. In section 2, we looked at three considerations that are commonly put forward as motivations for internalism about epistemic justification, or the kind of justification required for knowledge. In each case, we saw that the consideration in question failed to motivate internalism. In fact, each consideration motivated externalism about epistemic justification. In section 3, we considered a general argument against internalism in all its interesting varieties. The argument was that all interesting epistemic evaluations are made from the objective point of view or the subjective point of view – they concern questions about objective fit, or subjective appropriateness, or both. But all such evaluations involve considerations about the accuracy of beliefs and/or their etiology, and these are paradigmatically externalist factors. The conclusion is that there are no interesting internalist evaluations. Put another way, all interesting epistemic evaluations are externalist evaluations.[11]

Notes

1 This is what Alston calls "access internalism" (see Alston, 1985, pp. 57–89, 1986, pp. 179–221). See also Ginet (1975), Chisholm (1977) and Goldman (1980, pp. 27–51).
2 This is Earl Conee's and Richard Feldman's understanding (see Conee and Feldman, 2001, p. 233).
3 If we understand "internal to S's perspective" in terms of privileged access, we get:

> (I-PA) Whether b is subjectively appropriate for S is entirely a matter of factors to which S has a privileged epistemic access.

If we understand "internal to S's perspective" in terms of what goes on in S's mental life, we get:

> (I-M) Whether b is subjectively appropriate for S is entirely a matter of factors that constitute part of S's mental life.

In the remainder of the essay I will ignore this distinction, since it is not important to the arguments that follow.
4 For arguments along these lines see Ginet (1975) and BonJour (1985).
5 For an extended discussion of this distinction and its importance, see Audi (1993, esp. chapter 7).
6 For arguments along this line see Foley (1984) and Luper-Foy (1988, p. 361).
7 See Fumerton (1995, esp. chapter 6). BonJour (1985, pp. 36–7 and 56–7) hints at this sort of objection. See also Cohen (2002).
8 Many internalists believe that all knowledge requires evidential grounds, in which case the following considerations apply to knowledge in general.
9 For further discussion along these lines see Greco (1999, 2000). An alternative response to Hume might challenge premise 2 of each argument, claiming that the assumption in question is known because it is reliably formed or because it meets some other externalist criterion for justification and knowledge. It is hard to see how the internalist could

pursue an analogous strategy, however. For further discussion of this alternative response to Hume, see Greco (2002, esp. section V).

10 Another possibility is that there is some interesting status that is a component of epistemic justification. The arguments below will count against this possibility as well.

11 Thanks to Richard Feldman, Stephen Grimm, and Ernest Sosa for helpful comments and discussion.

References

Alston, W. (1985) Concepts of epistemic justification. *Monist*, 68, 57–89.

Alston, W. (1986) Internalism and externalism in epistemology. *Philosophical Topics*, 14, 179–221.

Alston, W. (1989) *Epistemic Justification*. Ithaca, NY: Cornell University Press.

Audi, R. (1993) *The Structure of Justification*. Cambridge: Cambridge University Press.

BonJour, L. (1985) *The Structure of Empirical Knowledge*. Cambridge, MA: Harvard University Press.

Chisholm, R. (1977) *Theory of Knowledge*, 2nd edn. Englewood Cliffs, NJ: Prentice Hall.

Cohen, S. (2002) Basic knowledge and the problem of easy knowledge. *Philosophy and Phenomenological Research*, 65, 309–29.

Conee, E. and Feldman, R. (2001) Internalism defended. In H. Kornblith (ed.), *Epistemology: Internalism and Externalism*. Oxford: Blackwell.

Conee, E. and Feldman, R. (1985) Evidentialism. *Philosophical Studies*, 48, 15–34.

Foley, R. (1984) Epistemic luck and the purely epistemic. *American Philosophical Quarterly*, 21, 113–14.

Fumerton, R. (1995) *Metaepistemology and Skepticism*. Lanham, MD: Rowman and Littlefield.

Ginet, C. (1975) *Knowledge, Perception and Memory*. Dordrecht: D. Reidel.

Goldman, A. (1980) The internalist conception of justification. *Midwest Studies in Philosophy*, 5, 27–51.

Greco, J. (1990) Internalism and epistemically responsible belief. *Synthese*, 85, 245–77.

Greco, J. (1999) Agent reliabilism. In J. Tomberlin (ed.), *Philosophical Perspectives 13*. Atascadero, CA: Ridgeview Press.

Greco, J. (2000) *Putting Skeptics in Their Place*. Cambridge: Cambridge University Press.

Greco, J. (2002) How to Reid Moore. *Philosophical Quarterly*, 52, 544–63. Reprinted in J. Haldane and S. Read (eds, 2003), *The Philosophy of Thomas Reid*. Oxford: Blackwell.

Luper-Foy, S. (1988) The knower, inside and out. *Synthese*, 74, 361.

Justification Is Internal

Richard Feldman

Internalism in epistemology is a view about what sorts of things determine or settle epistemic facts. As its name suggests, it holds that "internal" things determine epistemic facts. To say that the internal things "determine" the epistemic facts is to say that if two things are alike with respect to internal factors, then they must also be alike in the relevant epistemic ways. But we are not clear about just what internalism amounts to until we are clear about what counts as an internal thing and which epistemic facts are in question. In this essay I will say a little about what counts as an internal thing and considerably more about which epistemic facts are, according to internalism, determined by them. I will argue that internal factors do determine some epistemic facts, and thus my conclusion will be in stark contrast to the thesis John Greco defends in his essay, "Justification Is not Eternal."

I Background

To understand and assess the current debate about internalism and externalism in epistemology, it is useful to look briefly at the way in which the debate arose. A plausible starting point for this examination is the traditional analysis of knowledge and its rivals.

A The traditional analysis of knowledge

In Plato's dialogue *Meno* Socrates says, "That there is a difference between right opinion and knowledge is not at all a conjecture with me but something I would particularly assert that I know." Lucky guesses make vivid the difference to which Socrates refers. If I am a contestant on a game show, I might have the belief that the valuable prize is behind door 1 rather than door 2 or door 3. Suppose my belief turns out to be true. Still, it is clear that I did not know that the prize was behind door 1 until the door was opened and I saw it. This prompts the question, "What is the difference between mere true belief and knowledge?"

Many philosophers thought that knowledge required true belief plus good reasons or good evidence. Thus, Norman Malcolm (1963) wrote, "Whether we should say that you knew, depends in part on whether you had grounds for your assertion and on the strength of those grounds." Roderick Chisholm (1957, p. 16) wrote that "'S knows that *h* is true' means: (i) S accepts *h*; (ii) S has adequate evidence for *h*; and (iii) *h* is true." These remarks are entirely typical.

The two quotations just presented reveal a generally shared outlook on what is required for knowledge in addition to true belief. Philosophers put the point in a variety of ways. Some say that knowledge requires adequate evidence, others say that it requires good reasons, and others say that it requires strong grounds. And, more commonly, philosophers have expressed this idea by saying that a true belief must be *justified* in order to be knowledge. Thus, a standard way to formulate the traditional analysis of knowledge is by saying that knowledge is justified true belief. This, then, is our starting point. I will sometimes refer to the traditional analysis as "the good reasons" analysis.

There are difficult issues to resolve if the traditional analysis is to be spelled out in detail. For one thing, one must say how much evidence is adequate (or how good the reasons must be or how strong the grounds must be). This detail will not affect the discussion that follows. Another issue has to do with what counts as reasons (or evidence or grounds). This will matter in what follows. It will be discussed briefly in section C, after some rivals to the traditional analysis are introduced.

B Rival accounts of knowledge

Some philosophers have proposed analyses of knowledge that contrast sharply with the "good reasons" type analyses just described. According to one of these alternatives, knowledge requires true belief plus an appropriate type of causal connection to the fact that the belief is about. The details of the causal theory need not concern us here. In the words of one of its leading proponents, a central fact about it is that it "flies in the face of a well established tradition in epistemology, the view that epistemological questions are questions of logic or justification, not causal or genetic questions" (Goldman, 1967, p. 372). David Armstrong (1973, p. 166) defended a similar view. He said that the difference between knowledge and true belief was that knowledge involved "a *law-like connection* between the state of affairs [of a subject's believing that p] and the state of affairs that makes 'p' true such that, given the state of affairs of [the subject's believing that p], it must be the case that p." The idea, then, is that whether you have knowledge depends not on what your reasons are but rather on what the cause of your belief is. People know about the world because there is a causal connection between states in the world and their beliefs. For example, a person can know that it is cold out because the person's belief that it is cold out is caused by its being cold out.

Another theory that differs significantly from the traditional good reasons view is reliabilism. According to a simple version of reliabilism, a person has knowledge when the person's true belief is caused by a method of belief formation that reliably (i.e. regularly) leads to true beliefs (for details, see Goldman, 1979). Thus, reliable processes such as perception and memory yield knowledge, but unreliable processes such as wishful thinking and guessing do not yield knowledge, even on those occasions that they result in true beliefs. Reliabilism allows that one can have knowledge even if one does not have any reason to think that the process that causes one's belief is a reliable one and even if one has no evidence for the proposition believed. What matters is just that the belief be caused in a reliable way.

Although there are differences between the causal theory and the reliabilist theory, for present purposes their differences are far less significant than their similarities. In what follows, I will sometimes refer to all theories relevantly like these two as "causal" theories.

C A crucial difference between good reasons analyses and causal analyses

The discussion so far suggests that there are two distinct categories of theory about knowledge. One category includes the good reasons theories and the other includes the causal theories. A preliminary way to see the internalism/externalism debate is as a debate between defenders of good reasons theories (the internalists) and the defenders of causal theories (the externalists). However, as is so often the case, things are far more complicated than this initial formulation suggests. Before we look at why things are more complicated, it will be useful to make more explicit the key difference between good reasons theories and causal theories. This will bring to light something about what counts as an internal factor.

Good reasons theorists initially thought that what needs to be added to true belief in order to get knowledge is evidence or reasons. Reasons can include other beliefs, perceptual experiences, apparent memories, and so on. Consider your belief that there is a maple tree outside your window. According to the good reasons theorists, your reason for this belief might be another belief, say the belief that the tree has leaves of a particular shape. Or your reason might include the way the tree looks – how it appears to you. While we might ordinarily say that your reason for thinking that the tree is a maple is that its leaves are a particular shape, the fact that the leaves are that shape is not part of your evidence. What you are going on in judging the tree to be a maple is your belief that it has leaves of particular shape, and perhaps ultimately you are going on how the tree looks to you (your perceptual experience). These are internal, mental states you are in. As another example, suppose you believe that it is warm outside now. Your reason for this belief is your feeling of warmth. And this is an internal factor, while the actual outside temperature is not an internal factor. A person's reasons for a belief are things that the person can, at least in the typical case, describe to someone else and cite in support of the belief. In some cases, however, people may have reasons that they cannot describe, perhaps because they lack the proper vocabulary.

The idea, then, is that a person's reasons are the things the person has to go on in forming beliefs, and they will include how things look and seem to the person, the person's apparent memories, and the person's other beliefs. These are mental things. And internalism, at least as it will be construed here, is the idea that these mental things determine certain crucial epistemic facts. As noted earlier, this implies that if two people are alike with respect to the mental factors, then they must also be alike in the relevant epistemic ways. Thus, if an internalist holds that justification is an internal epistemic matter, then that internalist is committed to the view that if two people are mentally alike in all ways that bear on the justification of a particular proposition, then either they are both justified in believing that proposition or they are both not justified in believing that proposition. Equivalently, if they differ with respect to justification, then there must be an internal or mental difference.

Notably, the things that the causal theorists emphasized in constructing their theories are external factors. The fact that one's belief is causally connected in some particular way to some state of the world is not a fact internal to one's mind. Nor is it, by itself, an evidential fact. (More will be said about this topic in section IIIB.) Of course, one can have evidence about causal connections, but that is different. Thus, the good reasons theorists said that knowledge required true belief plus the right kind of internal factors, namely good reasons or evidence to support the belief. The causal theorists said that knowledge required true belief plus the right kind of external factor, namely a causal connection of the right sort.

As a first pass, then, we might take internalism to include theories relevantly like the good reasons theories and externalism to be theories relevantly like the causal theories. One way to state the idea is that internalism is the idea that knowledge requires justification whereas externalism is that the idea that it requires the right kind of causal connection rather than justification. But framing the issue this way is adequate only if we are careful about several key terms and we set aside some issues that some philosophers have seen as central. In the next section, I turn to those matters.

II Clarifications

A Knowledge and justification

The discussion so far conforms to one way philosophers use the word "justified." This usage necessarily associates justification with good reasons and evidence. On this way of speaking, a belief is justified only if one has good reasons for it. Accordingly, when the word is used this way, we can say that causal theorists hold that knowledge requires true belief plus the right kind of causal connection, and not true belief plus justification. The preliminary statement of the internalism/externalism theory works out well on this usage (setting aside complications to be described later).

However, it is possible for causal theorists to use the word "justified" in a different way. They can agree with traditionalists that knowledge requires justified true belief, but differ with traditionalists over what is required for justification. These causal theorists would say that a belief is justified when it is caused in the right way and deny that justification always requires good evidence. When the word is used in this way, the dispute between internalists and externalists cannot be formulated as dispute about whether knowledge requires justification, since all sides agree that it does.

There is no point in arguing about the proper use of the word "justified." What does matter is to be clear about which way we are using the word here. It will be somewhat more convenient in what follows to follow this first way of describing things. On this alternative, then, the controversy between internalists and externalists is, in its initial formulation, over whether knowledge requires justification.

B Justification and well foundedness

Supporters of versions of the traditional good reasons views acknowledge a distinction between merely having good reasons for believing a proposition and believing that proposition on the basis of those good reasons. The difference emerges in cases in which a person has good reasons for believing some proposition, but ignores or misevaluates those reasons yet believes the proposition out of wishful thinking or on the basis of some mistaken inference. This has a moral analogue: doing the right thing for the wrong reasons. In the belief case, we might say that the person believes the right thing on the wrong basis. Some philosophers will say that the person is justified in believing the proposition (since she has good reasons) but that she does not believe it justifiably (since she bases her belief on something other than good reasons). Another way to put the latter point is to say that the belief is not *well founded* (see Feldman and Conee, 1985, pp. 23–5). I will use this terminology here.

Chapter Nine

Internalists will agree that whether a person is justified in believing a proposition is an internal matter. It is less clear what to say about whether a belief's being well founded depends only on internal factors. At this point, some lack of clarity about exactly what counts as internalism emerges. Suppose a person is mixed up about what one of his own beliefs is actually based on. He has some good reasons for believing some proposition and he thinks that he believes it on the basis of those reasons. In fact, it is vanity or wishful thinking rather than those reasons that actually causes him to have the belief. This shows that he is justified in believing the proposition but his belief in it is not well founded. Perhaps this makes well foundedness not a fully internalist notion. This depends upon whether the fact that his belief is based on wishful thinking rather than his good reasons counts as a mental (or internal) fact. It is hard to say. This a fact about the causal relations among one's mental states. Perhaps no causal facts count as internal. On the other hand, one might also say that these causal facts are about mental causes, and thus are internal to the person's mind. It is unclear, therefore, whether internalists will count well foundedness as an internal matter.

Rather than attempt to resolve what really counts as internal, it may be better for present purposes to grant that well foundedness is not a purely internal concept. Still, a belief is well founded only if the believer is justified in believing the proposition. And an internalist will argue that whether a person is justified in believing a proposition is determined by reasons or evidence, where these are internal matters in even the most restrictive sense. Thus, their view is that justification is an internal matter, and it is necessary for knowledge. Externalists, presumably, will deny this. They will say that justification, so construed, is not necessary for knowledge.

C The Gettier problem

Internalists have long recognized that a well founded true belief can fall short of knowledge. That is, they realized that one can base a true belief on excellent reasons yet it can still be not a case of knowledge. It is easiest to see how this can happen by noticing first that well founded beliefs can be false. Consider anything that you do know. Take as an example the proposition that your neighbor owns a Ford. You have excellent reasons for this: you have seen him driving a Ford, he often talks about the Ford he owns, he has proudly shown you a title to the car with his name on it, and so on. You know that he owns a Ford. Now, imagine an odd but possible alternative example. You have exactly the same reasons, with exactly the same reasons to trust your previously honest neighbor. But, in this alternative case, he is faking Ford ownership. The car he drives is owned by his wealthy uncle, the ownership papers he has are forged, and so on. He has pulled off an elaborate hoax. We need not speculate on his motives for this. In this second example, you have a well founded belief that he owns a Ford, but your belief is false. You don't know that he owns a Ford, and the traditional analysis gets this case right. It implies that you don't know because your belief is not true. Of course, you did have knowledge in the original, normal, case. And the traditional analysis gets this example right as well.

There is, however, an even odder variation on the case. This case makes life difficult, but interesting, for epistemologists. In this odder case, your belief that your neighbor owns a Ford is true, but not for the reasons you have. Suppose that, in addition to the Ford your neighbor drives, his wealthy uncle also has recently bought a Ford and had the ownership of this other Ford assigned to your neighbor. So it is true that he is a Ford owner, but not for the reasons you are aware of. In this situation, you have a well founded true belief that he is a Ford owner, but you lack knowledge of this fact. Examples like this one are called "Gettier cases," after Edmund Gettier (1963), who first brought them to the attention of epistemologists.

The reason why Gettier cases are important for the present discussion is as follows. Philosophers who are firmly in the good reasons tradition agree that knowledge is not justified (or even well founded) true belief. They think that there is something else to be added as well. We need not dwell on the details of the possible fourth conditions such traditionalists will place on knowledge. It will suffice to examine briefly one line of thought. One idea is that knowledge requires, in addition to justified true belief, that there be no *defeater* for one's belief. According to one prominent account, a defeater is a true proposition such that, if the person were justified in believing it, then the person would not be justified in believing the target proposition. The idea is that this is a missing truth that ruins the person's knowledge. So, on this view, knowledge is undefeated well founded true belief.

Whether a belief is defeated or not is by all accounts something external to the mind of the believer. That is, things could be exactly the same from the perspective of two believers, yet one might be subject to a defeater and the other not. Two people could be internally alike, yet one is the victim of a Gettier case and the other is not. The examples about your neighbor's Ford illustrate this. Thus, good reasons theorists do not think that what must be added to true belief in order to get knowledge is merely something internal. Instead, what they think is that what must be added is good reasons (which are internal) plus two other conditions: that the belief is based on those good reasons, and that there be no defeaters. The latter is definitely an external condition and the former may be, depending upon just how "internal" and "external" are understood.

In modifying the traditional theory in these ways, good reasons theorists are not abandoning their original approach and accepting something like a causal theory. Good reasons remain essential for knowledge. We can, however, continue to interpret the internalism/externalism debate as the debate between the modified good reasons theories on the internalist side and the causal theories on the externalist side. The causal theorists may also have to say something to deal with the Gettier problem. Or, they may think that the causal connection condition replaces the combination of the justification condition and the condition internalists use to deal with the Gettier cases. In any case, the plausible internalist thesis is that justification is an internal epistemic matter, while knowledge requires something external, such as lack of defeat, to deal with the Gettier problem.

D Deontology

Some philosophers identify internalism with the view that justification involves fulfilling obligations or duties. Similarly, some say that justified belief is epistemically responsible belief. For example, Alvin Plantinga (1993, p. 19) has written that one central internalist idea is that "epistemic justification is *deontological* justification. ... All that it requires is that I do my subjective duty, act in such a way that I am blameless." Exactly how one connects this conception of justification to internalism is a matter of some controversy. I will not pursue it here. What is crucial to note is that the view that epistemic facts depend upon internal facts is logically distinct from the view that epistemic facts are in some sense matters of duty (for discussion, see Conee and Feldman, 2001). That is, it is one thing to say that justification is a matter of doing one's duty or doing what one ought to do. It is another thing to say that the relevant epistemic duty is determined by internal facts (such as evidence). It is possible to emphasize either the duty fulfillment aspect of the view or the internal factors aspect of the view when one characterizes what internalism is. The present discussion takes the second approach. In what follows it is not assumed that internalists are committed to a deontological approach.

As I and Earl Conee have argued elsewhere (Conee and Feldman, 2001, section I), any decision about what aspect of the traditional theories to emphasize in characterizing internalism is somewhat arbitrary. Internalism is the name given to the traditional theories. But those theories were stated prior to the names "internalism" and "externalism" being used to designate epistemological theories. Armstrong introduced the term "externalism" to characterize his causal theory and contrast it with the traditional theories. One could think that what was crucial to the traditional theories was the fact that they made good reasons necessary for knowledge. One could think that what was crucial was that they made justification a deontological matter. One could think that one of these aspects – say the deontology – was supposed to support the other. In this essay, I am identifying internalism with good reasons theories and their descendants, and setting aside the deontologism.

III Internalism Vindicated

Before turning to my general defense of internalism, I want to respond to John Greco's radical claim, in his contribution to this debate, that "all interesting epistemic evaluations are externalist evaluations."

A Some internalist epistemic evaluations

It is, of course, difficult to argue effectively about which evaluations are "interesting," since what is of interest to one person may not be of interest to another. In this section I will describe some evaluations that are internalist, at least in the way characterized earlier. I believe that these count as interesting evaluations, but I do not contend that they are among the necessary conditions for knowledge.

1 Consistency. A person's overall set of beliefs can be evaluated for *consistency* and each individual belief can be evaluated in terms of whether or not it is consistent with the rest of the person's beliefs. Although it is unclear exactly what counts as an epistemic evaluation, this would seem to be one. And it is internalist: it depends only upon the relations among the person's beliefs. Of course, whether the beliefs are consistent is a logical matter, and it may be that people are in some cases ignorant

of the logical relations among their beliefs. This shows that people may, for example, fail to realize that a new belief is inconsistent with some previously held beliefs. Still, whether the belief is inconsistent with another belief is an internal matter in at least the following sense: two people who are internally alike, in that they have the same mental states, cannot differ with respect to this property. If one has a belief that is inconsistent with the rest of her beliefs, then the other does as well.

2 Identifiable good reasons. A person might at times think about something he believes and ask whether he has any good reason for that belief. The ability to identify (or think of) such a reason is a mental fact about the person. Again, two people who are mentally alike in that they have the same beliefs and are able to identify the same reasons are alike with respect to this epistemic evaluation. And, once again, it is not assumed here that people are infallible with respect to whether they can identify a good reason. They may be mistaken about what counts as a good reason. Nevertheless, whether a person can identify such a reason is an internal mental fact about the person. Thus, this is a second internalist epistemic evaluation. By and large, the ability to identify a good reason one has will coincide with the more familiar property of being able to state a good reason. But these two evaluations will diverge in rare cases in which a person has a reason but, somehow, is unable to say what it is. In assessing someone else's beliefs, we may often be interested in whether they can state reasons for them. But it is difficult to see why the ability to identify such reasons should be ruled out as "not interesting." We might wonder, for example, whether a person can think of any good reasons for some unusual beliefs, even if we know that the person is unable to communicate those reasons.

There are, then, some internal epistemic evaluations that are of interest. This refutes Greco's extreme thesis. But it leaves open the question of whether there are any internal evaluations that are directly relevant to knowledge. I turn next to that.

B Knowledge without reasons

Some ordinary uses of the word "knows" clearly fit an externalist picture. We sometimes say such things as "The thermostat knows that it is time to turn on the furnace" or "The plants know that winter is over." Presumably, the truth about the thermostat and the plants involves only facts about the reliability of their responses to certain environmental factors. These uses of "knows" do not imply that the thermostat and the plants have any true beliefs, nor do they imply that they have good reasons for believing anything. One might liken ordinary attributions of knowledge to what is said in these cases, and affirm externalism as a result.

Arguably, however, these uses of "knows" are non-literal (see Conee and Feldman, forthcoming). We often use psychological terms in ascribing properties to things that do not actually have psychological states. We might say of a car that only runs on premium gas that it "does not like standard grades of gas" even though cars are not capable of literally liking or disliking anything. What we say is just a colorful way of saying that the car does not run well on standard grades of gas. Similarly, then, it may be that the knowledge attributions to the thermostat and the plants are not literally true. The thermostat does not *know* that it is time to turn on the furnace. It just is set up to turn on the furnace at the desired time. Similarly, the plants do not *know* that winter is over. They just come out of winter dormancy when winter is over. If this is right, then these uses of "knows" provide no support for externalism as we are currently understanding it.

Perhaps some epistemologists think that the uses of "knows" currently under discussion are literal and that they refute the traditional analysis. Perhaps they think that this resolves the debate in favor of externalism. However, at most it shows that not all kinds of knowledge require reasons, and perhaps that there is no particular kind of internal state that is necessary for all knowledge. (See Ernest Sosa's, 1997, discussion of animal knowledge.) This leaves open the possibility that we can plausibly divide all cases of knowledge into two kinds. One kind includes only the cases that are mere regular reactions to environmental stimuli. The other kind might be termed "discursive knowledge" or "reflective knowledge." It does seem to require good reasons, and thus to support a kind of internalism. So, it is open to internalists to argue that there is a kind of knowledge for which there is an interesting internalist necessary condition.

Finally, even if one does not say that there is a kind of knowledge that requires the possession of reasons, it is difficult to see why having reasons is not a matter of considerable epistemological interest in its own right. Arguably, this is what the traditional debate about skepticism has concerned (see Conee and Feldman, forthcoming, for discussion). That is, skeptics have asserted, and their critics have denied, that we have good reasons to believe many of the things we ordinarily believe. If we concede knowledge to the externalists, then skepticism is best transformed into a debate directly about the quality of our reasons. Since skepticism, so transformed, is interesting, this epistemic evaluation continues to be of interest.

C Knowledge with reasons

While discussing an argument for internalism based on deontological considerations, Greco points out that "we can make a distinction between (a) *having* good reasons for what one believes, and (b) believing *for* good reasons" (p. 261). This is the same as the distinction drawn earlier between a proposition being justified for a person and the person having a well founded belief in that proposition. Greco argues that for a belief to be responsibly formed, and thus justified according to a deontological view, it must be that it comes about in the right way. That is, it must be held for good reasons. And this, he assumes, is not an internal matter. I will grant that this is correct.

Greco makes similar claims about a view closer to the non-deontological internalism defended here. He considers the idea that two believers who are internally alike are equally well justified. He replies that

> The considerations about epistemic responsibility above suffice to counter this line of reasoning, however. The problem is that two believers might be alike internally, yet different regarding the causal genesis of their beliefs. And once again, etiology matters. Suppose that two persons arrive at the same perspective, but that one does so in a way that is epistemically responsible, whereas the other does [. . . not.] The two persons will not be alike with respect to epistemic justification, even though they share the same internal perspective. (p. 262)

Here, "epistemic justification" must be used to mean "well foundedness". Given that, the conclusion can be granted. However, this fails to show that the two believers will not be alike with respect to having good reasons, the epistemic evaluation to which Greco himself called our attention. Indeed, it seems clear that if they are internally alike, then they are alike with respect to having good reasons, and thus internally alike with respect to this epistemic evaluation. Furthermore, having good reasons is necessary for knowledge. Hence, it follows that there is an internal necessary condition for knowledge – having good reasons, or justification.

This does not quite clinch the case for internalism, if the issue is whether there is an "important" or "interesting" internal necessary condition for knowledge. Since Greco himself calls our attention to the property of having good reasons, one might conclude that he thinks that it is interesting. However, I can think of two reasons for denying that justification is an interesting or important necessary condition for knowledge. Greco explicitly discusses only one of them.

Consider first the reason Greco does not discuss. An externalist might argue as follows. Consider two rival analyses of knowledge:

Analysis 1: Knowledge is undefeated justified true belief.

Analysis 2: Knowledge is undefeated well founded true belief.

Philosophers who support anything along the lines of the traditional analysis will prefer Analysis 2 to Analysis 1. Thus, the interesting necessary condition for knowledge, the one that shows up in the best analysis, is well foundedness rather than justification. It follows that well foundedness, rather than justification, is the interesting epistemic evaluation in this vicinity, and it is an externalist evaluation. Justification, while internal, is not interesting.

This argument fails. Not all interesting necessary conditions for knowledge show up in a properly spelled out statement of the conditions for knowledge. Note that having good reasons, or justification, is necessary for well foundedness. So having good reasons is necessary for knowledge. From the fact that justification is not listed as a separate or independent element in Analysis 2, it does not follow that justification is not an interesting genuinely necessary condition for knowledge. What shows up as an "independent" necessary condition of knowledge depends upon inconsequential details about how we happen to write out our analysis of knowledge. Here is a way to rewrite Analysis 2:

Analysis 3: Knowledge is undefeated justified true belief in which the belief is based on justifying reasons.

Given that well founded beliefs are justified beliefs that are based on the justifying reasons, Analysis 2 and Analysis 3 are equivalent. Analysis 2 does not explicitly include a specifically internalist component. But this is because it makes use of well foundedness. Analysis 3 spells out what this element depends on, and in doing so it does make use of an explicitly internalist element. Thus, the (presumed) adequacy of Analysis 2 does not show that knowledge does not have an important necessary condition that is internalist. It only shows that there is a way to write down this analysis that does not make explicit appeal to this element.

There is not the slightest reason to think that justification (or good reasons) is not "interesting" or not "important" just because we can restate the analysis of knowledge in terms that mask its presence. It is not that Analysis 2 makes having good reasons not necessary for knowledge. It just does not make that factor explicit. It puts it inside the "well foundedness" requirement.

Greco presents a different reason for thinking that justification is not interesting in section 3 of his essay. He argues that all interesting epistemic evaluations are either objective or subjective. The objective evaluations have to do with truth or "fit with the world" and are not internal. The subjective evaluations are the ones that have the best chance of being internalist. But he argues that all such evaluations involve responsibility and this involves etiology and is therefore external as well. However, as I pointed out earlier, an evaluation in terms of whether one has a good reason – what I have been calling "justification" – does not depend upon either responsibility or etiology. I see no reason to reject this evaluation as "uninteresting." Consider some beliefs of importance, say religious beliefs or beliefs that figure centrally in your views about morality. A question you might ask yourself is whether you have any good reason to think that these beliefs are true. The claim that the evaluation that results is uninteresting is without merit.

D Externalist accounts of good reasons

The argument of the preceding section depends upon an assumption about reasons that should be made explicit. It is that what counts as a good reason is not an external matter. This is not to say that everyone always knows what counts as a good reason. It is just to say that external factors cannot make one thing a good reason in one case but not in another. External factors cannot make it the case that two believers who are internally alike differ in what they have good reasons to believe. Some externalists, such as Christopher Hill (1999), reject this assumption.

We can use an example Greco describes to develop this point. Suppose that a person learns the history of the country from a source that is unreliable but which he has every reason to trust. Greco says that there is a clear sense in which this person's historical beliefs are "subjectively appropriate." He goes on to argue that subjective appropriateness depends upon past factors. But the key thing to notice here is that in this example, the beliefs are subjectively appropriate when they are formed (since the person has every reason to trust his source) and they remain that way later on. This is just what an internalist would say about the case.

To reject the idea that this internalist evaluation is an "interesting" epistemic evaluation, one would have to say that the belief is not subjectively appropriate, either when formed or later on, simply because the source was not in fact reliable. Now, that is not a judgment Greco is prepared to make. However, it is possible that some externalists will say that the person has a good reason only if the source actually is reliable, no matter what information the person happens to have about its reliability. But this response is surely implausible. There is, of course, a difference between relying on a reliable source that one has reason to trust and relying on an unreliable source that one has equally good reason to trust. Yet there surely is something common to the cases, something favorable to be said of the person who does accept the word of both sources. The person who accepts what one such source says and rejects what the other says might, by chance, hit upon the truth. But such a person would surely not have reason on his side.

E Forgotten evidence examples

Examples in which people forget their original basis for a belief provide a key element of some objections to internalism. I examine them in this section.

Greco describes an example of a person, Maria, who has a clear apparent memory that Dean Martin is Italian and no current reason against the proposition that he is Italian. However, she initially formed this belief irresponsibly and unjustifiably, relying on the testimony of someone she knew to be untrustworthy. She has, however, forgotten that this is her source. Greco's example resembles one put forward by Alvin Goldman (1999, section III) in a critical discussion of internalism.

Greco says that Maria is not blameless in holding the belief that Dean Martin is Italian. His point is that whether a current belief is blameless depends upon its history, not just the believer's current situation. This case comes up as part of his response to an argument for internalism that makes use of premises about blameless belief. I do not endorse any such argument and will not dispute this part of his evaluation of the case.

However, I do want to examine more carefully whether Maria's belief is justified. I will consider two possible responses open to internalists.

Reply 1. Maria's belief is justified, given that her current evidence does clearly support the proposition that Dean Martin is Italian. There is an important assumption that gives this response credibility, and it is worth making this assumption explicit. The assumption is that there is some attitude toward this proposition that it is reasonable for Maria to take (and, more generally, for any person to take toward any proposition the person considers). Suppose Maria considers the proposition that Dean Martin is Italian and wonders what attitude to take toward it. She has a clear memory of learning of this, and has good reason to trust her memory. She has, as the statement of the example makes explicit, no reason to think otherwise. It would be absurd for her to think, in spite of all this, that he is not Italian. So, disbelieving the proposition is clearly not a reasonable option, given the situation she is in. Perhaps a critic thinks that she would be most reasonable to suspend judgment. But this, too, is quite implausible. She has reasons to think he is Italian and no reason to think otherwise. Nothing competes with her reasons in favor. She might appeal to some general skeptical worries – one's memory can always lead one astray – but this is not relevant here. Thus, of the options open to her – believing, disbelieving, suspending judgment – believing is the only sensible option. Her belief is justified after all. This justification is determined by internal factors.

As noted, an assumption behind this argument is that some attitude or other is the reasonable one for her to take. This is a plausible assumption. How could it be that no option is reasonable, that whatever attitude she takes, it would be epistemically bad? Of course, it could be that no attitude will give her knowledge. She might not be in a situation in which she can know the truth of the matter. Still, some attitude or other must be reasonable for her. It is very hard to see how any attitude other than belief could be the one that is epistemically best in her situation. It is true that she made a mistake earlier. And perhaps this mistake would prevent her from having knowledge even if her belief is true. That is, if her belief is true, then, as Conee and I (2001) argue, this is a Gettier case.

I conclude that, whatever we say about blamelessness, Maria is currently justified in believing that Dean Martin is Italian, just as an internalist view suggests. Perhaps some readers will not be convinced. Perhaps they will insist that Maria's belief is a bad one, epistemically speaking. Another response suggests an additional point about the resources open to internalists.

Reply 2. Notice that as Greco describes the case, Maria previously had reason to distrust her source for this belief. Internalism implies that her belief was not justified when she still had this reason. Greco's view is that having this origin makes her belief not justified at the later time, after all information about its bad origin is forgotten. Suppose we go along with this. What exactly this would show about internalism is far from clear. Much turns on just what counts as internalism. At most, what this argument shows is that past internal states matter. So suppose one holds that justification is a matter of one's history of internal states, not just one's current internal states. This presents a puzzling question: is such a view a kind of internalism?

As I see it, there is no definitive answer to this, since what counts as internalism is at least in part a matter of stipulation. But it is worth noting that such a view does not vindicate anything very close to the causal theories. It differs from current state internalism only in that it makes past internal states matter. Reasons still matter. It is just that one's history of reasons matters, as well as one's current reasons.

IV Conclusion

I conclude that the case for internalism in epistemology is very strong. The internalism in question is the view that certain interesting and important epistemic evaluations depend entirely on internal factors, namely reasons or evidence. There are, of course, epistemic evaluations that are not internalist. These include knowledge, being defeated (or undefeated), and, perhaps, well foundedness. Still, justification, construed along traditional lines, remains an important necessary condition for knowledge. And this suffices to vindicate internalism.

References

Armstrong, D. (1973) *Belief, Truth and Knowledge*. Cambridge: Cambridge University Press.
Chisholm, R. M. (1957) *Perceiving: A Philosophical Study*. Ithaca, NY: Cornell University Press.
Conee, E. and Feldman, R. (2001) Internalism defended. In H. Kornblith (ed.), *Epistemology: Internalism and Externalism*. Malden, MA: Blackwell.
Conee, E. and Feldman, R. (forthcoming) Making sense of skepticism. In *Evidentialism*. Oxford: Oxford University Press.

Feldman, R. and Conee, E. (1985) Evidentialism. *Philosophical Studies*, 48, 15–34.

Gettier, E. (1963) Is justified true belief knowledge? *Analysis*, 23, 121–3.

Goldman, A. (1967) A causal theory of knowing. *Journal of Philosophy*, 64, 357–72.

Goldman, A. (1979) What is justified belief? In G. S. Pappas (ed.), *Justification and Knowledge*. Dordrecht: D. Reidel.

Goldman, A. (1999) Internalism exposed. *Journal of Philosophy*, 96, 271–93.

Hill, C. (1999) Process reliabilism and Cartesian skepticism. In K. DeRose and T. A. Warfield (eds), *Skepticism: A Contemporary Reader*. Oxford: Oxford University Press.

Malcolm, N. (1963) Knowledge and belief. In *Knowledge and Certainty: Essays and Lectures*. Englewood Cliffs, NJ: Prentice Hall.

Plantinga, A. (1993) *Warrant: The Current Debate*. Oxford: Oxford University Press.

Sosa, E. (1997) Reflective knowledge in the best circles. *Journal of Philosophy*, 94, 410–30.

CHAPTER
T E N

Is Truth the Primary
Epistemic Goal?

Truth Is not the Primary Epistemic Goal

Jonathan Kvanvig

Question: What is the primary
epistemic goal?

The question before us concerns the epistemic goal, standardly taken in epistemology over the past fifty years or so to be that of getting to the truth and avoiding error. In order to assess the plausibility of any answer to this question, it will be useful to begin by thinking about the question itself to make sure that it is properly understood. Asking about goals is asking about values or goods. To ask what one's goals are in, say, going to college, we inquire about the perceived values or goods that are being pursued. So the first thing to note about our question is that it asks about the values or goods that are epistemic in character.

The second point to note about the question is that it can be addressed from two quite different perspectives. One perspective is that of the theoretician. From this perspective, the question concerns what goods or values are central or primary for the theoretical task undertaken by the epistemologist, whatever that task may be. There is also another perspective, however, and that perspective is the point of view of those organisms about whose cognitive activity the epistemologist is theorizing. From this perspective, the question concerns the values or goods involved in the type of states and activities investigated by epistemologists.

It is important to keep the difference between these perspectives in mind when addressing this question, for there is no reason to assume that the answer to the question will be the same from either perspective. For example, it might be the case that truth is the primary good that defines the theoretical project of epistemology, yet it might also be the case that cognitive systems aim at a variety of values different from truth. Perhaps, for instance, they typically value well-being, or survival, or perhaps even reproductive success, with truth never playing much of a role at all.

Our question arises primarily from the perspective of the theoretical project of epistemology, and I will address the question from that point of view. We will see that the perspective of the cognitive system itself plays a role in this investigation, but only an ancillary one. In addressing the question before us I will be arguing for a negative answer to it. I will be arguing, instead, that there is a plurality of epistemic values and goals, and that though truth is an important epistemic goal, it has no claim to being the primary such value or goal. In order to argue for this plurality view, it is important to begin with a general account of the subject matter of epistemology, for the narrower one's conception of epistemology, the easier it is to defend the idea that truth is the primary epistemic goal. After explaining the appropriate domain of epistemological theorizing, I will take up the task of defending the pluralistic view.

What Is Epistemology?

Epistemology is often taken to be the theory of knowledge, but that conception is too narrow. At the most general level of characterization, epistemology is the study of certain aspects of our cognitive endeavors. In particular, it aims to investigate *successful* cognition. Within its purview, then, are various kinds of cognizing, including processes such as thinking, inquiring, and reasoning; events such as changes in one's world view or the adoption of a different perspective on things; and states such as beliefs assumptions, presuppositions, tenets, working hypotheses, and the like. Also within its purview is the variety of cognitive successes, including true beliefs and opinions, viewpoints that make sense of the course of experience, tenets that are empirically adequate, knowledge, understanding, theoretical wisdom, rational presuppositions, justified assumptions, working hypotheses likely to be true, responsible inquiry, and the like.

Two notes of caution are in order here. First, not just any kind of inquiry into kinds of cognizing and varieties of cognitive success counts as epistemology. Presumably, one can investigate these issues scientifically as well as philosophically, and I assume that they can be investigated in other ways as well (religiously, politically, morally, aesthetically, etc.). Epistemology is the result when these issues are investigated philosophically, but I will not here attempt any general characterization of the difference between philosophical and other forms of investigation.

The second point to note is that what kinds of success in cognition are relevant to epistemology is somewhat controversial. Beliefs that contribute to the well-being of the organism are successful in some sense of that term, and yet some will hold that such success is not the kind of success within the purview of the discipline of epistemology. Notice that success of a practical sort will advert to the causal consequences of holding the beliefs in question, and a common view is that epistemology is more concerned with intrinsic features of cognition, the kind reflected in talk of inquiry for its own sake. When we engage in inquiry for its own sake, successful results will partake of a kind of success that is independent of any causal contribution to well-being or other practical concerns. When epistemologists reflect on the nature of successful contribution and the extent to which an organism achieves it, the predominant approach has been to reflect on a kind of success that abstracts from the consequences of cognition, whether those consequences are practical, moral, religious, political, or social. I am inclined here to make a terminological restriction that what I mean by the use of "epistemology" and related terms is just this study of success which abstracts from the consequences of cognition, but I do not wish to be understood to denigrate more pragmatic approaches that claim to be epistemological yet deny that there is any value in, or value in thinking about, inquiry for its own sake. In part, my decision to limit a discussion of epistemology to one involving reflection on success of this rather rarefied sort rests on an attempt to consider the best case available to those who defend a positive answer to the question of whether truth is the primary epistemic goal. On these pragmatic approaches, such a positive answer has nothing to recommend it, but I will ignore such approaches here.

In slogan form, my characterization of epistemology is that it is the study of purely theoretical cognitive success, where the notion of what is purely theoretical is understood as above in terms of abstraction from the causal consequences of the success in question. As already noted, I grant that this characterization has a mild stipulative dimension in that it refuses to count as epistemology certain types of pragmatic approaches to the study of successful cognition. Even with this mild stipulation, however, the point I am trying to bring across is the breadth of this conception of epistemology, breadth with ramifications for the question before us. Once we notice this breadth, we will be struck by the strong reductionist flavor of the claim that truth is the primary epistemic goal. One's first inclination should be to maintain that each independent kind of cognitive success within the purview of epistemology identifies a cognitive goal in its own right. From this viewpoint, epistemic goals include knowledge, understanding, wisdom, rationality, justification, sense-making, and empirically adequate theories in addition to getting to the truth and avoiding error. Once we have seen the variety of cognitive successes, the proper answer would seem to be that the class of epistemic goods is manifold, as wide as the class of cognitive successes. To answer otherwise would seem to engage in Procrusteanism involved in mild humor that begins with "there are two kinds of people in the world," except that this particular truncation would begin by trimming the number from two to one. Given this initial variety, how could the reductionist viewpoint be sustained?

According to Kvanvig's view, all of these things are epistemic goals.

Kvanvig says: There appear to be many epistemic goals. Why do some claim that there is only one (truth)?

Epistemic Values and Goals

One place to turn for a defense of the reductionist thesis is to the needs of epistemology itself. Perhaps in theorizing about cognitive success, there is a need for appeal to the goal of getting to the truth and avoiding error. I think something along these lines underlies the standard view that the epistemic goal is that of getting to the truth and avoiding error. The *Reader's Digest* condensed version of this approach goes like this: epistemology is the theory of knowledge, and knowledge includes, but is something more than, true belief. What more is required provides a connection between truth and belief. For example, it is well accepted that knowledge requires that the connection between belief and truth is *non-accidental*. Furthermore, for those who think that knowledge has a normative ingredient such as justification, rationality, responsibility, or the like, there will be a theoretical need to distinguish the sense of such terms from senses which have no place in an account of knowledge, such as practical senses. Perhaps that epistemic sense of the term should be characterized in terms of the goal, or good, of truth itself. If so, then perhaps the best way to think of the conditions needed for knowledge in addition to belief and truth are conditions best conceived in terms of some connection to truth.

Marian David provides an account of the matter along these lines. He says:

> Knowledge, the epistemic concept par excellence, is usually defined in terms of belief, truth, and some other epistemic concept, say, justification: S knows p iff p is true, S belief p, and S is justified in believing p in a manner that meets a suitable anti-Gettier condition. Belief and truth, although fundamental to epistemology, are not themselves epistemic concepts. They are the nonepistemic ingredients in knowledge. This means that epistemology is not responsible for them; that is, as far as epistemology is concerned, belief and truth are *given* and can be invoked to account for epistemic concepts. The distinctly epistemic ingredient in knowledge is justification: the concept of S's *being justified* in believing p. . . . Epistemology is certainly responsible for this concept. Indeed, once an account of knowledge is at hand, the task of epistemology pretty much reduces to the task of giving a theory of justification. (David, 2001)

David here endorses several of the claims noted earlier. First, his conclusion that epistemology's task reduces to that of giving a theory of justification requires the assumption that epistemology is the theory of knowledge. So David endorses

(1) Epistemology is the theory of knowledge.

Second, David endorses the strong claim that

(2) The only epistemic concept in an account of knowledge is justification.

David argues for (2) by claiming that belief and truth are not epistemic concepts, though he does not explain why they are not. Perhaps he is thinking as follows. Truth is a *semantic* notion and belief a *psychological* notion. As such, they should be investigated by semanticists and psychologists, not epistemologists.

Even if we accept this explanation, David's claim is a bit strong since it ignores the condition needed to solve the Gettier problem. (2) denies that attempts to solve the Gettier problem fall within the domain of epistemology, and that claim is mistaken. This point is more important than it might seem initially to be, since David's approach to showing that truth is the primary epistemic goal requires focusing exclusively on the theory of justification. Once we alter (2) to accommodate this point about the Gettier problem, no claims about the theory of justification can establish on their own the claim that truth is the primary epistemic goal.

I want to stress that we should not overestimate this difficulty, however. One approach to the Gettier problem, the defeasibility approach, explains the condition needed to handle that problem as a function of truth and justification. The simplest example of this approach says that having knowledge requires, in addition to justified true belief, there being no true information which, if learned, would result in the person in question no longer being justified in believing the claim in question. Though complications arise for this overly simple approach,[1] the point to note here is that the central concepts in this approach – truth and justification – already appear in the account of knowledge. If David's point can be sustained that justification is the only epistemic concept among the concepts of justification, truth, and belief, then this approach to the Gettier problem will be quite useful in the attempt to argue that truth is the primary epistemic goal by focusing on its role in the theory of justification. So even though David's account cannot succeed without some discussion of the Gettier problem, there is some hope for the idea that the Gettier problem will not force an alteration of his view that providing a theory of justification is the central task of epistemology. Perhaps David finds the defeasibility approach to the Gettier problem attractive, and it is this attraction that leads him to bypass any discussion of the Gettier problem in his defense of the claim that truth is the primary epistemic goal.

The defense of (2) is still troublesome even if we allow this explanation of why the Gettier problem does not undermine it. One problem with this explanation is that it proves too much. Justification is a property not only of beliefs but also of other things (such as actions) not within the domain of epistemology. According to the above explanation, if a concept is suitable for investigation by disciplines other than epistemology (such as semantics or psychology), then that concept is not an epistemic concept. Insofar as justification is also a property of actions, it is suitable for investigation by action theorists, a subclass among philosophers of mind. So it appears that the above defense of (2) implies that there are *no* epistemic concepts in the proper account of the nature of knowledge!

One might reply that there is a distinctive concept of justification that is at home only in epistemology, and that concepts of justification which apply to other things such as actions are simply different concepts. In this way, the concept of justification needed in an account of knowledge is at home only in epistemology and is thus the only epistemic concept in an account of knowledge.

Such a view faces serious difficulties. Consider a simple juridical example such as the O. J. Simpson case. Some who watched the case closely say that contrary to the actual finding of not guilty, the evidence justified both their position that Simpson was guilty (beyond a reasonable doubt) and a decision by the judge to send him to prison for life. This claim predicates justification of two things: the first is a position of the speaker, i.e. a belief, and the second is an action by a legal authority. On the view proposed in support of (2) above, we would need to treat this juridical pronouncement as semantically awkward, in the way it is semantically awkward to say that both sides of rivers and certain financial institutions are banks.

Let us put these difficulties aside for the moment, however, to see how (2) is supposed to take us to the idea that truth is the primary epistemic goal. On this issue, David provides us with two quite different answers. His first answer appeals to the idea of supervenience:

> However, it is usually held that, at some point, the theory of justification has to "break out of the circle" of epistemic concepts and provide a nonepistemic "anchor" for justification by connecting it in some significant manner with nonepistemic concepts. . . . It is not hard to see how the truth-goal fits into this picture. It promises to provide a connection between the concept of justification and the concept of true belief, tying together the different ingredients of knowledge. (David, 2001)

Is Truth the Primary Epistemic Goal?   289

This attempt to find a central place for the truth goal in epistemology is unsuccessful. The need to anchor epistemic concepts in the non-epistemic is more plausibly taken as a demand that evaluative concepts supervene on non-evaluative concepts, and there is no reason to identify truth with the supervenience base of evaluative concepts in epistemology, any more than there is reason to identify the concept of the good as the supervenience base of evaluative concepts in ethics. For example, one answer to the demand for a supervenience base is broadly empiricist: justification supervenes on experiential states and logical (or quasi-logical) relations between propositions. In this view, what *makes* a belief justified is that it stands in the right logical or quasi-logical relationship to another belief or to (the propositional content of) an experience. One may be tempted to maintain that the concept of truth will still enter into this picture when we try to characterize logical relationships, but that reply is a red herring. First, logical relationships can be characterized syntactically as well as semantically. Second, and more important, even if truth is an ingredient in our account of this supervenience base, it is not present in the manner of a *goal* or anything of the sort. To argue that because truth is needed to explain logic, it must be that a primary epistemic goal would also commit one to the view that because the concept of a sensation is necessary to explain experience, sensation itself must be a primary epistemic goal according to empiricism.

There is a particular kind of approach to the nature of justification that fits David's picture a bit better than the empiricist example. Alvin Goldman's reliabilism of 1979 begins with the same demand to break out of the circle of epistemic concepts in order to clarify the nature of justification, and the way in which Goldman prefers to break out of the circle is in terms of the concept of reliability. The central non-epistemic concept in his theory is that of the reliability of a process or method of belief formation, the percentage of times that process or method generates a true belief. Given that it is percentage of truth over error by which we favor some processes and methods over others, we might wish to characterize our theoretical preference for some processes or methods over others in terms of the goal of truth over error, thereby securing the idea that truth is the primary epistemic goal.

This way of defending the claim that truth is the primary epistemic goal thus requires the subconclusion that reliabilism is the correct approach to the nature of justification, a position that is far from trouble-free.[2] But the particular problems one might cite for reliabilism are not the central difficulty. The deeper problem is that the question we are attempting to answer arises at a different point in epistemological inquiry than the question of the adequacy of some particular theory of justification. The question whether truth is the primary epistemic goal is a meta-epistemological question, whereas the question of the adequacy of reliabilism is not. When we ask about the primary epistemic goal, we are asking whether there is a way of defending the idea that truth is the primary epistemic goal that is neutral between competing epistemological theories, and given that interpretation of the question, the approach that relies on the adequacy of a reliabilist approach in epistemology must be judged to be unsuccessful.

David seems to recognize the meta-epistemological character of the issue, for he provides another and quite different answer to the question of the relationship between justification and truth. He says:

Why is truth typically cast as a goal...? Alston provides the reason. It is generally agreed that being justified is an evaluative concept of some sort: To say that believing p is justified or unjustified is to evaluate belief p, in some sense, as a good thing or as a bad thing, as having some positive status or some negative status. The suggestion is that this type of evaluation, epistemic evaluation, is most naturally understand along broadly teleological lines, as evaluating beliefs relative to the standard, or goal, of believing truth and avoiding error. (David, 2001)

David here endorses Alston's claim that the evaluative character of justification should be understood teleologically, and this explanation of the relationship between truth and justification is a suitably meta-epistemological account in contrast to the previous account which seems to depend on the particular epistemological theory of reliabilism.

What we need to know, however, is how this point about the teleological character of justification helps to show that truth is the primary epistemic goal. David's argument proceeds by contrasting the idea that truth is the goal with the idea that knowledge is the goal:

Although knowledge is certainly no less desirable than true belief, the knowledge-goal is at a disadvantage here because it does not fit into this picture in any helpful manner. Invoking the knowledge-goal would insert the concept of knowledge right into the specification of the goal, which would then no longer provide an independent anchor for understanding epistemic concepts. In particular, any attempt to understand justification relative to the knowledge-goal would invert the explanatory direction and would make the whole approach circular and entirely unilluminating. After all, knowledge was supposed to be explained in terms of justification and not the other way round. This does not mean that it is wrong in general to talk of knowledge as a goal, nor does it mean that epistemologists do not desire to have knowledge. However, it does mean that it is bad epistemology to invoke the knowledge-goal as part of the theory of knowledge because it is quite useless for theoretical purposes: The knowledge-goal has no theoretical role to play *within* the theory of knowledge. (David, 2001)

David's argument thus proceeds as follows. We have already seen his claims that (1) epistemology is the theory of knowledge and (2) justification is the only epistemic concept within the theory of knowledge. These points imply that the central epistemic concepts are knowledge and justification, so the primary epistemic goal will have to be one related to these concepts. David's teleological conception of justification makes truth a contender for being the primary epistemic goal, and if the only epistemic concepts are justification and knowledge, the central competitor of the idea that truth is the primary epistemic goal would be that knowledge itself is the goal. Once we see the implication from (1) and (2) to the point that the central task of epistemology is to construct a theory of justification, the knowledge goal cannot be the primary epistemic goal on pain of rendering our epistemology viciously circular. Only the truth goal can be central if our theory has any hope of adequacy, so truth must be the primary epistemic goal.

The form of argument here bears scrutiny since the particular argument in question relies on the false assumption that epistemology is the theory of knowledge.

Given this assumption, the competitor to the idea that truth is the primary epistemic goal is the idea that knowledge is also an epistemic goal. Given the more general conception of epistemology outlined earlier and the variety of cognitive successes it implies, we will need a generalization of David's argument in order to conclude that truth is the primary epistemic goal. Such a generalization could begin by allowing that any purely theoretical cognitive success is of value and hence a suitable epistemic goal. But for each such goal, it has no theoretical goal to play within the project of theorizing about it, for such an account would make the theory "circular and entirely unilluminating." Moreover, it would have to be claimed, any goal that would render a theory circular and unilluminating in this way cannot be an epistemic goal, leaving truth as the only standing candidate for that role.

So, on this view, nothing of epistemic value can be an epistemic goal. Instead, only values that fall outside the domain of cognitive successes can legitimately be cited when explaining epistemic success. It also follows from this point that truth and belief cannot themselves be epistemically valuable, for otherwise getting to the truth cannot itself be an epistemic goal.

Contrast this result with an alternative picture. For simplicity, let us grant David's claims that epistemology is the theory of knowledge and that knowledge is to be understood in terms of justified true belief plus a Gettier condition. The alternative picture holds that each element in the theory of knowledge should isolate some epistemic good (something whose value contributes to and helps explain the value of knowledge). So, for example, truth itself must be an epistemic good, implying that it has value exceeding that of mere empirical adequacy. In a similar vein, belief must be an epistemic good, implying that Pyrrhonian counsel to abandon beliefs in favor of acquiescing to the appearances cannot, in any literal sense, accord with the facts about what is important from a purely theoretical point of view. Similar points could be voiced about the other two conditions as well, and the accumulated result of these points is that if truth is an epistemic goal so are the other values just mentioned. As a result, truth is not the primary epistemic goal, but rather one among several epistemic values that have equal claim to being epistemic goals. This alternative picture strikes me as much more plausible than the idea that nothing that is epistemically valuable can itself be an epistemic goal or good.

The generalization of David's argument above has a further problem. This generalization requires that for any epistemic value V other than truth itself, the fundamental goal in terms of which a theory of V is constructed is truth itself. Once we put the view in these terms, I think it is fairly easy to see that it is false, though it may be more plausible in some parts of epistemology than in others. Perhaps, for example, it has some plausibility with respect to the value of belief itself. One might maintain that the value of belief is in some way dependent on the value of truth in that cognitive activity in general is prompted by the *desire* to get to the truth, and that belief is the result of such alethic motivation. Alternative alethic accounts are also available, ones which posit something sub-intentional as the driving force behind such activity, perhaps a need or interest or drive or perhaps even an instinct to get to the truth. One might even hold that it is the *function* of cognition to get to the truth and avoid error, whether the organism in question can be properly characterized by any of the intentional or sub-intentional descriptions just noted.

Such a view is not without difficulties, however, for there are alternatives to this truth-based account with some plausibility. To the extent that an organism has explicitly intentional motivation for cognitive activity, it may be more plausible to characterize those motivations in terms of a desire for knowledge or understanding rather than in terms of a desire to get to the truth, for we typically view mere true belief as something less than what we really want. Moreover, this point about fully intentional cognitive activity carries over to subintentional contexts as well. If the function of cognition is to be given a factive characterization – one which implies truth, as opposed to one which requires only adequate coping with an environment for purposes of survival and reproduction – the factives of knowledge and understanding have at least as much going for them as truth itself. That is, it may be more plausible to hold that the function of cognition is to produce knowledge or understanding of one's surroundings than it is to maintain that the function of cognition is to get to the truth about one's surroundings.

I do not wish to rest my negative answer to the question of whether truth is the primary epistemic goal on a rejection of truth-based accounts of cognition, however. My own view is that something close to a truth-based account is correct. Since my answer to the question before us does not depend on my view of this matter, I will present only the briefest account of it here. In my view, the fundamental function of cognition and the fundamental intentional attitudes involved in cognitive activity can be characterized without appeal to the concept of truth. The function in question is that of determining, for any claim p, whether p, e.g. whether it is raining, or whether a particular object is a predator. Such a characterization appeals to no factive concepts stronger than truth, however. Moreover, even though the affective states underlying cognitive activity often involve factives such as knowledge or understanding, such states are not universal – not everyone wants knowledge, for example, and not everyone is motivated by a concern for understanding. What is fundamental to explicitly intentional cognitive activity as such is a weaker state, for even small children and animals engage in fully intentional cognitive activity. We characterize curiosity as the desire to know, but small children lacking the concept of knowledge display curiosity nonetheless. The conclusion to draw from these considerations is that an adequate characterization of cognition as such will appeal to no motivational structure, either intentional or non-intentional, involving a factive element stronger than truth. To the extent, then, that we are persuaded that such a motivational structure must involve facticity of some sort, we should have no objection to characterizing cognition in terms of the goal of truth.[3]

Let us return to the main issue, arising from the fact that the argument we are considering requires that for any epistemic value V other than truth itself, the fundamental goal in terms of which a theory of V is constructed is truth itself.

See Next page

Even if we grant that truth is in some way fundamental to our understanding of cognition itself, much more is needed to sustain this generalization. In particular, one would have to be able to argue that truth is fundamental to any of the kinds of purely theoretical cognitive successes noted earlier. Some such successes clearly involve the concept of truth, concepts such as knowledge, understanding, wisdom, likely hypotheses, and justified beliefs; and if these concepts involve the concept of truth, there is some hope that the goal of truth is somehow fundamental to an adequate account of these concepts. There are also cognitive successes that are not obviously truth-related, such as the concepts of making sense of the course of experience and having found an empirically adequate theory. Both of these concepts can be explained without recourse to the goal of truth. An empirically adequate theory is one that will never be refuted by the course of experience, and one makes sense of the course of experience by developing a classification system for experiences together with a theory of explanation of how the various categories are explanatorily related.

Another example of a cognitive success that is not obviously truth-related is that of responsible inquiry. Explaining why will take a bit of work, and we can begin by distinguishing deontic concepts from evaluative ones. Most ethical theories are teleological, explaining deontic notions such as obligation, permission, and forbiddenness in terms of evaluative notions such as the good. Not all do, however. Deontological theories refuse such definitions, explaining deontic concepts in other ways, the paradigm example being a Kantian theory that explains forbiddenness in terms of internal contradictions between universal maxims.

Epistemology has seen defenders of what is termed deontologism, and here Chisholm is the paradigm example. Epistemic deontologists have not been deontologists in the sense defined in the previous paragraph, however, for they have defined epistemic duties in terms of epistemic values such as truth. Chisholm, for example, says our epistemic duties arise from the fundamental duty to (do one's best to) believe the truth and avoid error (Chisholm, 1977).

What would real deontologism look like in epistemology? A good example of such can be developed along Bayesian lines. According to one kind of Bayesianism,[4] each of us has a complete theory of evidence in our heads, encoded in the form of conditional probabilities. Such a theory can explain the forbiddenness of a (degree of) belief in terms of logical notions such as logical inconsistency, rather than in terms of value terms. A degree of belief is forbidden when, in the face of new experience, it becomes logically inconsistent with the relevant conditional probabilities.

Other examples are available as well. Though Richard Foley[5] wholeheartedly endorses the standard epistemic goal of getting to the truth (now) and avoiding error (now), his theory doesn't require this teleological aspect. On his theory, a belief is justified if and only if it conforms to one's deepest epistemic standards. These standards are epistemic principles one would endorse given as much time to reflect as is needed to reach a stable point of view.[6] Once we have such internal standards playing a theoretical role, real deontologism can emerge, for it is in conforming to these standards that one's epistemic duties are satisfied.

Teleology in epistemology is needed only when the epistemic principles are licensed in some other, non-subjective way. If one's theory is truly subjective, then consistency with an internalized theory of evidence is all that is needed for defining key epistemic concepts such as justification. If, however, the theory of evidence is objective, then one needs some standard against which to assess its adequacy. It is here that epistemic teleology has its natural home.

Given this background, let us return again to the concept of responsible inquiry. The concept of epistemic responsibility can have strong subjective overtones, though it need not. A theory of epistemic responsibility may be modeled on the ethical notion of responsibility, which is to be contrasted with the notions of praiseworthiness and blameworthiness. In the moral sphere, one can be blameless in failing to live up to one's responsibility, and if we analogize to epistemic responsibility, we will be willing to say that one's inquiry might be irresponsible but blameless. If we refuse to distinguish epistemic responsibility from epistemic blamelessness, our theory of epistemic responsibility will be much more subjective, and the possibility of a non-teleological account of it will emerge.

Not much turns on this issue in the present context, however, for even in the face of a compelling argument that responsibility should be identified with blamelessness, there will still be an epistemic concept of value that can be understood in non-teleological terms – namely, intellectually blameless inquiry. So not only are there the notions of sense-making and empirical adequacy that do not presume the goal of truth, there are other, normative notions that can equally be clarified without appeal to the goal of truth.

Conclusion

The slogan that truth is the epistemic goal has influenced much of epistemology in recent history, and we have seen that there is some truth in this idea. In particular, the idea of truth as a goal will play a significant and fundamental role in our understanding of cognition itself. The claim that truth is the primary epistemic goal, however, goes well beyond such a claim. It implies that the concept of truth plays a fundamental role in any adequate theory of any cognitive success of a purely theoretical sort. The view I have defended is that such a position has too narrow a view of the variety of epistemic values and goods, and that once we appreciate this variety and the broadened conception of the domain of epistemological inquiry, we will go no further than to embrace the idea that truth is an important and central epistemic value and goal.

Notes

1 For discussion of these complications, see Klein (1981).
2 To my mind, the most serious such problem is that reliabilism cannot explain adequately the concept of propositional justification, the kind of justification one might have for a proposition one does not believe or which one disbelieves (believes the opposite). I have argued this point in several places (e.g. Kvanvig, 1990, 1992, 1996, 2000, 2003).
3 For a more complete investigation of these issues, see the chapter on the value of truth in my 2003.
4 For an intuitive account of Bayesianism and its commitments, see van Fraassen (1990).
5 The view I discuss here is from Foley (1986).
6 This "operational" definition of the concept of one's deep standards leads to various objections to Foley's view, of the sort that usually plague counterfactual accounts. For example, if one's deepest standards are chary of reflection of any kind, what results from Foley-reflection will be self-stultifying. To avoid these problems, one could develop a Foley-like view where the counterfactuals in question were taken to be evidentially related to the question of what one's deep standards are, but deny that they are related definitionally.

References

Chisholm, R. (1977) *Theory of Knowledge*, 2nd edn. Englewood Cliffs, NJ: Prentice Hall.

David, M. (2001) Truth as the epistemic goal. In M. Steup (ed.), *Knowledge, Truth, and Duty. Essays on Epistemic Justification, Virtue, and Responsibility*. Oxford: Oxford University Press.

Foley, R. (1986) *The Theory of Epistemic Rationality*. Cambridge, MA: Harvard University Press.

Goldman, A. (1979) What is justified belief? In G. Pappas (ed.), *Justification and Knowledge*. Dordrecht: Reidel.

Klein, P. (1981) *Certainty*. Minneapolis: University of Minnesota Press.

Kvanvig, J. (1990) The basic notion of justification. Christopher Menzel, co-author. *Philosophical Studies*, 59, 235–61.

Kvanvig, J. (1992) *The Intellectual Virtues and the Life of the Mind: On the Place of the Virtues in Contemporary Epistemology*. Savage, MD: Rowman and Littlefield.

Kvanvig, J. (1996) Plantinga's proper function theory of warrant. In J. Kvanvig (ed.), *Warrant and Contemporary Epistemology*. Savage, MD: Rowman and Littlefield.

Kvanvig, J. (2000) Zagzebski on justification. *Philosophy and Phenomenological Research*, 60, 191–6.

Kvanvig, J. (2003) Propositionalism and the perspectival character of justification. *American Philosophical Quarterly*, 40(1) 3–18.

Kvanvig, J. (forthcoming) *The Value of Knowledge and the Pursuit of Understanding*. New York: Cambridge University Press.

Pappas, G. (ed.) (1979) *Justification and Knowledge*. Dordrecht: Reidel.

Steup, M. (ed.) (2001) *Knowledge, Truth, and Duty. Essays on Epistemic Justification, Virtue, and Responsibility*. Oxford: Oxford University Press.

van Fraassen, B. (1990) *Laws and Symmetry*. Oxford: Oxford University Press.

Truth as the Primary Epistemic Goal: A Working Hypothesis

Marian David

I Possessing Truth

Let us first consider what it means to talk of truth as a goal, without worrying about its being the primary epistemic goal. "I want truth" is a bit like "I want fruit." Like fruit, truth comes in pieces. We have separate words for the different sorts of pieces fruit comes in. The pieces truth comes in we can just call *truths*. Philosophers often call them true *propositions*. The term is convenient because it also fits the pieces falsehood comes in. Say you are looking at the monitor and assert that the flight is leaving. I am looking too and I also assert that the flight is leaving. We both assert the same thing, the same proposition: the proposition that the flight is leaving. The proposition is either true or false. If it is true, we are both right; if it is false, we are both wrong. So, "I want truth" says that I want true propositions. "I want *the* truth," taken literally, says that I want exactly the truth, the whole truth and nothing but the truth; that is, taken literally, it says that I want all the true propositions and only the true propositions, no false ones. Of course, normally one would not take it literally; one would assume that what I really wanted is all and only the true propositions relevant to some salient subject matter not explicitly specified.

"I want truth" and "I want the truth" do not mention what I want with the truth. But it is clear that I want at least to have it, to possess it. How does one possess truth? We can possess truth by way of *believing* it, by believing true propositions. We can possess truth by way of *knowing* it, by knowing true propositions. "I want truth" can be understood either way. So the broad idea of truth being a goal comes in two versions, corresponding to the two ways of possessing truth. Let us call them the *true-belief goal* and the *knowledge goal* respectively. They are both truth goals.

On the believing-way of possessing truth, "I want truth" comes out as: "I want to believe true propositions." The more colloquial alternative, "I want to have true beliefs," is fine too as long as we remember that using the word "belief" for the things possessed can be awkward if believing is the mode of possessing them. We would not want to say: "I want to believe true beliefs." The noun "belief" is, as one puts it, act/object ambiguous. It might be used to refer to the act, or attitude, of believing a proposition. It might also be used to refer to the object, or content, of the attitude, to the proposition believed. If you believe that the flight is leaving, and someone says that your belief is true, then the noun "belief" refers to the proposition you believe. If someone were to say that your belief was silly, the noun would refer to your attitude of believing the proposition. The desire for truth relevant to the true-belief goal is a desire directed more at the attitude than the propositions; it is a desire for believing what is true, rather than for the truth of what one believes.

Propositional knowledge entails truth. One cannot know a proposition unless it is true: you cannot know that the flight is leaving at eight, unless it is leaving at eight (of course, you might *think* you know it is leaving at eight even though it is not). Since propositional knowledge entails truth, we can express the knowledge goal simply as "the goal of having knowledge," without mentioning truth. It is a truth goal nevertheless: it is the goal of possessing truths by way of knowing them.

The true-belief goal and the knowledge goal are both truth goals. Are there really two distinct goals here? Propositional knowledge entails true belief: one cannot know a proposition unless one believes it. (Sure enough, we sometimes say things like: "I don't believe it; I know it." But this is short for: "I don't *merely* believe it; I know it." We wouldn't say: "I know it, but I don't believe it.") Since propositional knowledge entails true belief, the goal of having knowledge and the goal of having true beliefs are not entirely distinct. They are at least "overlapping" goals in this sense: if you want to have knowledge, you want something you cannot have without having true beliefs.

Epistemologists like to emphasize that knowledge requires something in addition to true belief: justified or warranted or rational belief, or belief based on good reasons or on adequate evidence (and they usually add that more is required still). This seems right for many typical uses of the word "know." There also seem to be uses of "know" that do not require more than true belief. Alvin Goldman (1999) calls this the *weak* sense of "knowledge": when an unfaithful husband greets his lover with the words

"She knows," he is not worried about whether his wife is justified in believing that he is cheating on her; all he is worried about is that she believes it and that it is true. The goal of having knowledge in this weak sense coincides with the goal of having true beliefs. But let us reserve the term "knowledge" for the *strong* sense, the sense in which it requires more than true belief.

We can say, then, that the knowledge goal and the true-belief goal are different, albeit overlapping, truth goals.

Invocations of truth as a goal, as something desired or aimed at, show up fairly frequently, especially in religious, philosophical, and broadly scientific contexts: phrases like "the search for truth" and "the pursuit of truth" are almost commonplaces there. Such invocations usually leave open which of the two truth goals is intended. In general, any reference to truth as a goal might be taken to refer to the goal of believing truths or to the goal of knowing truths – our title is a case in point – and even when the word "knowledge" is used, it is often difficult to tell whether it is intended in the weak or the strong sense. Compare William James's (1911) commandment, "We must know the truth; and we must avoid error"; which he rephrases almost immediately as "Believe truth! Shun error!"

II Truth Goals

The goal of having true beliefs, the goal of believing true propositions, is an indefinite or indeterminate goal: it is vague about how much of the truth is being aimed at. The most ambitious determinate goal would be the one corresponding to "I want to believe *the* truth"; it would be the goal of believing all the true propositions and not believing any false ones. Using "$\forall p$" to abbreviate the universal quantifier "for all propositions p," it might be represented like this:

(1) G $(\forall p)$ (Tp $\rightarrow$ Bp & Bp $\rightarrow$ Tp),

but we must keep in mind that the relevant desire is supposed to be directed at the attitude rather than the propositions. So the goal represented in (1) should be understood in terms of wanting to believe all and only true propositions, or wanting to be such that one believes all and only true propositions, rather than wanting all propositions to be such that they are true if and only if one believes them.

It is fairly clear that we don't actually have this goal. The first part, the part about believing all the truths, looks like an absurd thing to want – partly because it is too obvious that there must be way too many truths for it to be humanly possible to believe them all, partly because there are vast numbers of unimportant and boring propositions which, it seems, we wouldn't particularly want to believe even if they were true (and the truths are so redundant: any conjunction of true propositions is itself a true proposition). The second part, though, believing only truths, not believing any falsehoods, does look like something we want – though we might say "I would like that," rather than "I want that," signaling that we don't think the chances of reaching this state are at all good. Still, because of its first part, (1) looks like an overly ambitious goal – verbal "commitment" to it ("Tell me the truth!") would normally be neither taken nor meant literally. One would automatically assume that it was meant to be restricted to all the relevant truths about some salient subject matter not explicitly specified. (But we should also remember that theists typically attribute omniscience to God, which involves believing all and only the truths. This indicates that we do tend to regard this state as something valuable, as some sort of ideal, albeit a remote one.)

Explicitly restricting the first part of (1) to "important and interesting" propositions would yield a goal that might be ascribed to us with some plausibility.

The indefinite goal mentioned earlier, the goal of "having true beliefs," can be regarded as a tacitly as well as indeterminately restricted version of (1). Indeed, this indefinite goal may well be the one most plausibly ascribed to us; it looks like a goal we actually have – maybe just because it is so vague. It is naturally understood with a suppressed rider about falsehood. Say like this: it is the goal of having true beliefs and few, or no, false ones (or maybe the goal of having a large stock of true beliefs containing few, or no, false ones; or maybe simply the goal of having true beliefs rather than false ones).

There might be some propositions that are so discomforting (painful, upsetting, disgusting) to believe that we wouldn't want to believe them even if they be true, and some so comforting to believe that we would want to believe them even if they be false. Would this show that we don't have the indefinite goal? No. It would not even show that we don't have unrestricted (1) as a goal. We have various goals. In some cases different goals come into conflict and one "loses out." In some cases a goal can be "neutralized" by contrary emotions. This does not show that we don't have the beaten or neutralized goal; it merely shows that the goal is not an absolute one.

The goals considered so far are "collective" goals. They refer not to individual propositions but to whole collections of propositions, e.g. unrestricted (1) refers to the collection containing all and only the true propositions; the indefinite goal refers to some "fuzzy" collection, or fuzzily refers to a collection. But talk about wanting to have true beliefs can also be intended "distributively." Consider the generalization:

(2) $(\forall p)$ G $(Tp \rightarrow Bp$ & $Bp \rightarrow Tp)$,

which says that, for every proposition p, one has the goal (wants) to believe p if and only if p is true. Whereas (1) represents a single goal referring to a collection of propositions, (2) itself does not actually purport to represent any goal at all; rather, it represents a (false) statement ascribing to us a huge number of individual relativized goals, one for each proposition p. It is clear that we can't have all these goals: there are way too many propositions.

But we can at least say this. For each proposition p such that we are seriously asking whether p is true, we will have the relativized true-belief goal with respect to p; that is, for each such proposition p, we have the goal (want) to believe p if and only if p is true: the very fact that we are seriously asking (ourselves or others) whether p is true shows that this is one of our goals with respect to p, at least at the time at which we are asking. Actually, what we want with respect to any such p is more completely captured like this: to believe p, if and only if p is true, and to believe ¬p, if and only if ¬p is true, where "¬p" refers to the negation of p. (Unlike Williams (1978, p. 38) and Sosa (2003), I take the "only if" parts to be important. Assume that, having asked whether p is true, you are being told that p is true and also, maybe by someone else, that ¬p is true. Since one of them must be true, you are being told the truth with respect to p/¬p. But this is not what you wanted. You wanted *only* the truth with respect to p/¬p: you did not want to get both, the truth and the falsehood.)

Note that there is something funny about how collective true-belief goals relate to goals concerning individual propositions. Say you are looking through a list of bargain CDs, wanting to buy all but only the ones by Eminem. You have reached the next item; it is called *Slim Shady*. You will want to buy *Slim Shady* if and only if it is by Eminem. Now assume you come to believe that *Slim Shady* is by Eminem: then you will (probably) want to buy *Slim Shady* (unless you believe that getting it would interfere with a more important goal, like not spending more than a certain amount). Here the collective goal relates fairly straightforwardly to a non-conditional goal with respect to one particular thing via your belief that the thing belongs to the collection of things you want. Now assume you are going through a list of propositions, wanting to believe all and only the ones that are true. You have reached the next item: the proposition p. Like before, we can say that you will want to believe p if and only if it is true. But now assume you come to believe that p is true. Can we again go on and say, non-conditionally, that you will (probably) want to believe p? This seems odd at best. Having come to believe that p is true, you already believe p (it is hard to see how you could believe that p is true without believing p); and once you believe p, it is at best odd to say that you *want* to believe p. Sosa (2003) suggests this shows that collective true-belief goals can play no role in "guiding" us about what to believe – whereas the collective Eminem goal can play a role in guiding you about what record to buy.

Let us briefly consider the knowledge goal too. Begin with the ambitious goal of having all knowledge; that is, the goal of knowing everything. To know everything would be to know everything there is to know. What is there to know? Truths, that is, true propositions, but no falsehoods: a false proposition cannot possibly be known (although it can be known to be false, but that would be knowing a truth about a falsehood). So part of the ambitious goal can be represented as "$(\forall p)(Tp \rightarrow Kp)$," which brings out that the knowledge goal is directed at possessing truths, just like the true-belief goal. What about a second, negative, part for the knowledge goal, a part corresponding to the $(Bp \rightarrow Tp)$-part of (1)? I am not quite sure. There seem to be two options:

(3.1) G $(\forall p)$ $(Tp \rightarrow Kp$ & $Bp \rightarrow Tp)$,
(3.2) G $(\forall p)$ $(Tp \rightarrow Kp$ & $Bp \rightarrow Kp)$.

According to (3.1), the ambitious knowledge goal would be the goal of knowing all the truths and not believing any falsehoods (avoiding error). But one might hold that the second part of the goal should be stronger than the second part of (1); that it should be about not believing something unless one knows it. Accordingly, (3.2) describes the goal in terms of wanting to be such that one knows all the truths and believes only what one knows. Note that, just as the condition (Tp → Kp) subsumes the condition (Tp → Bp), due to knowledge requiring true belief, so the condition (Bp → Kp) subsumes the condition (Bp → Tp), and for the same reason.

Problems about the plausibility, or rather implausibility, of thinking that the (3)s describe goals we actually have arise here in just the same way as they did with respect to unrestricted (1). To get goals more plausibly ascribed to us, the first parts of the (3)s would have to be restricted to important and interesting propositions. The collective knowledge goal most plausibly ascribed to us may again be an indefinite one, say, the goal of having knowledge (and avoiding error, or not believing things unless one knows them); which can again be regarded as some sort of tacit fuzzy weakening of an ambitious goal. And again collective goals should be distinguished from relativized goals:

(4.1) (∀p) G (Tp → Kp & Bp → Tp),
(4.2) (∀p) G (Tp → Kp & Bp → Kp).

These statements ascribe goals that are relativized to individual propositions p. Of course, no one can have all these goals, one for each proposition p. But we can say that, for each proposition p such that we want to know whether p is true, we will have such a relativized goal with respect to p – again, the full goals we have with respect to such p's should add clauses about wanting to know ¬p, if ¬p is true.

III Epistemic Goals

Among the many goals we have, or might have, only some appear to be directly relevant to the subject matter of epistemology. Let us call them *epistemic* goals. The primary epistemic goal would then be the goal that is the most important or most fundamental of the goals directly relevant to the subject matter of epistemology. What are the candidates? Epistemology is the theory of knowledge. So the main candidates should be the goal of having knowledge, the goal of having true beliefs, and some goal relating to the other main requirement for knowledge, say *having justified beliefs* (or warranted or rational beliefs, or beliefs based on good reasons or on adequate evidence – for convenience, I will often use the concept of justified belief as representative of this group).

It is difficult to be precise about the goal of having justified beliefs – in part that is because there is little agreement about what justification actually amounts to. Maybe the following will suffice for the indefinite version of the goal: it is the goal of believing a proposition, if one has justification for believing it, and only if one has justification for believing it (but we should not assume that one *has* a justification only if one has *given* one's justification). Alternatively, we might say that it is the goal of believing a proposition, if one has adequate evidence for it, and only if one has adequate evidence for it. Again we should distinguish between the single collective goal of having justified beliefs and the relativized goals we have, or might have, with respect to individual propositions p, to believe p if and only if we have justification for believing p.

The goal of having knowledge and the goal of having true beliefs are both truth goals. What about the goal of having justified beliefs? Is it also a truth goal? No: having justified belief is not a way of possessing truth. This is because, unlike true belief and knowledge, justification does not entail truth: a belief can be justified even though it is false. This does not mean that there aren't some forms of justification that do entail truth – justification by mathematical proof might be one. Such forms of justification are called "infallible" justification. But most forms of justification are fallible: they don't entail (guarantee) truth; e.g. justification by induction, or by the evidence of our senses. So, in general, having a justified belief does not entail that the justified belief is true.

We have identified three main epistemic goals: having justified beliefs, having true beliefs, and having knowledge. Which one, if any, can be regarded as the primary epistemic goal?

Many of our goals are connected. Often we want something because we want something else and because we realize that if we get the former we will (probably) get the latter, or because we realize that without getting the former we can't get the latter. Chains of goals we have because of other goals we have terminate in "basic" or "intrinsic goals," things we want, or value, just for their own sake and not for the sake of anything else. So, considering our epistemic goals, we might ask whether our epistemic goals are connected in some such way. If there is a single one at the bottom of such a chain, then that would be the primary epistemic goal.

Note that to claim that something is the primary *epistemic* goal does not imply that it is a basic goal all things considered, that we want it only for its own sake, that it is an "absolutely" intrinsic goal. Take the idea that possessing truths (by believing them? by knowing them?) is the primary epistemic goal. We want to possess truths in part for their own sake (we tend to be simply curious about things) and in part, or maybe mostly, because we think that having truths will increase our chances for securing our other, non-epistemic, goals (in particular, we want truths about the most effective means for securing our other goals). The idea that possessing truths is the primary epistemic goal does not commit itself on this issue beyond the claim that there are no other *epistemic* goals for the sake of which we want truths – never mind any non-epistemic goals for the sake of which we might want truths. It only commits itself to the claim that possessing truths is a "relatively" intrinsic goal, that it behaves like an intrinsic goal within the domain of epistemology.

Actually, it commits itself even less, or rather, to something slightly different. The idea that something is the primary epistemic goal has more the force of an "ought" than the force of an "is." It says that, to the extent that we do have epistemic goals, we *ought* to have them because we have the one singled out as primary. Obviously, it is rather risky to make claims about what we actually want and about why we want what we want, without asking or studying many of "us." Even if all of us do have the epistemic goals discussed earlier (or at least closely related ones), and even if these goals are in fact connected in the manner mentioned above, some of us might not realize that their epistemic goals are so connected. It would then be wrong to say that *we* have the other goals because we have the goal that is in fact the primary one; all that can be said is that we ought to. One can then go on and say that, to the extent that we realize this, we will tend to have the other epistemic goals because we have the primary one.

IV The True-belief Goal and the Justified-belief Goal

The goal of having justified beliefs is not a truth goal: having justified beliefs is not a way of possessing truths. Still, it is very plausible to think that it is a truth-oriented goal in the sense that it derives from, or depends on, a truth goal. The truth goal most often mentioned in this connection is the goal of having true beliefs. Consider the following claims:

A1 If you want to have TBs you ought to have JBs.
A2 We want to have JBs because we want to have TBs.
B1 If you want to have JBs you ought to have TBs.
B2 We want to have TBs because we want to have JBs.

Assume we want to have true beliefs and want to have justified beliefs. A1 would give us a reason for connecting these goals in the manner described in A2: if we believe what A1 says, we ought to and probably will connect these goals in the manner described in A2. If, on the other hand, we believed what B1 says, we ought to and probably would connect these goals in the manner described in B2.

Comparing these pairs, it is obvious that the A's are way more plausible than the B's. Indeed, initially one may even think that the B's have nothing going for them at all, that they are just false. That is not quite right, however. True beliefs are generally useful; hence, they can be instruments for acquiring new justified beliefs as well as for acquiring justifications for old beliefs, provided they are true beliefs of the right sort: viz, true beliefs about how evidence, old or newly acquired, bears on propositions we don't yet believe; true beliefs about how the evidence we already possess bears on our old beliefs; true beliefs about where to find new evidence for or against old beliefs; and so on. (If you come to believe, correctly, that some evidence e you have just acquired adequately supports some proposition p, and you then come to believe p in part because of your true belief about how e bears on p, then this belief contributed causally to the fact that you now hold the justified belief p – this is not the typical case though: more typically, acquiring e will just make you believe p, without going through the higher-level belief about e's bearing on p). True beliefs of this special sort – roughly, true beliefs about epistemic matters – have a certain measure of instrumental value relative to the JB goal. They have "epistemic utility" (Firth, 1998b) insofar as they tend to have causal consequences (namely the acquisition of justified beliefs) that contribute to the realization of one of our epistemic goals. So, the B's are not simply wrong. Still, compared to the A's, they look tenuous. They apply only to true beliefs of a special sort, whereas the A's apply quite generally to justified beliefs of all sorts.

Moreover, the rather weak reason B1 provides for wanting to have true beliefs because we want to have justified beliefs seems itself to take us back to the desire for true beliefs: to some extent we want true beliefs (namely true beliefs about epistemic matters) because we want justified beliefs (about many things); and we want justified beliefs (about many things) because we want to have true beliefs (about many things). In short: we want true beliefs about epistemic matters because we want true beliefs about many things. The A's have much more going for them than the B's.

The claims above are put in terms of collective epistemic goals. The B's are not entirely wrong because, collectively speaking, having true beliefs tends to have some epistemic utility relative to the JB goal: to the extent that a collection of true beliefs contains special true beliefs about epistemic matters, the collection will tend to promote the acquisition of justified beliefs. The A's, on the other hand, are much more plausible than the B's, because they stay plausible even when taken as claims about particular goals relativized to individual propositions p – read "iff" as "if and only if":

A3 For any p: if you want to ⟨believe p iff p is true⟩, then you ought to ⟨believe p iff you have justification for believing p⟩.

The corresponding claim for B1, the claim that results from exchanging the parentheses, has no plausibility at all. Note that A3 does not talk about the instrumental value of having justified belief in p relative to the goal of having true beliefs. It does not talk about the causal consequences justified belief in p has, or tends to have, for acquiring other beliefs that are true: it does not talk about any causal consequences of having justified belief in p at all. Where, then, does A3 "come from," as it were, if not from the epistemic utility of having justified beliefs *vis-à-vis* the goal of getting true beliefs? The intuitively most plausible answer to this question is surely something like:

A4 You ought to have justified beliefs rather than unjustified beliefs, given that you want to have true beliefs rather than false ones, because justified beliefs are likely to be true, at least considerably more likely to be true than unjustified ones.

The intuitive plausibility of A1 is grounded largely in A3, which seems to rest on A4. Note again that A4 does not talk about the causal consequences of having justified beliefs. It says that justified beliefs *themselves* are likely to be true. This claim is much stronger than the claim that, collectively speaking, having justified beliefs tends to make it likely that one has true beliefs. The latter would hold even if having justified beliefs merely tended to promote the subsequent acquisition of true beliefs. Although, somewhat confusingly, having justified beliefs does tend to do that too. In addition to A4 (justified beliefs being themselves likely to be true), there is also an "epistemic utility"-aspect to having justified beliefs, but this aspect depends on A4. Justification is transferable: to the extent that you acquire new beliefs properly based on justified beliefs, your new beliefs will themselves be justified; hence, because of A4, they will themselves be likely to be true. So, because of A4, having justified beliefs tends to have a measure of general epistemic utility relative to the TB goal: it tends to promote the growth of true beliefs. This epistemic utility of having justified beliefs, which itself depends in part on A4, adds to the plausibility of A1.

It is tempting to talk of justification as if it were essentially a *means* to the truth (e.g. BonJour, 1985, pp. 7–8). But note that such talk can be seriously misleading. It connects with the *less* important aspect, the "epistemic utility"-aspect, underlying A1. Though it is correct to say that having justified beliefs, collectively speaking, tends to lead to true beliefs (via the transfer of justification), this instrumental value that accrues to justified beliefs in virtue of their tendency to have desirable consequences itself depends on the point that (A4) justified beliefs themselves are likely to be true – and this latter relation between justified beliefs and true beliefs is not like the relation between means and the (desired) consequences they tend to produce; it is not a causal "productive" relation at all.

If one really wanted to say that the epistemic status of a belief as justified or unjustified derived from its power as a means to truth in the ordinary sense of "means," i.e. from the tendency of the belief to produce true beliefs, one would be in serious trouble. A belief might causally contribute to the acquisition of any number of false beliefs even though it is justified. Say you are about to watch a news-show because you believe it to be a good source of information: your belief may well be justified even though it will soon lead you to acquire lots of false beliefs through watching a show that is in fact a source of massive misinformation. Conversely, a belief might causally contribute to the acquisition of any number of true beliefs even though it is unjustified. Say you are about to watch a news-show because you believe it to be a good source of information: your belief may well be unjustified even if it will soon lead you to acquire lots of true beliefs through watching a show that is in fact a good source of information.

I should mention a problem that arises with respect to A4. On the one hand, A4 is highly plausible; on the other hand, it is unclear whether it can remain plausible while keeping the promise to connect justification to truth. The problem is this. What does it mean to say that a justified belief is "likely" to be true? Justified beliefs are based on grounds, typically referred to as evidence: mainly other beliefs, memories, perceptual experiences, and introspective experiences. To say that a justified belief is likely to be true can mean that its truth is likely *relative* to its grounds. This seems to fit with our concept of justification. Unfortunately, a belief that is likely relative to some grounds may be unlikely relative to other grounds, and may not be likely at all in any absolute sense. So, on this construal, it is not quite clear whether A4 really manages to connect the JB goal to the goal of having true beliefs. Alternatively, one might propose that justified beliefs are likely in some *absolute* sense, which would seem to secure the connection to the TB goal. Unfortunately, this may not fit well with our ordinary concept of justification. Suppose, as Descartes did, that a powerful evil demon leaves our perceptual experiences and memories just as they are but makes all the perceptual beliefs we base on them false. In this scenario, our perceptual beliefs would not be likely to be true in the absolute sense. So they are all counted as unjustified, even though they would still be based on the same grounds as our beliefs are actually based. This goes against widely shared, though not universal, intuitions about the concept of justification.

The problem is a tangled one, especially since it is not even clear whether it really is a problem. How much weight should really be given to intuitions about far-fetched scenarios like demon worlds? Why isn't relative likelihood of justified beliefs enough to secure the connection between the JB goal and the TB goal? It turns out that these issues are rather complex, and I will have to set them aside for now. It should be remembered, in any case, that they pertain to A4 rather than A1 and A3. To acknowledge that the plausibility of A1 rests largely on A3 is one thing. To uncover difficulties with the additional idea that the plausibility of A3 rests on A4 is another thing.

V The True-belief Goal and the Knowledge Goal

Given the considerations of the previous section, we can say that we (ought to) want to have justified beliefs because we want to have true beliefs, rather than the other way round. Let us conclude from this, at least as a working hypothesis, that the goal of having true beliefs is more basic than the goal of having justified beliefs; that the latter can be derived from the former. Even if this is correct, it does not follow that the goal of having true beliefs is the most basic epistemic goal. We still have to ask how it relates to the goal of having knowledge. Consider, then, the following claims:

C1 If you want to have TBs you ought to have K.
C2 We want to have K because we want to have TBs.
D1 If you want to have K you ought to have TBs.
D2 We want to have TBs because we want to have K.

If the C's were clearly more plausible than the D's, we could say that we (ought to) want to have justified beliefs *and* (ought to) want to have knowledge because we want to have true beliefs, but not the other way round. This would give us a reason for thinking that the TB goal is the basic epistemic goal.

However, there is something odd about the C's. Consider C1. It is quite OK when taken collectively, as a claim about the general epistemic utility of having knowledge *vis-à-vis* the goal of having true beliefs. For knowledge itself constitutes evidence (Williamson, 2000): to the extent that you acquire beliefs properly based on knowledge you already possess, your new beliefs will tend to be true. But taken as a general claim about arbitrary individual propositions p, C1 seems deviant. The reason is not hard to find. Since knowledge requires true belief, part of what C1 tells you is that, if you want to believe p iff it is true, then you ought to believe p iff it is true.

It looks like the D's are much more plausible. Consider D1. Quite independent of any instrumental value true beliefs might tend to have for acquiring knowledge (e.g. special true beliefs about how to acquire knowledge or evidence), D1 is plausible because true belief is a necessary condition for knowledge. It derives from a general claim about relativized goals with respect to individual propositions p: for any p, if you want to ⟨know p if it is true, and believe p only if you know it⟩ then you ought to ⟨believe p if it is true, and believe p only if it is true⟩. On the face of it, it looks like we should say that we (ought to) want to have true beliefs because we want knowledge, rather than the other way round. This would give us a reason for thinking that the K goal is a more basic goal than the TB goal. We should, then, consider the competing hypothesis that the K goal is the basic epistemic goal: we (ought to) want justified beliefs because we want true beliefs, and (ought to) want true beliefs because we want knowledge.

The knowledge goal and the true-belief goal are both truth goals. So our two hypotheses are but two versions of the idea that truth is the primary epistemic goal. Nevertheless, they would seem to be competing hypotheses. Most philosophers who have advanced or considered the idea that truth is the primary epistemic goal have taken this to mean that the true-belief goal is the primary one. Only a few – Williamson (2000) being the most recent – have explicitly advanced the view that it is rather the knowledge goal that is the primary one. Which view is the more plausible one?

Consider this thought: having true belief is a simpler, and in this sense, more basic state than having knowledge; having true belief is also a goal; hence, having true belief is a more basic goal than having knowledge. If "X is a more basic goal than Y" just means that X is somehow a more basic thing and is also a goal, then the true-belief goal may indeed be "more basic" than the knowledge goal. But this is not what one would normally mean when saying that X is a more basic goal than Y. Rather, what one would normally mean is that X is more basic *as a goal*; that we want, or ought to want, Y for the sake of X, rather than the other way round; or that the goal of having Y is in some other way derivable from the goal of having X. So, even if the state of having true belief is somehow more basic than the state of having knowledge, this does not show that it is more basic as a goal.

Let us try a different line of thought. The concept of knowledge is but the concept of justified true belief. So to want knowledge is not to want anything more than justified true beliefs. We have already seen that we want justified beliefs because we want true beliefs, rather than the other way round. Hence, we want justified true beliefs because we want true beliefs. The TB goal is the most basic goal after all. The impression that the K goal might be more basic than the TB goal is an illusion created by the complexity of the concept of knowledge.

This line of reasoning immediately faces the objection that, as Gettier (1963) shows, knowledge isn't merely justified true belief. Assume you believe that one of your friends owns a Corvette because you have adequate but nevertheless misleading evidence for the belief that your friend Smith owns a Corvette. Your friend Smith does not own a Corvette; but your friend Jones does. Then your belief that one of your friends owns a Corvette is both justified and true, but it isn't knowledge. Intuitively, your belief falls short of knowledge because it is only accidentally true.

Maybe we can make constructive use of this objection by turning it into a suggestion for how best to conceive of the goal of having true beliefs. Consider an initial diagnosis of Gettier cases: they show that knowledge requires *non-accidentally* true belief. Maybe this indicates that the true-belief goal is best conceived as the goal of having non-accidentally true belief. The goal might then be characterized by using subjunctives: we want to be such that we would believe p, if p were true, and would not believe p, if p were not true. Or, as Sosa (2003) might rather put it: it is the goal of being such that one would believe p if and only if p were true. (As a proposal for an analysis of the nature of knowledge that is responsive to Gettier cases the non-accidentality condition seems little more than a first step. However, it may well be good enough for paraphrasing our ordinary concept of knowledge and – more pertinent to the concerns of this paper – for describing the content of the true-belief goal). With the goal reconceived in this manner, the line of thought given above can be revived – now starting from the claim that to want knowledge is to want nothing more than justified non-accidentally true belief. As a result we get a defense of the idea that the true-belief goal is the primary epistemic goal in the slightly revised (improved?) version that the goal of having non-accidentally true beliefs is the primary epistemic goal.

VI *Meno* Problems

The view that the goal of having true beliefs is the primary epistemic goal appears to be committed to the claim that we *ought* to want knowledge and justification *only* because, and insofar as, we want true beliefs. In other words, the view seems committed to a version of epistemic "value monism" (DePaul, 2000): the sole basic epistemic value, or good, is true belief; and the sole basic epistemic disvalue, or bad, is false belief. The other epistemic goods, knowledge and justified belief, are derived goods; they are valuable only because true belief is valuable; they are extrinsic epistemic goods, whereas true belief is the sole intrinsic good, epistemically speaking.

This view has to face Meno's question: "It makes me wonder, Socrates, this being the case, why knowledge is prized far more highly than right opinion" (Plato, *Meno*, 97d). Meno has observed that intuition speaks in favor of value judgment (a) (below). One can make additional observations concerning intuitive judgments about epistemic value that will give rise to similar questions:

(a) Knowledge seems better than mere true belief.
(b) Justified true belief seems better than unjustified true belief.
(c) Unjustified false belief seems worse than justified false belief.
(d) Unjustified true belief versus justified false belief? Intuition hesitates.

If knowledge and justification derive their whole value from the epistemically basic value of true belief, then their presence shouldn't add (and their absence shouldn't subtract) any value from states already containing true belief or false belief. But then, why (a)? And why doesn't intuition tell us that the states mentioned in (b) and (c) are equally good and bad respectively? And why does intuition waver about (d)? Why doesn't it speak firmly in favor of true belief, however unjustified?

The value monist might ward off Meno's original question, the one concerning (a), by citing the revised true-belief goal, the goal of having non-accidentally true belief: knowledge is better than mere true belief, because knowledge contains non-accidentally true belief. Of course, this will lead to another difficult question: Why is non-accidentally true belief better than mere true belief? (Timothy Williamson, who is not a true-belief monist, holds a view reminiscent of Plato's own view: knowledge is better than mere true belief because it is more stable, less vulnerable to rational defeat by future evidence; cf. Plato's *Meno*, 97–8, and Williamson, 2000, pp. 62, 78, 86). In any case, the revised (improved?) true-belief goal doesn't seem to be of much help to the true-belief monist when it comes to the questions concerning (b), (c), and (d): these questions remain, even if the true-belief goal is reconceived.

Consider the other version of epistemic value monism, the one according to which knowledge is the sole basic epistemic good with true belief and justified belief as derived goods, valuable only because they are required for having knowledge. In a way, this view seems to fit with (a) to (d). Knowledge is better than mere true belief, because the whole value of the latter derives from the value of knowledge. Items (b) to (d) would be accounted for in terms of how many goods required for knowledge the states mentioned there contain or lack. But in another way, this version of monism seems deeply strange. How does knowledge get its basic value if true belief and justified belief don't have any basic value themselves? This seems like adding 0 to 0 to get 1. Does it get its basic value from the non-accidentality of true belief? But then that wouldn't be value *monism*: non-accidentally true belief would have to be a second basic epistemic value in addition to knowledge (cf. DePaul, 2002, p. 181). Or is the view simply that knowledge boils down to nothing more than non-accidentally true belief?

Now consider a pluralistic view about basic epistemic value. There are two basic epistemic goods, together with their accompanying bads: true belief and justified belief; false belief and unjustified belief. Knowledge, on this view, is a derived good, valuable only because it contains the basic goods. Evidently, this picture makes for the most natural fit with (a) to (d). Knowledge and justified true belief are better than mere true belief because they contain all the goods. Unjustified false belief is worst because it lacks all the goods. Intuition wavers about unjustified true belief versus justified false belief, because each contains one of the two goods and one of the two bads, and we can't decide, at least not right away, whether one of the two should weigh more heavily than the other.

Of course, on this pluralistic picture truth is not the primary epistemic good or goal after all. Instead, having justified beliefs is an additional epistemic value independent from true belief; it is at least as basic an epistemic good as having true beliefs. What, then, about the earlier considerations from section IV, supporting the view that the goal of having true beliefs is more basic than the goal of having justified beliefs? The pluralistic picture needs an alternative diagnosis of the plausibility of A1 – the claim that you ought to have justified beliefs, if you want to have true beliefs. The pluralist, it seems, has to say this: A1 is indeed highly plausible; but not because of A3 and A4. Rather, A1 is plausible because it is trivial. You ought to have justified beliefs anyway, never mind whether you want to have true beliefs or want to have false beliefs or neither: you just ought to have justified beliefs, period. You ought to want justified beliefs for their own sake.

This alternative diagnosis of A1 is off the mark. It confuses epistemology with ethics (Firth, 1998a). If there is a proper place for absolute *oughts* – for *oughts* that have a hold on us no matter what – then their place must surely be in ethics. (Pointing out that the *ought* in question is the "epistemic" *ought* does not help; for this just leads to a reformulation of the very issue under discussion: What is the epistemic *ought*, if not the one that has a hold on us insofar as we want to possess truth?) Moreover, the position that justified belief is valuable for its own sake leads straight into a mystery: Why is it that, when we do attempt to justify our beliefs, we produce evidence we take to be indicative of their truth? Why do we regard something as evidence for a proposition, only if we take it to indicate that the proposition is true, or at least likely to be true?

So let us return once more to the idea that having true beliefs is the sole basic epistemic good and the primary epistemic goal. Bernard Williams (1978, pp. 37–46) attempts to give an account of how a "pure inquirer," an inquirer who starts out with the basic desire for having true belief about some issue, would on reflection be led to want knowledge. Much adapted to our present framework, the account goes roughly like this. Assume you want true belief with respect to a certain question. Assume you are aware that (A1) if you want to have true beliefs, you ought to have justified beliefs. This gives you a reason for wanting justified belief on the issue in question. You now have two desires ("wants"): you want to have true belief on the issue, and you want to have justified belief on the issue. If you are minimally reflective, you will notice this: having both your desires satisfied requires being in the state of having justified true belief on the issue in question. This gives you a derivative reason for having justified true belief on the issue, which gets us close to an explanation of why it is that you might want knowledge because you want true belief (C2). But wait, knowledge isn't merely justified true belief. Fair enough, so we should give a slightly revised account starting from the goal of having non-accidentally true belief.

The account offers the true-belief monist a fairly natural interpretation of C2: the claim that we want knowledge because we want true beliefs. If you want (non-accidentally) true belief and are aware of A1, then a desire for knowledge will tend to come along with the ride. The desire for knowledge turns out to be an offshoot of the desire for true belief.

Does the account also help the true-belief monist with the *Meno*-problems raised by the intuitions catalogued under (a) to (d)? Here is a proposal (see Sosa, 2002, for a different proposal). If you want to have true belief with respect to some question and are aware of A1, then you will have *two* desires: a desire for true belief on the issue and a desire for justified belief on the issue. Note that both are real desires. Even though one desire, the desire for justified belief, is directed at a derived good without basic epistemic value, it is nevertheless a real desire, just as real as the desire for true belief – desires for derived goods are no less real *as desires* than desires for basic goods. But we usually want our desires to be satisfied; and we prefer it if more of our desires are satisfied rather than fewer. This – I am inclined to propose – is the source of the intuitions catalogued under (a) to (d). The intuitions arise due to a confusion of sorts. They do not reflect any bonus of intrinsic value accruing to knowledge over and above (non-accidentally) true belief, nor do they reflect any intrinsic value accruing to justified belief that would be independent from the value of (non-accidentally) true belief; rather, they reflect our desire to have our desires satisfied.

References

BonJour L. (1985) *The Structure of Empirical Knowledge.* Cambridge, MA: Harvard University Press.

DePaul, M. (2001) Value monism in epistemology. In M. Steup (ed.), *Knowledge, Truth, and Duty: Essays on Epistemic Justification, Responsibility, and Virtue.* Oxford: Oxford University Press.

Firth, R. (1998a) Are epistemic concepts reducible to ethical concepts? In J. Troyer (ed.), *In Defense of Radical Empiricism: Essays and Lectures by Roderick Firth.* Lanham: Rowman and Littlefield.

Firth, R. (1998b) Epistemic utility. In J. Troyer (ed.), *In Defense of Radical Empiricism: Essays and Lectures by Roderick Firth.* Lanham, MD: Rowman and Littlefield.

Gettier, E. (1963) Is justified true belief knowledge? *Analysis*, 23, 121–3.

Goldman, A. (1999) *Knowledge in a Social World.* Oxford: Clarendon Press.

James, W. (1911) The will to believe. In *The Will to Believe and Other Essays in Popular Philosophy.* New York: David McKay.

Plato (1976) *Meno.* Indianapolis: Hackett.

Sosa, E. (2001) For the love of truth. In A. Fairweather and L. Zagzebski (eds), *Virtue Epistemology: Essays on Epistemic Virtue and Responsibility.* Oxford: Oxford University Press.

Sosa, E. (2003) The place of truth in epistemology. In M. DePaul and L. Zagzebski (eds), *Intellectual Virtue: Perspectives from Ethics and Epistemology.* Oxford: Clarendon Press.

Williams, B. (1978) *Descartes: The Project of Pure Inquiry.* London: Penguin.

Williamson, T. (2000) *Knowledge and Its Limits.* Oxford: Oxford University Press.

Further reading

Alston, W. P. (1989) Concepts of epistemic justification. In *Epistemic Justification: Essays in the Theory of Knowledge.* Ithaca, NY: Cornell University Press.

Alston, W. P. (1993) Epistemic desiderata. *Philosophy and Phenomenological Research*, 53, 527–51.

Chisholm, R. M. (1957) *Perceiving: a Philosophical Study.* Ithaca, NY: Cornell University Press.

David, M. (2001) Truth as the epistemic goal. In M. Steup (ed.), *Knowledge, Truth, and Duty: Essays on Epistemic Justification, Responsibility, and Virtue.* Oxford: Oxford University Press.

Feldman, R. (1988) Epistemic obligations. *Philosophical Perspectives*, 2, 235–56.

Firth, R. (1998) Epistemic merit, intrinsic and instrumental. In J. Troyer (ed.), *In Defense of Radical Empiricism: Essays and Lectures by Roderick Firth.* Lanham, MD: Rowman and Littlefield.

Foley, R. (1993) *Working without a Net: A Study of Egocentric Epistemology.* Oxford: Oxford University Press.

Fumerton, R. (2001) Epistemic justification and normativity. In M. Steup (ed.), *Knowledge, Truth, and Duty: Essays on Epistemic Justification, Responsibility, and Virtue.* Oxford: Oxford University Press.

Goldman, A. (1986) *Epistemology and Cognition.* Cambridge, MA: Harvard University Press.

Goldman, A. (1992) What is justified belief? In *Liaison: Philosophy Meets the Cognitive and Social Sciences.* Cambridge, MA: MIT Press.

Haack, S. (2001) "The ethics of belief" reconsidered. In M. Steup (ed.), *Knowledge, Truth, and Duty: Essays on Epistemic Justification, Responsibility, and Virtue.* Oxford: Oxford University Press.

Kvanvig, J. L. (1998) Why should inquiring minds want to know? *Meno* problems and epistemological axiology. *Monist*, 81, 426–51.

Kelly, T. (forthcoming) Epistemic rationality and instrumental rationality. *Philosophy and Phenomenological Research.*

Maitzen, S. (1995) Our errant epistemic aim. *Philosophy and Phenomenological Research*, 55, 869–76.

Nietzsche, F. (1989) *Beyond Good and Evil: Prelude to a Philosophy of the Future* (trans. W. Kaufmann). New York: Vintage Books (original work published 1886).

Steup, M. (1996) *An Introduction to Contemporary Epistemology*. Upper Saddle River, NJ: Prentice Hall.

Velleman, D. (2000) On the aim of belief. In *The Possibility of Practical Reason*. Oxford: Oxford University Press.

Wedgwood, R. (2002) The aim of belief. *Philosophical Perspectives*, 16, 267–97.

Williams, B. (1973) Deciding to believe. In *Problems of the Self*. Cambridge: Cambridge University Press.

Williams, B. (2002) *Truth and Truthfulness: An Essay in Genealogy*. Princeton, NJ: Princeton University Press.

Zagzebski, L. T. (2003) Intellectual motivation and the good of truth. In M. DePaul and L. Zagzebski (eds), *Intellectual Virtue: Perspectives from Ethics and Epistemology*. Oxford: Clarendon Press.

Zimmerman, M. J. (2002) Intrinsic vs extrinsic value. In E. N. Zalta (ed.), *The Stanford Encyclopedia of Philosophy* (http://plato.stanford.edu).

Is Justified Belief
Responsible Belief?

Justified Belief as Responsible Belief

Richard Foley

The concepts of justified, warranted, and epistemically rational belief, along with the notion of knowledge, form the core subject matter of epistemology. Despite their centrality, these concepts are used in the literature in strikingly different ways and often with little regard for how they interrelate.

In what follows, I will be making recommendations for how to understand and distinguish these three concepts. The account I will be developing situates the concept of epistemically rational belief into a well integrated and philosophically respectable general theory of rationality; it links the concept of warranted belief with the theory of knowledge; and it insists that the concept of justified belief should be relevant to the assessments of each other's beliefs that we are most interested in making in our everyday lives, namely, assessments where the focus is not so much on whether one has fulfilled all the prerequisites of knowledge but rather on whether one has been a responsible believer.

These are the conclusions I will be moving towards, but the place to begin is with a quick history of recent epistemology. In his influential 1963 article, "Is Justified True Belief Knowledge?," Edmund Gettier (1963, pp. 121–3) designed a pair of counter-examples to show that knowledge cannot be defined as justified true belief. Gettier pointed out that one can be justified in believing a falsehood from which one deduces a truth, in which case one has a justified true belief but does not have knowledge. His article started a search for a fourth condition of knowledge, which could be added to justification, truth, and belief to produce an adequate analysis of knowledge.

Various fourth conditions were proposed, many of which were variants of the idea that knowledge requires one's justification to be either non-defective or indefeasible. However, a different kind of response to Gettier's counter-examples was to wonder whether something less intellectual than justification, traditionally understood, is better suited for understanding knowledge. Justification had been traditionally associated with having or at least being able to produce an argument in defense of one's beliefs, but critics pointed out that we are often inclined to say that someone knows something even when the person is not in a position to defend what he or she believes. This observation prompted these epistemologists, in their attempts to understand knowledge, to shift their focus away from questions of one's being able to justify one's beliefs intellectually and towards questions of one's being in an appropriate causal or causal-like relation with one's external environment. The philosophical task, according to this way of thinking about knowledge, is to identify the precise character of this relation.

This shift in focus led to reliability theories of knowledge. According to reliabilists, the processes, faculties, and methods that produce or sustain a belief must be highly reliable for the belief to count as an instance of knowledge. In turn, reliability theories of knowledge led to externalist accounts of epistemic justification. Initially, reliabilism was part of a reaction against justification-driven accounts of knowledge, but an assumption drawn from the old epistemology tempted reliabilists to reconceive justification as well. The assumption is that by definition justification is that which has to be added to true belief to generate knowledge, with some fourth condition added to handle Gettier-style counter-examples. If knowledge is reliably produced true belief and if justification is by definition that which has to be added to true belief to get knowledge, then epistemic justification must also be a matter of one's beliefs having been produced and sustained by reliable cognitive processes.

There is now an enormous literature arguing the pro's and con's of externalism and internalism in epistemology (for example, see BonJour, 1980; Audi, 1988; Fumerton, 1988; Goldman, 1988; Alston, 1989, esp. chapters 8 and 9; Sosa 1991). For the most part, the literature assumes that the two approaches are rivals, but an alternative and more charitable interpretation is that externalists and internalists have different interests. Externalists are principally interested in understanding what knowledge is, but in the process of developing an account of knowledge, many externalists feel compelled also to propose an account of justified belief, because they assume that by definition knowledge is justified true belief (again, with some fourth condition added to handle Gettier cases). Internalists, by contrast, are principally interested in explicating a sense of justification that captures what is involved in having beliefs that are defensible from one's own perspective, but along the way they see themselves as also providing the materials for an adequate account of knowledge, because they too assume that justification is by definition that which has to be added to true belief to get knowledge, with some fillip to handle Gettier problems. For internalists, the primary desideratum for an account of epistemic justification is that it provide an explication of internally defensible believing, and it is a secondary benefit that it also capture what has to be added to true belief in order to get a good candidate for knowledge, whereas for externalists that primary desideratum and secondary benefit are reversed.

This confusing state of affairs is the direct result of both sides accepting as the methodological assumption that the properties which make a belief justified are by definition such that when a true belief has those properties, it is a good candidate to be an instance of knowledge. This assumption has the effect of placing the theory of justified belief in service to the theory of knowledge; a proposed account of justified belief is adequate only if it contributes to a successful theory of knowledge. The theory of justified belief is thereby divorced from our everyday assessment of each other's opinions, which tend to emphasize whether we have been responsible in forming our beliefs rather than whether we have satisfied the prerequisites of knowledge.

The assumption has equally unhappy consequences for the theory of knowledge. To give due recognition to the fact that most people cannot provide adequate intellectual defenses for much of what they know, the assumption forces the theory of knowledge into awkward attempts to read back into the account of knowledge some duly externalized notion of justified belief.

And to make matters worse, the assumption also does damage to the theory of rational belief. The concepts of rational belief and justified belief ought to be closely linked, but if justified belief is closely linked with knowledge, then so too will be rational belief. But the more closely the concept of rational belief is connected with the prerequisites of knowledge, the more the concept will be cordoned off from our ways of understanding the rationality of actions, decisions, strategies, plans, and other phenomena whose rationality we regularly assess. The regrettable implication is that the conditions that make a belief rational have little to do with the conditions that make an action, decision, strategy, plan, etc. rational. I say "regrettable" because it ought to be possible to understand the rationality in a way that closely parallels our understanding of the rationality of actions, decisions, strategies, and plans.

The remedy is to jettison the idea that knowledge can be adequately understood in terms of rational or justified true belief plus some condition to handle Gettier problems, and, correspondingly, to jettison also the idea that there is a simple, necessary tie between either the theory of justified belief or the theory of rational belief and the theory of knowledge. Discarding these assumptions constitutes a first step towards an epistemology that is both theoretically respectable and relevant to the assessments of each other's beliefs that we actually make in our everyday lives.

A second important step is to recognize that rationality is a goal-oriented notion. Whether the question is one about the rationality of beliefs, decisions, intentions, plans, or strategies, what is at issue is the effective pursuit of goals. Questions about the rationality of a decision, for example, are in the first instance questions about how effectively the decision seems to satisfy some presupposed set of goals. I say "seems" because it is too stringent to insist that a decision is rational only if it in fact satisfies the goals. Rational decisions can turn out badly. Likewise, it is too stringent to insist that a decision is rational only if it is probable that the plan will satisfy one's goals, because it may be that no one could be reasonably expected to believe that the decision was likely to have unwelcome consequences. Considerations such as these suggest a general schema of rationality: a decision (plan, action, strategy, belief, etc.) is rational for an individual if it is rational to believe that it will satisfy his or her goals.

An obvious drawback of this schema, however, is that it makes reference to the notion of rational belief, thus leaving us within the circle of notions we wish to understand and, hence, without an adequate general account of rationality. I will return to this problem shortly, but I want first to look at some other issues about the schema.

One such issue is whether for a decision, plan, strategy, etc. to be rational, it must be rational to believe that it does a better job of achieving one's goals than any of the alternatives, or whether something less than the very best will do. As I will be using the terms, "reasonability" admits of degrees whereas "rationality" does not. In particular, reasonability varies with the strengths of one's reasons, and the rational is that which is sufficiently reasonable. This usage leaves open the possibility that several options might be rational for an individual even though there are reasons to prefer some of these options over the others. A decision, plan, strategy, etc. is rational if it is rational to believe that it will do an acceptably good job of achieving one's goals.

To say that a decision, plan, strategy, etc. will do "an acceptably good job of achieving one's goals" is to say its estimated desirability is sufficiently high, where estimated desirability is a matter of what it is rational to believe about its probable effectiveness in promoting one's goals and the relative value of these goals. More precisely, a decision, plan, strategy, etc. is rational if its estimated desirability is acceptably high given the context, where the context is determined by the relative desirability of the alternatives and their relative accessibility. The fewer alternatives there are with greater estimated desirabilities, the more likely it is that the decision in question is rational. Moreover, if these alternatives are only marginally superior or are not easy to implement, then it is all the more likely that the decision, plan, or strategy is rational. It will be rational because it is good enough, given the context.

Another important issue is that the set of goals we take into account when evaluating a decision, plan, strategy, etc. can vary with the context. We are sometimes interested in assessing what it is rational for an individual to do, all things considered, and we thus take into consideration all of the individual's goals. In other contexts, however, we take into consideration only a subset of his goals, because we are interested in a specific type of rationality. For example, we may want to evaluate someone's actions with respect to goals that concern his or her economic well-being. If we judge that doing A would be an effective means of promoting this subset of goals, we can say that A is rational, in an economic sense, for the individual. We can say this even if, with respect to all the person's goals, both economic and noneconomic, it is not rational to do A.

Thus, the above general schema of rationality can be refined: a decision (plan, strategy, etc.) is rational in sense X for an individual if it is rational for him or her to believe that the decision (plan, strategy, etc.) will do an acceptably good job of satisfying his or her goals of type X.

This distinction among different types of rationality is especially important for epistemology. When assessing each other's beliefs, we are typically not interested in the total constellation of our goals. Rather, our interest typically in only those goals that are distinctly intellectual. For example, as a rule, in assessing what it is rational for you to believe, we would regard as irrelevant the fact (if it is one) that were you to believe P, it would make you feel more secure. More notoriously, in assessing whether it might be rational for you to believe in God, we are unlikely to join Pascal in regarding as relevant the possibility that you might increase your chances of salvation by being a theist.

But why is it that in our discussions and deliberations about what it is rational to believe, the working assumption seems to be that the practical benefits of belief are not even relevant to the issue of what it is rational for us to believe? On the face of the matter, this working assumption seems puzzling. After all, beliefs have consequences for the quality of our lives and the lives of those around us. Why shouldn't such consequences be taken into account in deliberations about what it is rational to believe? Yet our intellectual practice is to regard these consequences as irrelevant to the rationality of our beliefs.

In what follows, I will be proposing a general theory of rationality, and within the context of this theory providing a resolution to this puzzle. But, first, I need to distinguish among various kinds of intellectual goals. In evaluating the rationality of beliefs, epistemologists have traditionally been concerned with not just any intellectual goal, but rather a very specific goal, that of now having beliefs that are both accurate and comprehensive. Notice that the goal is not to have accurate and comprehensive beliefs at some future time but rather to have such beliefs now. To understand the significance of characterizing the goal in this way, imagine that one's prospects for having accurate and comprehensive beliefs in a year's time would be enhanced by believing something for which one now lacks adequate evidence. For example, suppose a proposition P involves a more favorable assessment of my intellectual talents than the evidence warrants, but suppose also that believing P would make me more intellectually confident than I would be otherwise, which would make me a more dedicated inquirer, which in turn would enhance my long-term prospects of having an accurate and comprehensive belief system. Despite these long-term benefits, there is an important sense of rational belief, indeed the very sense that traditionally has been of the most interest to epistemologists, in which it is not rational for me to believe P. Moreover, the point of this example is not affected by shortening the time period in which the benefits are forthcoming. It would not be rational, in this sense, for me to believe P if we were instead to imagine that believing P would somehow improve my prospects for having accurate and comprehensive beliefs in the next few weeks, or in the next few hours, or even in the next few minutes. The precise way of making this point is to say that in such a situation, it is not rational in a purely epistemic sense for me to believe P, where this purely epistemic sense is to be understood in terms of the present tense goal of now having accurate and comprehensive beliefs.

Foundationalists, coherentists, reliabilists, and others have different views about what properties a belief must have in order to be epistemically rational. I am not going to try to adjudicate among these various views, because what matters for my purposes here is not so much their differences but rather something that they have in common. In particular, each of these accounts explicates the concept of epistemically rational belief without reference to any other concept of rationality. For example, foundationalists understand epistemic rationality in terms of a notion of basic belief and a set of deductive and probabilistic support relations by which other beliefs are supported by the basic ones, and they would view it a defect if they had to make use of some other notion of rationality (or a related notion, such as reasonability) in characterizing basicality or the support relations. Coherentists try to provide an explication of epistemic rationality in terms of a set of deductive and probabilistic relations among beliefs and properties such as simplicity, conservativeness, and explanatory power, but they too would view it a defect if their explication smuggled in any reference to a concept of rationality or a related concept. And the same is true of other accounts of epistemically rational belief.

This point is of relevance for the above general schema of rationality, because it provides the schema with an escape route from circularity. In particular, if we substitute the concept of epistemic rationality into the schema, the schema becomes: a plan, decision, action, strategy, etc. is rational in sense X for an individual just in case it is *epistemically rational* for the individual to believe that the plan, decision, action, strategy, etc. will do an acceptably good job of satisfying goals of kind X. Because accounts of epistemically rationally belief do not make use of any other notion of rationality or any of its close cognates, the schema is now theoretically respectable. It makes no non-eliminable reference to a concept of rationality or any of its close cognates.

The revised schema thus allows the concept of epistemically rational belief to serve as a theoretical anchor for other concepts of rationality. Moreover, the schema is perfectly general. The rationality of plans, decisions, strategies, etc. can all be understood in accordance with the schema, and in addition different kinds of rationality (economic rationality, rationality all things considered, and so on) can all be understood in accordance with the schema. Most relevant for my present purposes, the rationality of belief is itself an instance of the schema. Let me explain.

According to schema, a decision, plan, strategy, etc. is rational in sense X if it is epistemically rational for one to believe it will do an acceptably good job of satisfying goals of kind X. Recall, however, that "X" can refer to all of one's goals or only a subset of them. This creates a risk of confusion. If we take into consideration only economic goals, for instance, we may judge that it is rational (in an economic sense) for one to do X, but if we take into consideration all of one's goals, both economic and non-economic, we may well conclude that it is not rational (all things considered) for one to do X.

These same possibilities for confusion arise when it is the rationality of beliefs at issue. Beliefs can be assessed in terms of how well they promote the epistemic goal, but there is nothing in principle wrong with assessing them in terms of how well they promote the total constellation of one's goals. If it is epistemically rational for an individual to believe that believing a proposition P would effectively promote her overall constellation of goals, then it is rational for her to believe P, all things considered. There are two notions of rational belief at work here. The first is the notion of epistemic rationality, which is defined in terms of the purely epistemic goal. The second is a derivative notion, which is defined in terms of the concept of epistemically rational belief and one's total constellation of goals.

The puzzle that I raised above is why we so rarely evaluate beliefs in terms of this second notion if there is really nothing improper about doing so. In thinking about this puzzle, it is important to keep in mind that many of our discussions and debates concerning what it is rational to believe take place in a context of trying to convince some person, perhaps even ourselves, to believe some proposition. In an effort to persuade, we point out the reasons there are to believe the proposition in question. But notice that, insofar as our aim is to get someone to believe a proposition, the citing of practical reasons is ordinarily ineffective. Suppose that you are skeptical of the claim that there is intelligent life elsewhere in the universe, and I am trying to get you to believe it. Even if I succeed in convincing you that you have strong pragmatic reasons to believe the claim (perhaps someone will give you a million dollars if you come to believe it), this will ordinarily not be enough to make you to believe it. The prospects of the million dollars may get you to behave as if you believed that there is intelligent life elsewhere, but it will not be enough to prompt genuine belief. By contrast, if I marshal evidence and information in such a way that you become convinced that you have strong epistemic reasons in support of the claim – that is, reasons that indicate that the claim is likely to be true – this usually is sufficient to generate belief.

Thus, insofar as our concern is to persuade someone to believe a proposition, there is a straightforward explanation as to why we are normally not interested in the pragmatic reasons she may have to believe it, namely, it is normally pointless to cite them, because that they are not the kind of reasons that normally generate belief. Similarly, in our own deliberations about what to believe, we ordinarily do not consider what pragmatic reasons we might have for believing something, and the explanation is similar to the third-person case. Deliberations concerning our pragmatic reasons for belief are ordinarily inefficacious and hence pointless. Hence, our practice is to ignore them in deliberations about what to believe.

There is a second, complementary explanation for why in general we do not deliberate about the pragmatic reasons we have for believing something, namely, such deliberations are ordinarily redundant. Although we can have pragmatic reasons as well as epistemic reasons for believing propositions, ordinarily our overriding pragmatic reason with respect to our beliefs is to have and maintain a comprehensive and accurate stock. All of us are continually faced with a huge variety of decisions, but we do not know in advance in any detailed way the kinds of decisions that we will need to make, and we likewise do not know in advance the kinds of information we will need in order to make these decisions well. This might not be terribly important if, when faced with decisions, we had the opportunity to gather information and deliberate about which alternative is best, or at least the time to seek out the opinions of those who are better informed. But ordinarily, we do not. Most of the decisions we make have to be made without the luxury of extensive information gathering, consultations, or deliberations. We are instead forced to draw upon our existing resources and in particular upon our existing stock of beliefs. If that stock is either small or inaccurate, we increase the likelihood that our decisions will not be good ones.

So, ordinarily, the beliefs that are likely to do the best overall job of promoting the total constellation of our goals are beliefs that are both comprehensive and accurate. Only by having such beliefs are we likely to be in a position to fashion effective strategies for achieving our various goals. But then, since by definition beliefs that are epistemically rational for us are beliefs that are rational for us insofar as our goal is to have accurate and comprehensive beliefs, it is ordinarily rational, all things considered, that is, when all of our goals are taken into account, to believe those propositions that it is also epistemically rational for us to believe. Thus, for all practical purposes, taking this phrase literally, we can usually safely ignore pragmatic reasons in our deliberations about what to believe.

To be sure, there are conceivable examples in which our epistemic reasons and our overall reasons for belief are pulled apart. Pascal famously argued that belief in God is such an example, but it is also not hard to concoct non-theistic examples as well. Suppose you are aware that a madman will kill your children unless you come to believe, and not merely act as if you believe, some proposition P which is clearly epistemically irrational for you; that is, irrational insofar as your goal is to have accurate and comprehensive beliefs. Nonetheless, in such a situation, it is presumably rational for you to find some way of getting yourself to believe P. The importance of saving your children overrides all your other concerns.

In the vast majority of cases, however, the pragmatic benefits of belief are not so powerful. So, although it is in principle possible for what it is rational for one to believe, when all one's goals are taken into account, to be at odds with what it is epistemically rational for one to believe, in practice this tends not to happen.

However, this is not to say that pragmatic considerations do not deeply influence what it is rational for us to believe. It is only to say that they do not very often do so in the direct way that Pascal's wager envisions. They instead do so indirectly. In particular, pragmatic considerations are critical for determining the extent of evidence gathering and deliberating it is rational for us to engage in with respect to a particular issue, and in doing so, they shape what we are justified in believing, but in an indirect rather than direct way. They do so by imposing constraints on inquiry, but subject to these constraints, our goal is to determine which beliefs would be true, not which beliefs would be useful. We rarely engage in Pascalian deliberations which weigh the pragmatic costs and benefits of believing as opposed to not believing some proposition. On the other hand, it is anything but rare for us to weigh the costs and benefits of spending additional time and resources investigating a topic.

In buying a used car, for example, I will want to investigate whether the car is in good condition, but I need to make a decision about how thoroughly to do so. Should I merely drive the car? Should I look up the frequency of repair record for the model? Should I go over the car with a mechanic, or perhaps even more than one mechanic? Similarly, if I am interested in how serious a threat global warming is, I need to decide how much time to spend investigating the issue. Should I be content with looking at the accounts given in newspapers, or should I take the time to read the piece in *Scientific American*, or should I even go to the trouble of looking up articles in the relevant technical journals? And if it turns out that in order to understand these articles, I need to brush up on my statistics, should I do that? The reasonable answer to such questions is a function of how important the issue is and how likely it is that additional effort on my part will improve my reliability with respect to it. As the stakes of my being right go up and as the chances for improving my epistemic situation with respect to the issue go up, it is reasonable for me to increase my efforts.

So, it is not at all unusual for pragmatic considerations to influence the rationality of our beliefs, but it is rare for them to do so in the crass, direct way that Pascal's wager envisions. Instead, they determine the direction and shape of our investigative and deliberative projects and practices. When engaged in these intellectual projects and practices, we in general regard it as irrelevant whether or not believing the claim in question would be useful. The internal practice encourages us to be concerned only with the truth or likely truth of the hypothesis, but the practices themselves are thoroughly shaped by our overall needs, interests, and abilities and by the situations in which we find ourselves. They are thoroughly shaped, in other words, by pragmatic considerations.

Keeping this observation in mind, consider again the concept of epistemic rationality. To say that it is epistemically rational for an individual to believe a proposition P is to say it is rational for her to believe P insofar as her goal is to have accurate and comprehensive beliefs. But, of course, no human being is a purely intellectual being. All of us have many goals. Epistemic rationality is in this sense an idealized concept and as such is not particularly well suited for our everyday evaluations of each other's beliefs. Our everyday evaluations tend to be concerned with whether one has been responsible in arriving at one's beliefs, where being responsible is in turn a function of responding appropriately to the full complexity of one's situation, including the complexity that one has to balance the costs and benefits of trying to have accurate and comprehensive beliefs about an issue against the costs and benefits of trying to satisfy one's other goals, interests, and needs. On the other hand, the idealized character of the concept of epistemic rational belief also has its advantages, one of the most important of which is that the concept is suitable to serve as a theoretical anchor for other concepts that are less idealized and, hence, potentially more relevant to our everyday intellectual concerns.

The complication, as I have been pointing out, is that the most straightforward way of introducing a derivative concept of rational belief is too crude to be of much relevance to these everyday intellectual concerns. According to the general schema, it is rational, all things considered (that is, when all of the individual's goals are taken into account), for an individual to believe P if it is epistemically rational for her to believe that the overall effects of believing P are sufficiently beneficial. But it is rare for epistemically rational belief and rational belief, all things considered, to come apart in a crass Pascalian manner. There are powerful pressures that keep the two from being in conflict with one another in all but the most unusual circumstances. So, if the concept of epistemic rationality is to be used to explicate a concept that is relevant for our everyday intellectual assessments of each other's beliefs, it will have to be employed in a more subtle way.

A first step is to note that our everyday evaluations of each other's beliefs tend to be reason-saturated. We are interested, for example, in whether someone in forming her beliefs about a topic has been *reasonably* thorough in gathering evidence and then *reasonably* thorough in deliberating over this evidence. The standards of reasonability at work in these assessments are realistic ones. They reflect the fact that all of us have non-intellectual interests, goals, and needs, which place constraints on how much time and effort it is appropriate to devote to investigating and deliberating about an issue. Only a concept that is sensitive to questions of resource allocation is capable of capturing the spirit of these everyday evaluations.

I will be arguing that the concept of justified belief is just such a concept, but as I understand it, the concept is more closely associated with the everyday notion of responsible believing than it is with the notion of what is required to turn true belief, absent Gettier problems, into knowledge. Following the usage of Alvin Plantinga, I will reserve the term "warranted belief" for what turns true belief into a serious candidate for knowledge (see Plantinga, 1993).

Is Justified Belief Responsible Belief? | 321 |

Justifiably believing a proposition is a matter of its being rational, all things considered, for one to have acquired (and subsequently retained) the belief. More precisely, one justifiably believes a proposition P if one has an epistemically rational belief that one's procedures with respect to P have been acceptable; that is, acceptable given the limitations on one's time and capacities and given all of one's goals. Thus, if an individual has an epistemically rational belief that, all things considered, she has spent an acceptable amount of time and energy in gathering evidence about P and evaluating this evidence and has used acceptable procedures in gathering and processing this evidence, it is justifiable for her to have this belief.

This explication of the concept of justified belief makes reference to a concept of rationality, but because the concept it makes reference to is that of an epistemically rational belief, which itself can be explicated without reference to any other concept of rationality or any of its cognates, the result is a theoretically respectable account of justified belief, that is, an account that make no non-eliminable use of another notion of rationality.

An important related concept is that of non-negligently believing a proposition. Whereas justifiably believing a proposition P is a matter of its being rational to have acquired (and subsequently retained) the belief, non-negligently believing P is a matter of its not being irrational to have acquired (and subsequently retained) the belief. Having this second concept in addition to the concept of justified belief is important, because we often do not have a very good idea of how it is that we came to believe what we do. We may not remember or perhaps we never knew. Consequently, with respect to many of our beliefs, we may not think that the processes which led to them were acceptable, but by the same token we may not think, and need not have evidence for thinking, that these processes were unacceptable either. The beliefs in question are thus not justified, but there nonetheless is something to recommend them, namely, they are non-negligent.

In particular, I shall say that one non-negligently believes a proposition P if (a) one believes P and (b) one does not believe, and it is not epistemically rational for one to believe, that one's procedures with respect to P have been unacceptable, that is, unacceptable given the limitations on time and capacities and given all of one's goals. For example, if an individual does not believe, and if it is not epistemically rational for her to believe, that all things being considered she has spent an unacceptably small amount of time in gathering evidence or evaluating this evidence, or that she has used unacceptable procedures in gathering and processing this evidence, then her belief P is non-negligent.

These concepts of justified belief and non-negligent belief are far less idealized than the concept of epistemically rational belief. They recognize that given the relative unimportance of many claims, the scarcity of time, and the pressing nature of many of our non-intellectual ends, it would be inappropriate to spend significant time and effort gathering information and thinking about these claims. A large proportion of our beliefs are acquired without much thought, and there is nothing untoward about this. I believe that there is a chair in front of me because I see it. I do not deliberate about whether or not to trust my senses. I simply believe.

Of course, some topics are important enough and complex enough that it is appropriate to devote considerable time and effort in investigating and thinking about them, but even in these investigations and deliberations we make use of an enormous number of opinions, skills, and habits, most of which we have to rely on without much thought. Even when we are being our most vigilant, as, for example, in scientific inquiry, the bulk of our intellectual proceedings has to be conducted in a largely automatic fashion. We have no realistic choice in this matter. Only a fraction of the various intellectual methods, practices, and faculties that we make use of in any significant intellectual project, and only a fraction of the wide range of pre-existing opinions that we bring to bear in reaching our conclusions, can be subject to scrutiny.

Similarly, every new situation that we confront in our everyday lives presents us with new intellectual challenges, if only because we will want to know the best way to react to the situation. The everyday flow of our lives thus potentially swamps us with intellectual projects and questions. Fortunately, not all are equally important. Given the total constellation of our goals, some of these projects are more significant than others, and likewise, given the scarcity of time, some are more pressing than others. These are the ones on which it is reasonable to devote time and attention.

Because of the relative unimportance of many topics and the pressing nature of many of our non-intellectual ends, we can have justified beliefs about these topics even when we have spent little or no time gathering evidence about them or deliberating about them. Indeed, we can have justified beliefs about them even if we are in the possession of information which, had we reflected upon it, would have convinced us that what we believe is incorrect. This is one of the ways in which justified belief and epistemically rational belief can come apart. Even if an individual has evidence that makes it epistemically irrational to believe P, she might nonetheless justifiably believe P, because given the unimportance of the topic, it would have been inappropriate for her to have taken the time and effort to sift through this evidence. What we believe about an unimportant topic may not meet the standards of epistemically rational belief, which are concerned with what it is rational to believe insofar as one has the goal of having accurate and comprehensive beliefs, but it nonetheless can meet the standards of justified belief, which are concerned with the level of effort it is appropriate to devote, given the full panoply of one's goals, to gathering evidence and thinking about a topic.

Having justified beliefs requires one to be a responsible believer, but being a responsible believer does not require one to go to extraordinary lengths in trying to discover the truth about an issue. More exactly, it does not require this unless the issue is itself extraordinarily important. The standards that one must meet if one's beliefs are to be justified slide up or down with the significance of the issue. If nothing much hangs on an issue, there is no point in going to great lengths to discover the truth about it. Accordingly, the standards one must meet are low. These are the kinds of cases I have been discussing until now. On the other hand, when weighty issues are at stake, it takes more to be a responsible believer and, hence, the standards of justified belief become correspondingly higher. Indeed, they can even become more stringent than those of epistemically rational belief. The more important the issue, the more important it is to reduce the risk of error. For example, if having inaccurate opinions about a given topic would put people's lives at risk, one should conduct especially thorough investigations before settling on an opinion. If one fails to do so, the resulting beliefs will not be justified even if they are epistemically rational.

This is possible because epistemically rational belief does not require certainty, not even moral certainty, whereas moral certainty sometimes is required for one to be a responsible believer. To be epistemic rational, one needs to have evidence that reduces the risks of error to an acceptable level insofar as one's goal is to have accurate and comprehensive beliefs. But the risks might be acceptable in this theoretical sense even if one's procedures have been unacceptably sloppy, given that people's lives are hanging in the balance. If so, the beliefs in question will not be justified despite the fact that they are epistemically rational.

The concept of justified belief is also able to give expression to the way in which in our everyday assessments of each other's beliefs, the intellectual standards we expect one to meet vary not only with the importance of the topic at issue but also with one's social role. If it is your job but not mine to keep safety equipment in good working order, the intellectual demands upon you to have accurate beliefs about the equipment are more stringent than those upon me. My belief that the equipment is in good working order might be justified even if I have done little, if any, investigation of the matter. I need not have tested the equipment, for example. A cursory look might suffice for me, but this won't do for you. It would be unreasonable for you not to conduct tests of the equipment. The standards of justified belief are higher for you. You need to do more, and know more, than I in order to have a justified belief about this matter.

One's social role can be relevant even when the issue at hand is primarily of theoretical interest. For example, my justifiably believing that the principle of conservation of energy is not violated in the beta decay of atomic nuclei is a very different matter from a theoretical physicist justifiably believing this. My familiarity with the issue derives exclusively from popular discussions of it in *Scientific American* and *The New York Times* science section. This kind of information is presumably enough for me to be a responsible believer; no more can be reasonably expected of me. On the other hand, much more is reasonably expected of the authorities themselves. They are part of a community of inquirers with special knowledge and special responsibilities, and as a result they should be able to explain away the apparent violations in a relatively detailed way.

In these and other ways, non-epistemic ends help to determine what one can justifiably believe, but they do not do so in the way that Pascal envisioned. The idea is not that they give one good reasons to believe a proposition for which one lacks good evidence. Rather, they define the extent of evidence gathering and processing that it is reasonable to engage in with respect to a particular issue. They thus shape what it is justified for one to believe in an indirect way rather than a direct, Pascalian way. They do so by imposing constraints on inquiry, but subject to these constraints one's aim will be to determine which beliefs are true, not which beliefs are useful.

One of the significant advantages of the distinctions I have been making among epistemically rational belief, justified belief, and non-negligent belief is that they are all parts of a philosophically respectable theory of rationality. At the heart of the theory is the following schema: a decision, plan, strategy, or whatever is rational in sense X for an individual S if it is epistemically rational for S to believe that the decision, plan, strategy, etc. will do an acceptably good job of satisfying her goals of type X. This schema is perfectly general. It can be used to distinguish different kinds of rationality and reasons; for example, economic rationality and reasons can be distinguished from rationality and reasons, all things considered. And it can be used to understand the rationality of different kinds of phenomena; for example, the rationality of decisions and the rationality of strategies and plans.[1]

Because the concept of epistemically rational belief is explicated without reference to another concept of rationality or any of its close cognates, it serves as a theoretical anchor for introducing other, derivative concepts, including the concepts of justified and non-negligent belief. The result is a cluster of concepts that is both theoretically respectable and relevant to our actual intellectual lives. The cluster is theoretically respectable in that it is based on a perfectly general schema of rationality that can be explicated without recourse to any further notion of rationality or any of its cognates. The cluster is a relevant to our actual intellectual lives, because it is capable of giving expression to the everyday concerns we have in evaluating our own and each other's beliefs. These concerns tend not to focus on whether we have met all the prerequisites of knowledge but rather on whether we are reasonably careful, reasonably cautious, and reasonably thorough in our opinions, where the standards of reasonability can vary from one situation to another and from one belief to another.[2]

Notes

1   Even epistemically rational belief is an instance of the schema. The concept of epistemically rational belief is concerned with what it is rational to believe insofar as one's goal is now to have accurate and comprehensive beliefs. Inserting this epistemic goal into the general schema for "goals of type X" results in the following: believing P is rational in an epistemic sense if it is epistemically rational for one to believe that believing P would acceptably contribute to the epistemic goal of one's now having accurate and comprehensive beliefs. This instantiation of the schema is uninformative, but for the sake of the generality of schema, this uninformativeness is just what is called for. It ensures that every belief that satisfies the requirements of a proposed account of epistemically rational belief will also be an instance of the general schema, where the relevant goal is that of now having accurate and comprehensive. The schema is thus compatible with all the major theories of epistemically rational belief. For example, according to coherentism, it is epistemically rational for one to believe that believing P would acceptably contribute to the epistemic goal of one's now having accurate and comprehensive beliefs only when the proposed coherentist conditions are met with respect to the proposition P, that is, only when P coheres appropriately with one's other beliefs and hence it is epistemically rational to believe that P is true; similarly for other accounts of epistemically rational belief.

2   For a closely related discussion of these matters, see Foley (2002).

References

Alston, W. (1989) *Epistemic Justification*. Ithaca, NY: Cornell University Press.
Audi, R. (1988) Justification, truth and reliability. *Philosophy and Phenomenological Research*, 49, 1–29.

BonJour, L. (1980) Externalist theories of empirical knowledge. In French, Uehling and Wettstein (eds), *Midwest Studies in Philosophy V*. Minneapolis: University of Minnesota Press.

Foley, R. (2002) Conceptual diversity in epistemology. In P. Moser (ed.), *The Oxford Handbook of Epistemology*. Oxford: Oxford University Press.

Fumerton, R. (1988) The internalism–externalism controversy. In J. Tomberlin (ed.), *Philosophical Perspectives*. Atascadero, CA: Ridgeview.

Gettier, E. (1963) Is justified true belief knowledge? *Analysis*, 25, 121–3.

Goldman, A. (1988) Strong and weak justification. In J. Tomberlin (ed.), *Philosophical Perspectives*. Atascadero, CA: Ridgeview.

Moser, P. (ed.) (2002) *The Oxford Handbook of Epistemology*. Oxford: Oxford University Press.

Plantinga, A. (1993) *Warrant: The Current Debate*. New York: Oxford University Press.

Sosa, E. (1991) Knowledge and intellectual virtue. In *Knowledge in Perspective*. Cambridge: Cambridge University Press.

Tomberlin, J. (ed.) (1988) *Philosophical Perspectives*. Atascadero, CA: Ridgeview.

Obligation, Entitlement, and Rationality

Nicholas Wolterstorff

I

My reflections begin from a feature of our life in the everyday. We say to each other such things as, "You should have known better than to think that Borges was an English writer," "You should be more trusting of what our State Department says," and "You should never have believed him when he told you that the auditors had approved that way of keeping books." Not only do we *regret* the knowledge and ignorance of our fellow human beings, their beliefs, disbeliefs, and non-beliefs; we *reproach* them, *blame* them, *chastise* them, using the deontological concepts of ought and ought not, should and should not. Of course we also praise them for believing and not believing, knowing and not knowing, as they do.

The English twentieth-century philosopher H. H. Price remarks in one of his writings (1954) that "we are all far too much addicted to blaming people as it is. If we are to be allowed, or even encouraged, to blame them for the way they direct their thoughts, as well as for their actions, there will be a perfect orgy of moral indignation and condemnation, and charity will almost disappear from the world." Price was opposing those philosophers who speak of an "ethic of belief." His objection was that if we were allowed, not to mention *encouraged*, to blame each other for how we direct our thoughts, social life would become intolerably judgmental. But contrary to what Price suggests, our situation is not that certain philosophers propose that we blame each other for "how we direct our thoughts," whereas at present we do not do that. Our situation is that we all engage in this practice in our everyday lives. The challenge facing the philosopher is not whether or not to recommend to his fellow human beings the introduction of this practice. The challenge is to understand this ongoing practice, and perhaps to make some proposals for improvement.

Our everyday practice of blaming or reproaching people for their belief, disbelief, and non-belief is not confined to reproaching them for the mere fact of their having taken up one of those attitudes toward a particular proposition. Sometimes we reproach a person for *how she came* to her belief (disbelief, non-belief). "Yes, she's right in thinking that Borges was an Argentinian writer; but rather than just asking the person next to her in the library, she should have looked it up." Sometimes we reproach a person for the degree of firmness with which she holds the belief or disbelief. "Yes, she's right that this unremarkable plant is a member of the orchid family; but she should not have been so cocksure about it." Sometimes we reproach a person for the imprecision of her belief. "Yes, she's right that it is around four o'clock; but if she is going to be a responsible member of the faculty, she had better get herself a watch and be far more precise about the time of day than that." And let us not overlook the fact that sometimes we reproach them for their knowledge; people know things they should not know, or should not know in the way in which they came to know them. Governmental employees know things about citizens that they should not know, politicians, about their opponents, parents, about their children.

Let me introduce a term that will make discussing these matters a bit less cumbersome. If a person ought not to have the knowledge or ignorance that she does in fact have, let me say that she is not *entitled to* that knowledge or ignorance; let me likewise speak of a person not being *entitled* to her belief, disbelief, or non-belief. And if it is something about the *mode* of knowledge or ignorance, belief, disbelief, or non-belief, that is wrong, let me likewise say that the person is not *entitled to* that mode.

II

In his essay "The Foundational Role of Epistemology in a General Theory of Rationality," Richard Foley (2001, p. 214) remarks about the concept of a rational belief that "An unfortunate methodological assumption of much recent epistemology is that the properties that make a belief rational are by definition such that when a true belief has these properties, it is a good candidate for knowledge." The preoccupation of philosophers in the twentieth-century analytic tradition with knowledge has worked itself out in such a way that accounts of rationality (and of justification) have been in thrall to attempts to render an account of knowledge. The accounts offered of rationality have been framed with an eye on that use, and often thereby distorted. Foley's plea is that we set our discussion of rationality of belief within the context of a discussion of rationality in general – the rationality of plans, decisions, actions, strategies, and so forth – and then at the end of the day ask how rational belief, thus understood, is related to knowledge.

I make the same plea for the concept of entitlement. Probably discussions of entitlement have been less in thrall to attempts to render an account of knowledge than discussions of rationality and justification have been, mostly because a good number of philosophers have thought that entitlement doesn't really have anything directly to do with knowledge. The effect on the concept of entitlement of the hegemony of knowledge has not so much been distorted analyses of that concept as very few analyses.

Beliefs have many distinct merits and demerits – many distinct *truth-relevant* merits and demerits: true, reliably formed, rational, entitled, and so forth. Often it is important for us to determine whether a belief has the merit of being a case of knowledge; the preoccupation of analytic epistemologists with knowledge is by no means preoccupation with the trivial. But it is also true that often it is important for us to determine whether a case of knowledge or ignorance, of belief, disbelief, or non-belief, is an instance of entitlement. Indeed, I am myself inclined to think that in our lives in the everyday, entitlement and its lack are overall more important to us than whether or not some belief is a case of knowledge. In fact, to a considerable extent our interest in entitlement and its lack absorbs into itself our interest in knowledge and ignorance. We do not merely praise the presence of knowledge as a good thing and dispraise ignorance as a non-good thing; we *reproach* people for their ignorance, sometimes even for their knowledge.

The importance for our lives in the everyday of the practice of reproaching people for lack of entitlement in their doxastic and cognitive lives, and of praising them for its presence, is not the only reason for reflecting on that practice philosophically. What makes such reflection doubly important is that a fundamental feature of the modern world has been philosophers and other intellectuals offering to all of us, not just to each other, highly general rules to be followed in the practice. "It is wrong, everywhere, always, and for anyone, to believe anything upon insufficient evidence," W. K. Clifford (1986) famously remarked. Those who have offered such general injunctions have felt that there was something unsatisfactory about our everyday practice of reproaching each other for our beliefs; the practice itself must be reformed, shaped up. The philosopher launches a reproach against the practice itself as it is currently employed and offers suggestions for improvement. These suggestions have not only attracted adherents but evoked counter-suggestions from other philosophers, and those counter-suggestions, yet other counter-suggestions, and so forth. Thus it is that entitlement is on the agenda of the philosopher.

III

There is a well known challenge that immediately confronts anyone who wishes to develop an account of entitlement. When we reproach people for their actions – not their beliefs now but their actions – it is always intentionally undertaken actions that we reproach them for. It is true that we blame a person for crashing into another car even if, instead of intentionally undertaking to do so, he did so because he fell asleep when driving while drunk; but a full analysis of the situation makes clear that what we are really blaming him for is the intentionally undertaken actions of drinking as much as he did and then driving while drunk, the not-at-all-surprising consequence of the last being that he fell asleep and crashed. Had he crashed because of a completely unanticipated epileptic seizure, we would not blame him.

But beliefs are not intentionally undertaken actions. Truth is, they are not actions at all; they are *states*. So let me put the point properly. Believings seldom come about as the result of undertaking to believe the thing believed – far too seldom for this to be what accounts for entitlement and non-entitlement.

The first point to be made is that there is no such *basic* action as believing P just by deciding to believe P. It never happens that somebody comes to believe some proposition just by deciding to do so.

All by itself, that point is not very important. Though turning on the light is an intentionally undertaken action on my part, it too is not and could not be a *basic* action; I can turn on the light only by initiating a causal chain of events that eventuates in the light coming on. So the relevant question is whether people do sometimes enact the intention to bring it about that they believe or disbelieve something and succeed in that attempt, initiating a causal chain which eventuates in that belief or disbelief.

Let's be clear, before we proceed, what such an intention actually comes to. One may have some proposition in mind and then act on the intention to acquire some doxastic stance or other toward that proposition. For example, after wondering whether the population of China is over a billion, I may want to acquire some doxastic attitude or other toward that proposition, it makes no difference which. So I look up China in a reliable atlas and emerge with a definite doxastic stance toward that proposition. I have achieved my goal. This sort of thing happens all the time. Conversely, I may want to *believe* some proposition or other on some topic. For example, I may want to believe some proposition or other about the population of China, it makes no difference which. So again I go to a reliable atlas and emerge believing some specific proposition on the matter. I have achieved my goal. This sort of thing happens all the time.

It is neither of those sorts of projects that we are talking about here. We are talking about someone acting on the intention to bring it about that she has a specific doxastic attitude toward a specific proposition – believing that China has more than a billion people – when at the time of setting that goal for herself she does not have that attitude toward that proposition. Perhaps she firmly believes that China's population is considerably less than a billion.

Though there is something profoundly odd about such an intention, let me on this occasion refrain from developing that point and concede that probably such intentions are sometimes enacted and are sometimes successful. Pascal's suggestion about how to become a believing Catholic is regularly cited. Some people who are not presently believing Catholics may become that if they regularly attend an attractive mass, steep themselves in appealing Catholic literature, read around in truly offensive atheist and Protestant tracts, and so forth. I think the agent has to be rather gifted at self-deception for such a project to work; but perhaps there are some people so gifted. What strikes me as happening far more often and naturally is a person successfully enacting the intention of *maintaining* some belief that he has.

But be all that as it may – the issue has been discussed voluminously over the past twenty-five years – it is irrelevant to our purposes here. When I say you should have known that Borges is not an English writer, I am not implying that you should have formed the intentional undertaking of knowing that Borges is not an English writer.

Is Justified Belief Responsible Belief?

IV

One possibility to consider at this point is that, contrary to what I have been assuming, the "ought" of entitlement is not really the deontological "ought." Definitive of the *deontological "ought"* is that failure to act, believe, and so forth in accord with the "ought" implies culpability and blameworthiness on one's part. What is to be noted, then, is that there is a standard use of the word "ought" (and its corollary, "should") such that being or doing as one ought *not* to be or do does not imply culpability and blameworthiness on one's part. This is the "ought" that is being used when the surgeon says to his patient, "You should be back at work in three weeks," and when the botanist says about the trillium, "It ought to have three petals." What is in the background of this use of "ought" is the notion of a *properly formed* or *properly functioning* entity. If the healing progresses properly, you will be back at work in three weeks; if the trillium were properly formed, it would have three petals. Given the background reference to proper formation or functioning, one might call this the *propriety "ought"* (I have on occasion called it the *paradigm "ought"* on the ground that in the background there is the notion of paradigmatic formation and functioning).

It is clear that the "ought" of entitlement is not the propriety "ought." When I say of someone that she should have known that Borges was not an English writer, I am not suggesting, implying, or presupposing that there was something about her belief-forming dispositions that was not working properly; instead I imply that she did not *employ* those dispositions as she should have employed them. I hold her *responsible* for her ignorance, as I do not hold the color-blind person responsible for not being able to discriminate certain colors, or the trillium before me for not having three petals. And more than holding her responsible, I regard her as culpable and hence blameworthy. I do not chastise the color-blind person for his failure to make certain color discriminations; neither do I chastise the malformed trillium.

V

In the course of arguing just now that the "ought" of entitlement is the deontological "ought," I tipped my hand on what in the self, as I see it, that "ought" attaches to. It attaches to the way in which one directs or fails to direct those dispositions of the self that form and maintain beliefs. Underlying my chastising someone for her ignorance in thinking that Borges was an English writer is my conviction or assumption that there is something she did not do, or did not do well enough or in the right way, with respect to her belief-forming or belief-maintaining dispositions. Our challenge will be to move beyond this vague talk about entitlement and the lack thereof having "something to do" with how one directs or fails to direct one's belief-forming and belief-maintaining dispositions – to move beyond the vagueness toward clarity.

But first I must say something about those dispositions themselves, and more generally, about belief-forming and belief-maintaining processes – meaning by "processes" both dispositions and practices. Let me start with dispositions. And for the sake of economy, let me pretty much ignore belief-maintaining processes and focus on belief-forming processes; the reader can easily draw out the analogues.

I think of belief-forming dispositions along Reidian lines. Each of us has a panoply of dispositions such that, when a disposition is activated by some event, a belief is produced. Reid believed that a great deal of learning lies behind the belief-dispositions that a person actually has at any time after infancy. Though a good deal of this learning happens more or less automatically, some is the result of quite deliberate undertakings. As the consequence of lots of hard work, the logic student eventually is able to discern the structure of arguments which, at the beginning of her studies, were completely opaque to her. Belief-forming dispositions also deteriorate, as the result of aging, disuse, and so forth; and one acquires some dispositions just by virtue of maturation, not by way of learning. In all these ways, we as belief-forming selves are never static; we are always undergoing formation.

What Reid himself emphasized rather more than any of the above points is that there have to be some innate belief-forming (and concept-forming) dispositions in us for the learning even to get going. Consider one example of the point. Reid called that disposition which we all have, to believe what we discern others to be telling us, the "credulity disposition." The credulity disposition, as we find it in any adult, is highly complex: we believe what certain sorts of people tell us on certain sorts of topics, we have no disposition whatsoever to believe what those same people tell us on other topics, and so forth. Reid argued that the formation of the highly complex and sophisticated credulity disposition of an adult presupposes the existence of a rather crude innate credulity disposition that gets refined in the course of one's experience of people saying true and false things to one.

Belief-forming and belief-maintaining processes come not only in the form of dispositions but also in the form of practices. All of us, in the course of our lives, learn from others and discover for ourselves a wide variety of *practices of discovery*, as I shall call them – that is, strategies for finding out what is the case on some matter. We acquire and employ practices for finding out the true color of objects, the time of day, the population of China, the number of the earth's moons, and so forth. The acquisition and employment of such practices characteristically presupposes the acquisition and employment of certain *practices of attention*. We learn how to listen, how to look, how to taste. In addition to practices of discovery we also acquire and employ certain *practices of retention*; that is, strategies for not forgetting what we know. Such strategies are far fewer in number than practices of discovery, and not especially reliable. (Or so, as least, it seems to me!) Nonetheless, there are strategies one can employ that make it somewhat more likely that one will remember something.

It goes without saying that the self which employs practices of discovery and retention is that same self of which we spoke earlier, namely, the self which, at any moment in its life, possesses a distinct panoply of belief-forming and belief-maintaining dispositions. More specifically, in the employment of those practices, those capacities are activated. To employ the practices is to *direct* the activation of those dispositions, to *steer* their activation in one direction rather than another.

Is Justified Belief Responsible Belief?

VI

One more matter must be considered before we can discuss the grounds of entitlement and non-entitlement. Entitlement to believe so-and-so is very much a situated phenomenon, varying from person to person, from stage to stage of a person's life, from situation to situation. To the question, "Is one entitled to believe so-and-so?" the answer is always "It all depends."

In the second edition of his *Theory of Knowledge*, Roderick Chisholm (1977, p. 14) wrote that "We may assume that every person is subject to a purely intellectual requirement – that of trying his best to bring it about that, for every proposition h that he considers, he accepts h if and only if h is true." This seems to me much too expansive in one respect and too constricted in another. Too expansive in this respect: can it really be the case that for *every* proposition I *consider*, I am under obligation to try my best to bring it about that I believe it if and only if it is true? I don't have the time or energy for that; often I have more important things to do. The principle is too constricted in the following respect: our obligations with respect to our believings do not pertain just to propositions that we happen to consider; sometimes it is our obligation to get new propositions in mind.

It would be possible for Chisholm to respond by saying that he and I are just missing each other. He is talking about a "purely intellectual requirement," as he calls it; I am talking about moral requirements. But if that were his response, then he must tell us why we may assume, as he says we may, that every person is subject to a purely intellectual requirement. What reason is there to suppose that there is any such requirement? Apparently Chisholm thinks of the requirement as bringing with it accountability, culpability, blameworthiness, and the like. But is there really any such pattern of culpability and meritoriousness pertaining to our believings as Chisholm says we may assume there is – a pattern entirely divorced from our lives as practical beings with moral obligations? I see no reason to suppose there is.

Which deficiencies in a person's system of beliefs that person is under obligation to remove or try to remove is very much a matter of where that person is situated in the space of moral obligation. This, in turn, is one reason why it is also true that which practices of discovery and retention a person is under obligation to employ or try to employ is a matter of where that person is situated in the space of moral obligation – the other reason being that it also very much depends on which practices are concretely available and morally acceptable to that person.

VII

All the issues thus far considered deserve a great deal more discussion than I have given them; but we must move on. In an essay to which I have already referred, "The Foundational Role of Epistemology in a General Theory of Rationality," Richard Foley first rehearses and refines the account of *rationality in belief* that he had developed in earlier writings, and then employs that account to offer an account of what I call *entitled* belief. It will prove instructive to look at Foley's account of entitlement. Let me reverse the order of his own discussion, beginning with entitlement and then backing up to get hold of as much of his account of rational belief as is necessary to understand his account of entitlement.

Foley does not use the term "entitled." Instead he divides what I call "entitled" beliefs into two groups, and then gives an account of each. One group he calls "responsible" beliefs. Here is his analysis:

> One responsibly believes a proposition P if one believes P and one also has an epistemically rational belief that the processes by which one has acquired and sustained the belief P have been acceptable, that is, acceptable given the limitations on one's time and capacities and given all of one's goals, pragmatic as well as intellectual and long term as well as short term. (Foley, 2001, p. 223)

Foley observes that often one does not have the meta-belief that responsible belief, thus understood, requires – that is, one does not have a belief about the identity or acceptability of the processes whereby one's belief that P was acquired and sustained. One acquires the belief without reflecting on the identity or acceptability of those processes; or one reflects on those matters but arrives at no conclusion. It is for those circumstances that Foley articulates his concept of non-negligent belief:

> One non-negligently believes a proposition P if (a) one believes P, and (b) one does not believe, and it is not epistemically rational for one to believe, that the processes by which one has acquired and sustained the belief P have been unacceptable, that is, unacceptable given the limitations on one's time and capacities and given all of one's goals. (Foley, 2001, p. 223)

The pivotal concept in these accounts of rational and non-negligent belief is, of course, that of *epistemic rationality*. So let us back up to see what Foley has in mind by that. Rationality in general, so Foley suggests, is concerned with the "effective pursuit of valuable ends" (ibid., p. 215). Eventually it becomes clear that, in spite of the diachronic connotations of these words, Foley means to include the situation of something in the present contributing effectively to one of one's present desiderata. But until we reach the point in the discussion where it will be important to take note of the synchronic situation, let me go along with Foley and speak of means and ends.

A plan, strategy, or whatever may be rational for one to undertake even though it will in fact make no contribution to any of one's goals; the best-laid plans go sometimes amiss. This leads Foley to explain the rationality of plans and the like in terms of beliefs *about* those plans; specifically, in terms of one's belief, about the plan in question, that it is *sufficiently likely* to be successful.

The notion of *being likely* to be successful refers to the fact that, within the total population of plans of this sort, there is a certain frequency of successful ones. The frequency that is *sufficient* in a given case is then determined by one's goals and desiderata overall. How important is it that one achieve this goal? How important is the negative factor of the likely costs of implementing this plan for achieving that goal? Are there other plans for achieving this goal whose likelihood of success is greater or whose likely costs are lower? It may be that achieving the goal is so important, and alternative plans so unattractive in one way or another, that one sets the bar for *sufficient likelihood* very low. The ambulance attendant may think it very unlikely that, with the techniques available to him, he will succeed in saving the patient's life; but he tries anyway. Alternatively, the goal may be so unimportant that one sets the bar for sufficient likelihood very high; it's just not worth bothering unless one is very likely to succeed.

On Foley's view it is not only the *content* of certain beliefs that determines the rationality of plans but the *quality* as well. For example, some beliefs to the effect that the plan in question is sufficiently likely to be successful will be too whimsical to make it rational for the person to accept the plan. Foley unfolds his strategy for dealing with this issue of quality in stages; until we get to the final stage, all the formulae that he offers must be regarded as provisional.

Begin with this: it must be *rational* for the person to hold the belief. The rationality of plans and the like is determined by the *rationality* of the beliefs, about those plans, that they are sufficiently likely to be successful. Here is what Foley says: "A plan (decision, action, strategy, belief, etc.) is rational for an individual if it is rational for the individual to believe that it would acceptably contribute to his or her goals" (ibid., p. 216).

Before I proceed, I should make it clear that it is not Foley's view that a condition of its being rational for some person to adopt some plan for achieving some goal is that the person *actually have* the belief that that plan is sufficiently likely to be successful. Though I do not find him entirely clear on the matter, the idea seems to be that the rationality of the plan is determined by whether or not, *if the person did* believe that, he or she *would be* doing so rationally.

Rational belief comes in various sorts; the rationality of a plan is determined only by a certain sort of rational belief about the sufficient likelihood of the plan, not by any sort of rational belief whatsoever. Let me bypass Foley's account of rational belief in general and head straight for the relevant sort.

Foley observes that "when assessing the rationality of a decision, strategy, etc., we can take into consideration all of the individual's goals or only a subset of them" (ibid., p. 216). If we do the latter, then we can speak of a plan's being rational *in an economic sense*, meaning thereby that it is rational with respect to one's economic goals, of its being rational *in a professional sense*, meaning thereby that it is rational with respect to one's professional goals, and so forth.

This brings Foley to the point where he can introduce the concept of what he calls "the epistemic goal." It is here especially that the diachronic suggestions of "plan" and "goal" are misleading; what Foley has in mind is a certain *desideratum* with respect to *beliefs*. The *epistemic desideratum*, he says, is now having a set of beliefs that are individually accurate and collectively comprehensive – or in other words, now believing as much as possible of what is true and as little as possible of what is false. A belief will be epistemically rational if it is sufficiently likely to be successful in advancing this epistemic desideratum.

And what must a belief be like so as to be sufficiently likely to be successful in advancing the purely epistemic desideratum? In the article under discussion, Foley does no more than hint at how he would answer this question. His answer appears to be that the propositional content of the belief must be more probable than not on the evidence available to the person. *How much* more probable? Foley does not say.

The answer will presumably be determined by how one thinks the competing values of not having false beliefs and of having true beliefs should be weighted relative to each other.

With the concept of epistemic rationality in hand, we can now present Foley's full and final analysis of the rationality of plans, strategies, and the like: "A plan (decision, action, strategy, belief, etc.) is rational in sense X for an individual if it is epistemically rational for the individual to believe that it would acceptably contribute to his or her goals of type X" (ibid., p. 218). An ingenious feature of this general account of rationality is that we can now use it to give an account of when it is epistemically rational for a person to believe something. Believing P is epistemically rational in case a certain *meta-belief about believing* P is epistemically rational. It goes like this: "Believing P is rational in an epistemic sense if it is epistemically rational for one to believe that believing P would acceptably contribute to the epistemic goal of one's now having accurate and comprehensive beliefs" (ibid., p. 218).

The explanation, as it stands, is obviously circular. Foley says that such epistemological theories as foundationalism, coherentism, reliabilism, and the like provide an exit from the circle by virtue of offering "competing views about how this purely epistemic sense of rational belief is best explicated" (ibid., p. 217). It appears to me that the exit is instead provided by the fact, noted above, that a belief acceptably contributes to the epistemic desideratum just in case its propositional content is, to some degree, more probable than not on the evidence available to one.

VIII

With this conceptuality in hand, let us now return to Foley's account of entitlement. Recall that after dividing entitled beliefs into two groups, responsible beliefs and non-negligent beliefs, he then offered a separate account of each; in both cases, the concept of epistemic rationality occupied central position.

The first comment I wish to make about Foley's proposal is that its scope is too narrow. Though it offers an account of entitled and non-entitled *beliefs*, and by rather natural extension, of at least some kinds of entitled and non-entitled *modes* of belief, it offers none of non-entitled non-belief and ignorance – nor indeed of non-entitled knowledge. I submit that a satisfactory theory of entitlement must give us a unified account of all these different applications of the concept of entitlement.

But let's move on to consider whether Foley's analyses yield the right results for the cases that fall within their scope. One responsibly believes a proposition P, Foley suggests, in case one has the epistemically rational meta-belief that the processes whereby one acquired and sustained the belief that P were sufficiently likely to be successful. Now suppose that in a given case one has just such a meta-belief. One believes the requisite thing about the processes that led to the formation of one's belief that P, and it is epistemically rational for one to hold that meta-belief – which is to say, on the evidence available to one the propositional content of that meta-belief is considerably more probable than not. Does it follow that one is entitled to believe P? It seems to me that it does not.

Here is one reason: perhaps you were irresponsibly sloppy in your acquisition of evidence concerning the identity and/or acceptability of the processes that led to your belief that *P*; then, no matter how probable on your evidence is the propositional content of your meta-belief, you should not hold that meta-belief. And if you do not believe that the processes which led to your believing *P* were sufficiently likely to be successful, then in some cases at least you should not believe *P*.

Here is another reason: perhaps you are not to be faulted in any way for the evidence you have available to you concerning the identity and acceptability of the processes that brought about your believing *P*. And perhaps it is probable on that evidence that your belief about that identity and acceptability is true; your meta-belief is thus epistemically rational. Nonetheless, you may have been irresponsibly sloppy in coming to that meta-belief. If so, you are not entitled to that meta-belief. And then in turn, in at least some cases you will not be entitled to believe *P*.

Combine the two points: only if your meta-belief about the formation of your belief that *P* is itself entitled will it be relevant to the determination of the entitlement of your belief that *P*. But that meta-belief may be epistemically rational without being entitled.

The point has its counterpart for Foley's non-negligent beliefs. Suppose I believe *P*; and suppose I do not believe, nor would it be epistemically rational for me to believe, that the processes which led to my believing *P* were unacceptable. On the evidence available to me, it is unlikely that they were unacceptable. It may nonetheless be the case that I *ought* to believe they are unacceptable. Here is one way that could happen: I should have collected or attended to good evidence concerning the acceptability of those processes; had I done what I ought to have done on that score, I would believe that it is unlikely that they are unacceptable. But if I ought to believe that the processes generating my belief that *P* were unacceptable, then I ought not to believe *P*.

IX

My own view, which here I can only state and not develop, is that what brings it about that a person is not entitled to some feature of his belief- or knowledge-system is that either: (i) there is some practice of discovery or retention that he failed to employ but ought to have employed with a seriousness and competence such that, had he done so, the presence of that feature would have been forestalled or eliminated; or (ii) there is some practice of discovery or retention that he employed with a certain seriousness and competence but ought not to have (thus) employed, and which is such that, had he not employed it thus, the presence of that feature would have been forestalled or eliminated.

The formula is not intended as an *explanation* of the concept of entitlement. Neither are Foley's formulae thus intended. The intent, in both cases, is to identify some phenomenon on which entitlement supervenes – and another on which non-entitlement supervenes. My own attempt at such identification forthrightly makes use of that very same concept of the deontological "ought" which the concept of entitlement incorporates; there is no attempt to move outside the circle of the deontological "ought."

Foley, by contrast, does not employ the deontological "ought" in his identification of the phenomena on which, so he suggests, entitlement and non-entitlement supervene.

Though I have no way of showing it, I very much doubt that any such attempt as Foley's will prove successful. As far as I can see, entitlement is radically deontological, in the sense that no attempt to identify the phenomenon on which it supervenes without making use of the deontological "ought" will be successful. The point at which Foley's attempt fails is instructive. One is entitled to a certain belief, says Foley, if one has a belief of a certain sort about that belief; but that proves to be true only if one is *entitled* to that meta-belief. Or one is entitled to the belief if one does not hold a belief of a certain sort about that belief; but that proves to be true only if one is *entitled to that non-belief.* And so forth.

X

In conclusion, I want to return to Foley's account of epistemic rationality. Suppose that I believe *P*, and that the meta-belief about that belief, to the effect that it acceptably contributes to the epistemic desideratum, is epistemically rational; then, so Foley claims, the belief that *P* is itself epistemically rational.

A number of challenging questions come to mind. How are we to understand the implicit counterfactuals? And is Foley's epistemic desideratum *really* a desideratum; I am dubious. But here I will confine myself to an issue suggested by our discussion in the preceding section.

Suppose I believe *P*. Suppose I also believe, *about* that first belief, that it contributes acceptably to the epistemic desideratum – assuming there to be such and that it is what Foley says it is. Suppose further that that meta-belief on my part is epistemically rational, as Foley explains that. Does it follow that my belief that *P* is rational, specifically, *epistemically* rational?

I think not. That meta-belief is epistemically rational for me if, on the evidence available to me, its propositional content is more probable than not. Now suppose that it is highly probable on that evidence, but that the evidence has been very sloppily acquired, so that, moving now to entitlement, I am not entitled to the meta-belief. Is my belief that *P* nonetheless epistemically rational? Though I judge my grasp of the concept of rationality to be rather infirm, I would say that it is not rational in any sense, hence not in the epistemic sense.

The conclusion I draw is that if Foley is correct in his fundamental thesis, that the rationality of plans, beliefs, and the like is to be explained in terms of the rationality of a certain sort of belief *about* those plans, beliefs, etc., then rationality is an implicitly deontological concept. An implication is that the order of explanation has to be first entitlement, then rationality, rather than the reverse.

References

Chisholm, R. (1977) *Theory of Knowledge*, 2nd edn. Englewood Cliffs, NJ: Prentice Hall.
Clifford, W. K. (1986) The ethics of belief. In G. D. McCarthy (eds), *The Ethics of Belief Debate.* Atlanta: Scholars Press.

Foley, R. (2001) The foundational role of epistemology in a general theory of rationality. In A. Fairweather and L. Zagzebski (eds), *Virtue Epistemology: Essays on Epistemic Virtue and Responsibility*. Oxford: Oxford University Press.

Price, H. H. (1954) Belief and will. *Proceedings of the Aristotelian Society*, 28, supplement.

Further reading

Alston, W. (1989) The deontological conception of epistemic justification. In W Alston, *Epistemic Justification*. Ithaca, NY: Cornell University Press.

Foley, R. (1987) *The Theory of Epistemic Rationality*. Cambridge, MA: Harvard University Press.

Foley, R. (1993) *Working without a Net*. New York: Oxford University Press.

Wolterstorff, N. P. (1984) Can belief in God be rational if it has no foundations? In A. Plantinga and N. P. Wolterstorff (eds), *Faith and Rationality*. Notre Dame, IN: University of Notre Dame Press.

Wolterstorff, N. P. (1997) Obligations of belief – two concepts. In L. E. Hahn (ed.), *The Philosophy of Roderick M. Chisholm*. Chicago and LaSalle, IL: Open Court.

Response to Wolterstorff

Richard Foley

Although Nicholas Wolterstorff and I have our differences, we are in agreement that a notion such as entitlement (his preferred notion) or responsible belief (my preferred notion) is much more important for our everyday evaluations of each other's beliefs than whether or not a belief is an instance of knowledge. On this fundamental point, which stands in opposition to most of the recent tradition in epistemology, Wolterstorff and I are in deep agreement. But there are significant differences as well.

One complaint that Wolterstorff makes against my account is that it says nothing about irresponsible ignorance. I agree that this is an omission which a full blown account would need to rectify, but the general approach I take to issues of irresponsible belief can be readily extended to provide an account of irresponsible ignorance as well. A first step is to recognize that irresponsible ignorance is often simply the flip side of irresponsible belief. If it is your job to keep the safety equipment in working order but you have not conducted tests of the equipment and hence have not discovered the loose valve, then your belief that the safety equipment is in working order is irresponsible, and so is your ignorance of the loose valve. On the other hand, irresponsible ignorance is not always associated with a corresponding irresponsible belief. I may have no opinions one way or the other about an issue that is so pressing that I should have opinions about it. My account, however, can be easily enough adapted to cover such cases. In particular, if I do not have beliefs one way or the other about P, but it is epistemically rational for me to believe that I have not expended enough time and effort in arriving at an opinion about P, given its importance, then my ignorance is irresponsible. Of course, sometimes ignorance is irresponsible and sometimes it is not, and my account is also readily able to explain the difference. I have no beliefs one way or the other about whether the number of grains of salt in the shaker in front of me is odd or even. I could have taken the time to count them but have not done so. Nevertheless, my ignorance is not irresponsible. Why not? Because it is not epistemically rational for me to believe that in light of all my goals and the limitations on my time and capacities, it is worth the effort to have an accurate belief about this issue.

My position on justified belief, expressed loosely, is that S justifiably believes P if S responsibly believes P, where S responsibly believes P if S believes P and also has an epistemically rational belief – call it belief P* – that her treatment of P has been acceptable in light of the relative importance of having accurate beliefs about P, that is, given the relative importance of P, she has been acceptably thorough in gathering evidence, acceptably careful in evaluating the evidence, and so on. But Wolterstorrf raises an intriguing question about the belief P*. Suppose S was irresponsibly sloppy in arriving at belief P*. Wouldn't this also contaminate her belief P, making it irresponsible as well?

The answer is not necessarily. To see why, consider a pair of cases. In each case it is the month of April and S believes P. In each case S began investigating P in January; and in each case she had evidence in January that she was inappropriately dealing with P, but she ignored this evidence. As a result, in each case she in January irresponsibly acquired the belief P* (the belief that she used acceptable procedures with respect to P), and in each case she still has this belief P* in April.

Let's now stipulate that the two cases differ in the following respect: in Case 1 she in April still has evidence that her data gathering and processing in January was inappropriate, whereas in Case 2 she in April no longer has any evidence that anything she did in January was inappropriate. In Case 1 her April belief P is irresponsible, and it is irresponsible for precisely the reason implied by my account. Although she believes P and also believes P*, this latter belief is not epistemically rational, because she still has evidence that her past methods with respect to P were unacceptable. By contrast, in case 2 her April belief P is not irresponsible, and again my account explains why. She no longer has evidence to the effect that there were any improprieties in January. To be sure, she had such evidence in January and thus it may well be that she should have taken corrective actions in January. It also may be true that had she done so, she would not believe P in April. But this mistake is in the past. At the current moment in April, there is (by hypothesis) nothing in her current situation that provides her with any reason to be suspicious of the way she acquired her belief P. Hence, it is no longer irresponsible of her to believe P.

One of the lessons to be learned from such cases is that responsibly believing a proposition is not equivalent to having responsibly acquired the belief. If at the time I acquired a belief I had evidence that my procedures with respect to it were unacceptably sloppy but I ignored or in some way downplayed the significance of this evidence, then I acquired the belief in an irresponsible manner. Still, my current situation may be such that I can no longer be reasonably expected to be aware or remember that these procedures were unreasonably sloppy. If so, it can be responsible for me to go on believing the proposition even though my belief was originally acquired irresponsibly. This can be the case because the evidence of the original sloppiness has been lost with time, but it can also be the case – and this is an interesting and often overlooked point – that my overall treatment of the issue has begun to look less inadequate with time. Even if I was sloppy in acquiring a belief, if the belief leads to no significant practical difficulties or theoretical anomalies, the relevance of the original sloppy treatment may be diluted over time, not because I have done anything concrete to correct the original sloppiness but simply because the original sloppiness seems less and less problematic when viewed in the context of my overall history with the belief. Like people, irresponsible beliefs tend to become respectable with age as long as they don't cause serious problems.

Often enough there is even a self-fulfilling mechanism at work in these cases. The belief that was originally irresponsible may itself help to generate other opinions that help to undermine the suspicions about it. This isn't an especially unusual phenomenon, however. Whenever issues of rationality and related notions are at stake, phenomena of this kind tend to occur. Even if you have irrationally chosen some course of action over others that would have been better alternatives, this course of action can become rational for you at a later time just by virtue of your having stuck with it. It originally may have been rational for you to drive to New York rather than California, but if the irrational decision has already been made and you are now two-thirds of the way to California, it may very well be rational for you to continue on your way to California rather than turn around. Actions can have snowballing effects; they can engender subsequent actions that create momentum which make it increasingly unreasonable to reconsider the original ill-chosen course of action. So too beliefs can have snowballing effects; they can engender other beliefs, the collective weight of which may make it increasingly unreasonable to reconsider your original belief, even if it was sloppily acquired.

Snowballing is by no means inevitable. Often the shortcomings of the original decision or original belief continue to dominate over the costs of reconsideration. When this is so, it is irresponsible not to reconsider. The point here is simply that this is not always and everywhere the case; sometimes beliefs as well as actions can produce such snowballing effects. And the more general point is that irresponsible actions do not necessarily contaminate everything that follows from those actions, and neither do irresponsible beliefs. Sloppy evidence gathering decades earlier in your life does not necessarily imply that all of your subsequent beliefs are also irresponsible, even if it is true that these subsequent beliefs would have been different had you been a more responsible believer decades ago. There is a statute of limitations on irresponsibility.

An even more fundamental difference between Wolterstorff and me concerns whether it is even possible to provide a philosophically respectable account of responsible believing, "philosophically respectable" in the sense that the account makes no use of notions that are as much in need of explication as the notion being explicated. Wolterstorff maintains that any attempt to explicate the notion of responsible (or entitled) belief without making use of the notion of what the person ought to have done or believed (what he calls the "deontological ought") is doomed to failure. Responsible believing is, he says, radically deontological; it is deontological all the way down.

This position starkly contrasts with my own. I have not tried here to defend a specific theory of epistemically rational belief, although I have done so elsewhere.[1] Rather, I have pointed out that despite their many differences, foundationalists, coherentists, reliabilists, and others are all engaged in the project of trying to explicate the concept of epistemically rational belief without reference to any other concept of rationality or any of its cognates. I further point out that this is a feasible project only because the concept of epistemically rational belief is so narrowly defined; it is concerned only with the goal of having accurate and comprehensive beliefs, whereas all of us have many other goals and needs as well. Because it is so narrowly defined, the concept of epistemically rational belief is not directly relevant to our everyday evaluations of each other's beliefs. On the other hand, because it is explicated without reference to another concept of rationality or any of its close cognates, the concept of epistemically rational belief can potentially serve as a theoretical anchor for introducing other, derivative concepts, including the concepts of justified and non-negligent belief, which are relevant to our everyday intellectual lives. The result is a cluster of concepts that are both theoretically respectable and relevant to the assessments of each other's opinions that we need to make in our everyday lives. Or at least so I argue.

Who is correct on this point? Wolterstorff or me? The jury is still out. A negative claim such as Wolterstorff's can be decisively refuted only by actually generating an account of responsible believing that is both philosophically respectable and stands the test of time, and it is far too early to make any such claim for my account. On the other hand, I am comfortable in stating that the working hypothesis for epistemologists ought to be, *contra* Wolterstorff, that it is indeed possible to develop an account of responsible believing that is both relevant to our everyday assessments of each other's beliefs and philosophically respectable. If in the end this project turns out to be impossible, as Wolterstorff suggests, then so be it. But whether in science or philosophy or any other intellectual endeavor, progress is often the result of adopting a working hypothesis and seeing how far one can progress in defending that hypothesis.

Note

1 Most recently, in Foley (2001, esp. chapters 1 and 2).

Reference

Foley, R. (2001) *Intellectual Trust in Oneself and Others.* Cambridge: Cambridge University Press.

Response to Foley

Nicholas Wolterstorff

In my discussion of Richard Foley's theory of responsible belief, I observed that whereas a full blown theory of responsibility in believing would include an account of irresponsible ignorance, Foley's theory did not include such an account. Foley concedes both points, but goes on to offer an account of irresponsible ignorance which is a straightforward extension of his way of accounting for irresponsible belief. His account goes like this: "if I do not have beliefs one way or the other about P, but it is epistemically rational for me to believe that I have not expended enough time and effort in arriving at an opinion about P, given its importance, then my ignorance is irresponsible." It is not clear to me whether Foley intends that one's being irresponsibly ignorant concerning P entails that one has entertained P. If so, it seems to me that this formula will not do. It may be that the particular nature of my ignorance of P is not that I do not have beliefs one way or the other about P, but that P never so much crossed my mind. It should have; but it didn't.

Perhaps the account Foley gives here of irresponsible ignorance can be repaired to circumvent this particular objection. If so, then we return to my basic objection to the general pattern of his theory – the objection to which Foley devotes the bulk of his time in his response.

The basic strategy of Foley's theory is to account for what I call a person's *entitled* and *non-entitled* beliefs in terms of the presence or absence in the person of certain meta-beliefs. It will be satisfactory here to concentrate on those that he classifies as *responsible* beliefs. S responsibly believes P, Foley suggests, if S believes P and also has the epistemically rational meta-belief P* that, given the relative importance of P, she has been acceptably thorough in gathering evidence, acceptably careful in evaluating the evidence, and so on. My objection was that S might have been irresponsibly sloppy in arriving at the meta-belief P*; if so, then that irresponsibility infects P, so that P too is irresponsible.

Foley's response is: not necessarily. He is right about that; his cases establish his summary conclusion that "irresponsible actions do not necessarily contaminate everything that follows from those actions, and neither do irresponsible beliefs." His cases all trade on changes that take place over time: the belief remains, but one's memory of the evidence changes, or one's assessment of its evidential force changes, with the result that whereas originally the belief was irresponsible, now it is no longer that. But this still leaves us with those cases in which no such changes occur; Foley does not even attempt to answer my criticism for such cases. And even for those cases in which such changes do occur, whether later it becomes responsible for one to believe P, when earlier it was not, depends in part on whether or not at that later date one is responsible for having allowed one's memory of the poor evidence to recede into forgetfulness. For these reasons my suspicion, that responsible believing is deontological all the way down, has not been alleviated.

In his conclusion Foley says that an account of responsible believing is "philosophically respectable" just in case the account makes no use of "notions that are as much in need of explication as the notion being explicated." Thus an account of responsible believing that makes use of the concept of *obligation* is not, by his lights, a philosophically respectable account. He indicates that it was a philosophically respectable account that he was after in his theory. And he concedes that my objections to his account leave it an open question whether such an account of responsible belief is possible.

On this understanding of a philosophically respectable account of some concept, thinking of possibility and necessity in terms of possible worlds proves not to be a philosophically acceptable account of those concepts – since in possible worlds thought one uses those very concepts. Yet thinking about possibility and necessity in terms of possible worlds has proved undeniably illuminating. Accordingly, though one way of achieving philosophical illumination concerning some concept and its application is by offering what Foley calls "a philosophically acceptable account," it has to be conceded that sometimes such philosophical illumination is achieved instead by showing how one sort of application of the concept fits into a larger pattern of applications. My hunch is that such illumination, and only such illumination, is available to us with respect to the concept of responsible belief. But as Foley says, the jury is still out.

Index